Health &
Healing
for
African-Americans

Health &
Healing

for
African-Americans

Straight Talk and Tips
from More Than *150* Black Doctors
on Our Top Health Concerns

Edited by Sheree Crute

Foreword by Joycelyn Elders, M.D.,
former U.S. Surgeon General

Rodale Press, Inc.
Emmaus, Pennsylvania

Copyright © 1997 by Rodale Press, Inc.

Illustrations copyright © 1997 Yvonne Buchanan

Prevention Health Books is a trademark of Rodale Press, Inc.

Printed in the United States of America on acid-free (∞), recycled paper ♻

"The Birth Control Basics" on page 44 is adapted with permission of Planned Parenthood Federation of America, Inc. Copyright ©1996 PPFA. All rights reserved.

Library of Congress Cataloging-in-Publication Data

Health and Healing for African-Americans : straight talk and tips from more than 150 black doctors on our top health concerns / edited by Sheree Crute.
  p. cm.
Includes index
ISBN 0–87596–365–X hardcover
ISBN 1–57954–044–9 paperback
1. Afro-Americans—Health and hygiene. I. Crute, Sheree
RA778.4.A36H43 1997
613'.08996'073—dc21   97–5716

Distributed in the book trade by St. Martin's Press

4 6 8 10 9 7 5 3   hardcover
2 4 6 8 10 9 7 5 3 1 paperback

OUR PURPOSE

"We inspire and enable people to improve their lives and the world around them."

Health and Healing for African-Americans Editorial Staff
Editor: Sheree Crute
Managing Editor: Ann Gossy Yermish
Writers: Kirk A. Johnson, Harriet Washington
Contributing Writers: Claire McIntosh, Yanick Rice-Lamb, Lauren Swann, R.D.
Lead Researcher: Jennifer Barefoot
Editorial Researchers: Tanya Bartlett, Kelly Coffey, Christine Dreisbach, Jan Eickmeier, Joely Johnson, Nicole Kelly, Kathryn Piff, Jenny Schaeffer, Margo Trott, Michelle Szulborski Zenie
Senior Copy Editor: Jane Sherman
Associate Art Director: Darlene Schneck
Cover and Interior Designer: Elizabeth Youngblood
Cover Photographer: Dennis Mitchell
Illustrator: Yvonne Buchanan
Technical Artist: William Allen
Manufacturing Coordinator: Melinda B. Rizzo
Office Manager: Roberta Mulliner
Office Staff: Julie Kehs, Bernadette Sauerwine

Rodale Health and Fitness Books
Vice-President and Editorial Director: Debora T. Yost
Executive Editor: Neil Wertheimer
Research Manager: Ann Gossy Yermish
Design and Production Director: Michael Ward
Copy Manager: Lisa D. Andruscavage
Studio Manager: Stefano Carbini
Book Manufacturing Director: Helen Clogston

Contributing Physicians and Health Professionals

Our ancestors on African soil and in the American South brought babies into the world, eased the aches and pains of their elders, and helped their children grow up strong with home remedies and ingenuity passed on through the generations. One man built a bridge between those traditions and the world of conventional medicine when he became America's first African-American physician. James Derham—the son of slaves—proudly opened the doors of his medical practice in New Orleans in 1783.

Since that time, hundreds of thousands of African-American men and women have trained to become physicians, surgeons, psychologists, and researchers to help us live longer, healthier lives. That's why this book does more than just report on the latest medical findings—it gives you first-hand advice from some of the leading Black doctors in the country about managing the health concerns that have the greatest impact on our well-being.

All of the 163 African-American health experts cited in this book are listed here in recognition of their contributions, expertise, and commitment to helping improve our health as individuals and as a community.

Sheree Crute

Chester Aikens, D.D.S., a dentist in private practice and past president of the National Dental Association

Carol Archie, M.D., assistant professor of obstetrics and gynecology at the University of California at Los Angeles School of Medicine

Mark Baganz, M.D., assistant professor of radiology and director of neuroradiology at Howard University Hospital in Washington, D.C.

Alise Jones Bailey, M.D., an obstetrician and gynecologist with Buckhead Women's Medical Group in Atlanta

Richard S. Baker, M.D., assistant professor of ophthalmology and assistant dean of research at Charles R. Drew University of Medicine and Science, King-Drew Medical Center in Los Angeles

Neal Beckford, M.D., an otolaryngologist and head and neck surgeon in private practice in Memphis, Tennessee

Carl Bell, M.D., professor of clinical psychiatry at the University of Illinois College of Medicine, clinical professor of public health at the University of Illinois School of Public Health, and president and chief executive officer of the Community Mental Health Council, all in Chicago

Georges Benjamin, M.D., deputy secretary for public health in Maryland and a former emergency physician in Silver Spring

Carol Bennett, M.D., associate professor of urology at the University of California at Los Angeles School of Medicine

Richard Bensinger, M.D., an ophthalmologist at Swedish Hospital in Seattle and spokesperson for the American Academy of Ophthalmology

Deborah L. Bernal, M.D., a TMD physical medicine and rehabilitation specialist in private practice in Washington, D.C.

Louis J. Bernard, M.D., former director of the Drew-Meharry-Morehouse Consortium Cancer Center in Nashville

JudyAnn Bigby, M.D., assistant professor of medicine at Harvard Medical School and a physician in the Division of General Medicine at Brigham and Women's Hospital in Boston

Kevin L. Billups, M.D., assistant professor in the Department of Urologic Surgery and director of the National Institute for Men's Health at the University of Minnesota in Minneapolis

Lorraine Bonner, M.D., general practitioner and a founding member of On-Call Physicians Medical Group at Summit Medical Center in Oakland, California

Linda Bradley, M.D., a staff gynecologist at the Cleveland Clinic Foundation in Ohio

Otis W. Brawley, M.D., director of the Office of Special Populations at the National Cancer Institute in Bethesda, Maryland

Rovenia Brock, Ph.D., nutritionist and health correspondent for Black Entertainment Television (BET) News in Washington, D.C.

Yvonne L. Bronner, R.D., Sc.D., assistant professor of maternal and child health at Johns Hopkins University School of Hygiene and Public Health in Baltimore and spokesperson for the American Dietetic Association

Annette M. Brown, M.D., a diagnostic radiologist in private practice in Manhattan

Clinton D. Brown, M.D., director of the ambulatory dialysis unit and the hypolipidemia clinic and assistant professor of medicine at the State University of New York Health Science Center in Brooklyn

Gina Brown, M.D., assistant professor of obstetrics and gynecology at Columbia University College of Physicians and Surgeons in New York City

Arthur L. Burnett, M.D., director of the Male Dysfunction Clinic at Johns Hopkins Hospital in Baltimore

Richard Casey, M.D., chief of ophthalmology at Charles R. Drew University of Medicine and Science, King-Drew Medical Center in Los Angeles

Dennis E. Castillo, D.P.M., a podiatrist and clinical assistant professor of surgery at the State University of New York Health Science Center in Brooklyn

Zerline Chambers-Kersey, M.D., an obstetrician and gynecologist in private practice in Annandale, Virginia

Wayman Wendell Cheatham, M.D., chief of the Diabetes Treatment Center at Howard University Hospital in Washington, D.C.

Joy Church, M.D., assistant professor of family and preventive medicine at Emory University in Atlanta

Greta F. Clarke, M.D., a dermatologist in private practice in Berkeley, California

L. Anita Cone, M.D., associate physician at Georgia Spine and Sports Physicians in Marietta

Edward Cooper, M.D., professor emeritus of medicine at the University of Pennsylvania Medical Center in Philadelphia and the first African-American president of the American Heart Association

Sadye B. Curry, M.D., gastroenterologist and associate professor of medicine at Howard University College of Medicine in Washington, D.C.

Cheryl Doyle, M.D., a pediatric pulmonologist at Woodhull Medical and Mental Health Center in Brooklyn

William Emikola Richardson, M.D., medical director and president of the Atlanta Clinic of Preventive Medicine

Keith C. Ferdinand, M.D., medical director of the Heartbeats Life Center at the Medical Center of Louisiana in New Orleans

John M. Flack, M.D., associate professor of surgery, medicine, and public health sciences and associate director and medical director of the hypertension center at Bowman Gray School of Medicine of Wake Forest University in Winston-Salem, North Carolina

Debra Ford, M.D., assistant professor and chief of the Division of Colon and Rectal Surgery at Howard University Hospital in Washington, D.C., and the first board-certified female African-American colorectal surgeon

Margaret A. Fountain, M.D., an arthritis specialist in private practice and the health editor for a local television station in Baltimore

Patricia A. Fraser, M.D., a rheumatologist and assistant professor of medicine at Harvard Medical School

Kenneth M. Frontin, M.D., a gastroenterologist and assistant professor of medicine at Morehouse School of Medicine in Atlanta

James Gavin III, M.D., Ph.D., senior scientific officer at the Howard Hughes Medical Institute in Chevy Chase, Maryland, and the first African-American president of the American Diabetes Association

Richard F. Gillum, M.D., special assistant for cardiovascular epidemiology at the National Center for Health Statistics in Hyattsville, Maryland

Marcia Glenn, M.D., a dermatologist at the King-Drew Medical Center in Los Angeles

Samuel Gordon, Ph.D., clinical psychologist at the National Rehabilitation Hospital in Washington, D.C.

Sandra Gordon, M.D., assistant clinical professor of medicine at Boston University School of Medicine

Ellsworth Grant, M.D., an oncologist in private practice in Pasadena, California

Wayne L. Greaves, M.D., associate professor of medicine at Howard University Hospital in Washington, D.C.

Jennifer Y. Greene, M.D., an obstetrician and gynecologist in private practice in Akron, Ohio

Kevin C. Greenidge, M.D., professor and chairman of the Department of Ophthalmology at the State University of New York Health Science Center in Brooklyn

Elwyn Grimes, M.D., chairman of the Department of Obstetrics and Gynecology at Meharry Medical College School of Medicine in Nashville

Andame Guillaume, M.D., assistant professor of otolaryngology at the King-Drew Medical Center in Los Angeles

Rebat M. Halder, M.D., professor and chair of the Department of Dermatology at Howard University College of Medicine in Washington, D.C.

Ruth Louise Hall, Ph.D., assistant professor of psychology at The College of New Jersey in Trenton

Rodney Hammond, Ph.D., director of the Division of Violence Prevention at the Centers for Disease Control and Prevention in Atlanta

Margarita Hanser Gardiner, M.D., assistant professor of medicine at the Medical College of Pennsylvania and Hahnemann University in Philadelphia

Barbara Harmon, M.D., an internal medicine specialist and associate attending physician at Harlem Hospital in New York City

Hazel Harper, D.D.S., assistant professor of community dentistry at Howard University College of Dentistry in Washington, D.C., and president-elect of the National Dental Association, an organization of Black dentists

Jules P. Harrell, Ph.D., professor of psychology at Howard University in Washington, D.C.

James Leo Harry, M.D., director of the Owings Mill branch of the Vein Clinics of America in Maryland

Elaine Hart-Brothers, M.D., an internist in private practice in Durham, North Carolina

Ronnie Hawkins, M.D., a family practitioner in Des Moines, Iowa

Lester Henry, M.D., retired Howard University endocrinologist

Carla Herriford, M.D., a dermatologist in private practice in Los Angeles

Eve Higginbotham, M.D., professor and chair of the Department of Ophthalmology at the University of Maryland School of Medicine in Baltimore

B. Gerald Hoke, M.D., chief of urology at Harlem Hospital Center and assistant professor of clinical urology at Columbia-Presbyterian Medical Center in New York City

Patricia Holsey, M.D., a family practitioner with the Henry Ford Medical Center in Royal Oak, Michigan

Portia Hunt, Ph.D., professor of psychology at Temple University in Philadelphia

Harold Jackson M.D., an orthopedic surgeon in private practice in California

Cage Johnson, M.D., professor of medicine (hematology) at the University of Southern California in Los Angeles

Edwin T. Johnson, M.D., author of *Breast Cancer/Black Woman* and a retired general surgeon and honorary staff member of the Department of Surgery at the Columbia Regional Medical Center in Montgomery, Alabama

Ervin E. Jones, M.D., Ph.D., associate professor of obstetrics and gynecology at Yale University School of Medicine and clinic chief of the Yale In-Vitro Fertilization Programs

Ruth Jones, J.D., former adjunct professor of law at Fordham University Law School in the Bronx and director of the university's Domestic Violence Clinic

Sandra J. Jones, M.D., an otolaryngologist in private practice in Atlanta

Wilbert Jordan, M.D., director of the Oasis Clinic at King-Drew Medical Center in Los Angeles

Margaret Kadree, M.D., chief of infectious diseases and director of clinical research at Morehouse School of Medicine in Atlanta

Anthony Kalloo, M.D., director of gastrointestinal endoscopy at Johns Hopkins School of Medicine in Baltimore

William Keith, M.D., clinical assistant professor of medicine at Drew Medical School/Martin Luther King, Jr., Hospital and medical director of the Institute for Aesthetic and Cosmetic Dermatology, both in Los Angeles

Terence Killebrew, Ph.D., a clinical psychologist at the Manhattan Vet Center in New York City

Willie Kindred, D.C., a chiropractor in Tempe, Arizona

Gary King, Ph.D., assistant professor and coordinator of the Urban Health Research Program at the University of Connecticut Health Center in Farmington

Shiriki Kumanyika, R.D., Ph.D., professor and head of the Department of Human Nutrition and Dietetics at the University of Illinois at Chicago

Darlene A. Lawrence, M.D., a family physician and associate professor at Georgetown University Medical School and Family Practice Residency Program in Washington, D.C.

James Lawrence, M.D., a clinician and assistant professor of pediatric and adult rheumatology at the University of South Alabama College of Medicine in Mobile

William Lawson, M.D., Ph.D., professor of psychiatry at Indiana University School of Medicine, chief of psychiatry at the Richard L. Roudebush Veterans Administration Medical Center, both in Indianapolis, and president of the Black Psychiatrists of America

Judith R. Lee-Sigler, M.D., assistant professor of medicine at the University of Illinois College of Medicine at Urbana-Champaign and staff physiatrist at Carle Clinic Association in Urbana

Michael LeNoir, M.D., immunologist and allergy specialist at Comprehensive Allergy Services in Oakland, California

Evelyn Lewis, M.D., assistant professor of family medicine at the Uniformed Services University of the Health Sciences in Bethesda, Maryland

James P. Lewis, M.D., of the Department of Family and Community Medicine at St. Paul-Ramsey Medical Center in St. Paul, Minnesota

Vivian Lewis, M.D., an obstetrician and gynecologist and director of the Reproductive Endocrinology Unit at the University of Rochester Medical Center in New York

Charles Littlejohn, M.D., chief of the Division of Colon and Rectal Surgery at Stamford Hospital in Connecticut

Marc Lowe, M.D., chief of urology at the Group Health Cooperative of Puget Sound (central division) in Seattle

Stephenie Lucas, M.D., an endocrinologist at the Center for Preventive Medicine in Detroit

Richard M. Lynch, Ph.D., assistant professor of industrial hygiene in the Department of Urban Studies and Community Health at Rutgers University in New Brunswick, New Jersey

Andrew D. McBride, M.D., director of health for the City of Stamford, Connecticut

Cheryl R. Martin, M.D., assistant clinical professor of cardiovascular medicine at the Medical College of Wisconsin in Milwaukee

Nicholette Martin, M.D., a physiatrist at the Orthopedic and Sports Medicine Center in Annapolis, Maryland

Celia J. Maxwell, M.D., an infectious disease specialist at Howard University in Washington, D.C.

A. R. Mays, M.D., staff orthopedic surgeon at the Student Health Center of the University of Southern California at Los Angeles

Lois V. Melchior, M.D., a family practitioner and member of Dimensions Affiliated Physicians in Hyattsville, Maryland

Janet L. Mitchell, M.D., chairperson of the Department of Obstetrics and Gynecology at Interfaith Medical Center in Brooklyn

John P. Mitchell, M.D., assistant professor of clinical ophthalmology at Columbia University College of Physicians and Surgeons in New York City

Nelli L. Mitchell, M.D., a psychiatrist in private practice in Rochester, New York

Sherry Molock, Ph.D., associate professor of the clinical psychology program at Howard University in Washington, D.C.

Ronald A. Morton, Jr., M.D., director of laboratories at the Baylor Prostate Center and assistant professor of urology at Baylor College of Medicine in Houston

Linda James Myers, Ph.D., associate professor of African-American and African studies, psychology, and psychiatry at Ohio State University in Columbus and past president of the Association of Black Psychologists

Shawna Nesbitt, M.D., assistant professor of internal medicine at the University of Michigan School of Medicine at Ann Arbor

James E. C. Norris, M.D., a New York plastic surgeon formerly with the Harlem Hospital Burn Center

Keith Norris, M.D., vice chairman of the Department of Medicine and Science at King-Drew Medical Center in Los Angeles

Joanne A. Peebles Wilson, M.D., gastroenterologist, professor of medicine and associate chief of gastroenterology at Duke University Medical Center in Durham, North Carolina

Elliott Perlin, M.D., chief of hematology at Howard University Hospital in Washington, D.C.

Robert T. M. Phillips, M.D., Ph.D., associate professor of psychiatry in the School of Medicine and Law at the University of Maryland in College Park, deputy medical director for the American Psychiatric Association, and a visiting lecturer at Yale University

Rogsbert F. Phillips, M.D., clinical professor of surgery in the Department of Surgery at Emory University School of Medicine in Atlanta

Harold Pierce, M.D., a dermatoplastic surgeon at the Pierce Cosmetic Surgery Center in Philadelphia

Thomas L. Pitts, M.D., instructor of medicine at Northwestern University Medical School and the University of Illinois College of Medicine in Chicago

O. D. Polk, Jr., M.D., a pulmonary disease specialist and assistant professor of medicine at Howard University College of Medicine in Washington, D.C.

Winston S. Price, M.D., National Medical Association trustee and assistant professor of pediatrics at the State University of New York Health Science Center in Brooklyn

Beny Primm M.D., executive director of the Addiction Research and Treatment Corporation in Brooklyn

Lawrence Prograis, Jr., M.D., deputy director of the Division of Allergy, Immunology, and Transplantation at the National Institute of Allergy and Infectious Diseases in Bethesda, Maryland

Edward A. Rankin, M.D., clinical professor of orthopedic surgery at Howard University Hospital in Washington, D.C.

Elena R. Reece, M.D., chief of allergy and clinical immunology at Howard University Hospital in Washington, D.C.

Nancy Roberson, M.D., clinical associate professor of obstetrics and gynecology at the University of Rochester School of Medicine in New York

John Robertson, Ph.D., executive director of the National Black Alcoholism and Addictions Council in Washington, D.C.

Adam M. Robinson, Jr., M.D., a colorectal surgeon and Force Surgeon for Commander Naval Surface Force, U.S. Atlantic Fleet, in Norfolk, Virginia

Michael F. Robinson, M.D., an endocrinologist in private practice in Inglewood, California

Robert G. Robinson, Dr. P.H., associate director for program development for the Office on Smoking and Health at the Centers for Disease Control and Prevention in Atlanta

Lemuel A. Rogers, M.D., clinical assistant professor of obstetrics and gynecology at the University of Rochester in New York

Myra E. Rose, M.D., associate professor of clinical medicine at Morehouse School of Medicine in Atlanta

William H. Rutherford, D.P.M., clinical instructor at Howard University College of Medicine and chief of the podiatry section at Howard University Hospital in Washington, D.C.

Elijah Saunders, M.D., associate professor of medicine and head of the Division of Hypertension at the University of Maryland School of Medicine in Baltimore

Edward W. Savage, Jr., M.D., medical director and chief of gynecology at the King-Drew Medical Center in Los Angeles and professor of obstetrics and gynecology at the medical center and the University of California at Los Angeles

Victor Scott, M.D., chief of gastroenterology at Howard University Hospital in Washington, D.C.

Jessie L. Sherrod, M.D., pediatric infectious disease specialist at King-Drew Medical Center in Los Angeles and a member of the Advisory Committee on Immunization Practices of the Centers for Disease Control and Prevention in Atlanta

Cuthbert Simpkins, M.D., trauma surgeon, director of the violence and victimization prevention program at Erie County Medical Center in Buffalo and associate professor of surgery at the University of Buffalo

D. Kim Singleton, Ph.D., a clinical psychologist in private practice in Washington, D.C.

LaFayette Singleton, M.D., assistant professor of neurology at the University of Chicago School of Medicine

Delaney E. Smith, M.D., of the Baldwin Hills Medical Group in Los Angeles

Henry T. Smith, M.D., chief of the Division of Internal Medicine at Hennepin Faculty Associates and director of the Hypertension Clinic at Hennepin County Medical Center in Minneapolis

Duane Smoot, M.D., a gastroenterologist and associate professor of medicine at Howard University Hospital in Washington, D.C.

Lauren Swann, R.D., president of Concept Nutrition Consulting in Bensalem, Pennsylvania

Anne L. Taylor, M.D., associate professor of medicine and cardiology at Case Western Reserve University in Cleveland

Duane J. Taylor, M.D., lead physician for otolaryngology-head and neck surgery at the Mid-Atlantic Permanente Medical Group in Landover, Maryland

Emmet Taylor, M.D., director of a sexually transmitted disease clinic in the urban area around New Orleans

Susan C. Taylor, M.D., of Society Hill Dermatology in Philadelphia

Terry L. Thompson, M.D., assistant professor of orthopedic surgery at Howard University College of Medicine in Washington, D.C.

Yvonne Thornton, M.D., director of perinatal diagnostic testing at Morristown Memorial Hospital in New Jersey

Debra Thurmond, M.D., a family practitioner in Morrow, Georgia

Patricia Treadwell, M.D., associate professor of dermatology and pediatrics at Indiana University School of Medicine in Indianapolis

Lucius Tripp, M.D., a neurosurgeon and specialist in occupational and preventive medicine in Detroit

Nadu Tuakli, M.D., a family practitioner in Columbia, Maryland

Wayne B. Tuckson, M.D., assistant professor of surgery at the University of Louisville in Kentucky

Ernest A. Turner, M.D., director of the Comprehensive Sickle Cell Center at Meharry Medical College in Nashville

Donald Vereen, M.D., medical officer and special assistant at the National Institutes of Health in Bethesda, Maryland

Nsenga Warfield-Coppock, Ph.D., a psychologist and assistant visiting professor at Catholic University of America in Washington, D.C.

W. Bedford Waters, M.D., professor of urology at Loyola University Medical Center in Maywood, Illinois

Marlene F. Watson, Ph.D., a couple and family therapist in private practice in Philadelphia

Leonard Weather, Jr., M.D., director of the Omni Fertility and Laser Institute in New Orleans

Lennox S. Westney, M.D., director of the Division of Obstetrics at Howard University Hospital and professor at Howard University College of Medicine, both in Washington, D.C.

Calvin B. Wheeler, M.D., clinical instructor in the Department of Neurology and Pediatrics at the University of California, San Francisco, School of Medicine and child neurologist and assistant physician-in-chief at Kaiser Permanente Medical Center in Fremont, California

Clarence M. Wiley, M.D., clinical assistant professor of dermatology at the University of Kansas School of Medicine and medical director of the Center for Skin Health and Beauty, both in Wichita

Lillie R. Williams, R.D., Ph.D., chairperson of the Department of Nutritional Sciences at Howard University in Washington, D.C.

Kathy Williamson, N.D., a naturopathic physician in private practice in Los Angeles

Isaac Willis, M.D., professor of dermatology and head of dermatologic research at Morehouse School of Medicine in Atlanta

La Pearl Logan Winfrey, Ph.D., associate professor and director of clinical training at the American School of Professional Psychology in Arlington, Virginia

Gerald M. Woods, M.D., professor of pediatrics at Children's Mercy Hospital in Kansas City, Missouri

Raymond B. Wynn, M.D., assistant professor in the Department of Radiation Oncology at the Louisiana State University Medical Center in New Orleans

Mark Yerby, M.D., associate clinical professor of neurology and public health at Oregon Health Sciences University in Portland

Roscoe C. Young, Jr., M.D., a pulmonary health specialist and faculty development fellow at National Health Service Corps and professor at Meharry Medical College in Nashville

Contents

M

N

O

P

R

S

Foreword

A Message from Joycelyn Elders, M.D.

There's an old saying that promises, "What you don't know can't hurt you." Well, I'm here to tell you that when it comes to health care, nothing could be further from the truth. With the right knowledge, you can do more for your health than all of the well-trained physicians, miraculous medical discoveries, and well-equipped hospitals in America.

For most African-Americans, that message may come as a surprise, but it's absolutely true. We've all heard the reports that say we have more health problems and higher disease risks than just about any other group of people in America. But it doesn't have to be that way. All it takes to turn these disheartening statistics around is the knowledge, desire, and willingness to take better care of ourselves.

This book gives you the advice you need to get started on the road to better health. It is a valuable resource that shows you how to take control by giving you advice on ways to prevent and treat 100 health conditions of concern to African-Americans. And the advice comes from people we can trust—more than 150 of the nation's leading African-American physicians and health professionals.

No matter how successful we may be in other endeavors, without good health, nothing else really matters. You must make health your top priority. Whenever I get sick, I don't fret about the next speech I have to give or the next deadline that I'm trying to make. I think only about getting well. Feeling better is number one—it's paramount to a happy life.

Now, I admit that taking charge of your health does require time and effort. It's a whole lot easier to come up with excuses for skipping exercise, avoiding the doctor, and eating the wrong foods. Some folks, for example, think that there's no sense in trying to prevent a condition if it runs in your family. Well, that's poor logic. We can't choose our ancestors, but we can choose our lifestyles, and by learning healthy habits and passing them along to our family and friends, we can actually "catch" good health and spread it around.

No matter how busy you are, try to find small ways to improve your health. I get my exercise by gardening—I plant shrubs, take care of the lawn, and lay my flower beds. My favorite pastime is working in my vegetable garden. I call it my sanity patch because it's calming and satisfying to me.

Gardening is hard work, and

that makes it exercise. But the pleasure you get from doing something you like is good for your health, too. When I dig around in my begonia bed, I can actually feel the stress dissolve. My blood pressure goes down. It even helps me lose a little weight. This book is full of small but important healthy habits—like gardening—that can help you improve how you feel each day.

You'd be amazed at how much information there is out there about maintaining good health. You probably never even think about the fact that learning to use that information is a lost art among many African-Americans. Self-care used to be part of our culture. When I was young, we learned about taking care of ourselves because, like many Black families, we had to. We lived on a farm in rural Arkansas, so there were no doctors close by. I was actually in college before I had my first doctor's appointment! That may not have been an ideal situation, but it taught me, and perhaps many other people who experienced similar situations, to recognize symptoms, practice prevention, and know when it's time to go to the doctor.

These days, we have all kinds of talented doctors at our disposal, but many of us use this valuable health resource only as a last resort. Granted, no one wants to go the doctor for no reason, but too many African-Americans have allowed emergency room care—or no care at all—to become commonplace in their lives.

The information in these pages is the next best thing to having a doctor at your disposal 24 hours a day. This book offers practical prevention and treatment strategies and advice for scores of problems. It helps you know when to go to a physician and how to find one that's right for you. You'll also learn how to understand symptoms and figure out whether or not they are serious.

HEALING THE HEART OF OUR COMMUNITY

In these pages, you will also find solutions to many of the public health concerns facing our families and communities. There's advice on preventing and managing tough problems such as the spread of HIV/AIDS, the emotional fallout of violence in our neighborhoods, and the poor health of our babies.

Good medical care is important throughout our lives, but it has special value at the beginning of life, especially for African-Americans. Too many of our babies are born with low birthweights, and our infant mortality rates are approximately twice that of the White population. On page 343, you'll find an entire chapter dedicated to helping Black mothers have the healthiest and safest pregnancies so we can give our newborns the best possible head start in the world.

And, whether you're a teen or adult, one of the most important health issues in your life should be protecting yourself from HIV/AIDS, a disease that has become the leading cause of death among African-American men and women ages 25 to 44. HIV transmission can be prevented with the use of a latex condom. I know that it is sometimes hard for many young Black women to have the strong self-esteem needed to get the men in their lives to practice safe sex. Men may also find it difficult to adjust to using condoms. So on page 231, there are suggestions for how to manage uncomfortable situations. Throughout the book, there is also good, solid advice on avoiding other sexually transmitted diseases that can lead to heartbreaking circumstances such as infertility or even cervical cancer.

As you think about nurturing your physical health, do not forget the importance of mental health. Many people may not realize it, but one of the greatest threats to the well-being of African-Americans of all ages is the impact that experiencing violence has on our lives. For many of us, it is on our very doorsteps, day after day. We're even afraid to go to a neighborhood park or walk along our sidewalks. Some people may even face it within their own families.

I know violence all too well. My brother died of a gunshot wound and my sister lost her life in an automobile accident. Kindness, support, and empathy from others helped me through these tragedies. That taught me that we can all learn to be more sensitive to one another. Such support is the root of good health.

THE TOTAL HEALTH APPROACH

In this book, there are hundreds of helpful health messages, but most important, it teaches us that there *is* hope for improving our health and that ultimately, it resides in education. To improve the overall health of African-Americans, we must all work together to increase individual and community responsibility for health, stress comprehensive health education, place emphasis on prevention and primary care, and push for universal access to health care services.

We may not be able to change

the world, but we each have it in our power to stop our own risky behaviors. We know what they are: smoking, drinking, taking drugs, using weapons, being overweight, refusing to exercise, and eating unhealthy foods, among others.

There is no government agency, no church, and no kindly benefactor who can change the health care system without our intervention. We must arm ourselves with education, speak with authority, and act with determination to flourish in this life. Whoever you are, wherever you live, rich or poor, young or old, this is the time to educate yourself.

We can't be wealthy unless we're healthy, and we can't be healthy unless we are wise. As Emerson put it, "The first wealth is health."

—Joycelyn Elders, M.D.
former Surgeon General of the United States and currently professor of pediatric endocrinology at Arkansas Children's Hospital in Little Rock

Acne

Putting an End to Problem Skin

andra Wilson, a 25-year-old nurse from Philadelphia, took pride in always looking her best, and she loved to party. That's why her buddy Keisha was shocked when Sandra backed out of the biggest and best party in town.

"I told her that I wasn't going," recalls Sandra, "and she nearly had a fit. She said, 'What do you mean, you're not going? Girl, I jumped through hoops to get these tickets, and Steppin' Out is the Black social event of the year. Don't tell me you bought that gorgeous beaded dress to wear at home. You *are* going!'" Sandra remembers.

"'My face looks awful, and I'm not going,' I told her. She asked me about the new makeup I'd tried, and I told her that it covered up the dark spots. But on top of all the pimples I had, it just looked like chunky peanut butter. I felt like crying," Sandra says.

"I had tried just about everything to get a clearer complexion. But, my skin is beyond oily—it's greasy. I scrubbed my face religiously, morning and evening, with an abrasive facial puff, but all that seemed to do was make my skin red and make the blemishes more noticeable," Sandra laments. "The pimple creams that I bought at the drugstore sometimes worked, but often they'd leave dry, scaly patches of skin."

Finally, out of desperation, Sandra says, she decided to see a dermatologist and get serious about her acne.

Clean Doesn't Mean Clear

"Acne is not a hygiene problem. It's not necessary to scrub the skin ten times a day to get rid of it," advises Marcia Glenn, M.D., a dermatologist at the King-Drew Medical Center in Los Angeles. The real problem isn't dirt on the skin but an overproduction of oil, a common problem for African-Americans. "It's very rare that people with dry skin have problems with acne. Those with oily skin (like Sandra) tend to," says Dr. Glenn.

Sebaceous glands in our skin secrete oils in order to provide protection against the elements. The problem arises when this oil doesn't find its way to the surface of the skin, where it's intended to form that protective barrier. Instead it gets trapped in the pores, clogging ducts and causing the swelling we know as pimples. Plugged-up pores can also show up as blackheads or whiteheads.

Sometimes the accumulated oil attracts bacteria, and the resulting infection causes red, blotchy eruptions called cysts or pustules. African-Americans are more prone to blackheads and whiteheads, while Whites tend to have the reddened, inflammatory type, says Dr. Glenn.

The Road to a Better Complexion

The first step in dealing with acne is to control the excess oil. That means cleansing your face thoroughly but gently twice a day. Avoid abrasive cleansing products such as apricot scrubs, acne cleansing puffs, and facial brushes, advises Carla Herriford, M.D., a dermatologist in private practice in Los Angeles. "Use a mild cleanser, cold water, and your fingertips only," she says.

Keep the soap simple. If you are prone to oily skin, you probably don't need the moisturizing ingredients in expensive, superfatted beauty bars, says Dr. Glenn. She recommends plain old body soaps such as Ivory, especially for her acne patients under 30 who tend to have very oily complexions. Since hormonal changes make skin less oily as we age, try a less-drying soap such as Aveeno, Basis, or Purpose if you're in your thirties or forties.

Dr. Herriford recommends Neutrogena (original formula) and unscented Dove for all skin types. Both are available in bars or liquid. Cleansing washes such as pHisoderm, available at drugstores and cosmetics counters, may also be good choices for oily complexions.

Protect your beautiful back. If you have acne on your back or other oily areas, try SalAc soap. It contains salicylic acid, which acts as a mild peeling agent to smooth problem skin. Or try Sastid soap; it contains salicylic acid and sulfur, which are also gentle exfoliants. Many pharmacists will order this product, says Dr. Glenn. Talk to your doctor before trying either of these products if you are allergic to aspirin, since salicylic acid is related to aspirin and could cause a reaction.

Apply astringent. As a cleanser, Dr. Glenn recommends an over-the-counter astringent such as Aquaglycolic, Neostrata, or any other brand that contains glycolic or fruit acids, also known as alpha hydroxy acids (AHAs). Since astringents can irritate or dry the skin initially, she recommends using them once a day or every other day for a few days, then increasing to twice a day if you don't notice any reaction. Although these astringents are available over the counter, you may need to ask your pharmacist to order them for you.

Avoid pore-clogging cosmetics. Stay away from products such as cream blushes and oil-based foundations, says Dr. Glenn. Use oil-free powder or water-based formulas, and make sure your cosmetics are labeled "oil-free" or "noncomedogenic," which means that they are formulated with fewer pore-clogging ingredients. Keep in mind, though, that while these cosmetics are less likely than oil-based cosmetics to cause problems for women with oily complexions, even they can cause breakouts in some women.

Lose the lubricants. "If you wash your face in the morning and notice a shine by lunchtime, your skin produces enough natural oils so that you don't need a moisturizer," says Dr. Glenn.

Try out drugstore cures. Drug treatment of acne breakouts depends on the individual and also on the severity of the problem. Over-the-counter preparations are suitable for low-grade acne (five to ten lesions at a time). Benzoyl peroxide products such as Persa-Gel and PanOxyl AQ 5 are effective at controlling breakouts, says Dr. Glenn. Stick with a 2 or 5 percent concentration, as the 10 percent extra-strength formulations can be very irritating and therefore contribute to pigment problems.

Dr. Glenn says that you can also try a glycolic acid product such as Lac-Hydrin as a moisturizer if you have very dry skin. Ask your pharmacist to order it for you if your drugstore doesn't carry it.

Deal with those dark spots. Fade creams containing hydroquinone can help clear up the hyperpigmentation (dark marks) that often shows up after an acne breakout, says Dr. Glenn. However, misuse of these products can also cause skin sensitivity, irritation, or discoloration. That's why it's important to consult your doctor and follow her directions carefully. Most important, don't cause new dark spots by picking, popping, or squeezing pimples, says Dr. Herriford.

Sandra's dark spots turned out to be stubborn, so her dermatologist recommended that she use a glycolic acid cream along with a fade cream. She saw improvement after several weeks.

Have a dialogue with your dermatologist. If these treatments don't clear up the problem or if your acne is quite extensive, your dermatologist can offer several other options, one of which should work for you. "Acne is something we've learned to treat very successfully," says Dr. Herriford. "You don't have to live with problem skin." Also, if you have the type of acne that leaves pockmarks or pitted scars, delaying treatment will make it more difficult to smooth out your skin.

Many patients respond well to tretinoin (Retin-A) treatment. Because Retin-A cream makes skin extra-sensitive to sunlight, it should be used at night and in conjunction with a sunscreen. Dr. Glenn often recommends using it every other night and staying out of the sun on the following day. Sandra's doctor recommended that she use a glycolic acid product during the day and Retin-A at night. Ask your doctor about this regimen, since Retin-A is available only by prescription. If you have the red, lesion-type acne, your doctor will probably prescribe a topical antibiotic to control the bacteria and aid in healing. Erythromycin (Erycette pads) and clindamycin (Cleocin-T solution) are two commonly prescribed types. Oral antibiotics may be prescribed for very severe acne lesions, says Dr. Glenn.

Isotretinoin (Accutane), a prescription oral drug, is effective, but it is generally the treatment of last resort because it can cause serious side effects. Besides leading to skin irritation and sensitivity in some patients, Accutane can elevate cholesterol and triglyceride levels and contribute to heart disease, which is more common in African-Americans than in Whites. Taking Accutane during pregnancy may also cause severe birth defects. "Women undergoing Accutane treatment must be extremely responsible about birth control," says Dr. Glenn.

With the skin-care regimen that her doctor customized for her needs, Sandra is enjoying a beautiful, clear complexion. "My only regret is that I didn't check with a dermatologist years ago," she says as she gets ready to step out for the fourth time in a month. "I could have looked this fly all along."

Alcoholism

BEATING THE BOTTLE

arbara Brown often felt disconnected from people—and from herself—but she was never quite sure why. "There was a lot of dysfunction in my family," explains the soft-spoken Miami resident. As the daughter of an alcoholic father and a prescription drug–abusing mother, Barbara survived a childhood of sexual and physical assault only to become pregnant by age 15 and a substance abuser by age 21.

As a young adult, Barbara never really understood the scope of her problems until her compassionate landlady sat her down and said, "Look, you're drinking too much and abusing drugs. Get some help before you ruin your life."

Barbara was stunned. "No one had ever told me that before," she says. "Having grown up around substance abuse, I just took it for granted. It seemed almost normal to me." Within days, Barbara sought help through her company's employee assistance program. Eventually, she entered a 28-day substance abuse treatment program. There, for the first time in her life, she began to confront the feelings that she had so desperately tried to escape through alcohol and drugs. For her, it was the start of a new life.

Today Barbara counsels men who have committed felonies while under the influence of alcohol and other drugs, and she's tearin' it up on her way to a bachelor's degree in social work. But best of all, she's learned to love and respect herself. "I've come a long way and I've got a ways to go, but I feel great about my journey," she says.

As Barbara and many other African-Americans who are in recovery will tell you, kicking alcohol is tough, but it can be done.

The Making
of an Alcoholic

No one knows what causes alcoholism. But psychologists have noted that loneliness, shyness, depression, hostility, self-destructive impulses, and sexual immaturity seem to be recurring traits in alcoholics. Alcoholism also tends to run in families, and many clinicians believe that it has a genetic component, which helps to explain why the biological children of alcoholics are more prone to alcoholism than are adopted children.

But nearly everyone agrees that alcoholics initially turn to alcohol to help relieve some form of stress. For Blacks, that stress can come from just about every direction. And that doesn't apply only to those who live in economically disadvantaged communities. "Many middle-class brothers and sisters face the day-to-day stress of competing in the work world without the social supports that their White colleagues may have," says John Robertson, Ph.D., executive director of the National Black Alcoholism and Addictions Council in Washington, D.C., "so many turn to the bottle for a little helping hand."

That works for a while, occasional hangovers notwithstanding. "The alcohol was great," Barbara recalls. "It helped me feel good, it helped me feel pretty, and it helped me deaden the pain and guilt and shame of being sexually abused as a child." But like most problem drinkers, Barbara soon went from drinking to relieve stress to drinking just to feel normal and get through the day. Once a person begins to drink heavily (about 2 or more drinks a day or 14 or more drinks per week), their tolerance for alcohol increases, and they have to increase their consumption in order to achieve the same results.

That's when you know you have a problem with alcohol. Health professionals use two criteria to determine if someone is an alcoholic. The first is whether someone is dependent on alcohol. The second is a pattern of behaviors associated with alcoholism (see "Test Your Alcohol IQ" on page 8).

The Toll
on Blacks and Women

Of the 75 percent of Americans who drink, an estimated 1 in 10 experiences some degree of alcoholism. African-Americans actually drink less than Whites, but in our urban communities, the rates of cirrhosis of the liver (a deadly alcohol-related disease) are more than double the rates among the rest of the American population. And death rates due to cirrhosis are three times greater in Black men than in White men.

Moreover, many serious, chronic conditions are caused or made more severe by alcohol abuse, including high blood pressure, heart disease, and cancer. "In the Black community, the health consequences of alcoholism are often more severe, entanglements with the justice system are more profound, and linkages with domestic violence are more visible," says Dr. Robertson.

Men taste alcohol's bitter fruit more often than women: An estimated 9 percent of all men are alcoholics, compared to only about 4 percent of women. And the startling fact is that women seem to become intoxicated more easily and suffer more extreme health effects from alcohol than men, even when both drink the same amount. And Black women, like all women who drink heavily, face special health risks. The list begins with higher rates of breast cancer (because alcohol increases estrogen levels in the bloodstream), and then there's depression and possibly early menopause.

For women in their childbearing years, alcohol consumption can cause infertility. And drinking while you're pregnant can cause miscarriage, stillbirth, and premature birth as well as put your baby at risk for fetal alcohol syndrome, which causes physical and mental defects. And if you're watching your weight, watch out. Alcohol slows down your metabolism and makes it harder for you to burn fat (even if you work out), and studies show that people tend to eat more when they drink alcohol with a meal. All in all, chronic alcohol abuse can knock 15 years off a woman's life.

HALTING
THE CYCLE

To get sober or avoid developing a drinking problem, substance abuse prevention experts recommend the following strategies.

Step in early. Since alcoholism develops over time, early intervention can stop the process before things get out of hand. It helps to know the warning signs of trouble. It's even more important to be honest enough to admit a potential problem.

Trust your peers. "Alcoholics Anonymous, or AA, has helped

This self-test will help you review the role that alcohol plays in your life. Most people are unaware or unwilling to acknowledge that they have an alcohol problem. Use the test to determine whether you (or someone you know) need to find out more about alcoholism. Be honest, because if you don't face the problem, you can't solve it. If you answer yes to even one of these questions, you need help.

1. Do you drink in the morning?

2. Do you drink excessively without really feeling any ill effects?

3. Is alcohol interfering with other parts of your life?

4. Do you feel that you can't enjoy social activities without alcohol being involved?

5. Do you get drunk alone?

6. Do you experience repeated withdrawal symptoms—nausea, sleep disturbance, tremors, irritability, and anxiety—that are only relieved by drinking?

7. Are you are losing control of your drinking and you can't stop?

8. Has drinking become more important to you than your job, family, and friends?

alcoholics help themselves more effectively than any other approach," says Dr. Robertson. AA offers mutual support and encouragement in a nonjudgmental, nonthreatening atmosphere.

Consider a private counselor. "AA meetings are an important part of recovery, and we encourage people to participate in them," says Dr. Robertson. "But sometimes we need more. That's where individual counseling can help." If your employer has an employee assistance program, you may already have access to free confidential counseling. Or phone a local hospital, health department, or community mental health center for a referral. You can also arrange a confidential visit with your local affiliate of the National Council on Alcoholism and Drug Dependence. Finding your local affiliate is easy: Just call 1-800-NCA-CALL.

Find treatment that suits your needs. Alcohol treatment services are increasingly offering culturally appropriate services that speak to African-Americans' concerns, so be sure to check with the treatment center that interests you to see what they have available. When it comes to the length and scope of treatment, there are lots of options, so scout around for the type of care that feels right to you. If you find it hard to refrain from drinking after you've had outpatient treatment, for example, you might consider partial hospitalization. With this option, you can go to your job during the day and return to a therapeutic setting in the evening.

There are also day rehabilitation programs in which you participate in structured activities at a health care facility during the day and return home at night. Finally, there are inpatient rehabilitation facilities (like the famed Betty Ford Center). To find services, look under "Alcoholism" in the Yellow Pages for treatment centers and other facilities near you, or call a local addictions hotline.

Recognize the good. It's natural to feel a sense of loss when you stop drinking. But remember what you're gaining, too. For example, cutting out alcohol can help reduce high blood pressure and bring it into the normal range without the use of medicines. You're not just giving up alcohol; you're gaining a whole new life.

Expand your world. If alcohol has become your one-stop source of confidence, self-esteem, and pain relief, you will probably wonder how you will face life without it. In time, however, alcoholics discover an entire new spectrum of healthy pleasures and activities.

Barbara enriched her life by attending a church that she says works hand in hand with AA to give her a sense of purpose. She also does step aerobics and treats herself to manicures and pedicures. "I'm 46 and look 35, honey," she says. And she sets goals for herself. First it was a high school equivalency degree. Then it was getting physically fit. Now it's getting her college degree and buying a car. "Keeping those goals in front of me gives me a sense of direction," she says.

Anemia

Ironing Out a Pressing Problem

oressa Williams is a busy woman and proud of it. She's one of those fast-moving, hard-working, up-by-the-boot-straps sisters that you read about in the local paper because she's always getting an award from the church, a sorority, or other good folks.

She's also no stranger to fatigue. "It took 12 years for me to build my publishing company—years of working overtime, overnight, and over every other kind of problem to make sure I took care of business," says the 46-year-old Chicago native.

One day, however, Loressa realized that she was more than just tired. "I was almost in a stupor," she remembers. "I usually walked at least 10 miles a week to keep in shape (I'm proud of this sleek, size 12 figure), but I got to the point where I'd get out of breath just thinking about stepping around the park."

By the time she made it to a doctor, she was starting to suspect that she had a serious disease. Needless to say, she was relieved—and surprised—to discover that her problem was iron-deficiency anemia. "After I started taking my prescribed iron pills and making a few changes in my diet, my energy returned and I was fine," Loressa says.

Figuring Out Anemia

When you develop iron-deficiency anemia (which is not related to sickle cell disease), it means that your blood is deficient in one of two important components, either red blood cells or hemoglobin. Red blood cells contain hemoglobin molecules. As blood flows through your lungs, the hemoglobin picks up oxygen so that it can be delivered throughout your body.

Viewed under a microscope, a hemoglobin molecule resembles a twisted mound of spaghetti. At the center of the mound lies a single molecule of iron. Iron is an essential element of hemoglobin: No iron, no hemoglobin.

Because iron is so important, you can imagine what happens when you're iron-deficient: Your body can't manufacture enough hemoglobin, so you don't get enough oxygen. That's why people with anemia feel so weak and fatigued. Anemia can also cause dizziness, headache, ringing in the ears, and in some cases, heart palpitations as the heart pumps faster in an attempt to compensate for poorly oxygenated blood.

What causes iron deficiency? The most common cause is losing too much blood. A red blood cell lives for about 120 days, after which it bites the dust and the body manufactures a replacement. Our bodies normally recycle the iron in aging red blood cells. In fact, 97 percent of our daily iron requirement comes from our own recycled blood. The rest comes from food. If you run low on blood or your diet is consistently iron-poor, you end up exhausted and run-down, like Loressa.

WHO'S IN DANGER OF DEFICIENCY?

Women deal with iron deficiencies far more often than men. After age 55, only about 0.2 percent of men are affected, while the rate for women in this age group is 2 percent. In other words, for every ten women with iron deficiencies, only one man is affected.

Among menstruating women, the rate is about 3 percent. The reason, of course, is the blood lost during the monthly menstrual cycle. Women lose a milligram of iron each day they're menstruating. "This is a special problem among premenopausal African-American women because they, like other premenopausal women, may have menstrual disorders. There does seem to be an increased incidence of uterine fibroids in African-American women that cause irregular and excessive bleeding," explains Elliott Perlin, M.D., chief of hematology at Howard University Hospital in Washington, D.C.

Pregnancy places women at risk, too, because the developing fetus takes iron from the mother. And the blood lost during childbirth can contain as much as 250 to 300 milligrams of iron. It's because women experience blood loss in these ways that they account for the majority of cases of anemia.

Occasionally, anemia can signal other health problems, especially when it appears in men and women in their fifties and sixties. "After age 55, men and postmenopausal women can develop bleeding-induced anemia from a peptic ulcer, hemorrhoids, or a malignancy like endometrial cancer or colon cancer. Sometimes this bleeding shows in bloody or black stools," says Barbara Harmon, M.D., an internal medicine specialist and associate attending physician at Harlem Hospital in New York City.

Iron-deficiency anemia can also stem from having a food intake that's insufficient to replace the iron we lose each day. While that may sound odd in a nation where food is fortified with a whole alphabet soup of nutrients, not everyone eats enough to satisfy their body's dietary needs. This is a problem mainly for young children (usually if they are fed milk for a prolonged period and don't get a variety of foods or supplemental iron), pregnant women, and people on a restricted diet, especially those who are dieting to lose weight and eat fewer iron-rich foods.

And even if you do eat enough, you may not receive high-quality iron. Dietary iron comes in two forms—heme iron, which is found only in meat, and nonheme iron, which is found in certain vegetables, fruits, and seeds. Your body absorbs around 20 percent of the heme iron in meats but only 3 to 5 percent of the nonheme iron in plant foods. Vegetarianism may be the best thing since sliced (whole-wheat) bread, but it deprives women and men of a top-notch iron source.

So anemia happens for lots of reasons. "The important thing is that anemia isn't a disease in itself," says Dr. Harmon. "It always reflects an underlying problem."

EMPHASIZING IRON

Anemia is easy to remedy, but the first order of business is to zero in on the cause. If you have symptoms of anemia, see your doctor and have your blood checked for iron content. Once you're diagnosed and your doctor identifies the source of your anemia, you can work at getting back to optimal health. Nutritionists and physicians recommend the following methods for safely upping your iron intake.

Get help with supplements. If you have anemia, your doctor will probably prescribe oral iron supplements. It generally takes two

Mining for Iron

Planning menus that include high-iron foods can help you meet your daily iron needs. Check the following table for iron-rich foods to incorporate into your meals. Keep in mind that your body absorbs about 20 percent of the heme iron in meat and seafood but only 3 to 5 percent of the nonheme iron in fruits, nuts, beans, and vegetables.

Food	Portion	Iron (mg.)
Meat and Meat Products		
Beef liver, braised	3 oz.	5.8
Beef bottom round, lean	3 oz.	2.9
Beef sirloin, lean, broiled	3 oz.	2.9
Ground beef, lean	3 oz.	2.3
Pork shoulder	3 oz.	1.3
Chicken, skinless, roasted	3 oz.	0.9
Turkey, roasted, light or dark meat	3 oz.	0.7
Seafood		
Clams, steamed	1 doz.	15.1
Oysters, Eastern, steamed	1 doz.	6.5
Sardines, Atlantic, canned	3 oz.	2.5
Vegetables and Nuts		
Tofu	¼ block (3 oz.)	6.2
Soybeans, boiled	½ cup	4.4
Miso	½ cup	3.8
Lima beans	½ cup	2.3
Pea (navy) beans	½ cup	2.3
Pinto beans	½ cup	2.2
Refried beans	½ cup	2.2
Cashews, dry-roasted	¼ cup	2.1
Great Northern beans	½ cup	1.9
Black beans	½ cup	1.8
Chickpeas	½ cup	1.6
Almonds, blanched	¼ cup	1.3
Fruits and Juices		
Prune juice	1 cup	3.0
Peaches, dried	5 halves	2.3
Apricots, dried	10 halves	1.7
Raisins, seedless	½ cup	1.5

to six months of iron supplementation to remedy the anemia and replace the missing iron.

Since vitamin C creates an acidic stomach environment that favors iron absorption, it's a good idea to take your iron with some C. You can take a daily 250- to 500-milligram supplement or wash down your iron tablets with citrus or tomato juice. Or look for Vitron C, an over-the-counter iron supplement that contains vitamin C, advises Dr. Perlin.

Beef it up. "Iron-deficiency anemia usually doesn't result from an iron-poor diet," says Dr. Perlin. The Daily Value for iron is 18 milligrams. In general, 6 to 7 milligrams is available with each 1,000 calories of food. Of this amount, however, only 10 percent is absorbed, so try to eat iron-rich foods such as clams, red meat (the best source of dietary iron), Cream of Wheat cereal, tofu, and soybeans.

Menstruating women should be sure to eat a diet that provides an adequate amount of iron. If you are pregnant, you should double your intake of iron-containing foods, according to Dr. Perlin.

Take calcium with care. Are you stocking up on calcium in your thirties to guard against osteoporosis in your sixties? It's not a bad strategy, but calcium and iron make such good bedfellows that they cozy up together in the digestive tract. That prevents iron from being absorbed into your bloodstream where it belongs. So if you're using an iron supplement, take it at least 90 minutes before or after you take a calcium supplement or eat calcium-rich foods, says Dr. Harmon.

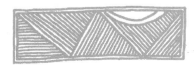

Anxiety Disorders

LEARNING TO CHILL

veryone thought I was losing my mind," explains Shari Green, while nervously tugging at the end of one of her long, black braids. "There I was, a law enforcement officer, and I was afraid to drive on a major highway!" Sometimes merely setting foot in an automobile was enough to make Shari's anxiety well up inside her. "It took every bit of concentration I could muster to stay in the car," she says. "I wanted to get out and run."

Shari's deathly fear of highways, triggered by on-the-job stress, was a typical anxiety disorder. Fortunately, she was able to find relief through psychiatric help and anti-anxiety medication, but the road to recovery was long and difficult. "I resisted going to a psychiatrist for eight months," says the 30-year-old California resident. "I'm so happy I finally reached out for help."

ANATOMY OF ANXIETY

Shari is back in the driver's seat, but her experience illustrates the disruptive power of an emotion that many of us take for granted as part of everyday life. Anxiety disorders strike about 5 percent of all Americans, but they're more common in young adults and in women, who are affected twice as often as men.

If anyone knows anxiety, it's African-Americans. After all, life can be a tense affair when simple activities such as earning a living or moving to a new neighborhood can mean dealing with discrimination. "The effects of racism are emotionally crippling and a main source of anxiety for Blacks," says Portia Hunt, Ph.D., professor of counseling psychology at Temple University in Philadelphia. "We're susceptible to all sorts of race-based scrutiny without having the power to eliminate the long-term effects racism can have on our lives."

But if you are suffering from an anxiety disorder, even small issues can become problems of major proportion. "You worry about things you can't solve, and you can't shut it off," says Dr. Hunt.

Even when race is not a factor, African-Americans have their share of bouts with chronic fear. "Anxiety put me in solitary confinement. It put walls around me," recalls Alan Mathis, a young city administrator in New York City. Alan dreaded unfamiliar places, an anxiety that may have stemmed from the unpredictability of growing up in an alcoholic household. The fear of being stranded by a train breakdown made his 90-minute commute a twice-daily test of nerves. "By the time I arrived at work, my freshly laundered clothes would often be soaked with perspiration," he remembers.

FIGURING OUT YOUR FEARS

If you suspect that you have an anxiety disorder, don't hesitate to see a therapist for a definite diagnosis. Your problem could be one or more of the following five types of anxiety.

Chronic anxiety. People with chronic anxiety are in distress 24-7, for months at a time. They're easily startled, uncomfortable around others, and often depressed. Other symptoms include chronic fatigue, headaches, and insomnia. And the cause of the anxiety may be unclear.

Phobias. Whether it's a fear of crowds or open places (agoraphobia), closed spaces (claustrophobia), or heights (acrophobia), phobias have three things in common.

▲ The fear is unrealistic. (It's highly unlikely that the elevator will plunge 29 floors to the ground the second you step inside.)
▲ The fear is persistent. (It lingers even after you've seen others ride safely all day.)
▲ The fear disrupts your life. (That is, unless you can leap 29 flights of stairs in a single bound.)

Obsessive-compulsive disorder. Unlike phobias, in which you're afraid of something in the world, people who are obsessive-compulsive are afraid of something inside themselves. They may also fear something outside themselves, such as dirt or lice. Obsessions are the thoughts that cause this type of anxiety, and compulsions are the behaviors that are done repeatedly to relieve the anxiety.

Stress disorders. These may be caused by either a current stressful situation (acute stress) or a stressful situation from the past for which the symptoms may be delayed in appearing (post-traumatic stress).

Panic attacks. A panic attack is a distinct period during which a person feels intense apprehension, fear, or terror. In the grip of a panic attack, you may be short of breath, have pain in your chest, feel smothering sensations, or feel as if you are going to lose control. Panic attacks may contribute to agoraphobia and make a person avoid leaving her home because she fears having an attack in a public place.

STAYING CALM AND COOL

One in three people with anxiety disorders eventually recovers, and men get better a bit more often than women. And since this is a disorder that tends to hit the young, it often settles down as you approach your late forties or fifties. Try these coping tactics, suggests Dr. Hunt.

Do the therapy thing. Sometimes anxiety disorders stem from an inner emotional conflict. For instance, your growing sexual attraction toward a co-worker might conflict with your no-sex-before-marriage upbringing, and now the thought of going to work sends you into a blind panic. Most anxiety sufferers don't consciously realize these connections, but working with a psychologist or psychiatrist can reveal them and suggest a way out, says Dr. Hunt.

Get it on tape. Imagining a catastrophe that you can't get out of your head? Describe the scenario on tape, then play it back over and over again. Chances are, this exercise will help you realize that your worries are greatly exaggerated, Dr. Hunt says.

Lose control. People with anxiety disorders are out of control about being in control. Often they are perfectionists who cannot delegate responsibility. Try to loosen up and learn to accept help.

Aspire to perspire. You can walk. You can swim. You can shoot some hoops. "It doesn't matter what kind of exercise you pick," says Dr. Hunt. "The important thing is to allow yourself to decompress."

Pamper yourself. "I often suggest that my Black women clients treat themselves to a massage," says Dr. Hunt. "Often they've never had permission to give themselves such a gift." It's a good idea to escape from the daily routine every once in a while. Dr. Hunt often sends clients to a nearby Quaker community to spend a weekend in quiet contemplation.

Anyone who's ever had a panic attack will tell you that they're terrifying. Panic attacks occur repeatedly in people with chronic anxiety, and they may last for several minutes or one or two hours, says Portia Hunt, Ph.D., professor of counseling psychology at Temple University in Philadelphia.

During a panic attack, you feel suddenly overwhelmed by a profound dread of impending catastrophe. The panic may be irrational—like the fear that your house will be blown to bits by a tornado in a matter of days—but it's so fierce that you can't think rationally. Your hands tremble. You feel sweaty. Your heart pounds, and you may hyperventilate. You could feel dizzy and nauseated, and you might have diarrhea. Sometimes you may fear that you're about to lose consciousness, experience a heart attack, or even die.

As debilitating as these symptoms can be, however, treatment can help keep panic attacks at bay. Here is a summary of the most effective remedies, according to Dr. Hunt.

Medication. Antidepressants and anti-anxiety drugs can prevent attacks or greatly reduce their frequency and severity.

Psychotherapy. Cognitive behavioral therapy brings relief to many. It works by teaching people to recognize the emotions that contribute to the attacks and learn to modify or even eliminate those feelings.

Group therapy. Talking things out in a self-help or support group may also be a great help.

Learn to de-stress. Alan's psychologist taught him to tune in to his body. "Now when I feel stress in my neck, temples, or forehead in the middle of a meeting, I'll massage those spots," he says. "Sometimes in my mind I'll go to another place, where I feel peace, or I'll recall a song I love. I'll play that song in my head and I'm okay."

Appendicitis

Knowing When You Need Help

Sunday dinner almost 13 years ago nearly cost young Libby Johnson her life.

"My mama was—and still is—one of the world's best cooks. My all-time favorite was her beef stew. One weekend, when I was 15, I ate so much of that beef stew that I was still feeling nauseated and nursing a stomachache the next day. Mama did what most sensible Black moms would do—she gave me a laxative," says Libby, who is now 28 and has two daughters of her own. "But when I got to school, my guidance counselor took one look at my face and sent me straight to the doctor." That night a surgeon removed a severely infected appendix from Libby's aching belly.

A Pouch with No Purpose

The appendix is a thin, finger-length pouch that extends from the large intestine (colon) in your lower right abdomen. Exactly what it does—besides getting inflamed and infected—is unknown. Doctors do know that like all colon tissue, the appendix produces mucus, which helps ease the passage of stool. Unfortunately, that mucus flow doesn't stop if the worm-shaped appendix happens to develop a kink or if a wayward fragment of food or stool clogs up the works. When that happens, the resulting buildup of mucus and bacteria can cause an infection.

Libby was lucky. Her mom's inability to recognize the symptoms of appendicitis in her daughter could have ended in disaster. Each year, approximately 1 in 500 Americans comes down with appendicitis, a severe infection of the appendix. If it's not treated quickly (usually within 24 hours), the inflamed or infected appendix can rupture, releasing bacteria into the abdominal cavity. This can lead to a potentially fatal infection of the lining of the stomach and intestines called peritonitis.

Doctors used to think that appendicitis, like other digestive dis-

Is It Gas . . . or Appendicitis?

You really overdid it at the family reunion. You put away enough ribs and collards to feed a family of four, and now your belly is dialing 911. Here are some warning signs that your distress may be appendicitis rather than overindulgence.

• Sudden onset of pain in the stomach or near the navel
• Pain that shifts after a few hours to the lower right side of the abdomen, which feels tender to the touch

You may also experience the following symptoms.

• Nausea and vomiting
• A low-grade fever of 99° to 100.5° F
• Pain that increases when you walk or jump up and down

In just about all appendicitis cases, there is pain. The last three symptoms appear in fewer than half of all appendicitis patients, so their absence doesn't necessarily mean that you're in the clear, says Georges Benjamin, M.D., deputy secretary for public health in Maryland and a former emergency physician in Silver Spring. When in doubt, get to a doctor—and pronto. Remember, an infected appendix can burst within 24 hours after the onset of symptoms.

If you suspect that you have appendicitis, don't eat anything before you go to the hospital. "They may want to operate on you as soon as possible," advises Dr. Benjamin. "If so, the anesthesiologist will want your stomach to be empty."

If you're pregnant, your doctor may be especially cautious because appendicitis often mimics the abdominal cramps that women have during pregnancy. If she is concerned about acute appendicitis, she may want to remove your appendix to be on the safe side, says Dr. Benjamin.

orders, was caused by too little dietary fiber. After all, the condition is rare in parts of the world where traditional staples like millet and yams haven't been edged out by white bread and junk food. But fiber may not be the smoking gun. One British study found a 50 percent lower risk of emergency appendectomy (removal of the appendix) among vegetarians than among people who eat meat. Although this study suggests that a nonmeat diet lowers the risk of appendicitis, researchers note that there may be other dietary or lifestyle factors that contribute to the reduced risk.

Cut
to the Chase

Prevention is not possible. The appendix is stubborn: If it wants to get inflamed, it will. So there's not much you can do to prevent a flare-up, says Georges Benjamin, M.D., deputy secretary for public health in Maryland and a former emergency physician in Silver Spring, but the best way to protect yourself is to know the warning signs (see "Is It Gas...or Appendicitis?").

Hold off on home remedies. As with many ailments, however, African-Americans often try a selection of home remedies for stomach pain before they will seek professional help. Dr. Benjamin has seen it all. "Folks will turn to enemas, laxatives, tea, alcohol, or warm milk if they think they have an ulcer. None of it will hurt you if you have an upset stomach, but if your discomfort is severe and lasts for more than a few hours, go to a doctor," he advises.

Say yes to surgery. If your doctor does discover that you have appendicitis, the only safe treatment is the surgical removal of the infected organ. This requires an abdominal incision that's usually a few inches long, but most patients are well enough to resume eating and drinking within 24 to 48 hours after the procedure and leave the hospital within a few days.

"Fear of surgery can be a major issue in some parts of the Black community," says Dr. Benjamin. But appendectomies are routine; they're performed more often than any other abdominal surgery except hernia repair. Besides, if your appendix is inflamed, refusing to have it removed can only lead to more serious health problems.

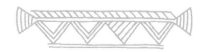

Ashy Skin

GETTING SKIN TO GLOW AGAIN

When C. J. Henderson met Laurita Frey for a shopping spree one Saturday afternoon at the mall, she was ready to shop. They hit Filene's Basement ahead of the crowds, made quick work of the sportswear racks, and met in the communal fitting room to try on their finds.

"I found a linen suit that was a steal. It was a size smaller than I am, but it was the last one they had, so I was praying that it would run large," C. J. remembers.

"And then, as I took off my slacks to try on the skirt, Laurita said to me, 'You'd also better pray you have some lotion for that ashy skin, C. J.,' pointing to my bare legs.

"I was mortifed," says C. J. "I looked in the mirror, and sure enough, my shins looked as if I had just stepped off a dry, dusty road, and my knees looked as if they were coated with chalk. In spite of all the lotion I used, my skin still dried up. No matter what I did, I was still ashy before the end of the day."

THAT AWFUL ASH

"Ashy skin is really a slang term, not something I'd diagnose medically," says Carla Herriford, M.D., a dermatologist in private practice in Los Angeles. "But it's a common concern among many of my African-American patients." Actually, the gray, chalky film we call ash, which most commonly occurs on the arms and legs, can result from two different skin conditions.

"It could simply be due to excessive dryness, meaning the skin does not produce enough natural oil," says Marcia Glenn, M.D., a dermatologist at the King-Drew Medical Center in Los Angeles. This typically is a milder form of ashy skin that simply appears as a dull, drained complexion. On the other hand, if the ashy area feels hard, rough, or itchy and appears very gray, it could be caused by accumulated dead skin that does not shed as quickly as it should, explains Dr. Glenn.

"Our skin normally renews itself every six weeks," says Dr. Herriford. "Sometimes this process is slower than normal so that as new layers of skin are formed underneath the existing layers, the dead outer layers stack up and create visible patches of dry, dusty-looking, or scaly skin."

GETTING BACK
TO BEAUTIFUL SKIN

Try these methods to keep your skin soft, supple, and glowing, says Dr. Herriford.

Take speedier showers. You may think that taking a bath or shower relieves dry skin, but bathing actually can set up a vicious drying cycle. Since bathing or showering can strip your skin's natural protective oils, your skin can end up drier after the bath water evaporates. To avoid this, limit baths or showers to five or ten minutes.

Be careful at bathtime. Bathe in lukewarm water—never hot. In the winter, when your skin is at its driest, consider washing only the odor-producing, hairy areas of your body daily and taking a whole-body shower or bath every other day. Since we don't sweat much in the winter, daily bathing is often excessive and unnecessary for hygiene purposes, say dermatologists.

Select a different soap. Most deodorant bars are too drying. Dr. Glenn recommends mild emollient brands such as Cetaphil, Dove (unscented), Oil of Olay, Neutrogena, Basis, and Alpha-Keri for ashy or dry skin. Most of these are available in bar and liquid form.

Pat dry. Don't rub yourself dry with your towel, says Dr. Herriford. Gently pat your skin dry instead.

Strike oil. An important step in combating dryness is to massage a pure, fragrance-free oil into your wet skin, Dr. Herriford suggests. Try fragrance-free baby oil, Neutrogena Body Oil (fragrance-free light sesame formula), or mineral oil, she adds.

Moisturize from the inside out. Dehydration can worsen dry skin. Be sure to drink about eight (8-ounce) glasses of water daily.

Drink more during periods of hot weather or heavy exercise, says Dr. Herriford. If your urine is dark yellow, that's an indication that you're not getting enough water, she adds.

Slough it off. C. J. made an appointment with a dermatologist, who advised her to use products that would help get rid of dead skin cells. "But I already use lotion all the time," C. J. said. Her doctor explained that for those of us with ashy skin, it's not enough to use a lotion that simply moisturizes. For stubborn ash, the best moisturizer is one that also speeds up the skin's sloughing process.

"Look for a lotion that contains glycolic acids, also known as alpha hydroxy acids or fruit acids. With continued use, these products help the skin to renew itself and shed dead cells more effectively," says Dr. Herriford. Eucerin Plus Alpha Hydroxy, Lubriderm Alpha Hydroxy Formula, and Lac-Hydrin Five are three brands to look for at your drugstore. C. J. switched to Lubriderm Alpha Hydroxy Formula and saw improvement after a few weeks.

See your doctor. If dryness continues even after you've tried these methods, get a medical checkup. "Persistent dry, itchy skin could signal an internal problem such as diabetes or thyroid disease," explains Dr. Herriford.

Asthma

BREATHING FREE

alarie Jordan, 38, was so sick as a child that she spent two years living thousands of miles from her hometown of Akron, Ohio. She stayed at a hospital in Denver, where asthma specialists could treat her. It was a hardship for her and her family, but for her generation, she was one of the lucky ones. "Patients like Valarie were the ones doctors lost 20 years ago," notes Cheryl Doyle, M.D., a pediatric pulmonologist at Woodhull Medical and Mental Health Center in Brooklyn.

In those days, there was more emphasis on treating the symptoms of asthma—the wheezing, coughing, and shortness of breath—and not enough on getting to the root cause. "I believe I survived because my symptoms softened with age and I gradually learned how to manage the disease," says Valarie. "But I also don't discredit the roles played by God, my parents, and two of the best doctors I could have had."

Like Valarie, more African-Americans have learned how asthma works and how to manage it so that they can lead productive, enjoyable lives. "I don't get sick as much as I used to," says Valarie, a data entry clerk for the U.S. Postal Service. "I still have to take medications, but I'm able to function normally. For me, learning to handle this disease was a double blessing, since my children have it and I am able to help them avoid some of the suffering that I went through."

HOW ASTHMA WORKS

Research, along with the experiences of people like Valarie, has helped a growing number of doctors gain a better understanding of asthma. They now know that it is caused primarily by inflammation in the lungs, and they're working with their patients to get them more involved in their own care. "There's more emphasis on preventive measures and home management and less on therapy after the fact," Dr. Doyle explains.

Asthma is a chronic inflammatory disease that obstructs airways (bronchial tubes) and makes them oversensitive to irritants. During an attack, the muscles that surround the airways tighten, causing the tubes to narrow inside as they become inflamed and swollen. To make matters worse, the glands within the tubes produce excess mucus. The passages become clogged, making it difficult to breathe air in and out. Some people say they become so short of breath that they feel as if they are suffocating or drowning.

The American Lung Association estimates that 14.6 million people in the United States have asthma, which is a 61 percent increase over the last decade. The asthma rate among African-Americans is 22 percent higher than the rate for Whites: 61 of every 1,000 Blacks have asthma, while only 50 of every 1,000 Whites are affected.

The mortality rate from asthma is three times higher among Blacks than among Whites. Blacks account for slightly more than one in five asthma deaths (21.5 percent), even though only one in eight people in the United States is Black.

TRACKING DOWN TRIGGERS

The American Lung Association reports that the reasons behind the differences between the races are unknown. There is also no known explanation for the increased rates of asthma over the last decade, but researchers have found critical gaps and barriers between asthma patients and health care resources. Eighteen U.S. states lack public or privately sponsored programs that target asthma care and education for low-income and minority populations. Additionally, most of the 50 states do not address the issues that can worsen asthma, such as smoking and poor-quality indoor air.

Lots of other things can also trigger an asthma attack, including pollen, mold spores in damp basements, or cold air, which can dry and irritate air passages. Valarie says that her triggers include cold weather, dust, smoke, feathers, pollen, and almost anything else outdoors.

"The interior environment is probably more important in triggering asthma reactions than it once was," says Elena R. Reece, M.D., chief of allergy and clinical immunology at Howard University Hospital in Washington, D.C. She notes that more people are spending more time inside and that wall-to-wall carpeting has grown in popularity. "Cockroaches and their droppings are also a major problem as an indoor allergen—similar to dust mites," Dr. Reece adds. "The reason we didn't know it before is that we didn't know to look for it."

Roughly only a quarter of childhood asthma sufferers outgrow the disease, according to the American Lung Association. "Patients are more likely to outgrow their pediatrician than outgrow their asthma," Dr. Reece says. Asthma can also flare up for the first time during pregnancy.

FINDING
THE RIGHT TREATMENT

"Treatment is improving, but one of the problems is that too many family physicians don't follow the guidelines established by the National Heart, Lung, and Blood Institute," Dr. Reece says. "People with asthma should be monitored with peak flow meters and have a treatment regimen. Many of the patients who have died may have lost their lives because the doctors who treated them really didn't know how sick they were," she says.

Too many doctors—and their patients—are still going for the "quick fix," she says, rather than the anti-inflammatory drugs that can eventually change the entire course of the disease. "They don't realize that just using a bronchodilator is good for 15 minutes or a couple of hours, but it has no lasting effect over the long haul.

"I'm terribly aggressive about treating patients," she continues. "I don't want my patients on the edge. I don't allow them to try the quick, temporary fixes."

The only over-the-counter asthma medications are low-level bronchodilators (Bronkaid Mist and Primatene Mist) and the comparable bronchodilator/expectorants (Bronkaid Caplets and Primatene Tablets). They help with mild asthma episodes but are not very useful for more serious attacks and can actually cause unpleasant side effects like heart palpitations. It is important that you talk with your doctor before taking any medications, explains Dr. Reece, especially because the treatment of asthma begins with identifying the cause. Different causes lead to different care plans.

A peak flow meter is a simple mechanical, handheld device that can give you an accurate measurement of how much airway obstruction and lung capacity you have at any time by recording the amount of air you blow into the meter. A peak flow meter is a crucial tool in obtaining an objective measurement of pulmonary function, says Elena R. Reece, M.D., chief of allergy and clinical immunology at Howard University Hospital in Washington, D.C.

Simple Self-Care

You can use a peak flow meter at home to help monitor your health, avoid potential attacks, and even spot the warning signs of an asthma attack a few days before you feel symptoms. The meters are available without a prescription, and most drugstores either carry them or will order one for you.

Once you and your doctor determine your maximum flow volume, the peak flow meter will tell you how you are doing on any given day. For example:

- If your lungs are operating at 80 to 100 percent of your maximum ability (green zone), you are doing well.
- If you're only managing 50 to 80 percent of your max (yellow zone), you should begin to monitor your peak flow more frequently. Most likely you will also have to alter your medications when you are in the yellow zone, says Dr. Reece.
- Anything below 50 percent of your max (red zone) is usually considered a medical alert, and aggressive therapy with medications is needed. Call your doctor.

Experts recommend measuring your lung capacity at least twice a day, at the same time every morning and evening, particularly if you plan some kind of strenuous activity. The measurement should be taken before you use your medications, but if your reading is lower than normal, take your asthma medications and retest after 30 minutes.

The main types of prescription asthma medications are bronchodilators, anti-inflammatory agents, and corticosteroids. They can be taken as liquids or pills, through a metered dose inhaler, or as a mist using a machine called a nebulizer.

Anti-inflammatory drugs include nedocromil (Tilade) and cromolyn (Intal), which, when taken at the same time every day, prevent asthma attacks but do not treat an active attack. Some bronchodilators, like albuterol (Proventil), start working after 5 minutes and last anywhere from 3 to 8 hours, making them effective during attacks. The bronchodilator salmeterol (Serevent) lasts up to 12 hours but takes about 20 minutes to work, making it unsuitable for emergencies but ideal for nighttime symptoms.

Corticosteroids like prednisone (Orasone) and dexamethasone (Hexadrol) play a role in managing chronic, severe asthma only when other medications have proven ineffective. There are side effects associated with corticosteroids, such as high blood pressure, cataracts, and muscle weakness, that can be reduced by limiting their use.

Another form of treatment, immunotherapy, involves injections of the very substances, such as pollens, molds, or dust, that cause asthma attacks. The idea is that the body will build up a resistance to the asthma-inducing factors.

AN ASTHMA
ACTION PLAN

If you think having a healthy, active life with asthma is impossible, think again. The next time you watch Olympian Jackie Joyner-Kersee in action, you'll see an example of how much energy a person with severe asthma can have at her disposal—with the proper medical attention, of course.

"An ounce of prevention is worth a couple of pounds of cures, medicines, and injections," Dr. Reece likes to say. Here, from Dr. Doyle and Dr. Reece, are a few ways to trounce the potential asthma triggers in your life.

Get the smoke out. First of all, says Dr. Doyle, no one should smoke in the house or in the car. Some people go so far as to get rid of pets, strip wallpaper, pull up carpeting, or vacuum until their arms are ready to fall off, but they won't give up cigarettes. It's terrible for adults with asthma and even worse for children.

"Some people say things like, 'I only smoke in the bathroom,' as if the smoke stays within the confines of the bathroom," Dr. Doyle says. But smoke is one of the most pervasive threats to people with

Here are the early warning signs that an asthma flare-up is on its way.

- Wheezing
- Difficulty breathing
- Restless sleep
- Tightness in your chest
- Itchy throat
- Fatigue
- Cough when you don't have a cold
- Headache
- Runny nose
- Change in the color, thickness, or amount of mucus
- Peak flow readings in the yellow or red zone

In the event of an actual asthma attack, you must increase the use of bronchodilating medications and institute the use of corticosteroids, according to your physician's instructions.

asthma, she warns, since it lingers for such a long time in clothing and hair and in the air. And these trace amounts are enough to trigger an asthma attack.

Plan on plastic. Get an airtight cover for your mattress (better yet, get a waterbed) or at least vacuum your mattress on a regular basis.

The problem here is dust mites, microscopic bugs that live in bedding and other dusty surfaces and can irritate your lungs. Getting rid of mites entirely is impossible, since about 2,000 of the little suckers can fit on the head of a pin, but you can buy covers made of airtight plastic or special allergen-proof fabric for pillows, mattresses, and box springs. Wash your bed linens weekly in water that is hotter than 130°F; cooler water will not kill dust mites.

Call the Asthma and Allergy Foundation of America at 1-800-7-ASTHMA for information on special air filters, bedding, household cleaners, and other products.

Live with leather. Mites also love couches and chairs because upholstered furniture collects more dust. If you don't mind vinyl or leather furniture, buy it. It's the best thing for your asthma, says Dr. Reece.

Can the carpet. Here's bad news if you're a wall-to-wall fan: Dust mites, mold, animal dander, and other unsavory substances love to hang out in carpets. Wood or linoleum floors are best because they provide less opportunity for allergens to survive than a carpet laid over a concrete floor.

Kill the clutter. Avoid dust catchers. Keep stuffed toys out of the rooms of children with asthma, and go light on the knick-knacks.

Scrub the spores. Periodically washing humid, moist areas like kitchens, bathrooms, and basements with bleach or another household cleaner that's slightly diluted with water is an excellent way to eliminate mold, says Dr. Reece. Pay particular attention to garbage containers, rotting wood floors, damp firewood, windowsills, and water-damaged wallpaper—they all harbor mold. And make sure that all bedding is washed at temperatures above 140°F.

Don't buy down. All of your pillows, comforters, and coats should be filled with synthetic fibers, as goose down is a common trigger for asthma. Wash your comforters and pillows regularly and replace synthetic pillows every two to three years, says Dr. Reece.

Clean the air. Use the air conditioner instead of opening the windows, and change the filters frequently. Better yet, purchase a HEPA (high-efficiency particulate) filter to clean your air. If you have a central heating or air-conditioning unit, you can purchase a HEPA filter to replace the regular air filter you use now. There are also portable HEPA air filtration systems that plug into regular household outlets and come in many different sizes so they fit almost anywhere. Look in the appliance section of most stores.

Watch what you eat. Ask your doctor to test you for food allergies. And beware of sulfites, preservatives that are used to eliminate bacteria, increase the storage life, and preserve the freshness and brightness of certain food products; they can lead to an asthma attack if ingested. There are a number of foods that contain sulfites, such as beer, wine products, salad bar items, and desserts, so pay special attention to food labels and check with restaurant managers when you go out to eat. Terms to look for on labels include sulfur dioxide, potassium bisulfite or potassium metabisulfite, and sodium bisulfite, sodium metabisulfite, or sodium sulfite.

Don't inhale. Stay away from aerosol vapors from cleaning solvents, deodorants, or perfumes. Whenever possible, use pump sprays instead of aerosols and always ventilate whenever cleaning products are used.

Delegate. Household cleaning jobs that involve disturbing dust or using chemicals should be passed on to other family members. Wear a filtration mask, available at most drugstores, for do-it-yourself jobs.

Be regular. See your doctor on a regular schedule for checkups and treatment. Asthma is a disease that should be watched and managed by a medical professional.

Protect yourself from pets. If you want to hold on to the family cat or dog, get them used to bathtime. An asthma-free family member (or a grooming service) should wash them regularly. Yes, cats can be scrubbed down; they don't like it, but they get used to it. Also, keep Brutus and Fluffy out of the bedroom. If these measures aren't practical or don't help, consider adopting a lizard or a few fish.

Atherosclerosis
Protecting the Pathways to Your Heart

Sharetha King nervously bit her lip as she described the long, dark brown scar that starts just below her Grandpa Eddie's right ear and snakes almost 6 inches down his neck. "At 78, my granddad is still a spry, handsome man who looks years younger than his age. I guess that's why it hurts me so much to see him struggling through surgery after surgery as the doctors try to keep his arteries open," Sharetha explains. "His spirits are still high when he's in the hospital, and he's always anxious to come home, but he's been suffering for years."

Grandpa Eddie's health troubles began in his late fifties with a mild heart attack. By the time he reached his seventies, his blood vessels were so clogged that surgeons had to remove fatty deposits from arteries in his neck and leg. "Now even the circulation to his heart is being slowed by a clogged and hardened vein," says Sharetha.

Sharetha and her grandmother listened to doctors warn Eddie for years about how his cigarette smoking and habit of eating fried fish, smothered pork chops, and other fatty foods were giving him atherosclerosis, or hardening of the arteries. He is the fourth relative in two generations of Sharetha's family to fall ill with heart disease. These days, though, she not only worries about her granddad, she is beginning to worry about herself.

The Risk
for African-Americans

Sharetha's fears aren't just needless worry, as her granddad might say. They are common sense. Atherosclerosis is a leading cause of cardiovascular (heart) disease, and heart disease is America's number one health threat. It's responsible for almost one million deaths each year.

Since most heart disease research focuses on White men, however, not too many people know that African-American women are the ones who suffer most from heart problems.

"Black women have the highest death rates from heart disease, and they develop it at earlier ages than any other population in the United States," says Anne L. Taylor, M.D., associate professor of medicine and cardiology at Case Western Reserve University in Cleveland. The death rate is 69 percent higher in Black women than in White women. And as Sharetha suspected, having a family history of heart disease adds to your risk.

There is more research on African-American men, but it also gives cause for alarm: 46 percent more Black men die of heart disease than White men.

How Does It Happen?

What causes atherosclerosis? Everyone's blood vessels, which are flexible in childhood, stiffen with age. But too many plates of soul food (or any fatty, cholesterol-rich food) can stiffen them even more. When we eat extra fat, some of it clings to the walls of our veins and arteries and hardens into a substance called plaque. Over time, plaque can narrow blood vessels or eventually block them completely. These blockages can cause a stroke or a heart attack. They can also cause numbness or extreme pain in the legs, feet, hands, or arms.

Even when plaque doesn't block a blood vessel, it can reduce its flexibility. That's important, because arteries normally expand with every heartbeat to accommodate each pulse of blood. In this way, the artery helps diminish the shock of the heartbeats and keep your blood pressure low. The stiffer the blood vessel, the greater the risk of hypertension (high blood pressure), which in turn contributes to everything from kidney disease to eye problems.

Rich food isn't the only culprit here. High blood pressure, smoking, excess alcohol consumption, obesity, diabetes, sedentary living, and premature menopause (from early hysterectomy) all play a role in atherosclerosis.

It's no wonder that heart disease has such an impact on us. "Compared to Whites, African-Americans have more hypertension, a disproportionate amount of cigarette smoking, and more obesity, starting in the teen years," says John M. Flack, M.D., associate professor of surgery, medicine, and public health sciences and associate director and medical director of the hypertension center at Bowman Gray School of Medicine at Wake Forest University in Winston-Salem, North Carolina.

PREVENTING
A "HARD" ATTACK

That's the frustrating news. The good news is that atherosclerosis—and the many health problems it can create—is preventable.

Fix it while you're young. The best prescription is to stop atherosclerosis before it starts. "You can reduce your risk later in life even if you haven't done everything right in your twenties and thirties," advises Dr. Flack. "But the best option of all is to adopt healthy lifestyles that prevent high risk in the first place." Although the consequences often aren't clinically evident until people reach middle age (women seem to enjoy some protection until they reach menopause), cardiovascular disease can begin before age 20. So it's never too early to plan ahead.

Play the numbers. Experts suggest that you keep track of your blood pressure and cholesterol levels and do your best to keep them low and under control.

One way to keep track is by getting tested. Anyone over age 20 should have his blood pressure checked every year and his cholesterol checked every three to five years. Everyone should be tested at least once in childhood or adolescence. If your blood pressure or cholesterol readings start to climb, Dr. Taylor suggests a healthy diet and exercise as a way to get them under control.

Ideally, your total cholesterol level should be less than 200 milligrams per deciliter (mg/dl); 240 mg/dl or higher is very hazardous, especially if you smoke, are overweight, or have high blood pressure. Normal blood pressure for an adult is a systolic reading (the top, larger number) of 140 or less and a diastolic reading (the bottom, smaller number) of 90 or less. (For more on high blood pressure, see page 222.)

Put those calories on a diet. You need to be especially careful of fat calories. The average American gets 40 percent of daily calories from fat, but nutritionists advise keeping fat intake at 20 to 30 percent. How? Watch what you eat. Substitute skim milk for whole, for example. Buy low-fat frozen yogurt instead of ice cream. Try mushroom and nonfat mozzarella cheese on your pizza rather than sausage and pepperoni. Go for fish and chicken over chops and burgers. Broil foods, don't fry them. Cook foods with vegetable or chicken broth rather than lard or bacon drippings.

Toss that salt shaker. "People with hypertension who exercise, lose weight, and lower their salt intake sometimes find that their blood pressures fall into the normal range without resorting to medication," says Dr. Flack. Giving up salt doesn't mean settling for food that tastes like cardboard. First try reducing the amount of salt in your recipes by half. Rinse the salt from canned tuna, sardines, and beans. Spice up your cooking with lemon juice, garlic, hot peppers, and other sassy seasonings. And slow down on fast foods, some of which are notoriously high in sodium.

Don't retire—perspire. "That doesn't mean training like Flo-Jo," reassures Dr. Flack. All you need to do is walk at a comfortable pace for 20 or 30 minutes three or four times a week. No one in America is more sedentary than Black women. The American Heart Association says that 67 percent of African-American women (and 62 percent of African-American men) get little physical activity. So get up and get moving for good health.

Teetotal most of the time. Research shows that a little alcohol may prevent heart disease, but too much can help to make your arteries rigid. Keep alcohol consumption to a moderate one drink a day for women and no more than two drinks a day for men (a drink can be 12 ounces of beer, 5 ounces of wine, or 1.5 ounces of liquor).

Even if you have a family history of atherosclerosis, like Sharetha, putting these tips to good use will dramatically increase your chances of keeping your arteries clean, clear, and plaque-free.

Back Pain

BEING KIND TO YOUR SPINE

he back is one body part that does lots of hard work but usually receives little attention. But for Willa Johnson, thinking—no, worrying—about her back was a full-time job.

"For years, with no warning, sharp pains would shoot from my lower back and down my left leg, leaving me temporarily unable to move without excruciating pain," says Willa. "And doctors offered little help: One told me I had phlebitis, another swore I had gout—you name it," recalls the young religion professor. "Then one day I was sitting in a hospital emergency room explaining my tale of woe to yet another physician when, to my amazement, he diagnosed me on the spot."

The source of her misery was a herniated disk, which Willa had suffered unknowingly in a fall. Now that she knows what she's dealing with, she takes extra precautions to protect her tender back. All of her footwear has soft soles to minimize jarring movements to her spine. And when she's able, she walks three miles a day to help strengthen her back muscles. "There's only one person who can treat my back with the ultimate loving care," she says. "And that's me."

BACK TO BASICS

For Americans, lower back pain is the second most frequent reason for doctors' visits (the first is the common cold). And it's the leading cause of disability for people under age 45.

Back pain can strike just about anyone at any time, but there are steps that you can take to protect yourself. First you need to get to know your body, and your back, a little better. You may be a prime candidate for backaches if you belong to one or more of the following categories.

▲ Are you female and over 45? Women's overall bone mass begins to decrease after menopause, which can mean an increased risk of back injuries.

▲ Are you in a love/hate thing with your bathroom scale? If you're obese (25 pounds over your ideal weight)—and 60 percent of Black women are by the time they reach middle age—your back may be paying the price.

▲ Are you cheered by the absence of "No Smoking" signs? Nicotine in tobacco smoke reduces the oxygen supply to the disks that cushion your backbone and heightens the risk of degenerative changes in your spine.

▲ Do you sometimes feel that the term *couch potato* was coined just for you? Sedentary folks suffer more back pain than people who get at least 30 minutes of aerobic exercise three times per week.

▲ Is your work more like a workout? Eight hours of standing or heavy lifting can be cruel and unusual punishment for your back if you are not fit.

As you can see, the source of back pain can be tough to diagnose because so many things can cause it. The underlying problem might be as minor as a muscle strain, as subtle as stress, as mysterious as the muscle disorder fibromyalgia, or as life-threatening as a tear in the aorta, the body's main artery. What's more, your doctor may not spend enough time with you to sort through all the possibilities.

"When White patients complain of back pain, physicians often perform a careful examination to rule out serious health problems," says Detroit neurosurgeon Lucius Tripp, M.D., a specialist in occupational and preventive medicine. "I feel Black patients are more likely to have their complaints dismissed."

RELIEVING THE ACHE

Should back pain strike—and it hits an estimated 80 percent of us at some point in our lives—forget the traditional remedies. Extended bed rest, surgery, prescription medications, and passive patients are passé, according to recent guidelines from the U.S. Agency for Health Care Policy and Research. The new approaches stress gentle exercise, over-the-counter painkillers, chiropractic care, and active patient involvement. Happily, 9 out of 10 people with acute lower back pain find relief within one month without costly medical intervention such as surgery. Here's Dr. Tripp's advice and prescription.

Get thee to a doctor. Severe back pain or any back pain associated with numbness in the groin, extreme leg weakness, or problems controlling your bowels or bladder warrants a visit to your doctor. Also see your doctor if your pain persists for more than a few days.

Learn how to lift. Take a back-friendly approach to hoisting. Keep your back straight, hold the object close to your body, and bend at the knees, not the waist.

Love those flats. Comfortable low-heeled shoes are infinitely kinder to your spine than high heels, which contort your back into an unnatural posture.

Give it a rest. When you're off your feet, sit erect in a high-backed chair and rest your feet on a low stool.

Hit the sack. If the problem is minor enough for home care, the best therapy begins with bed rest, but it should be limited to two days, says Dr. Tripp.

For the first two days of treatment, apply an ice pack to reduce any swelling. Put some ice in a freezer bag or use a package of frozen vegetables and wrap the cold pack in a towel to protect your skin. Find a comfortable position and apply the ice to your back for 15 minutes three or four times a day.

After two days, slowly resume your daily activities within tolerable and comfortable limits. Continue the cold treatments and alternate with heat by taking three or four 15-minute warm (not scalding) showers each day or applying a heating pad set on medium for a maximum of 15 minutes, also three or four times daily. (Do not sleep on a heating pad, as serious burns can occur). Check with your doctor to determine how long you should continue the treatments. Dr. Tripp finds that alternating heat and cold shortens the duration of therapy and reduces the risk of tissue damage.

Minimize further back strain whenever you're in bed by placing pillows under your knees while lying on your back. Do not lie on your abdomen, because this causes more strain on your spine. Use a firm mattress and a single pillow for your head, and place a pillow between your knees when you sleep on your side to keep your spine from bowing.

Pick a pain pill. There's no need to be a martyr. Use a painkiller like acetaminophen or a nonsteroidal anti-inflammatory drug such as aspirin, ibuprofen (Advil, Nuprin), or naproxen (Aleve).

Take an alternative route. Spinal manipulation by a chiropractor, osteopath, or other therapist can be helpful in the early stages of back pain, according to Dr. Tripp. Acupuncture is also increasingly accepted as a successful treatment for back pain. (To find an acupuncturist in your area, contact the American Academy of Medical Acupuncture at 5820 Wilshire Boulevard, Suite 500, Los Angeles, CA 90034.) But if the pain doesn't diminish within four weeks, return for a re-evaluation.

Move it around. Start stretching your back as soon as the pain permits. Be gentle, and don't bounce. Here's one good stretch: Lie on your back, hug your knees to your chest and hold for up to 20 seconds. You can expect a little discomfort, but if it hurts, stop. The stretching sets the stage for light exercise that will strengthen your muscles and prevent reinjury. Pick an activity that causes minimal back stress, such as are walking, biking, or swimming.

Two weeks or so after the onset of the pain, gradually add to your regimen of exercises to strengthen your stomach and back muscles. Ask your doctor or physical therapist to provide appropriate exercises.

Change your style. Often the most challenging aspect of recovery is making the lifestyle changes that help guarantee that the pain won't return. If you're not used to it, it's not always easy to incorporate regular exercise, good nutrition, and smoke-free living into your everyday routine. But you should try. Your back will thank you for your efforts.

"A low-fat diet rich in fiber, antioxidants, and carbohydrates gives your body the nutrients it needs to build strong muscles and bones," says Dr. Tripp. "And when you stop smoking, your blood carries more oxygen that allows injured muscles to heal and healthy muscles to operate at peak efficiency."

Birth Control

PROTECTING AGAINST UNWANTED PREGNANCY

vonne Miller already has three children, and she's only 22. All are loved, but not one was planned.

"After my first child was born in 1987, my doctor recommended the Pill," Yvonne explains. "I thought it would be easy and safe, but sometimes I'd forget to take it, and in 1988 I got pregnant again. After I had the baby, my doctor suggested a diaphragm, foam, and condoms, but I found them too complicated to use, so I stayed on the Pill instead.

"Because I was having terrible side effects, my doctor kept changing the dosage. With one formula I was soaking through pads. Another gave me really bad cramps. And somehow I still got pregnant: In 1991 I had another baby. Without a doubt, I needed a better method of birth control.

"The doctors at my clinic wanted everyone to have Norplant, but I'd heard a lot of horror stories about it. So in 1992 I decided to try 'the shot' (Depo-Provera). It was convenient, but no one warned me that it would make me feel as if I were pregnant. I had bloated breasts, and I was always angry. I had no period for six months, but when it came, it lasted two months! My body ballooned from a size 13 to a size 24. Then my hair started falling out—I even had bald spots!

"Well, my depression, weight gain, and hair loss ended when I ended the shots. Since 1993 I've used condoms, foam, jellies—whatever it takes."

BIRTH CONTROL BLUES

Stories like Yvonne's illustrate the problems that can occur with different forms of contraception, and most women of childbearing age (15 to 44) can relate to the confusion and difficulty of finding the right type of birth control. Although pregnancy itself has risks, the unfortunate fact is that even in our age of high-tech medical miracles, problems with contraception—from debilitating side effects to high failure rates—are still a common part of life.

Sixty percent of the 58 million women of childbearing age in the United States use contraception, yet one study revealed that 60 percent of pregnancies in this country are unplanned. And even if you do prevent pregnancy, you may not be able to prevent the serious side effects of many forms of birth control.

Why are so many women getting pregnant unintentionally? Unplanned pregnancies are largely due to what laboratories label contraceptive failures and the rest of us call accidents. One reason is that pregnancy risk is inseparable from sexual intimacy, explains Carol Archie, M.D., assistant professor of obstetrics and gynecology at the University of California at Los Angeles School of Medicine. "I think our age of technology gives you the idea that you can protect yourself against everything. That's not true. We have to realize that (sexual) intimacy is not to be taken lightly; there is a certain amount of risk that you just must accept."

The numbers illustrate Dr. Archie's point. Although many methods tout success rates of 99 percent or higher in the laboratory, their success rates in our bedrooms are far less impressive. To achieve the rates that are trumpeted in product advertising, you must use a method consistently and correctly *every* time. Even a low annual failure rate translates into a pregnancy risk for the average woman after years of use.

Making Contraception Work for You

When you select a form of birth control, you have to take many factors, including your lifestyle, health, and comfort level with certain methods, into account.

The contraceptive implant (Norplant), for example, is extremely effective: Fewer than 1 woman in 1,000 becomes pregnant while using it. But women who use it have experienced bleeding, weight gain, moodiness, sore breasts, headache, and nausea. It is also less effective for women who weigh more than 150 pounds, which is a consideration for a higher percentage of Black women than

White women. Keloids (scar tissue) can also form over the implants, making removal difficult for doctors and very painful for patients. In some of the worst cases, the implants have worked their way through the skin and caused bleeding.

And then there's the Pill. The Pill has many health benefits if you're a good candidate. Women who take it lower their risk not only of pregnancy but also of endometrial cancer, ectopic pregnancy, endometriosis, anemia, ovarian cancer, menstrual cramps, and even pelvic inflammatory disease. The Pill is also 99 percent effective in preventing pregnancy—*if* you take it as directed.

If you are like many Black women, however, and are at high risk for diabetes, high blood pressure, or heart disease, or if you have sickle cell disease, you should be carefully screened before considering oral contraceptives. Women who have an increased risk of developing breast or cervical cancer might also want to consider using another method, since the research into these risks is still inconclusive.

On top of all this, actual-use failure rates for the Pill are considerably higher than laboratory rates. About 5 out of every 1,000 women using the Pill become pregnant in a year's time, mostly because they forget to take it. If you have a foggy memory, the Pill is probably *not* for you. And neither the Pill nor the other methods mentioned above provide protection against sexually transmitted diseases (STDs) such as HIV/AIDS.

Even the simple, old-fashioned methods like condoms have their drawbacks. Latex condoms are the best protection, other than abstinence, against HIV/AIDS and other STDs, but research has shown that women are far more accepting of their use than men. The best bet for women is to learn to be comfortable with asking their partners to wear condoms or to protect themselves with female condoms. All types of condoms are cheap and readily available at any well-stocked drugstore.

As you can see, avoiding potential health and pregnancy problems, not to mention steering clear of STDs, is not exactly simple. To make it easier to sort out your options, the table on page 44 is designed to help you compare methods and gather the information you need to have an informed discussion with your doctor or health care provider and make the best possible choice.

Birth Control Pill (The Pill)

Effectiveness	97–99.9%
What It Is	A prescription pill that you take once a day, every day.
How It Works	Combination pills contain estrogen and progestin, which prevent the release of eggs. Mini-pills contain only progestin. Both types thicken cervical mucus to keep sperm from entering the uterus and prevent a fertilized egg from implanting in the uterus.
Advantages	There's nothing to put in place before intercourse. Periods are more regular. Protects against ovarian and endometrial cancers, pelvic inflammatory disease, noncancerous breast tumors, and ovarian cysts; reduces chances of tubal pregnancy.
Possible Side Effects	Irregular bleeding, depression, nausea, and other discomforts. In rare cases, blood clots, heart attack, and stroke. Women who are over 35 and smoke and those who are greatly overweight are at greatest risk.
Comments	Must be taken daily. Does not protect against STDs.

Cervical Cap

82–91% for women who have not had a child;
64–74% for women who have had a child

A thimble-shaped latex cap, fitted by a doctor, that is coated with spermicide, then inserted into the vagina to cover the opening of the cervix.

Acts a barrier to keep sperm from entering the uterus.

There are no major health concerns.

Allergies to spermicide.

Does not protect against STDs, can be messy, and cannot be used during vaginal bleeding or infection. There are only four sizes to choose from, which makes it difficult to fit some women. Other women may find it difficult to use.

(continued)

The Birth Control Basics—Continued

	Condom
Effectiveness	88–98% for male condom; 79–95% for female condom
What It Is	The male condom is a latex, polyurethane, or animal-membrane sheath that covers the penis during intercourse. The female condom is a polyurethane sleeve that fits into the vagina.
How It Works	Keeps sperm from entering the uterus. Spermicidal lubricants can be used with a condom to immobilize sperm.
Advantages	Latex condoms are effective protection against STDs, including HIV, the AIDS virus. The male and female polyurethane condom may offer some protection. They are relatively inexpensive and are widely available.
Possible Side Effects	Allergic reactions to latex and loss of sensation for men.
Comments	Condoms can break. Do not use oil-based lubricants like petroleum jelly on latex condoms. Instead, use a water-based lubricant like K-Y Jelly. To prevent sperm leakage, hold the male condom against the penis when withdrawing from the vagina. Animal-membrane condoms do not protect against STDs.

Depo-Provera	Diaphragm
99.7%	82–94%
A hormone injection in a woman's arm or buttock that's given every 12 weeks by a doctor or nurse.	A shallow latex cup, fitted by a doctor, that is coated with spermicide, then inserted into the vagina to cover the opening of the cervix.
Prevents the release of eggs, prevents sperm from entering the uterus, and stops fertilized eggs from implanting in the uterus.	Acts as a barrier to keep sperm from entering the uterus.
Protects against pregnancy for 12 weeks. There's nothing to put in place before intercourse. Can be used during breastfeeding (6 weeks after delivery) and by some women who cannot take the Pill. Protects against endometrial cancer and iron-deficiency anemia.	There are no major health concerns.
Irregular bleeding, weight gain, headaches, depression, and abdominal pain. Side effects cannot be reversed until the medication wears off (up to 12 weeks). May cause a delay in conception after treatments are stopped.	Increased risk of bladder infection; allergies to spermicide.
Does not protect against STDs.	Does not protect against STDs, can be messy, and cannot be used during vaginal bleeding or infection.

(continued)

	Fertility Awareness Methods (FAMs) or Periodic Abstinence (Rhythm)
Effectiveness	80–99%
What It Is	Women learn from a professional how to chart their menstrual cycle and detect physical signs to help predict fertile days. It is necessary to abstain from sex on those days.
How It Works	Methods of charting a woman's cycle include checking temperature daily, checking cervical mucus daily, and recording menstrual cycles on a calendar.
Advantages	No pills or medications are needed.
Possible Side Effects	No medical side effects.
Comments	Do not protect against STDs. Women with irregular periods or temperature patterns cannot use these methods. Uncooperative partners and poor record-keeping can compromise effectiveness. Illness, lack of sleep, and other conditions and events can affect body temperature. Vaginal infections and douches change mucus.

Intrauterine Device (IUD)	Morning-After Pills or Emergency Contraceptives
97.4–99.2%	92-98%
A small plastic device inserted in a woman's uterus by a doctor.	A series of pills that can reduce risk of pregnancy if taken within 72 hours of unprotected intercourse.
Contains copper or hormones that keep sperm from fertilizing an egg and/or prevent a fertilized egg from implanting in the uterus.	Temporarily disrupts a woman's hormonal pattern and either prevents sperm from fertilizing an egg or stops a fertilized egg from implanting in the uterus.
There's nothing to put in place before intercourse and no daily pill to take. Copper IUDs may be left in place for up to 10 years. IUDs don't affect hormone levels. IUDs that contain hormones may reduce menstrual cramps and can be left in for 1 year.	Can be used after unprotected intercourse.
Increased cramps, spotting between periods, heavier and longer periods, and (rarely) a puncture in the wall of the uterus. Also an increased chance of tubal infection, which can lead to sterility.	Nausea, vomiting, and/or headaches.
Does not protect against STDs.	Most doctors and clinics know about this method, but many don't prescribe them unless a woman asks.

(continued)

	Norplant
Effectiveness	99.96%
What It Is	Six small capsules inserted under the skin of a woman's upper arm by a doctor.
How It Works	The capsules constantly release small amounts of hormone that prevent the release of eggs and thicken the cervical mucus to keep sperm from fertilizing an egg.
Advantages	Protects against pregnancy for 5 years. There's nothing to put in place before intercourse. Can be used during breastfeeding (6 weeks after delivery) and by women who cannot take the Pill. Can be removed at any time, but only by a doctor.
Possible Side Effects	Scarring can occur at the insertion site, and Black women run the risk of keloid scarring, a raised scar that has different pigmentation than the rest of the skin. Some women experience irregular bleeding, headaches, nausea, depression, nervousness, dizziness, weight gain, and (rarely) infection at the insertion site.
Comments	Does not protect against STDs.

Spermicides	Sterilization
72–97%	99.6–99.8%
Spermicides in the form of contraceptive foams, creams, jellies, films, or suppositories that can be purchased without a prescription	For women, tubal ligation blocks the fallopian tubes, where the sperm fertilizes an egg. For men, vasectomy blocks the tubes that carry sperm.
Spermicides are inserted into the vagina shortly before intercourse to keep sperm from fertilizing an egg. Spermicides also immobilize sperm.	Keeps sperm from fertilizing an egg.
Most products are easy to use and relatively inexpensive to buy in drugstores and supermarkets.	Provides permanent protection against pregnancy and does not affect sexual pleasure.
Can be messy. May cause irritation, allergic reactions, or mild vaginal infections.	No lasting side effects after recovery from the operation. Complications may include bruising at the incision site and (rarely) blood vessel or bowel injury. With vasectomy, complications may include blood clots in or near the testicles, bruising, swelling, or tenderness of the scrotum, or leaking sperm that may form temporary small lumps near the testicles.
A spermicide with nonoxynol-9 may provide protection against many STDs, but it must always be used with a latex condom.	Reversibility cannot be guaranteed. In rare instances, tubes can reconnect, allowing pregnancy to occur. Does not protect against STDs.

(continued)

Withdrawal

Effectiveness

81–96%

What It Is

The man removes his penis from the vagina before he ejaculates.

How It Works

Keeps sperm from entering the uterus.

Advantages

An option if no other method is available.

Possible Side Effects

None, but requires great self-control for optimum effectiveness.

Comments

Preejaculate can contain enough sperm to cause pregnancy. Pregnancy is also possible if the semen or preejaculate spills into the outer area of the vagina. Does not protect against STDs.

Breast Cancer

SAVING YOUR LIFE AND YOUR BREASTS

Wilhelmina Grant is 39, but she looks and moves like a young girl. The tall, lithe flight attendant, karate expert, and health advocate is known for her boundless energy and her wide, frequent smile.

"After my breast cancer diagnosis, I created a job description for myself. I decided to get the message out to other African-American women that breast cancer does not only affect middle-aged White women.

"I tell sisters, you, your mother, and your cousin are also at risk, so you need to be proactive in seeking health care. Bone up on the issues and get your mammograms as prescribed by your doctor," she says in a voice filled with determination. She knows the importance of high-quality medical care.

Wilhelmina, a volunteer outreach coordinator for SHARE Self-Help for Women with Breast or Ovarian Cancer , a New York City–based nonprofit organization that provides emotional and social support services for women, their friends, and families, shudders to think what might have happened had she not had a minor mishap in karate class.

"I was in a sparring match and my opponent inadvertently hit my breast. The unexpected pain brought my attention to a tumor that had been growing undetected in that spot for who knows how long," she explains. A visit to a doctor confirmed Wilhelmina's fears—she did indeed have breast cancer.

After undergoing a lumpectomy, chemotherapy, radiation, and hormone therapy, she is cured. She's also convinced that the karate incident was no accident. "It's that divine intervention thing," Wilhelmina says.

"Now here I am, doing outreach work and helping protect other women from dying of cancer," she says.

Black Women and Breast Cancer

Newspapers, television, and magazines focus on the fact that White women develop breast cancer at a higher rate than Black women. But Raymond B. Wynn, M.D., assistant professor in the Department of Radiation Oncology at the Louisiana State University Medical Center in New Orleans, questions this assumption.

When measured by race, the number of new cases is only slightly lower in Black females. The incidence rate is 112 per 100,000 White women and 95 per 100,000 Black women, says Dr. Wynn. For African-American women, even bigger problems arise after the diagnosis. We are 1½ times more likely to be diagnosed at a late stage of the disease, which is one of the reasons that our breast cancer death rates are almost 15 percent higher than those of White women.

Since the key to being cured is early detection, more African-American women need to adopt a can-do attitude when it comes to preventing and treating breast cancer, says Rogsbert F. Phillips, M.D., clinical professor of surgery in the Department of Surgery at Emory University School of Medicine in Atlanta. Breast cancer is a very terrifying disease because it surprises you. But some of the pessimism that people experience regarding breast cancer is unwarranted. "Early breast cancer is curable—that has been proven over and over. But you tie your doctor's hands when you get there too late," says Dr. Phillips.

Some of us see breast cancer as an older woman's disease, but as Wilhelmina can tell you, it's a threat to us at any age. The under-45 incidence is higher for Black women. "I have had three 29-year-old Black patients with breast cancer," says Annette M. Brown, M.D., a diagnostic radiologist in private practice in Manhattan. "I've seen several Black women in their thirties with breast cancer, but only one of them had a family history of the disease," she adds.

That's why Dr. Brown feels it's important to remind Black women that our attitudes toward breast cancer may be one of our greatest problems. "When many Black people hear cancer, they think it is a death sentence, so they don't bother to seek treatment," Dr. Brown observes. When we find a lump, we tend to pray. We should pray, but we must also go to the doctor.

Understanding
Your Risk

Here are the facts you should know to assess your risk.

▲ The chief breast cancer risk factor is being a woman: Fewer than 1 percent of victims are men.

▲ Age is the next most important risk factor. The 1-in-8 risk rate that you hear so often, for example, refers only to women who are 85 and over. At age 35, your risk is really about 1 in 622.

▲ If the women in your immediate family—your mother, sister, or daughter—have had breast cancer, you have an increased chance of developing it.

▲ If your periods began when you were 11 or younger, your risk is 20 percent higher than if they began at 14 or older.

▲ If you delay childbearing until after age 30 or never have children, your risk is two to three times that of women who become pregnant before age 20. Early menstruation and late childbearing increase a woman's lifetime exposure to estrogens, which some scientists believe could promote cell division in breast tissue and possibly increase the chance of cancer.

Working Out
a Prevention Plan

No one has figured out how to stop breast cancer in its tracks. A few reliable studies have shown, however, that there are certain lifestyle changes that you can make to help protect yourself.

Make exams a habit. Monthly breast self-examinations are your most powerful weapons against breast cancer. Many cancerous lumps are found by women, not by doctors or screening tests.

"You want to give us a chance to cure you, but you have to help us out. Start by knowing what your tissue feels like. Know its texture. Be comfortable with your breasts, then pick up changes from month to month. Otherwise, you are cheating yourself," says Dr. Phillips. Love yourself enough to do it.

Get a mammogram. Self-exams are critical, but so is having a regular mammogram once you're past the age of 40, even if you have no symptoms. "The American Cancer Society (ACS) and the National Medical Association (the nation's leading Black medical professional organization) recommend mammography starting at age

Many of us fear a breast cancer diagnosis because we are afraid of losing a breast. The first thing you need to know is that these days, that's a lot less likely to happen than it might have been just 10 years ago, says Raymond B. Wynn, M.D., assistant professor in the Department of Radiation Oncology at the Lousiana State University Medical Center in New Orleans. Many breast cancers are now treated in ways that conserve the breast. Many studies have shown that in early-stage cancer, lumpectomy (removal of the lump only) followed by radiation therapy has proven to be an effective way to treat the cancer without removing the entire breast.

For more advanced disease or as an option for early-stage disease, there is a procedure called modified radical mastectomy that removes the entire breast, a chest muscle, and the lymph nodes under the arm. This is less disfiguring than the radical mastectomies that were common in the United States 20 years ago. The earlier you seek treatment, the better your chances of avoiding a mastectomy, says Dr. Wynn. "If you come to the office with a grapefruit-size cancer, we can't save your breast," he warns.

Here are a few other tips for managing your recovery.

Get support. Breast cancer support groups run by and for Black women are springing up all over the country. While there is no national clearinghouse for these groups, you may be able to find one near you by contacting Rise, Sister, Rise, a program of the Breast Cancer Resource Committee, 1765 N Street NW, Suite 100, Washington, DC 20036.

Reduce stress. You will need all of your stamina to successfully complete breast cancer treatment and get your life back together, so try to cut as much stress as possible. Meditate, take

40," says Dr. Brown. The advantage of a mammogram is that it can sometimes detect cancer a good two years before you can feel a lump, which gives you an opportunity to get earlier treatment.

Because of the tendency of Black women to develop the disease when they are younger, some doctors will recommend a mammogram yoga, go to church, see your friends, or find something that makes you laugh, says Zora Brown, founder of the Breast Cancer Resource Committee. Exercise that helps you take the tension out of your body is also great for women undergoing breast cancer treatment.

Relax. Brown suggests that you take time out for this routine. "Close your eyes and pay attention to your breathing. Picture everything in your body relaxing, from the roots of your hair to the tips of your toes. Systematically focus on easing the tension out of each section of your body, especially your neck and shoulders."

Visualize. Ask a therapist to teach you guided imagery. This is a process that allows you to develop a picture of your cancer cells and then kill them off one by one in your mind's eye, says Brown. Studies show that it works.

Think positive. If you find yourself dealing with depression after your diagnosis, you should understand that it's perfectly normal, but you should seek therapy. Depression suppresses the immune system.

Plan a "cancer-free" day. Sometimes you need to remove yourself from cancer, suggests Brown. Surround yourself with positive people, get together with friends and do something you really enjoy, she advises. "I call it my play day. It's a great way to relax," she says.

Eat healthy. While the occasional treat can perk up both your spirit and your appetite, don't forget to stick to a healthy diet, says Brown. "You need good nutrition to build yourself up after treatment for cancer. A low-fat diet, rich in fruits and vegetables and vitamins and minerals, is important for recovery," she says.

when you have any lumps or pain, even if you are under 40. "If a young Black woman has symptoms of any kind, I won't hesitate to do a mammogram on her. You have to treat symptoms very seriously. For a Black woman, I will do a mammogram as young as age 29," says Dr. Brown.

Use the power of healthy eating. Many studies have suggested

Wilhelmina Grant, community outreach coordinator for SHARE Self-Help for Women with Breast or Ovarian Cancer, a New York–based nonprofit organization, says that one of the most important messages she delivers to the sisters who come to her breast-care workshops, health fairs, and outreach events is that there is life after cancer treatment. "One of the biggest barriers to getting well for African-American women is our mental and spiritual attitude toward cancer treatment. We hear family members say that breast cancer is a death sentence, but I'm living proof that it's not.

"I strongly believe in the power of prayer, but a lot of us want to believe that if we pray hard enough, we won't need chemotherapy or other treatment," she says. "I feel that you need to put your faith in the hands of a higher power and your doctor. I'm a Baptist, and before my surgery, radiation, and chemotherapy, I read the Scriptures. Every time, the Bible fell open to 'For they shall do it with joy.'

"After being diagnosed, I went to a support group and met with a kind, open, great bunch of women. They sat me down with a cup of tea and answered all my questions. I felt so comfortable with them; I felt the scripture verse referred to them.

"I went through a heavy experience with chemotherapy and radiation," Wilhelmina continues. "I chose a more aggressive course of drugs because I know cancer can recur, but I didn't suffer to the extent that others thought I would. All in all, it was not that bad.

"I did lose my hair 10 days after my first treatment, but I didn't look or feel sick. I refused to wear a wig, and in response to my exotic look, people would ask me if I was a dancer or a model. I took those comments as compliments. Now I'm strong again and people don't believe I've had cancer. You can bounce back and continue what you're here to do," she promises.

that a low-fat diet protects women against breast cancer. But researchers from the Harvard School of Public Health believe that it is difficult to pinpoint exactly how important the role of fat is in breast cancer, since people who follow a healthy diet don't only eat low-fat.

One study has shown, however, that there are benefits to eating light. Researchers at the University of Massachusetts Medical School in Worcester and the Harvard School of Public Health studied the effects of a two diets on a small group of Black women. One diet was low in fat (20 percent) and high in fiber (40 grams per day). The other was close to the women's usual high-fat, low-fiber diet. When the women ate the low-fat, high-fiber diet, their levels of estrogen, which is a known risk factor for breast cancer, decreased significantly.

The kind of fat is also important. Studies in Spain and Greece found that monounsaturated fats, specifically olive oil, are protective against breast cancer. In any case, a healthy diet involves eating high-fiber foods such as fruits, vegetables, and grains, which all help to reduce cancer risk.

Keep your weight down. Study after study of postmenopausal women shows that increased weight is associated with increased risk of breast cancer. A team of scientists headed by researchers from the National Cancer Institute (NCI) found that the risk of breast cancer for the heaviest 40- and 50-year-old women in the study was double that for the lightest women of the same age.

Banish the butts. Cancer specialists don't list smoking as a major risk factor for breast cancer, but one Danish study found a significant increase in breast cancer risk in women who had smoked for 30 years or more. If you smoke, quit. If you don't, don't start.

Stay fit. A study done by researchers at the University of Southern California in Los Angeles found that premenopausal women who get four hours of exercise per week can reduce their risk of breast cancer by 58 percent.

Watch the booze. According to researchers from the Harvard School of Public Health, alcohol is the best-established dietary risk factor for breast cancer. In their study, consumption of an average of one drink a day increased the risk of breast cancer 11 percent, and the risk increased about 11 percent for each additional daily drink (one drink equals a 5-ounce glass of wine, a 12-ounce can of beer, or a mixed drink made with 1.5 ounces of 80-proof distilled spirits). And, if a woman drinks the same amount of alcohol consistently throughout her life, according to studies by the National Institutes of

Good breast care begins with learning when and how to do a breast self-exam. The American Cancer Society (ACS) recommends that women over the age of 20 do monthly breast exams. "But I would teach women to examine their breasts even earlier," says Annette M. Brown, M.D., a diagnostic radiologist in private practice in Manhattan. "Girls should start examining their breasts when their periods start," she recommends.

"You should do the exam each month at the same point in your cycle, usually a week after your period begins," she says. If your periods have stopped, choose a day of the month, such as the first or last day, and do your exam then.

Start with a visual exam of your breasts, Dr. Brown advises. Stand in front of a mirror with your arms at your sides. Check for anything unusual such as puckering, redness, dimpling, or discharge from your nipples. Raise your arms and press your hands against the back of your head and repeat this check. Then place your hands on your hips, pull your shoulders and elbows forward, and repeat it again.

Next, examine your breasts by touch. You may wish to put lotion on your hands or do the exam in the shower with soapy hands so that your fingers slide smoothly.

Still standing, raise your right arm and use the pads on the fingers of your left hand to feel your right breast and the area surrounding it. Check for anything unusual such as lumps or thickening.

"You need to be methodical in order to examine yourself thoroughly," says Dr. Brown. Cover the entire breast and pay attention to the area between the breast and armpit as well as the

Health, the risk goes even higher—40 percent greater than for women who don't drink.

Talk to your doctor about HRT. Hormone replacement therapy (HRT), the most common treatment for the symptoms of menopause, can help women avoid osteoporosis, heart disease, and armpit itself. Also check above your breast up to the collarbone and over to the shoulder. Start by gently feeling for any superficial changes. Then press more firmly to feel deeper into the breast tissue. Finally, suggests Dr. Brown, press firmly to feel all the way back to your ribs. Then change positions and examine your left breast the same way.

Finally, lie on your back and repeat the exam. This position flattens your breasts and makes them easier to check. Put a pillow under your right shoulder, bend your right arm, and put your hand beneath your head. Use your left hand to examine your right breast, then repeat on the other side, putting your left hand under your head and using your right hand to examine your left breast. You should follow a definite pattern when you check, advises Dr. Brown. You can choose either vertical, wedge, or circular.

Vertical pattern. Starting at your breastbone and moving toward the side, slide your hand up and down over your breast and the area near your armpit and shoulder.

Wedge pattern. Start at the nipple and move your fingers toward the outside of your breast and then back in toward the nipple. Checking one small wedge at a time, continue around your entire breast.

Circular pattern. Starting at your nipple, move your fingers in increasingly larger circles toward the outside of your breast.

In addition to breast self-exams, the ACS recommends that you have an examination done by your doctor or nurse every three years if you are between the ages of 20 and 40 and once a year if you are over 40.

other health problems that can arise after menopause. The problem is that numerous studies have found an increased risk of breast cancer among women who took estrogens for a long period of time or who took relatively high doses. Many other studies, however, have found no increased risk. Two studies published in 1995 haven't cleared up the debate, either. One, based on the large Harvard Nurses' Health study, found that the risk of breast cancer was significantly higher among current users of HRT. The other, published just a month later, suggested that there was no increase in risk. According to *Cancer Rates and Risks*, published by the NCI, "it is difficult to draw firm conclusions" about HRT and breast cancer. The NCI does note that, for most women, many scientists think that the benefits of HRT outweigh the risks of cancer. The institute recommends that you discuss the pros and cons of HRT with your doctor.

With all the studies out there, it may seem as if figuring out how to reduce your risk of breast cancer is difficult. But it's actually pretty simple. According the ACS's *Guidelines on Diet, Nutrition, and Cancer Prevention*, "At the present time, the best advice to reduce the risk of breast cancer is to limit the intake of alcoholic beverages, eat a diet rich in fruits and vegetables, be physically active, and avoid obesity."

The National Black Women's Health Project can provide general information on breast cancer and assist in locating African-American support groups. Contact them at 1211 Connecticut Avenue NW, Suite 310, Washington, DC 20036.

Breast Changes

UNDERSTANDING YOUR BODY

ost mornings I barely have time to run a brush through my hair, throw on some clothes, and get the kids together," says Lindsey Watkins, a 34-year-old mother of two girls, ages 4 and 7. "But since my little scare, I make time to keep up with my breast exams." Lindsey's scare was the discovery of a lump in her breast right before her period about a year ago.

"It was so frightening and disorienting," says Lindsey. "I stepped out of the tub, reached for my towel, and spent a few quick seconds examining my breasts. I knew I was doing a rush job, but it had been months since I'd checked at all, so I thought that a quick pass was better than nothing. Then I discovered this hard little place that just wouldn't yield to pressure from my fingers. Immediately I thought 'cancer,' especially since I'd just learned that Black women frequently developed breast cancer as early as their thirties and their cancer is usually diagnosed at a later stage.

"My husband, Keith, and I will never forget sweating out the days until I got to my doctor and had him examine my breasts. As it turned out, I was lucky; it was just a cyst. But I still get a little chill every time I start the exam. It's just so hard not knowing what to look for," she says with a shake of her head. "My doctor says the important thing to remember is that breasts change naturally over the years, and most lumps are not a sign of cancer."

COMMON, NOT CRITICAL

Even the coolest sister may panic while sweating out the days between discovering a breast lump and having a doctor put her mind at ease. Sure, our breasts change naturally, but how are you supposed to know what's natural and what's not?

Neither you nor your doctor can distinguish a serious breast change from a harmless one simply by looking. It is important to make breast self-examination a monthly habit and to arm yourself with knowledge about the most common noncancerous breast conditions and their symptoms by referring to this table. Remember, though, that no amount of understanding is a substitute for a professional evaluation from your doctor, says Yvonne Thornton, M.D., director of perinatal diagnostic testing at Morristown Memorial Hospital in New Jersey.

Condition	Description
Abscess	Redness, hotness, and swelling caused by a blocked gland in the breast or on the nipple
Cyclical pain	Breast pain that occurs right before your period due to hormonal changes
Cyst	A lump (a fluid-filled sac that is smooth on the outside) that grows in the midst of breast tissue
Fibroadenoma	A smooth, hard lump that moves around easily within the breast tissue, caused by hormonal changes in the body
Fibrocystic breasts	General lumpiness of the breasts that may increase right before or during a woman's period
Lactational mastitis	Redness, hotness, and swelling caused by a blocked milk duct as a result of breastfeeding

The fact is that our breasts may often exhibit small, pea-size lumps and fleeting pains that have nothing to do with cancer. In Lindsey's case, a noncancerous cyst developed as a result of hormonal changes in her body. A cyst, a fluid-filled sac, forms in the midst of breast tissue and normally feels like a soft lump. If it is deeper within the breast tissue, it may feel like a hard lump. These lumps may form quickly and change in size. If you develop one, your doctor will probably perform a needle aspiration to confirm that it is a cyst. She will anesthetize the area of the breast over the lump and then insert a needle with a syringe attached into the cyst to draw out the fluid.

Harmless lumps like Lindsey's account for the great majority of breast changes that occur in women before age 50. Your breasts may become even more lumpy as hormone levels go up before your period and less lumpy afterward as the levels go down. This condition is known as fibrocystic breast disease, but since it is so common and it's not a true disease, doctors frequently refer to it as lumpy breasts.

Since breast changes do increase in the week before your period, don't perform your self-exam at that time. Wait until your period begins, says Yvonne Thornton, M.D., director of perinatal diagnostic testing at Morristown Memorial Hospital in New Jersey. "Over time, you will notice other changes, such as increased fattiness," she says. Women with lumpy breasts typically find that the lumps diminish or disappear after menopause because of declining estrogen levels.

Nursing mothers may experience redness and swelling, which usually turn out to be mastitis (an infection of the mammary gland) and can be treated with warm compresses and antibiotics, says Edwin T. Johnson, M.D., author of *Breast Cancer/Black Woman*.

KEEPING A WATCHFUL EYE

While Black women currently have higher breast cancer mortality rates than White women, there's no evidence that breast changes in general are more prevalent in Black women.

"The key is to monitor your breasts for changes with monthly breast exams and with mammograms," says Dr. Johnson. The National Medical Association, the nation's leading Black medical professional organization, recommends mammograms after age 40. Mammograms are best given to women over 30, as their breast tissue is less dense, and spots on the mammogram are easier to detect. Any changes should be evaluated by your doctor, although most are due to noncancerous conditions.

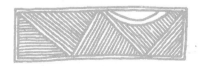

Bronchitis

KICKING A CONSTANT COUGH

ven though it feels like a cold and lasts like a cold, when I cough, I sound like a pit bull," Wes Michaels explains as a barking, repetitive spasm shakes his 6-foot, 2-inch frame. He had been a heavy smoker for at least 15 of his 36 years, and now the habit was beginning to catch up with him in more ways than one. "Not only am I sick more often, but in the past year, every time I get the sniffles, that nagging bronchitis cough shows up within days," he says. "I'm not the world's healthiest brother, but even I can see that I need to change my habits. This cough is kicking my butt."

WHERE IT BEGINS

Wes's problem is far more common in folks who puff on cigarettes, but bronchitis affects smokers and nonsmokers alike. An inflammation of the mucous membranes that line the bronchi (the breathing passages in your chest), bronchitis afflicts Americans about 18 million times each year. It's a condition that African-Americans need to be careful about, not because of our physiology—we start out in life with good, strong lungs—but because we are likely to live in crowded, congested cities. Poorly treated allergies, certain kinds of asthma, and exposure to air pollutants , which are common conditions in many urban neighborhoods, can predispose you to bronchitis.

What causes bronchitis? Take your pick: viruses, bacteria, or both. Sometimes these little troublemakers hide out in the mucus that drips down the back of the throat as the sinuses drain after a cold or the flu. Other times, an overstressed or sluggish immune system allows dormant cold viruses that are already in the respiratory tract to proliferate. Once these microorganisms make their way into the lungs, they invade the normally sterile membranes lining the bronchial passages. The membranes become inflamed and narrow, and they secrete mucus to protect the airways from further harm.

Like other upper respiratory infections, this one typically starts with a slight fever, a runny nose, malaise, aches, and chills. Then comes the signal for the onset of bronchitis: the telltale cough, which is initially dry. Over the course of a few hours or days, the cough produces steadily increasing amounts of phlegm. Other symptoms may include wheezing, breathlessness, and chest pain.

Unpleasant as it is, that mucus can be your first clue to what's making you ill. "Bronchitis phlegm can be thin and whitish to thick and yellowish or greenish depending upon the source of the infection," says Elena R. Reece, M.D., chief of allergy and clinical immunology at Howard University Hospital in Washington, D.C. For example, yellow or green phlegm can signal that bacteria are feeding on the surface of a virally inflamed bronchial tube that has lost its protective layer of cells and mucus, says Dr. Reece.

Acute bronchitis, in which fever and associated discomforts may last for five to seven days and a cough may linger for several weeks, is aggravating but benign as long as you don't have a history of lung disease and you don't smoke. Chronic bronchitis, an acute case that fails to heal, is more serious. Here the cold symptoms dissipate, but the mucus-producing cough typically persists for at least three months a year for at least two years. Chronic bronchitis damages the lungs and makes you susceptible to pneumonia, emphysema, and heart failure.

BLOCKING BRONCHITIS

The best way to deal with bronchitis is to avoid it. There's no guaranteed method for keeping this annoying lung condition at bay, but these tips can help to keep you breathing easy, says Dr. Reece.

Get a flu shot. If you can prevent the flu, you can prevent one of the main consequences of the flu, which is bronchitis. "I routinely suggest a flu shot each year to all of my patients," says Dr. Reece. "My colleagues and I have been surprised by how effective it is in reducing the incidence of bronchitis. The number of sick days taken by families declines dramatically."

Wash your hands. It's basic, but it works, says Dr. Reece. The viruses that cause colds are usually spread by hand contact with a surface that a sick person has touched. As soon as you touch your eyes or nose, your mucous membranes become a welcome mat for the virus. Before long, it's time to stock up on facial tissue and aspirin.

"You'd be amazed at the preventive power of old-fashioned hand washing. I can see 50 patients an evening in the emergency room during a flu outbreak," says Dr. Reece. "But as long as I wash my hands after I touch each patient, I won't get the flu."

Keep your lungs in shape. If, like many other African-Americans, you suffer from asthma or other respiratory conditions, see your doctor regularly and stick to your treatment program, says Dr. Reece.

COPING WITH COUGHS

If prevention fails to do the trick, you can still increase your odds of getting well quickly by following a smart treatment plan.

Hit the docs. Medicine can't do much against viruses, but if bacteria are the culprits, the remedy of choice is an antibiotic. "Antibiotics can help a person feel more comfortable as the body heals from bronchitis," says Dr. Reece. (Even though antibiotics are useless against viruses, doctors sometimes prescribe them for viral infections because a viral flare-up increases the risk of a secondary bacterial infection.) You can also ease some of the discomfort of acute bronchitis with aspirin or acetaminophen and by resting until the fever subsides.

Clear it out. As worrisome as the cough may sound, don't stifle it. It's essential for clearing your lungs. Use a vaporizer or hold your towel-draped head over a basin of hot water to moisten your air passages and loosen thick phlegm, suggests Dr. Reece. Another excellent way to thin mucus is to drink lots of liquids, on the order of 8 to 10 glasses of water or fresh fruit juice a day. Avoid coffee, tea, cola, and other caffeinated drinks, which only dehydrate you.

Toss the tobacco. Your lungs are already working overtime to cope with the infection; smoking only makes their job harder. Try to avoid secondhand smoke as well.

Think mellow. Stress can suppress your immune system, making you susceptible to colds and flu, so figure out a way to relax for a few minutes each day.

Carpal Tunnel Syndrome

DODGING THE PAIN AND STRAIN

I tried to ignore the pain, but it really started to bother me when I realized that my assistant, John, had figured out that something was wrong," says Chinwe Ellis, peering through her oversize horn-rimmed glasses. "I would do everything in my power to get him to go on and mind his business, but sometimes I'd look up and there he would be, watching me rub my aching wrists and fingers."

Like many people with carpal tunnel syndrome, Chinwe feared letting her co-workers know that she was having trouble at the computer terminal, especially because of the way she made her living. "I was only 37, and I had just been promoted to world news editor at the newspaper I was working for in Georgia. I was the first Black woman to hold the job," Chinwe says with pride. "The last thing I wanted was people suggesting that I couldn't do my job, so I guess I was in denial."

Late one afternoon, Chinwe got the awakening she needed to face the pain in her hands and arms. "I looked up and saw John gesturing toward the other side of the room, so I followed his glance. What I saw gave me that little kick in the belly that we all know as fear.

"Across the room, co-workers were helping Robyn, one of our best metro reporters, clean out her desk. Her right arm was held immobile by a complicated-looking brace that enveloped her entire lower arm. I knew that she had been out with a mild case of carpal tunnel," says Chinwe, "but as I watched her walk away from her career, John explained to me that Robyn's pain had gotten so severe that she could no longer touch her computer." The next morning, Chinwe made an appointment with a doctor.

FINGERS THAT
CAN'T FUNCTION

"Carpal tunnel is on the rise," says Richard M. Lynch, Ph.D., assistant professor of industrial hygiene in the Department of Urban Studies and Community Health at Rutgers University in New Brunswick, New Jersey. Repetitive strain disorders like carpal tunnel account for approximately two-thirds of workplace illnesses. According to the Bureau of Labor Statistics, this is a 10 percent rise over the 1993 figure.

Carpal tunnel syndrome is aptly named, says A. R. Mays, M.D., staff orthopedic surgeon at the Student Health Center of the University of Southern California at Los Angeles. The bones of your wrist and the overlying fibrous tissue form a tunnel through which your median nerve and nine tendons run. These important structures provide feeling and function for the thumb, index-, and middle-finger portion of the hand. Within the carpal tunnel, the tendons normally have plenty of room to slide back and forth without pressure on the nerve as you type, hold a dentist's drill, or comb your hair.

Problems begin with overuse or injury. The resulting inflammation and swelling, along with constricted blood flow, reduce the function of the median nerve. Later, scar tissue may form. The result is tingling, numbness, and pain that's occasionally severe enough to wake you from a sound sleep if you happen to put pressure on your hand.

As carpal tunnel syndrome progresses, your grip weakens until you are no longer able to effectively use your fingers. Eventually, the muscles of your hand, starting with the thumb, may begin to lose tone, size, and strength.

Carpal tunnel results from overuse and from adopting an awkward posture while working. It may be that more people are developing carpal tunnel syndrome because more and more people are sitting all day at a computer that has not been properly adjusted for their height and comfort, or it may be that we are diagnosing the condition more efficiently, says Nicholette Martin, M.D., a physiatrist (specialist in physical medicine and rehabilitation) at the Orthopedic and Sports Medicine Center in Annapolis, Maryland.

Risky Business

There is no specific genetic susceptibility for carpal tunnel syndrome, according to Dr. Lynch. But if we accept that throughout the centuries, Blacks have had tougher working conditions in general, we might find that Black women have been more likely to get jobs that require the most force and the most repetition, he says.

Among the people who are most prone to carpal tunnel syndrome are office workers, writers, and journalists, because they spend so much time at keyboards, often with a phone cradled awkwardly between their shoulder and head. Construction and factory workers, including the many Black women on assembly lines in chicken and meat-processing plants throughout the South, are at increased risk because of the high number of repetitive motions and awkward wrist movements they perform, points out Dr. Lynch.

Beauticians (and braiders) are also an important high-risk group of African-American women, adds Willie Kindred, D.C., a chiropractor in Tempe, Arizona.

Steering Clear of Repetitive Strain

"Carpal tunnel syndrome may be prevented and treated," says Dr. Mays. He offers these tips for prevention.

Get a (workplace) makeover. Ideally, you should have an ergonomic assessment done at your workplace. An ergonomic assessment uses interviews, surveys, and observation to identify the causes of muscular and skeletal problems in the workplace and provide solutions to these problems. Ask an expert who is both certified (a certified professional ergonomist, or CPE, or a certified professional ergonomic evaluator, or CPEE) and experienced to investigate everything from the height of your computer monitor to the possibility of using telephone headsets, which will free you from the need to cradle the receiver between your head and shoulder. A good place to start looking for an ergonomic specialist is *The North American Ergonomic Resources Guide*, which is available by calling 1-800-341-7874, extension 347. The cost is about $48 plus shipping and handling.

Learn the ropes. The more you know about which activities and postures can put you at risk, the better your chances of avoiding a bout of carpal tunnel syndrome. Usually your doctor will have brochures or information available for you to read.

Play ball. Buy a ball small enough to fit into the palm of your hand and soft enough to compress. A Nerf ball is good for this kind of exercise. The more you squeeze it, the more grip strength you'll develop. Better grip strength in turn will improve the strength of your wrist and hand and oppose the forces that cause carpal tunnel.

WORKING ON RECOVERY

If you think you have symptoms of carpal tunnel, which consist of pain and numbness in the hands and wrists, particularly at night, there are things you can do to ease your discomfort.

Take a break. Stop working, if you can. Take a leave of absence for a few weeks or months. Rest is what your wrists need. For many people, of course, this is impossible because of the financial hardship it would entail, but even a short vacation may help, says Dr. Kindred.

Change your style. It is paramount that you alter the offending motions. If the cause is still present, the carpal tunnel syndrome will return, or never stop. Your orthopedist, physical therapist, or workplace ergonomic specialist can show you how, says Dr. Lynch.

Adjust your board. If you spend long hours at a keyboard, adjust the height and angle of your keyboard to reduce awkward wrist positions. Your wrists should not be bent back or to the side, says Dr. Lynch.

Lose weight. There is limited evidence that the risk of carpal tunnel syndrome increases with obesity. Extra weight may reduce the amount of space within the carpal tunnel and increase the pressure on the median nerve, says Dr. Lynch.

GETTING TREATMENT

See a doctor at the first signs of carpal tunnel syndrome— frequent pain and tingling in the affected arm or hand. Don't wait, says Dr. Mays, because untreated carpal tunnel syndrome can become progressive neuropathy, a condition in which the affected hand becomes very painful, and may lead to permanent muscle loss.

You should go to an orthopedist, who specializes in disorders of the joints and connective tissues, says Dr. Mays. Physiatrists also treat repetitive strain injuries such as carpal tunnel syndrome.

Your doctor will take a detailed history and perform a thorough physical exam of your hand, including testing the nerve and analyzing your grip strength. You may then be given a splint to immobilize the wrist and hand and help minimize the offending movements, says Dr. Mays. A trial of anti-inflammatory medications may be prescribed.

If your case is advanced before you see the doctor, she may place the joint in an immobilization cast for four to six weeks. To help relieve the pain, she will also recommend nonsteroidal anti-inflammatory drugs (NSAIDs) such as naproxen or ibuprofen in either prescription (Anaprox, Motrin) or nonprescription (Aleve, Advil) strength.

In the worst cases, a surgeon will perform a carpal tunnel release operation. This procedure is performed in the hospital under general or regional anesthesia, explains Dr. Mays. The surgeon may use a scope or a more extensive open approach to cut the transverse carpal ligament, the fibrous band that encloses the median nerve. This relieves swelling, pain, and pressure but does not leave you impaired in any way. Most people can expect relief of up to 90 percent of their pain and a return of 85 to 90 percent of their grip strength. This procedure is reserved for advancing cases that do not respond to conservative measures, such as immobilization, NSAIDs, and changes in physical activities.

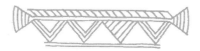

Cervical Cancer

SCREENING CAN SAVE YOUR LIFE

immy Alexander absolutely loved life in the city. When she was growing up in rural Kentucky, she spent just about every spare moment planning how she was going to move to New York and live a glamorous life as a single woman and successful graphic designer. "Since I'm only about three years out of college, my life is a little more grunge than glamour, but I am still thrilled to actually be in Manhattan," she says with more than a trace of a Southern accent and a bright smile. Her enthusiasm for her new life is especially impressive in the light of the ordeal she has endured over the past year.

"I didn't do the best job of taking care of myself when I got here," Kimmy admits. "Since I survive on freelance work, I've spent most of the past two years living on tuna and spaghetti, scraping together dollars to hit the latest clubs with my homegirls, and forgetting all about things like regular checkups. After all, I was young and healthy . . . or so I thought.

"Finally, I made an appointment with the gynecologist, but the visit resulted in the biggest shock of my life. My Pap smear revealed dysplasia—precancerous cell changes. When I had a biopsy, I learned I had cervical cancer—at age 24," Kimmy explains. "I had been sexually active in college, but I hadn't had a Pap smear in four years."

Kimmy ended up putting her New York life on hold and going home to Kentucky for treatment. Since cervical cancer is highly curable in its earliest stage, Kimmy was treated with laser surgery and was back on her feet within days. But she still has to watch carefully for a recurrence. "I'm back in good health and back in town," she says, "but from now on, I will find the time and money to get to the doctor, no matter what else I do."

EARLY DETECTION
IS THE KEY

There are more than 15,000 cases of cervical cancer diagnosed annually; in nearly 5,000 of those cases, women lose their lives. The saddest thing is, nearly all of these cancers could be prevented if women saw their gynecologists regularly.

Although past studies led some researchers to believe that a disproportionate number of cervical cancers develop in African-American women, more recent studies suggest that the risk for Black women is no greater then that for Whites.

"Much of the risk of developing cervical cancer is related to the number of sexual partners you have, and White women are as sexually active as Black women," explains Nancy Roberson, M.D., clinical associate professor of obstetrics and gynecology at the University of Rochester School of Medicine in New York. "But until recently, most of the research was conducted in urban areas, and the studies focused on large numbers of African-American women. That added to the impression that we had much higher rates of the disease," she says.

The incidence rate for Black women is slightly higher than that for White women, (12.6 per 100,000 compared to 7.9 per 100,000). But the rates for Black women are declining. At the same time, the rates for young White women are increasing, so the rates for women of both races are becoming similar.

Black women do run into trouble, however, when it comes to surviving cervical cancer. We may not get cervical cancer that much more frequently than White women, but some studies report that we are twice as likely to die of the disease—primarily because we fail to get treatment, says Yvonne Thornton, M.D., director of perinatal diagnostic testing at Morristown Memorial Hospital in New Jersey.

Even though a Pap smear will detect cervical cancer early enough for it to be cured, this early warning test is underutilized by African-American women. "Many of us die because we forget to see the gynecologist. Ours is a culture that often prefers home remedies to medical treatment," Dr. Thornton says.

"When women hear the words *cervical cancer*, they think, 'Oh, my gosh, I've got *cancer!*' People need to understand that the vast majority of abnormal Pap smears are not telling us that a patient has cancer," Dr. Thornton says.

At one end of the continuum is dysplasia, a condition in which new cervical cells grow in odd shapes and sizes and appear unstructured compared to healthy cells. Not all women with dysplasia develop cancer, but dysplasia is known to be a precancerous condition.

If abnormal cell growth continues, the dysplasia will evolve into cancerous cells that line the cervix. If the cancer is not detected and treated, it will grow and become invasive.

The most important thing for women to remember, however, is that cervical cancer is easily detected, easily treated, and, if caught early, relatively easy to cure. If your Pap smear reveals cancer, your doctor will measure its severity by determining the stage of the tumor. The earlier the stage, the greater your chance of complete recovery.

National Cancer Institute statistics show that the five-year survival rate for cancer caught before it spreads beyond the cervix is 91 percent; for cancers that have spread to nearby organs, it's 50 percent; and for cancers that have spread to distant organs, it's only 9 percent. The cure rate for early cervical cancer (where cancer cells are only on the surface of the cervix) is virtually 100 percent. "If women got regular pelvic examinations and Pap smears, virtually no one would die of cervical cancer," says Dr. Thornton.

GETTING A GRIP ON RISK

Women who have had human papillomavirus (HPV) or HIV and those who smoke, maintain a poor diet, and have multiple sex partners increase their risk for cervical cancer. The majority of cervical cancers are caused by certain types of HPV.

"The HPV virus is transmitted to women during intercourse with an infected man, but the tough part for a woman is that she can't recognize the virus in a man. HPV causes genital warts in women, but there are no visible symptoms in men," says Wilbert Jordan, M.D., director of the Oasis Clinic at the King-Drew Medical Center in Los Angeles.

That's why regular Pap smears are so critical for women. Cervical cancer is silent. A woman who has it doesn't feel pain or experience any symptoms until the later stages of the disease, when she may bleed after intercourse or douching or notice a heavier-than-usual menstrual period.

You are also at increased risk if you have ever had an abnormal Pap smear (from an inflammation of the cervix, for example) or if you became sexually active before age 18, says Dr. Thornton.

"Smoking cigarettes seems to increase your risk. One study found that nicotine, tar, and other cigarette-borne carcinogens are concentrated in the cervical tissues of smokers," explains Dr. Thornton.

PROTECTING YOURSELF

Doctors and researchers offer these suggestions for preventing cervical cancer.

Depend on the Pap. Regular Pap smears should begin when you are 18 or at whatever age you become sexually active, says Dr. Thornton. Using this procedure, your gynecologist can usually detect cervical cancer early and treat it successfully. Dr. Thornton recommends that you get a Pap smear yearly.

Although your Pap smear can be performed by a nurse practitioner, a midwife, or your family practitioner, Dr. Thornton recommends that you see a gynecologist, who specializes in this field of medicine.

Make a commitment. Because your cervical cancer risk increases with the number of sexual partners you've had—and the number of partners your partner has had—you should use a latex condom (preferably with spermicide).

"I have a 26-year-old patient now with cervical cancer who has had only one sexual partner, a man who has sex with many other women. Women need to start insisting on condom use," says Dr. Jordan.

"Multiple sexual partners definitely put a woman at increased risk for HPV infection and cervical cancer," says Dr. Thornton.

Keep it in check. If you have had one bout with cervical cancer, avoiding recurrences requires vigilance, says Dr. Thornton. Keep your follow-up exam appointments and have regular Pap smears and pelvic exams as directed by your gynecologist.

Select the circumcised. "Research shows that the partners of uncircumcised men have an increased incidence of cervical cancer," says Dr. Thornton. If your partner is not circumcised, Dr. Thornton recommends that you use a condom.

Eat for good health. Studies have suggested that vitamins C and E, beta-carotene, and particularly folate are important nutrients for cervical cancer prevention. Women who eat diets high in these nutrients have a lower risk.

Be aware that taking vitamin supplements is not as effective as eating natural food sources, says Dr. Thornton. Choose green leafy vegetables such as kale, spinach, turnip, and collard greens as well as beans, peanuts and peanut butter, broccoli, red peppers, and orange juice, all of which are good sources of these important nutrients.

Stress the positive. Relaxation and stress reduction boost the immune system, which helps you stay healthy or recover from disease, says Dr. Thornton. So try meditation, yoga, prayer, or any other mode of stress reduction that works for you.

WHAT TO EXPECT FROM TREATMENT

How your doctor chooses to handle cervical dysplasia or cancer depends on the severity of your disease. Your Pap smear will show if the cells from your cervix are normal, if you have mild, moderate, or severe precancerous changes, or if cancerous cells are present.

If your Pap smear is mildly abnormal, your doctor may choose to treat it conservatively. Your cervix will be viewed with a special microscope, called a colposcope, and your doctor will do follow-up Pap smears every four to six months to determine if the abnormal cells revert to normal or progress to more serious disease. In many cases, the cells revert to normal on their own.

For more serious precancerous changes, your doctor may either destroy or cut out the suspicious lesion. Destructive methods include a laser, which vaporizes the cells, and cryosurgery, which freezes off the affected cells. A cone-shaped biopsy can be cut out with a laser or scalpel or by electrosurgery. The biopsied tissue can be used to determine if the abnormal cells have invaded the cervix and you have cancer.

If you do have cancer, your doctor may choose surgery, radiation, or chemotherapy, depending on how far the cancer has spread.

Chronic Fatigue Syndrome

DEALING WITH AN ENERGY CRISIS

anessa Johnson remembers slumping onto the women's room couch and feeling her car keys drop from her limp hand. Her friend Sheila asked what was wrong.

"I had a splitting headache and had just been 'read' by my boss for the third time in a month," Vanessa says. "I had booked her on the wrong flight, then scheduled an editors' meeting for the day before she was due back in town, instead of the day after. 'I just can't concentrate anymore,' I told Sheila. 'I'm depressed and I'm tired, and I just want to get out of here. But I don't even have the energy to go home.'

"My troubles began when I had the flu in January. Then in June, I was still feeling weak, achy, feverish, and exhausted all the time. I though that maybe I was depressed, but whatever it was, I needed to see a doctor because, although I was only 28 years old, I felt as if I was pushing 75," she recalls.

MYSTERIOUS IDENTITY

Chronic fatigue syndrome (CFS) is an illness with an image problem. "Say 'CFS,' and the image that comes to mind is that of a middle-class, White female with a condition that's often called the yuppie flu, but CFS—a physical illness that may be caused by an overactive immune system—affects African-American women equally," says Sandra Gordon, M.D., assistant clinical professor of medicine at Boston University School of Medicine. "We'd find more African-American women with CFS if we asked more questions about their symptoms. Many African-American women who have the disorder have no idea that there's a name for what they're feeling. If the term *chronic fatigue syndrome* is not part of your social environment, you may not recognize what is happening to you," she explains.

CFS also affects men, who comprise 15 percent of its victims. The condition is described by doctors as an illness that follows an infection, lasts at least six months, and results in a level of fatigue so debilitating that it reduces a person to performing only half of their normal daily activities. Many doctors admit, however, that they are still struggling to fully define the condition, its source, and its many symptoms.

THE GREAT PRETENDER

There is a host of diseases that mimic CFS, and misdiagnosis is common. "Some doctors dismiss CFS as depression because its symptoms are so hard to pinpoint," says Dr. Gordon. CFS also resembles many other ailments, from fibromyalgia (a condition that causes chronic pain) to mononucleosis or low blood sugar, so diagnosing it is often tricky. "It is very important to exclude or rule out other identifiable conditions that may produce similar symptoms," he says.

Scientists and physicians are still trying to sort out the confusion about CFS. They do not have all the answers, but they have some clues. For one, they're sure that the immune systems of people who are fighting CFS seem to work overtime, as if they are on constant alert. Dr. Gordon adds that some doctors originally thought that CFS was caused by the Epstein-Barr virus (EBV), but this connection is now considered ambiguous.

There is hope, however, for CFS sufferers in search of a diagnosis. The clues discussed below can help doctors uncover this mysterious illness.

"If you have a flulike illness that doesn't go away after several weeks, see your doctor, because it could be CFS," says Dr. Gordon. Although CFS is not contagious, the muscle aches, low-grade fever, swollen glands, sore throat, and—most of all—the profound fatigue it brings feel like a perennial flu.

CFS can also lead to irritability and an inability to concentrate. "Patients often say that they feel as if they're in a fog," says Dr. Gordon. In some cases, these symptoms have caused doctors to dismiss the syndrome as being "all in a patient's head."

Other common symptoms are:

▲ Persistent fatigue that does not resolve with rest
▲ Mild fever
▲ Unexplained generalized muscle weakness
▲ Painful or swollen lymph glands
▲ Headaches, especially ones that are different from the type you usually experience
▲ Joint pain without swelling or redness
▲ Fatigue that lasts more than 24 hours after a previously tolerable level of exercise
▲ Sleep disturbances

Less common symptoms include severe premenstrual bloating and weight gain, blurred vision, and sensitivity to bright light.

HEALING
AND HELPING YOURSELF

"Since there's no medication for CFS itself, treatment consists of easing symptoms through medical techniques and self-help, including family and patient education. Rest, exercise, well-balanced meals, and stress reduction can all help," says Dr. Gordon. CFS is most severe in the first few months; it eventually reaches a plateau, although flare-ups, triggered by vigorous exercise, infections, or seasonal changes, can occur. Remember that most people with CFS do improve, so keep a positive attitude and give yourself permission to slow the pace of your life somewhat.

Seek support. If you are diagnosed with CFS, ask your doctor or check at your local hospital for information about CFS support groups in your area, suggests Dr. Gordon. Talking with other CFS patients and working with trained counselors can help you learn practical coping tips and give you a needed psychological boost.

There is an amazing amount of information available online, via computer, including medical databases and support groups for CFS.

Rely on rest. Give yourself the time and permission to get more sleep, says Dr. Gordon. You may need as much as, or more than, 10 hours of sleep a night.

Eat for energy. A low-sugar diet helps many CFS sufferers stay pumped, as does avoiding caffeine and alcohol, notes Dr. Gordon.

Lighten your load. Think of ways to slow down a bit and give your body time to recover, says Dr. Gordon. Consider a more flexible work schedule, if possible. Shop by mail, consider books on tape, order in instead of cooking. Do whatever you can to pamper and comfort yourself and make your life easier.

Take a chill pill. Over-the-counter painkillers such as ibuprofen (Advil, Nuprin) and aspirin will help relieve CFS-related headaches, muscle aches, and joint pain, says Dr. Gordon.

Talk to your doctor. CFS can hide other health problems, so if you have it, you should see your doctor regularly. Some antidepressants, such as amitriptyline (Elavil) and fluoxetine hydrochloride (Prozac) may bring some relief. "Tricyclic antidepressants are helpful, and that may be because the patients have underlying depression," says Dr. Gordon.

Chronic Pain

REGAINING CONTROL OF YOUR LIFE

When people meet Claudia Simmons, they are almost always impressed by her charisma and charm. She has the kind of personality that brings warmth and ease to just about any situation. And she certainly doesn't seem like someone who has experienced years of debilitating pain.

"I had been working for years as a computer data-entry technician at a hospital in Boston," Claudia says, "and I was basically in good health—until I developed a pain in my shoulder that gradually moved into my hands, wrists, and elbows. At first, doctors thought that I had carpal tunnel syndrome, so they sent me to an occupational therapist.

"But the pain just got worse, much worse. And none of the tests they conducted could reveal why. I'll never forget the day I had to give up my job," she explains. "At the time, I was going through a difficult divorce, so I was just terrified that I would end up sick, alone, and broke at age 34.

"I was out of work for a year, and for half of that time I was virtually immobilized by pain. Finally, I found a doctor who diagnosed a condition called reflex sympathetic dystrophy, or RSD. I'd never heard of it, but her assessment was on target. About a year before the pain started, I was in a car accident and broke my arm in several places. My doctor explained that the severe trauma from the accident caused damage to my nervous system that resulted in the chronic pain of RSD.

"My doctor prescribed various types of therapy—muscle massage and ultrasound treatments for the long muscle groups in my back, biofeedback, and meditation," says Claudia.

"Finally, the pain began to improve, but certain activities still cause pain in my fingers, wrist, and neck. But I'm grateful just to be functional again! And my doctor says there's a good chance of complete recovery," she says.

Claudia's doctor, JudyAnn Bigby, M.D., assistant professor of medicine at Harvard Medical School, explains that Claudia's aching arms and back are just one of many types of chronic pain, which is any persistent pain that you cannot eliminate with nonnarcotic painkillers.

By definition, if you have pain every day for longer than six months, you have chronic pain, says Nicholette Martin, M.D., a physiatrist at the Orthopedic and Sports Medicine Center in Annapolis, Maryland.

The insidious truth about chronic pain is that it can accompany many maladies, including cancer, arthritis, fibromyalgia (a condition that causes chronic muscle pain), carpal tunnel syndrome, repetitive strain injury, or RSD, the cause of Claudia's problems. It can also be exacerbated by stress, physical activity, or depression, adds Dr. Bigby.

Chronic pain strikes approximately 15 to 20 percent of adults from their thirties to fifties, but it can strike younger people, too. "I've seen some 29-year-olds with this condition, but it's very rare in children," Dr. Martin explains.

"People with chronic pain must understand that although they are often looking for a specific diagnosis—a pinched nerve, for example—we may not be able to find one," warns Dr. Bigby.

One of the chief causes of unexplained chronic pain, according to Dr. Martin, is RSD, also called sympathetically mediated pain. "There may have been a mishap—a sprained arm or leg or acute trauma (that's what happened to Claudia)—or an ongoing health problem that causes trauma in one part of the body. Whatever the cause, if the affected limb does not return to normal after the initial problem, you may be developing RSD," she says.

The sympathetic nervous system is normally switched on by emergencies. It kicks your body into the fight-or-flight response, which causes your pupils to dilate, your blood pressure to rise, and your muscles to tense.

When the initial trauma is over, the fight-or-flight response is supposed to shut down and let the body return to normal. In people with RSD, however, the abnormal nerve signals continue in the traumatized limb. "The pain associated with this state can last for months or years," says Dr. Martin.

If you are plagued by chronic pain, you should see a doctor. Here are some tips to help your doctor help you.

Demand attention. A badly healed or poorly treated injury is often the beginning of chronic pain. If your doctor says, "Oh, it's just a sprain or a strain," and your limb is still red, swollen, and hot after four weeks, make sure your physician takes additional steps to help it heal, or request a second opinion. "Pay attention to your body and make your doctors listen to you," says Dr. Martin.

Consider a specialist. Seek out a physiatrist, a doctor who specializes in physical rehabilitation. Moderate physical exercise and physical therapy programs may eliminate or greatly ease chronic pain in many people. "We also use oral nonsteroidals, local anesthetics, and steroids, which can soothe inflammation even when narcotics have failed to quiet a patient's pain," says Dr. Martin.

"The bottom line is that you must use the limb that's causing you pain as much as you can. If you do this, your pain probably won't get worse, and it may even get better," says Dr. Martin.

Try different drugs. Over-the-counter pain relievers don't always work for chronic pain, says Dr. Martin. If the nonprescription drugs you try don't give you relief, ask your doctor about prescription medication.

Investigate alternatives. Acupuncture may be very effective in relieving arthritis and other types of pain. Ask your doctor for a referral to a licensed acupuncturist or contact the American Academy of Medical Acupuncture (AAMA) at 5820 Wilshire Boulevard, Suite 500, Los Angeles, CA 90034.

Get in touch. Try meditation, hypnosis, or other stress-reducing techniques such as yoga to soothe away pain. "These techniques help you to connect your mind and spirit and give you a greater awareness of your body," says Lorraine Bonner, M.D., a founding member of On-Call Physicians Medical Group at Summit Medical Center in Oakland, California.

Colds and Flu

GETTING THE BEST OF THE BUGS

he employees at Jersey Percell's real estate office in suburban Detroit used to say that she could never sneak up on them. "I was one big sneezing machine," says Jersey. "I caught three or four colds every winter, and people hardly ever saw me without tissues in one hand and cough drops in the other." And forget about dating. "I keep myself in great shape for a woman of 43," she says, referring to her slender, 5-foot, 9-inch frame, "but have you ever tried to be cute with puffy red eyes and a runny nose? Forget it."

Then Jersey decided it was time to take her personal battle against microbes to new heights. "One of my girlfriends told me that cold and flu viruses are spread primarily by hand contact, so people might have thought I was crazy, but I started washing my hands after appointments. You shake an awful lot of hands in this business," she explains. And since cigarette smoke makes your lungs more susceptible to infections, Jersey quit her 14-year cigarette habit. "It's been a little more than a year since I last lit up," she says proudly.

Jersey's lifestyle changes paid off. Over the last two winters, she's had only one cold, and a mild one at that. "Believe it," she says with a triumphant smile. "Those little bugs didn't know what hit them."

FIGHTING BACK

Jersey was right to get serious about prevention. Cold and flu viruses cause more than their share of misery. Co-workers, school-children, and commuters are always infecting each other.

And please don't even mention the *S*-word (stress). African-Americans are under so many stresses from cradle to grave that they often have suppressed immune systems, says immunologist and allergy specialist Michael LeNoir, M.D., of Comprehensive Allergy Services in Oakland, California. Research shows that stress—especially stress that makes you feel powerless and not in control of your life—drains your immune system. Alcohol counts as an immune system stressor; so do sinus allergies. These factors can make it easier for you to catch 1 of the 200 viruses responsible for colds and flu, says Debra Thurmond, M.D., a family practitioner in Morrow, Georgia.

TAKING
THE OFFENSIVE

As you grow older, your immune system gradually learns to recognize viruses and stop them in their tracks. So while young adults typically weather two to three colds a year, their elders may get one or none. But there's no need to wait until your first Social Security check to build up your defenses against colds and flu. Here's how.

Accentuate the positive. "Research shows that your mental state has a lot to do with your physical health," says Dr. LeNoir. Find an activity that brings you inner peace. Whether it's a quiet walk in the morning or a few moments of soft jazz after work, taking time to relax will deliver peace of mind and body.

Beef up your immunity. "Caring for a cold starts before you get sick," reminds Dr. LeNoir. When you eat well, exercise regularly, and stay in good shape emotionally, your immune system stays strong. In one study, women who walked at a brisk but comfortable pace for 45 minutes a day got colds that lasted only half as long (3½ days versus 7 days) as the colds suffered by women who were sedentary.

Soap those hands. Cold viruses can survive for several hours on practically anything that people touch, including doorknobs, computer keyboards, and even money. Keep viruses at bay by washing your hands frequently during cold and flu season, says Dr. Thurmond.

Get needled. Flu shots can be lifesavers. "I recommend them for all of my patients," says Dr. Thurmond. And if you are in one or more of the following categories, you should be certain to get one each fall.

▲ You're over 65.
▲ You have chronic health problems, such as heart disease, respiratory problems, diabetes, severe anemia, or a compromised immune system (such as occurs in AIDS), or you care for someone who does.
▲ You work in the community or have an increased exposure to the flu.

COPING
WITH A COLD

Colds usually start with sneezing, a runny nose, and a stuffy head. You might feel sluggish and have watery eyes, a sore throat, or a slight fever. (If you have a fever of more than 101°F and/or a productive cough, call the doctor immediately.) The average cold lasts from 7 to 14 days. Try the following tips for surviving with minimum wear and tear.

Go easy on the meds. Forget antibiotics. They're only good against bacterial infections, and colds are caused by viruses. "Instead, aim to relieve symptoms, but don't drown yourself in medicine," advises Dr. LeNoir. "I don't take many medicines when I get a cold. I may use a pain reliever or a fever reducer, but otherwise I take it easy, drink plenty of fluids, and stay in a positive frame of mind," he says.

Throw in the towel. When a virus knocks you out, don't fight it. "Take some sick time or find someone to watch the kids. Get some rest," advises Dr. LeNoir. It'll help you recuperate faster.

Try tradition. Confused about whether to feed a cold, starve a cold, or do neither? "Listen to your body," advises Joy Church M.D., assistant professor of family and preventive medicine at Emory University in Atlanta. "If you feel like eating, don't forget a comforting dish like chicken soup," she says. You can also try Dr. LeNoir's favorite: pinto beans and hot sauce for a stuffy nose. They'll also fortify your soul and help you fill up on lots of vitamins and minerals.

Steam it out. The warmth and humidity of steam will help open up stuffy sinuses. "Lean over a sink full of hot water with a towel draped over your head, or steam up the shower," says Dr. Church.

Count on C. Taking vitamin C for a cold is still controversial, but one University of Wisconsin study suggests that it will help you experience milder, briefer colds with less coughing, sneezing, and nose blowing. "Because you also need fluids, try to drink some fruit juices that contain vitamin C," advises Dr. Church.

Soothe your throat. Calm a sore throat by gargling with a mixture of warm water and salt (¼ teaspoon of salt to ½ cup of warm water). Or drink a throat-coating mixture of honey and lemon or lime juice. "Try two tablespoons of citrus juice mixed with a dollop of honey," suggests Dr. Church.

Fighting the Flu

The flu doesn't mess around: It's a heavy hitter. It comes on like a bulldozer, with high fever (102° to 103°F), chills, headache, sore throat, cough, and muscle aches. The fever and other obvious symptoms usually subside after a few days, but weakness, sweating, and fatigue can last for days or weeks. If untreated, the flu can lead to a life-threatening case of pneumonia. Try these tips for relief.

See your doctor. He will want to make sure that your symptoms don't signal something even more serious than the flu. "Ask your physician to prescribe antiviral medicines for other family members who live with you," advises Dr. Thurmond.

Go OTC. Try drugstore medications that control congestion, fever, and coughs. Decongestant sprays that contain oxymetazoline (Dristan 12-Hour Nasal Spray) or pseudoephedrine (Sudafed) can help unclog that stuffy nose, but be sure not to use them longer than three days in a row. Many sprays can cause a rebound effect, leaving your nose stuffier than before you first used the medication.

There are many different cough preparations for different types of coughs. If you have a dry, hacking cough, choose a product containing dextromethorphan (Benylin Adult). If you have a cough with phlegm, use a product with an expectorant like guaifenesin (Robitussin). Expectorants help loosen and moisten phlegm, making it easier to expel, says Dr. Thurmond.

"For pain and fever, nonaspirin products are preferred, especially for children," says Dr. Church. Acetaminophen or ibuprofen (Advil, Nuprin) can help reduce the fever and relieve the muscle aches that are the hallmarks of flu.

Lock away the smokes. Flu patients who smoke are at high risk of contracting potentially fatal pneumonia, warns Dr. Thurmond.

Watch for complications. If your flu symptoms persist for more than three days and are not relieved by home remedies, see a doctor, says Dr. Church.

Colorectal Cancer

CATCHING IT EARLY IS THE KEY

oagie Thompson was always too embarrassed to agree to his doctor's suggestions that he have a yearly rectal exam. "To tell you the truth," says the tall, heavyset World War II veteran, "I wouldn't have gotten one if my wife hadn't insisted. She said that any man my age (a spry 68) had better go ahead and have the test, so I did."

Hoagie and his wife are both glad that he finally gave in. As part of the exam, Hoagie's doctor did a fecal occult blood test and discovered a little blood in the stool sample, so he performed a follow-up exam using a thin, flexible scope. The second test—a sigmoidoscopy—revealed a mass on Hoagie's colon.

The mass turned out to be cancerous. "The surgeons took it out, and because they caught it early, they say I'm cancer-free!" Hoagie exclaims. "And I don't have a colostomy bag, which is a real relief. My life is back to normal."

A DANGEROUS LEGACY

Hoagie is very fortunate, because colon and rectal (colorectal) cancer is the second leading cause of cancer deaths in America. It doesn't have to be that way, though. If it's caught early, there is an 80 to 90 percent survival rate, making this disease one of the most survivable cancers.

If you're a man, you have a 1-in-16 chance of getting colon or rectal cancer in your lifetime, according to the American Cancer Society (ACS); for women, the odds are 1 in 17. That's an estimated 133,500 new cases every year. Of these cases, an estimated 1 in 1,000, or 54,900 Americans, will die. Although men's odds of getting colorectal cancer are slightly higher, women are slightly more likely to die from it.

Overall, African-Americans are not only more likely to get any type of cancer than our White counterparts, we're also much more likely to die from it. Why? One difference in survival rates can be attributed to delayed diagnosis. Inadequate health insurance that often keeps us from making expensive visits to a doctor and a terrible fear that hospitals and surgery are the beginning of the end are also part of the problem. "We often turn to remedies like laxatives and enemas until we're too sick for a doctor to help us," says Debra Ford, M.D., assistant professor and chief of the Division of Colon and Rectal Surgery at Howard University Hospital in Washington, D.C., and the first board-certified female African-American colorectal surgeon.

Experts say that 90 percent of these cancers are diet-related (the other 10 percent involve a genetic predisposition). Many blame low-fiber diets, which slow the transit time of stool through the colon, thus allowing any cancer-causing substances in the stool to have prolonged contact with the colon wall.

Evidence also points to diets high in fat, which releases tissue-damaging (and potentially cancer-causing) substances called free radicals. "Some African-Americans think greasy diets are good for you because they lubricate your system," says Charles Littlejohn, M.D., chief of the Division of Colon and Rectal Surgery at Stamford Hospital in Connecticut. But it's not so. Researchers think that Africa's low-fat, high-fiber cuisine is the major reason that colorectal cancer is so rare on that continent.

TAKING
THE OFFENSIVE

How can you make colorectal cancer a rarity in your life? Heed the following advice.

Don't bring home the bacon. Most Americans get 40 percent of their calories from fat, but the ACS says that we should aim for less than 30 percent. The ACS recommends eating at least five servings of a variety of complex carbohydrates and fiber-containing foods (fruits, vegetables, and legumes) and six or more daily servings of grain products. This may seem like a lot, but the serving sizes are small. One serving is ½ cup of fruit, ¾ cup of fruit juice, ½ cup of cooked vegetables, 1 cup of leafy vegetables, 1 medium piece of fruit, 1 slice of bread, or ½ cup of cooked rice, cereal, or pasta.

There are three very common signs of colorectal cancer, according to the American Cancer Society (ACS). See your doctor without delay if you experience any of them.
• A change in bowel habits that lasts more than a few days, such as diarrhea, constipation, or narrower stools than usual
• Any fresh or dried blood in or on the stool
• Cramping or abdominal pain

Other signs of colorectal cancer are unexplained weight loss and constant tiredness, says Debra Ford, M.D., chief of the Division of Colon and Rectal Surgery at Howard University Hospital in Washingon, D.C. Dr. Ford stresses that any of these symptoms can be caused by a number of problems, so it is important to see a physician to determine the cause.

Treatment and Survival

There are three stages of colorectal cancer defined by the ACS; they are determined by the spread of the cancer cells.
• *Stage 1* is confined within the colon wall without spreading (five-year survival rate: 91 percent).
• *Stage 2* has progressed through the colon wall and involves adjacent organs or lymph nodes (five-year survival rate: 63 percent).
• *Stage 3* has metastasized to distant tissues (five-year survival rate: 7 percent).

Overall, survival continues to decline beyond 5 years, and 51 percent of people who have had colorectal cancer survive for 10 years.

"A lot of cancers, especially in the early stages, are curable," says Dr. Ford. Doctors use surgery, radiation, and chemotherapy or a combination of treatments, depending on the severity of the disease. Contrary to many patients' fears, colostomies are relatively rare. "Less than 15 percent of all colorectal cancer patients need a permanent colostomy bag," according to Dr. Ford. "We use them in cases where the cancer is located very low in the rectum."

Fill up on fiber. Most of us consume only about 15 grams of fiber a day; the ideal is more like 20 to 30 grams. "When I say high-fiber, my patients think of Metamucil," says Dr. Ford. "They don't always realize that a handful of raisins or a bowl of oatmeal provides fiber, too." It's not hard to boost a low-fiber diet.

"A small bowl of lettuce contains only 1 to 2 grams of fiber, which is less than people think," says Dr. Littlejohn. "But when you add a half-cup of kidney beans, you add 23 grams of fiber. If you add a half-cup of peas to the meal, you get almost 4 more grams." You may experience more gas when you move to a higher-fiber diet, but your body will usually adjust over the course of a few months. If you have cramps, that may mean you're overdoing it.

Know your risk. You're at higher risk for colorectal cancer if you're over 50 (90 percent of people diagnosed are 50-plus), have a history of inflammatory bowel disease such as Crohn's disease or ulcerative colitis, or have had breast, uterine, or ovarian cancer. Your risk is also higher if someone in your family has a history of colorectal cancer.

If you fall into any of these risk groups, take steps now to improve your diet and make sure that you adhere religiously to the recommended schedule of doctor's visits.

Get regular checkups. They're your number one tool for keeping colorectal cancer at bay. Here's what the ACS recommends for people who show no suspicious symptoms.

▲ After age 40, have your doctor do a digital rectal exam as part of your regular annual physical.

▲ At age 50, have a flexible sigmoidoscopy. In this test, the doctor passes a flexible tube through your rectum to examine your lower colon for polyps and other unusual growths. It's a common office procedure that doesn't require anesthesia. "The process takes 5 or 10 minutes in skilled hands," explains Adam M. Robinson, Jr., M.D., a colorectal surgeon and Force Surgeon for Commander Naval Surface Force, U.S. Atlantic Fleet, in Norfolk, Virginia. "Many first-time patients tell me that the procedure wasn't as bad as they imagined it would be," he says. If polyps are found, they can be removed painlessly. If the test is negative, it should be repeated every three to five years.

▲ After age 50, have a yearly stool test for hidden (occult) blood. One good home method is called a guaiac test. You can get a test kit from your doctor, who will give you a special diet that you should follow for three days before the test as well as during it to ensure the best results. You simply touch a swab to your stool after three consecutive bowel movements. Then you smear the samples onto three cards, seal the cards, and take them to your doctor for laboratory analysis.

Another test that detects occult blood, EZ-Detect, is available over the counter at your drugstore. With this test, there are no dietary restrictions and the results are immediate. After a bowel movement, you drop a specially treated pad into the toilet. If the test is positive for blood, a blue-green cross will appear on the pad. Consult your doctor if your test is positive.

Constipation

KEEPING YOUR BODY REGULAR

ohn Buchanan didn't realize how much constipation affected his life until he almost missed getting his son, who was the starting center on the basketball team, to the state championships. "I used to spend so much time in the bathroom that I never knew what I was missing and what others were missing because of me," says John, a portly cab driver who's known in his Philadelphia neighborhood for his trademark red suspenders.

"Sure, many times I would be late dropping Aaron off at school because I was in the bathroom. Aaron would just say, 'That's all right, Pop, I'll take care of it.' But when I almost didn't get him to the state championships, and I saw the apprehension and disappointment in his eyes, I knew it was time to talk to a doctor."

When his doctor suggested beefing up his intake of dietary fiber and water, John jumped on it. He traded in his morning doughnuts for two hearty bran muffins, and he started sipping water throughout the day from a plastic squeeze bottle that he kept in his cab. It didn't take long before his new regimen paid off. "I can't believe what a difference that little change made in my day and in my life. It was well worth letting go of some of my favorite foods," he says.

BEHIND THE BATHROOM DOOR

If you think that you're the only one who spends a little too much time sitting and straining, here are three words of comfort: Join the club. An estimated 50 million Americans have at least occasional constipation; 18 million of us get that plugged-up feeling pretty regularly. And African-Americans (with a special emphasis on *American*) suffer more than Whites. "In South Africa, for example, Whites have a lot of constipation, while Blacks have almost none due to their high-fiber diets," explains Anthony Kalloo, M.D., director of gastrointestinal endoscopy at Johns Hopkins University School of Medicine in Baltimore.

Why do Blacks in the United States have this problem? Not surprisingly, a big part of the reason is diet. Fiber boosts the bulk and water content of stool, allowing it to pass easily and quickly through the intestines. "Many high-fiber foods like whole-wheat bread, fruits, vegetables, and bran cereal aren't standard fare for many African-Americans," says Dr. Kalloo. We tend to fill up on fat instead, which crowds out high-fiber grains, vegetables, and fruits, foods that are staples among South African Blacks.

Women, whose surging estrogen levels during pregnancy or before menstruation can slow what doctors call bowel transit time, are twice as vulnerable as men. Couch potatoes are susceptible because transit time slows with inactivity. And constipation is a side effect of many medications, including blood pressure drugs known as beta-blockers, some pain medicines, antidepressants, and aluminum-containing antacids.

Even a sweet tooth can make chronic constipation worse. "Many sweets are little more than refined flour and sugar," explains Duane Smoot, M.D., a gastroenterologist and associate professor of medicine at Howard University Hospital in Washington, D.C. The digestive tract absorbs sugar so completely that what little fiber remains forms a hard stool that's difficult to pass. "My typical constipation patient has coffee cake for breakfast, a candy bar for lunch, and a little dinner with lots of dessert," says Dr. Smoot.

There's no precise definition of constipation, partly because what's regular differs greatly from person to person. But many experts say that you're constipated if you pass small amounts of hard, dry stool less than three times a week. "Once a week can be normal," stresses Dr. Smoot. "Frequency isn't as important as having soft stool that you can eliminate without straining."

UNBLOCKING THE WORKS

Most constipation sufferers find gratifying relief through the following simple lifestyle changes.

Experts recommend that we consume between 20 and 35 grams of fiber a day, which is about twice as much as most of us normally get. The foods listed here are great sources of fiber that are worth eating every day.

Food	Portion	Fiber (g.)
Kellogg's All-Bran cereal	⅓ cup	10.0
Black-eyed peas, boiled	½ cup	8.3
Kidney beans, boiled	½ cup	6.9
Lima beans, boiled	½ cup	6.8
Black beans, boiled	½ cup	6.1
Lentils, boiled	½ cup	5.2
Succotash	½ cup	5.2
Chickpeas	½ cup	4.4
Pear	1	4.3
Potato, with skin, baked	1	4.0
Oatmeal, cooked	¾ cup	3.9
Apple	1	3.7
Brussels sprouts	½ cup	3.4
Sweet potato, baked	1	3.4
Orange	1	3.1
Prunes	5	3.0
Acorn squash	½ cup	2.9
Corn	1 ear	2.9
Raisins	½ cup	2.9
Dried apricots	10 halves	2.7

Focus on fiber. Go with the American Dietetic Association on this one and aim for 20 to 35 grams of fiber each day. (Most of us get 5 to 20 grams.) Don't feel that you have to eat a heaping bowl of wheat bran at each meal, though. "I tell my patients, instead of drinking orange juice, eat an orange. Instead of french fries, have a baked potato with skin," says Dr. Kalloo. (See "20 Fiber All-Stars" above for more tasty options.)

Drink your share. Six to eight 8-ounce glasses of water or juice or the same amount of herbal tea or other refreshing liquid will help soften your stool and make for easier passage. You'd better skip the caffeinated stuff, though. "Caffeine can cause bowel spasms that prevent food from moving through the intestines," cautions gastroen-

Handling Diverticular Disease

Mary Caldwell wasn't exactly the picture of health. She smoked like a barbecue pit and never exercised, and the closest she came to eating a vegetable was nibbling at the sprig of parsley that came with her steak. So it didn't surprise Mary's doctor when she complained of gas and a dull, aching pain in her abdomen—two signs of diverticular disease.

The doc recommended a diet makeover. Mary rebelled. "I told him I liked my diet just fine the way it was, thank you!" says Mary, a large woman who strikes a defiant pose as she tells the story. "But then I remembered how much pain I'd been in for the past few months and decided to give it a try."

Poor eating habits and frequent constipation can lead to diverticulosis, a condition in which small pouches (diverticula) occur in the colon, usually near the rectum. Diverticulosis is painless and is frequently only detected by doctors during unrelated medical examinations. In fact, as many as 8 out of 10 people with diverticular disease never have any symptoms.

Occasionally, however, the pouches become inflamed, causing a dull, aching lower abdominal pain that may be relieved when you have a bowel movement or pass gas. This condition is called diverticulitis. Sometimes the pain is accompanied by fever and nausea. You might pass small, hard stools and occasionally have diarrhea. If the diverticula bleed, the stool might contain fresh red blood.

Researchers think that a meaty, fatty, low-fiber diet that provides little bulk sets the stage; straining to eliminate dry, hard stools may create the pouches. The condition usually appears in middle or old age and is rare before age 40.

"The best prevention is munching four or five servings of fruits and vegetables and washing them down with six to eight glasses of water or other liquids daily," advises Kenneth M. Frontin, M.D., a gastroenterologist and assistant professor of medicine at Morehouse School of Medicine in Atlanta.

If you notice persistent pain in your lower abdomen, particularly if it's accompanied by a change in bowel habits that persists for more than two or three weeks, see a doctor, says Dr. Frontin.

terologist Joanne A. Peebles Wilson, M.D., professor of medicine and associate chief of gastroenterology at Duke University Medical Center in Durham, North Carolina.

Keep moving. Moderate exercise, such as a brisk walk, will jump-start your colon, says Dr. Wilson. Sometimes just routine daily activity will also do the trick.

Follow the urge. Your body tells you when it's time to go, but the system only works if you listen. If you ignore the urge to defecate (say if you're away from home and you don't want to use an unfamiliar bathroom), you can hold back the stool long enough for the urge to disappear. "We see a lot of constipation in teachers, truck drivers, doctors, and so forth—people whose professions require them to keep going no matter what," says Dr. Wilson.

Rise and sit. Many people feel the urge to have a bowel movement in the morning, particularly after eating. Twenty or 30 minutes after a meal, something called the gastrocolic reflex starts your bowels moving. "Get up early enough to eat something and spend a little time in the bathroom," suggests Dr. Wilson.

Try a more natural laxative. Safe laxative alternatives are fiber supplements that contain psyllium or methylcellulose and work by drawing water into the stool, making it larger, softer, and easier to pass, says Dr. Wilson. Metamucil and Fiberall are two brands sold in drugstores and supermarkets. Avoid harsher, stimulant laxatives (such as Ex-lax and Correctol) that work by irritating the intestinal lining, she says. These laxatives can cause dependency if used too often, so generally you should avoid them and use them only as a last resort.

Watch for changing habits. Constipation can signal a serious problem, including cancer. "If you can pin constipation to a specific cause, like travel or a change in diet, it's less likely to be dangerous. However, if constipation persists or there is associated bleeding, a more serious problem could be present," says Dr. Wilson. "In that case, see your doctor."

Depression

Banishing the Blues

hen Callie Ferguson was told that she was clinically depressed, she stared at her psychiatrist in disbelief. Here she was, a hardworking bank officer in the prime of her career, with plenty of friends and an adoring husband.

But Callie knew something was wrong. She slept a lot, occasionally dozing straight through most of the weekend. Her appetite wasn't what it used to be, and on some days she felt totally blah. "The clincher came when I started to lose interest in sex," says Callie, lifting her wire-rimmed glasses from the bridge of her freckled nose to emphasize her point. "That had never happened before, so I realized I was in denial over a problem."

The problem was depression. After a few weeks of therapy, Callie discovered that her depression had started after she attended a performance by the renowned Dance Theatre of Harlem. Her psychiatrist helped her understand that the performance triggered an episode of depression by making her realize that at age 46, she had never lived out her childhood dream of becoming a dancer. "I feel infinitely happier these days, thanks to a good psychiatrist and twice-weekly dance classes," says Callie.

Living Off-Balance

African-Americans are the people who gave the blues a name, but we are unlikely to recognize, accept, or address depression when it happens to us. "Fifty percent of the African-Americans who suffer from clinical depression do not seek help," says William Lawson, M.D., Ph.D., professor of psychiatry at Indiana University School of Medicine, chief of psychiatry at the Richard L. Roudebush Veterans

Administration Medical Center, both in Indianapolis, and president of the Black Psychiatrists of America.

And that's no small number. At some point, 15 percent of the population is likely to experience what health professionals call clinical depression. Overall, nearly 12 million Americans experience some form of depression each year. You may have clinical depression if you experience any of the following symptoms for longer than two consecutive weeks.

▲ A failure to receive pleasure from things you usually enjoy (work, food, or sex, for example)
▲ Fatigue or decreased energy
▲ Sleep disturbances
▲ Changes in appetite or weight
▲ Feelings of hopelessness
▲ Feelings of guilt, worthlessness, or helplessness
▲ Thoughts of death or suicide
▲ Difficulty concentrating, remembering, or making decisions
▲ Chronic aches or other persistent bodily symptoms that are not caused by illness

WHO'S AT RISK?

Depression is more common in women than in men, but because of women's tendency to reach out and seek help, they are more likely than men to overcome it. African-Americans are also just as likely to become depressed as Whites. "Contrary to popular belief, it's as common in Black youngsters, especially males, as it is in White youngsters," says Dr. Lawson. "But the stressors may be different for African-Americans. Our youth are taught, erroneously, that racism is no longer an issue and that if they are not successful in life, it's their own fault." Living with unrealistic ideas like these instead of being shown how to develop effective coping strategies for life crises can bring on a case of the blues.

In addition, many conditions associated with depression are part and parcel of the Black experience. For example, psychologists say that you are more prone to depression if you have a low sense of self-esteem, if you view others as undependable, and if your environment is frustrating.

When Martin Luther King Day rolls around each January, do you feel too low to celebrate? If so, you may have seasonal affective disorder, or SAD. People with SAD experience seasonal depression that usually kicks in each autumn and subsides the following spring. They may overeat (especially carbohydrates), sleep much more than usual, feel sad or anxious, have extreme fatigue, withdraw from friends and family, and have difficulty concentrating and accomplishing tasks. Although the same symptoms are present in other forms of depression, it is the particular combination of symptoms occurring only at certain times of the year that are the hallmark of SAD.

SAD affects only about 1 percent of the population. However, in the northern latitudes, 25 percent of the population experiences at least some of the symptoms of SAD. While the cause is not clear, most theories point to the role of too little sunlight. SAD patients have reported symptom reversal within days of traveling from their winter climate to Florida, only to have the depression recur when they return home.

The most promising treatment for SAD is light therapy. Sixty to 80 percent of SAD sufferers show significant improvement after a few days of sitting in front of specially designed light boxes for 30 minutes to 2 hours a day.

The lights can be purchased through some mail-order companies and used in the home, but it is important to contact a doctor or mental health specialist for a diagnosis, says Robert T. M. Phillips, M.D., Ph.D., deputy medical director of the American Psychiatric Association. Two mail-order companies that offer information, light products, and services are The SunBox Company, 19217 Orbit Drive, Gaithersburg, MD 20879 (1-800-548-3968), and Apollo Light Systems, 352 West 1060 South, Orem, UT 84058 (1-800-545-9667). Call or write for more details.

"Well, if we internalize messages of racial inferiority, our self-esteem *is* low, people around us *are* undependable, and our environment *is* frustrating," says Linda James Myers, Ph.D., associate professor of African-American and African studies, psychology, and psychiatry at Ohio State University in Columbus and past president of the Association of Black Psychologists.

We are also deeply familiar with another key cause of depression—loss. "African-Americans have suffered the greatest loss of all—the loss of own cultural reality. We have an entire race for whom the typical stressors marking depression have become normal experiences," says Dr. Myers.

But racism and loss aren't the whole story. If they were, every African-American would be overwhelmed by depression, says Dr. Myers. Some people manage to avoid milder forms of clinical depression because of their emotional resilience and outlook on life.

"The learned helplessness that results from ruminating about racism can cause depression, not just because racism is such a sad legacy but also because focusing so much on it prevents us from taking constructive steps—like getting an education—that help buffer us against oppression," says Samuel Gordon, Ph.D., clinical psychologist at the National Rehabilitation Hospital in Washington, D.C.

Ignoring reality can be just as bad. Those of us who try to leave our culture behind in an effort to blend into mainstream America sometimes feel estranged when we are under stress or have a setback and feel that we do not have the support of our Black roots at home. The result? You guessed it: Depression.

And then, of course, there are people like Callie. Sometimes we fail to acknowledge our own hopes and dreams. Turning your back on your fondest desires can result in another occasion for feeling the blues, says Dr. Lawson.

For some people, even living under ideal circumstances is not enough to protect them from depression. Their pain has nothing to do with how well they can pull themselves up by their bootstraps. It stems from a chemical imbalance within the brain. "These people are very susceptible to depression," says Dr. Gordon. "Any small stress causes them to sink low."

Your genes and your childhood are the largest factors in your susceptibility to depression. Heredity plays a critical role: Your risk of depression is three times greater if one of your parents has experienced symptoms of depression. The other big predictor is whether you experienced a profound childhood trauma such as physical abuse or an emotional crisis.

Health professionals are often slow to identify depression in African-Americans, and we are less likely than Whites to self-identify it and ask for help. "When doctors see a man yelling that people are out to get him, for example, they might say he's psychotic," says Dr. Myers. "But his rage could be a sign of severe depression." In fact, unrecognized depression may be endemic among African-Americans, she says.

Rather than seeking help, Black men are very likely to try to tough things out by self-medicating their distress with alcohol or other mood-altering drugs, says Robert T. M. Phillips, M.D., Ph.D., deputy medical director of the American Psychiatric Association. Brothers who hang on the street corner passing around a bottle of cheap whiskey would probably be characterized as lazy by the average onlooker, says Dr. Phillips. But an astute mental health professional may see them as depressed. "And many men tend not to share their feelings with a physician," he says. "By the time men's feelings do emerge, their depression has become severe." It's especially important to pay attention to these feelings, as men with depression are twice as likely as women to commit suicide.

Black women, on the other hand, are more likely to seek help, but they rarely recognize their feelings as depression. "They may say they're stressed, or angry, or frustrated," says La Pearl Logan Winfrey, Ph.D., associate professor and director of clinical training at the American School of Professional Psychology in Arlington, Virginia. "Black women often feel that they have so many responsibilities, they can't afford to be depressed. Or if they're in a high-visibility professional position, they may feel that they can't afford to let White people see them sweat."

KEEPING YOUR SPIRITS HIGH

Want three quick tips for preventing depression? Here they are.

Hold on to your roots. "As you climb the social and professional ladder, hang on to the things that help you feel whole: your family, old friends, church, grade-school teachers, the old barber shop or beauty parlor," says Dr. Gordon.

Develop self-esteem. "Give youngsters important roles to play in the family," advises Dr. Lawson. "It builds their self-esteem and may guard against depression. Young Black males in particular may feel expendable."

Remember emotional needs. Depression is prevalent among people who have chronic health problems like AIDS or heart disease, which are disproportionately prevalent in our community. "But physicians and other caregivers often treat the physical ailments without tending to people's emotional problems," warns Dr. Lawson.

FINDING
A WAY OUT

Whether your depression is mild or serious, the result of a chemical imbalance or of negative thinking, self-care, treatment, and perhaps medication can help you find relief.

Be social. "Spending time with people you enjoy may be all you need to resolve mild depression," says Dr. Gordon. Family get-togethers and reunions, sororities and fraternities, and social clubs can surround you with people who appreciate you. "Church services can help, too," he says. "It gives you a lift to see people smiling at you."

Look for the good. Living in constant suspicion about other people's motives and actions is a tough way to go. "Try to believe that most people are essentially good and that those who aren't will probably avoid you anyway," suggests Dr. Gordon.

Sweat it out. Regular aerobic exercise helps ease depression by generating beneficial brain chemicals called endorphins, the body's natural mood-lifters. Try walking, biking, jogging, or swimming.

Reach out for help. Professional help from a psychiatrist, psychologist, psychotherapist, or social worker is essential for clinical depression. Among people with depression who seek help, 80 percent can be successfully treated. "It's virtually impossible to think through clinical depression on your own," advises Dr. Myers. If your depression is severe or is associated with an imbalance of brain chemicals, you may need to augment therapy with medication, which only a physician or psychiatrist can prescribe.

Be an informed consumer. Ask friends if they know of local mental health professionals with a good reputation, or call the Association of Black Psychologists at (202) 722-0808 for a free referral, advises Dr. Winfrey. Speak with the professional you are considering and ask how long he has treated depression, how many African-American clients he has worked with, what therapeutic philosophy he believes in, how long you can expect treatment to last, and whether payment arrangements are flexible. "Don't feel trapped," advises Dr. Winfrey. "You're purchasing a service, and you have the right to ask these questions."

Aim for a trusting relationship. Don't assume that any African-American therapist is automatically a good match for you. "We're a heterogeneous group of people," reminds Dr. Winfrey.

On the other hand, White therapists need to have special training and sensitivity to relate effectively to Black clients. "White therapists who say they're color blind can make you feel that your color—an essential part of your identity—is being denied," she says. "Yet if all the therapist wants to do is talk about race, that may not relieve problems that go beyond race and ethnicity. Try to find someone who's comfortable talking about race and with whom you feel you can build a trusting relationship," Dr. Winfrey advises.

Expect hard work, with good results. Successful therapy usually involves rethinking long-standing assumptions, which can be uncomfortable but ultimately rewarding. Remember, if you have signs of clinical depression, see a doctor. Most of the people who receive professional help for depression now achieve relief. "Depression can now be treated as successfully as pneumonia," says Dr. Lawson.

Dermatitis

COPING WITH A BAD REACTION

fter four weekends of hard work, Bill Pettigrew had finally completed his backyard deck. He leaned back in his newly installed hammock and admired his beautiful handiwork: All that sawing, sanding, staining, and sealing had been worth it. His hands, however, were much less attractive. "I was used to calluses after heavy work," he says, "but this time my skin was red, dry, cracked, and blistered all over my palms and fingers.

"I tried lotions and Vaseline with no luck. Finally, I took my wife's advice and went to the doctor," Bill says. The dermatologist prescribed a skin ointment, and his hands healed in about 10 days. But the problem still mystified him. "I've been doing woodwork for years without such a bad reaction. Why would building a deck destroy my skin?" Bill asked. The doctor explained that Bill had developed a reaction to one of the building materials— probably the weatherproofing finish that he'd used to seal the deck. "That makes sense," says Bill. "All my other projects were for indoor furniture, and I didn't use the sealant then."

CLOSE-CONTACT ALLERGENS

A skin reaction to contact with a specific substance or material is known as irritant contact dermatitis, says William Keith, M.D., clinical assistant professor of medicine at Drew Medical School/Martin Luther King, Jr., Hospital and medical director of the Institute for Aesthetic and Cosmetic Dermatology, both in Los Angeles. It is one of the most common types of dermatitis, an umbrella term for many skin problems.

Almost anything can cause a reaction, but common irritants include detergents and cleaning products, varnishes, nail polish, artificial nails, hair dyes, jewelry, and even the juice of certain fruits and vegetables, such as celery and tomatoes. If you've ever had an itchy red circle on your wrist where the skin came in contact with the nickel back of your watch, or your earlobe became red and irritated after you wore pierced earrings, you've probably had irritant contact dermatitis. The irritation is usually (but not always) limited to the site of contact.

The good news is, when the cause goes away, so does the problem. In Bill's case, discontinuing contact with the sealant and applying the prescription ointment allowed the rash to clear up.

AVOIDING
THE PROBLEM

"With contact dermatitis, the most important treatment is to find out what the irritant is so that you can keep it away from your skin," says Dr. Keith. Do a little dermatological detective work. Think about what substances or materials you may have recently come in contact with. If your left hand became inflamed over the weekend but not your right, your golf glove might be to blame, for example.

Once you think you've pinned down the culprit, see if you can find a safe substitute, or at least a way to lessen the negative effect. Dr. Keith offers these suggestions.

Steer clear of latex. Some people are allergic to latex condoms and gloves, so shop for products that are made of other materials.

Say no to nickel. If the nickel in your earrings bothers you, switch to ones with silver, gold, or surgical stainless steel posts. You can also paint the nickel posts with clear nail polish, but it wears off quickly, says Dr. Keith.

Check your paste. If you get small bumps around your mouth after using tartar-control toothpaste, switch to regular toothpaste.

Ditch the dyes. Avoid irritating dyes in tissues and toilet paper by buying only white paper products.

Minimize your makeup. If cosmetics are a problem for you, avoid wearing them, or at least purchase those that are hypoallergenic and fragrance-free. Products marked "unscented" are not necessarily fragrance-free: They usually contain a masking fragrance to cover up the natural smell of the product.

Patch it. If you can't figure out the source of the problem, visit a dermatologist. To identify the allergen you'll need to avoid, the doctor may do a series of tests by applying patches that contain a mixture of common allergens. He or she will try about 10 to 24 patches in an effort to find the guilty allergen. When one patch raises a telltale rash, you'll know you have the culprit.

SOOTHING IT YOURSELF

Since you can't avoid everything that may irritate your skin, Dr. Keith suggests subduing dermatitis with these smart skin strategies.

Rethink your notion of clean. In the winter months, when dry air can irritate skin, consider bathing less frequently. No matter what the season, take warm, not hot, baths to avoid stripping away the oils that protect your skin, says Dr. Keith. Use the mildest soap you can find, such as Dove or Neutrogena—never deodorant soap. And dry off gently with a patting motion, not by rubbing, which irritates skin.

Oil up. Moisturizers keep your skin soft and less itchy. You can keep it well-lubricated by having several bottles of lotion on hand—in your office, by your bed—so that you can lube up frequently. Most important, moisturize each time you step out of the shower or bath.

Soak in cereal. A warm bath with colloidal oatmeal added can soothe the itch. Aveeno is one brand to look for at drugstores.

Chill out. To relieve itching, you can place a cold compress or an ice pack on the irritated area for a maximum of 15 minutes.

Sit on your hands. Scratching makes irritation much worse by spreading the rash to a larger area and prolonging the healing process. If you just can't keep your hands away, press the spot, don't scratch.

Head to the drugstore. One percent hydrocortisone cream or ointment, available over the counter, will relieve the itch temporarily.

Get help. If self-help hasn't worked within a week or two, give your dermatologist a call. He or she will probably prescribe a stronger steroid cream or an oral steroid to help heal the rash.

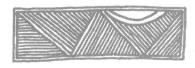

Diabetes

Learning to Take Charge

irst it was her aunt's leg, then her older brother's foot. Diabetes and its most fearsome complication—amputation—had cut such a terrible swath through her family that Zelda Jefferson just knew that her younger brother Andre, who was diagnosed with the disease as a teenager, was in for a big fall. "My 'little' brother had always been large; by the time he was 16, he was 6 feet 4 inches and weighed 310 pounds," says Zelda, a soft-spoken computer technician who was born and raised in Miami. "But he's such a teddy bear that I've always felt protective toward him." When she learned that Andre had diabetes, Zelda braced herself for the worst.

But the worst never came. Andre took the offensive against diabetes with daily walks and a more careful diet. Over time he lost so much weight that Zelda, who had moved to Los Angeles, didn't recognize her own brother in a family photo. "It was amazing," she recalls with a look of astonishment. "There were my parents and my other siblings, and I said to myself, 'Who's this guy?' It was Andre."

But the best part was his blood sugar profile, which went from alarming to perfectly normal. "Let me tell you—when Andre phoned to tell me the good news that his doctor was taking him off insulin, I was too excited," recalls Zelda. "It was one more sign that there's nothing inevitable about poor health."

Nothing Is Sweet about This Sugar

If Andre's happy ending were the rule instead of the exception, diabetes would be no big deal. But that's definitely not the case. More than 2.6 million African-Americans—and one in four Black women over the age of 55—have diabetes. More than half of all people with diabetes don't even know they have it.

How is it possible for one disease to stir up so much trouble? Well, diabetes interferes with something pretty fundamental—the way you metabolize a sugar called glucose, the body's principal fuel. After you eat a sugary or starchy food, glucose marches into the bloodstream, ready to refuel everything from your heart muscles to your brain cells.

Once it reaches your bloodstream, glucose needs a helping hand to complete its journey to each of the millions of hungry cells that need it. That helper is insulin, a hormone secreted by the pancreas. Insulin acts like a master key, latching on to cells and unlocking the gateways that allow glucose to enter and be converted to energy.

With diabetes, this delivery system goes haywire. In Type II (non-insulin-dependent) diabetes, the form of the disease that affects most Black people with diabetes (only 5 percent of African-Americans who have diabetes have Type I, or insulin-dependent, diabetes), the pancreas makes some insulin, but not enough. What's more, the body's cells become insulin-resistant, a condition in which your system does not respond to the insulin you make.

Without enough insulin to carry it away, the extra glucose in your blood can scar and thicken blood vessel walls, heightening the risk of high blood pressure, stroke, and heart attack. It can bruise delicate blood vessels in your eyes, causing a potentially blinding disease called diabetic retinopathy, and can wear out your kidneys, which have to work overtime to flush sugar from the blood.

Diabetes also weakens the immune system, making many people with diabetes susceptible to potentially life-threatening infections. It impedes blood circulation to the nerves, causing numbness and debilitating pain in the legs, feet, and skin (which, in serious cases, can lead to amputations). It makes pregnancy risky for both the mother and the unborn child. And diabetes-impaired nerves can even pull the plug on your sex life, making it difficult to achieve and maintain an erection or to experience vaginal lubrication.

You can see that diabetes isn't like most diseases. If you have heart disease, it affects one major organ. If you've got diabetes, it affects your entire body.

Cornelius Hopkins, a perky seventh-grader, was walking home from school one afternoon when he sensed something terrible coming over him. Suddenly he felt woozy, and it was awfully hard to think straight. "This must be how it feels to be drunk," he thought.

Alcohol wasn't the cause, though; it was low blood sugar. Like thousands of youngsters with Type I diabetes, Cornelius has learned the signals and now carries candy with him at all times for just such an emergency. He takes insulin as well.

Low blood sugar, or hypoglycemia, occurs when there is an imbalance between insulin and glucose in your body. This imbalance results from an excess of insulin in the bloodstream and can be caused by too long a period between meals or too much strenuous exercise. In each case, blood sugar levels drop so low that the body's cells are deprived of energy-packed glucose.

Hypoglycemia can occur with either Type I or Type II diabetes, but it's more common with Type I, a form of the disease in which the pancreas produces little or no insulin. This type of diabetes is primarily a disease of youth: 80 to 90 percent of patients are age 30 or under, and even infants can be affected, but the disease still lasts a lifetime.

"Type I diabetes is much rarer among African-Americans than Type II, but it does occur," says Thomas L. Pitts, M.D., instructor of medicine at Northwestern University Medical School

WHO GETS DIABETES?

Type II diabetes is usually accompanied by too much body fat in people who have a genetic tendency toward diabetes. "People who have an apple-shaped physique, with fat around their waists rather than on their thighs or hips, seem to be at greater risk for Type II diabetes, although a family history of diabetes is the best indicator," explains retired endocrinologist Lester Henry, M.D., formerly of Howard University in Washington, D.C. That explains why diabetes is so common in Black women, who are more likely than Black men to be heavy and less likely to exercise regularly. Both of these factors and the University of Illinois College of Medicine in Chicago. "And research suggests that it may be underdiagnosed in Black children, so it's important for parents to make regular visits to the pediatrician."

What are the warning signs of Type I diabetes in a child? "Watch for personality changes, a change in grades, loss of weight and growth, frequent urination, and vomiting," advises Dr. Pitts.

If your child has Type I diabetes, teach her the warning signs of low blood sugar, which can include uneasiness, confusion, dizziness, trembling, hunger, and difficulty performing such routine tasks as thinking, walking, or talking. Severe cases of hypoglycemia can cause loss of consciousness, says Dr. Pitts.

People with diabetes who experience these symptoms need sugar immediately in the form of candy, glucose tablets, or orange juice, followed by a meal. "If there's no meal to replenish the body's fuel supply, the hypoglycemia can recur in 30 minutes," warns Dr. Pitts.

As for preventing low blood sugar, you should help your child develop the habit of eating and taking insulin like clockwork. "The staples of good diabetes control are consistency of timing of meals and medicines and taking blood sugar readings faithfully," says Dr. Pitts.

heighten your risk of developing Type II diabetes.

Black women are also twice as likely as White women to experience short-term diabetes while pregnant. This condition, called gestational diabetes, results because the mother is unable to produce enough insulin response in her cells due to insulin resistance. Insulin resistance causes high levels of glucose to accumulate in the bloodstream, even though fairly high levels of insulin may be present.

Those high levels of glucose in the mother's bloodstream cross into the fetus, causing the pancreas of the fetus to produce a high

William Montgomery, a 63-year-old farmer from southern Georgia, seldom misses church and never misses his annual trip to the eye doctor. William has been visiting his ophthalmologist ever since he was diagnosed with Type II diabetes 14 years ago. So far, he's had the usual blurring of vision that comes with age but no eye complications from his disease. "I've been lucky," he says, his sun-etched skin betraying the hours he spends on his tractor. "But I work hard at it, too, so I guess you could say I'm lucky and diligent."

Diabetic retinopathy is degeneration of the retina, the eyeball's inner layer that collects light images for the brain. It occurs when the sugar-laden blood of someone with diabetes damages blood vessels in the retina, plugging them like corks in a bottle. The remaining blood vessels can leak blood into the retina, causing blurred vision, or into the vitreous humor, the jellylike interior of the eye, dimming or obliterating vision altogether.

If you have diabetes, controlling your blood sugar is the first step toward a terrific insurance policy for your eyes. The second step is having your eyes examined by an ophthalmologist once a year. "Begin five years after you're diagnosed with Type I diabetes and immediately after you're diagnosed with Type II diabetes," advises Richard S. Baker, M.D., assistant professor of ophthalmology and assistant dean of research at Charles R. Drew University of Medicine and Science, King-Drew Medical Center in Los Angeles.

"If an exam finds retinopathy, laser surgery, which shrinks or plugs the blood vessels that leak blood and fluid, helps prevent small problems from becoming big ones," says Dr. Baker.

concentration of insulin in reaction to too much glucose. The excess insulin causes the fetus to store extra fat, which leads to high birth weight. After the birth of the baby, the risk is that the mother may progress to full-blown diabetes in a relatively short period of time.

Around 3 to 5 percent of healthy women develop gestational diabetes, which also dramatically increases their risk of developing diabetes after pregnancy. Forty percent of women with gestational diabetes who are obese (more than 15 percent over their ideal weight) before pregnancy develop Type II diabetes within four years of their pregnancy. African-Americans are about twice as likely to have gestational diabetes as non-Hispanic Whites.

ARE YOU
AT RISK?

The first step in beating diabetes is to understand the disease and the ways in which it may affect you. These are the major risk factors for Type II.

▲ You're overweight (more than 10 percent over your ideal weight)
▲ You have a family history of diabetes
▲ You're over 45 years old
▲ You're sedentary
▲ You've ever given birth to a baby weighing 9 pounds or more or had diabetes only during pregnancy

These are the warning signs.

▲ Recurring or sluggishly healing skin, gum, or bladder infections
▲ Drowsiness
▲ Blurred vision
▲ Numbness or tingling in the hands and feet
▲ Itchy skin
▲ Frequent urination
▲ Excessive thirst
▲ Constant hunger
▲ Weight loss
▲ Irritability
▲ Fatigue and weakness

If you fit the risk profile, talk to your doctor about your potential for diabetes and ask her to test you once a year, even if you are symptom-free, says Wayman Wendell Cheatham, M.D., chief of the Diabetes Treatment Center at Howard University Hospital in Washington, D.C. If you are having some of these symptoms and fit the risk profile for Type II diabetes, see your doctor immediately. Diabetes is often a silent disease that sends few warning signs until you begin to have serious complications.

If you have diabetes, the doctor may prescribe oral insulin-enhancing medicines called sulfonylurea drugs or injections of insulin itself (especially if you have Type I), says Dr. Cheatham.

BEATING DIABETES

Your chances of controlling diabetes are excellent. Here's the formula.

Update your plate. Years ago, doctors prescribed special diets for people with diabetes. Today, they say your goal should just be an overall healthful diet. Choose foods that are low in fat and cholesterol (because diabetes can injure your arteries), high in fiber (which helps normalize blood sugar levels), and moderate in protein (to avoid straining your kidneys). Some food choices recommended by Dr. Cheatham include legumes, whole grains, fresh vegetables, and fruit.

Then make sure your overall calories are low enough to encourage weight loss. "People used to say diabetics couldn't eat cake or pie," says James Gavin, III, M.D., Ph.D., senior scientific officer at the Howard Hughes Medical Institute in Chevy Chase, Maryland, and the first African-American president of the American Diabetes Association. "That's rubbish. Sugar is fine when used in moderation as part of a healthful diet."

Exercise your options. Exercise is as close as you can get to a natural diabetes medicine. By reversing insulin resistance, exercise lets sugar flow into energy-starved cells. Treat yourself to 15 to 20 minutes of moderate exercise three times a week. Aerobic exercise is best. Walking, running, biking, swimming—anything that stimulates the heart and lungs and involves lots of muscles is good, says Dr. Gavin.

Go high-tech. Keeping track of your blood sugar and taking your insulin, if you need it, are essential to staying healthy. Extremely accurate, easy-to-use blood sugar monitors are as small as pocket pagers, and insulin injectors are as unobtrusive and convenient to carry as a ballpoint pen.

For more information, including church and community-based activities for African-Americans, check the White Pages for your local American Diabetes Association or phone 1-800-DIABETES.

Domestic Violence

TAKING BACK YOUR LIFE

"Y ou don't realize how bad it is until you see the frightened eyes of your child staring up at you, asking why you're hurt and crying," says Keesha Gore as she twists her wedding ring. "There were days when I would go to work thinking that I had concealed my latest black eye with makeup. Then I'd catch a look at my face in the mirror. I was in denial; there was no way to really cover that awful bruise. I remember seeing my smooth, caramel-colored skin, my carefully lined red lips—and this ugly black eye caked with powder.

"The morning I caught my daughter staring at one of those grotesque black eyes was the day I decided to leave," she continues. "I thought, 'I will never let Darryl or anyone else do this to me again. I'll start over with just the clothes on my back if I have to.'

"I put my child in the car, gunned the motor, and headed for the interstate. After a minute my little girl, Celine, said: 'I'm hungry. Where are we going, Mommy?' I told her, 'Someplace safe, baby. We're going to stay with friends for a while.'

" 'What about Daddy?' " she asked. " 'Are you and Daddy still mad?' It hurt my heart. It didn't make sense, but I felt sorry for Darryl. I thought of how he would feel when we didn't come home. I turned to Celine and said, 'Honey, we're not mad, but we're going to stay apart for a while. We're going to get help and so is Daddy. Then we'll be back together again. You'll see.' "

WHEN HOME IS WHERE THE HURT IS

Some people think that domestic violence is a Black issue. The truth is, domestic violence crosses all racial, ethnic, and socioeconomic lines. Abuse appears more frequently among the economically disadvantaged because educated, middle-class, and affluent women tend to have more resources that make it possible for them to avoid or leave violent relationships. They may also seek confidential professional help instead of counseling at residential shelters.

Because most incidents of domestic violence aren't reported, the statistics that are available are often inaccurate. Women fear that somehow the attacker will get back at them, or they worry that they will be shunned by their community. Some women feel it's a private matter and that the police can't or won't be able to help.

The U.S. Department of Justice estimates that each year women experience more than 10 times as many incidents of violence by an intimate partner or ex-partner than men. Annually, between one and four million American women are abused by a partner, and Black women and White women experience equivalent rates of violence committed by partners and ex-partners.

In addition, one out of every nine women who seek care in hospital emergency rooms is there because of injuries resulting from domestic violence, according to a study conducted at the Colorado Emergency Medicine Research Center in Denver. Even more incredible is the fact that every 9 seconds, a woman is physically abused by her husband, and 42 percent of slain women are killed by an intimate male partner, notes the National Resource Center on Domestic Violence in Harrisburg, Pennsylvania.

Clearly, domestic violence is an important public health issue, but when it comes to coping with domestic violence, African-American women tend to engage in denial rather than facing up to the problem. "We must admit that domestic violence happens to us," says Byllye Avery, founder of the National Black Women's Health Project in Washington, D.C. "Domestic violence will not disappear until it ceases to be hidden. Many women don't understand how to support a person in a violent relationship, but as more women tell their stories and as more women and men learn other ways to solve their problems, this will change."

RECOGNIZING TROUBLE

In the early stages, it can be hard to recognize yourself as someone in an abusive relationship, explains Ruth Jones, J.D. (doctor of law), former adjunct professor of law at Fordham University Law School in the Bronx and director of the university's domestic violence clinic. "It is particularly difficult to recognize an abusive relationship because many of the early warning signals are elements of what one could view simply as old-fashioned, traditional roles in a marriage (the male is more controlling or dominates the relationship)," she says.

"There is also often a link between drugs, alcohol, and domestic violence. People tend to make excuses and blame the abuse on a drinking problem or a drug problem. But it's not. It's an abuse problem," Dr. Jones explains.

"After an incident of abuse, a 'honeymoon' phase usually follows, during which the man promises to reform," she says. "He may promise not to hit his partner again and to enter treatment for drug or alcohol abuse. The couple may go through this cycle once or twice, then the relationship is usually characterized as abusive."

"Women may think of domestic violence as no more than a slap or punch, but they are underestimating how often it leads to serious injury and death," says trauma surgeon Cuthbert Simpkins, M.D., director of the violence and victimization prevention program at Erie County Medical Center in Buffalo and associate professor of surgery at the University of Buffalo.

Dr. Simpkins has seen the frightening effects of domestic violence firsthand. "Women often assume that the worst will never happen. 'He may hit me, but he would never cut, burn, or shoot me,' they say. Then when it happens, they are genuinely shocked.

"We tell the victims how close they were to death and that this is a serious matter. People sometimes just don't realize that until we lay it out for them," he says.

BREAKING
THE CYCLE

"If a woman is being abused, she should leave. If she is afraid for her life, she must leave right away," says Dr. Simpkins. But a woman may feel that she cannot make the move for emotional or financial reasons. "She should at least go to a domestic violence shelter for counseling," he advises.

Donald Vereen, M.D., medical officer and special assistant at the National Institutes of Health in Bethesda, Maryland, says, "The key is to bring the problem into the health arena and do something positive. Society mandates that the abuser should be punished, but we should also offer long-term therapy to the couple to stop the abusive pattern. Punishment alone will not fix the relationship. Batterers and victims have often witnessed abuse as children and grow up to enter abusive relationships. Helping the victim and the batterer to develop healthy relationships should be addressed as well."

"In most situations of domestic abuse, women can't or aren't ready to leave the relationship, and then we have to work within it," says Dr. Simpkins. "In these cases, we try to help families work through their issues. Each family is different, but the only way the relationship will work is to get help for the abuser."

The long-term effects of domestic violence on our community affect all of us, male and female. Men who watched a man beat their mothers are predisposed to act out violent behaviors; this cycle of violence hurts everybody because it makes men into what they don't want to be as well as damaging other family members, says Avery.

Domestic violence hurts children, too, says Dr. Vereen. "Girls who see Dad beat Mom may develop problems with trusting others and self-esteem. Boys who witness domestic abuse may grow up to copy the behavior in future relationships. They may develop conflicting feelings about seeing their loved ones physically and emotionally hurt one another. They may also feel personally threatened or perhaps even paranoid due to the violence they witnessed."

PREVENTING AND ENDING THE VIOLENCE

If you find yourself in an abusive relationship, here are some steps that experts suggest you take to safely free yourself.

Prioritize your needs. "An abused woman needs to go where she can't be found," Avery points out. To do this, she must start to disconnect from her belongings and surroundings. "So many women feel 'I can't leave because of my car' or 'I can't leave because of my house.' Figure out what's most important—you or the house," she says.

Seek support. Abuse is something you should not have to live through alone. "Reach out. Talk to someone. You can get free professional advice from a local hotline (almost every community or state has one). You can get specific information about resources in your area from the social or human services pages of the phone book and obtain legal information through your district attorney's office," advises Dr. Jones.

Make a plan. "If you know you are in an abusive situation, face it and start making a safety plan for leaving," says Dr. Jones. "How will you get the kids out in the middle of the night? How will you gain access to money, credit cards, hotels? Are there friends or a shelter where you can safely stay?"

Get professional help. If you're not ready to leave your partner, at least go for counseling. "If he won't go for counseling with you, go by yourself," says Delaney E. Smith, M.D., of the Baldwin Hills Medical Group in Los Angeles. "Make it clear to the therapist that you are being abused; don't try to hide it. Children who witness more than one violent incident between their parents should perhaps have counseling as well," he says.

Don't take time to talk. Once violence starts, don't negotiate with your abuser. Take threats seriously and get away if possible. Don't do or say anything that will escalate the situation or cause you further physical harm—just leave, says Dr. Simpkins.

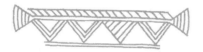

Drug Abuse

AVOIDING ADDICTION

Sonja Roberta and her husband had a home in the Poconos, sent their son to private school, and traveled three times a year. She had all the standard trappings of picture-perfect suburban prosperity—and a drug habit.

Sonja started experimenting with heroin at the age of 14 because she felt inadequate. "I also felt alone and insecure. I was withdrawn," recalls the 44-year-old corporate manager. "So as a young girl I searched to fit in somewhere, to be a part of something. I thought I had found acceptance in drugs and with those who used drugs. I felt as though I belonged. It was like being a member of a club."

It took Sonja years to come to grips with the complex pain that led her to drugs—years of depression, denial, and re-lapses. Sonja eventually entered a substance abuse treatment program, where for the first time in her life, she learned to live without drugs. "I knew I was dying spiritually," she says.

Completely drug-free for the first time since childhood, Sonja now co-facilitates the Women's Transition Lecture Series on Mondays, the Co-Ed Transition Lecture Series on Tuesdays, and the Women's Relapse and Prevention Support Group on Thursdays for African-American Family Services, the center in Minneapolis/St. Paul that helped her learn how to live without drugs. Sonja also sponsors other African-Americans who are struggling to live clean. "I realize now that my problems were all about how I felt about myself," Sonja says.

THE SURPRISING FACE OF DRUG ABUSE

The full story of drug abuse doesn't make it to the evening news. Sure, as a community we've got plenty of folks on drugs—more than our share. But not all African-Americans with drug problems are poor and struggling, and not every house with drugs is a crack house. "There's often more drug use in the suburbs than in the inner city," says Salimah Majeed, a licensed independent clinical social worker and executive director of African-American Family Services. Of all of the issues that affect the Black community, substance abuse may be the least understood.

African-Americans have many different reasons for turning to drugs, but one common element is cultural pain. "Lots of our clients use drugs to medicate the shame and anger and rage they feel from racism and the oppression that Blacks often inflict on each other," says Majeed.

Others may initially do drugs because it's daring and exciting. But eventually many drug abusers resort to antisocial or criminal drug-related acts such as stealing, lying, and manipulating, observes Majeed. These behaviors often make them so ashamed that getting high becomes a way to deaden their remorse.

Still others turn to drugs as part of a youthful search for identity. "Many middle-class kids buy into the media image that says Black culture is defined by the urban street life," says Majeed. "They feel ashamed of their affluence, so they get involved in drugs to try to identify with that life."

Finally, researchers point to four factors that seem to lead to drug abuse: sadness, poor self-esteem, social alienation, and stress—especially when people feel that they are powerless to change their circumstances.

Add it all up and you get a feel for why the rates of African-American drug abuse are so high. The majority of past drug abusers—37 percent—in the United States are White, while only 31 percent are Black and 5 percent are Hispanic. Yet a higher percentage—8 percent—of Black Americans currently use illicit drugs, according to data from the U.S. Department of Health and Human Services. That compares with 6 percent of Whites and 5 percent of Hispanics.

Drug abuse can be deceptive. It usually begins pretty innocently, says Beny Primm, M.D., executive director of the Addiction Research and Treatment Corporation in Brooklyn. Pressure from peers and youthful curiosity can start the ball rolling. So can emotional distress. Even after a drug habit is full-blown, it's easy for users to convince themselves that they're in complete control.

"For years I smoked pot, sniffed coke, and used heroin, but I never thought I had a drug habit. I'd find myself saying, 'I won't use for a couple of days' so I could feel as though I had it all under control. I still made it to work every day and paid my bills on time. Most important, I felt I could stop using drugs whenever I wanted to," Sonja remembers.

Of course, getting off drugs is rarely a simple matter. Physical addiction is only one component of a drug problem; there's a substantial psychological component as well. Dr. Primm predicts that some addicts would experience a genuine drug high and craving if they simply observed someone sniffing a line of plain white flour and feigning exhilaration. "They're so susceptible to the ritual that surrounds drug-using and so used to being taken to another place by drugs that their brains would actually tell them they were high or actually needed a fix themselves," he says.

DEEP-SIXING DRUGS

What should you do if you or someone you love is addicted to drugs?

Talk about it. "Black people don't like to talk with outsiders about troubling problems that are going on at home," says Majeed. "But until we confide in others, it can be difficult to get proper treatment."

Cut them off. It sounds cold-blooded, but it can work. "We need tough love. If a drug addict is homeless because he spent his rent money on drugs, let him sleep on the streets. If you believe in our inner resilience as a people, then believe that we must stop coddling people and let them hit rock bottom and decide to do something about their habits," says Majeed.

We know that our extended families and the larger community will always be there for us if we get in trouble, says Majeed, and it's a wonderful tradition. But with drug abuse, helping hands can prolong the addiction if they keep bailing out the abuser.

Get help. Phone the federal 24-hour Drug Information Hot Line toll-free at 1-800-662-HELP. You can talk with a counselor about a drug problem, get referrals to treatment programs in your state, and order printed material on substance abuse. It's a free service provided by the U.S. Center for Substance Abuse Treatment.

Go for treatment. If you have health insurance, your coverage may dictate where you can go for treatment. But you should scrutinize available programs for the following three elements: comprehensiveness, cultural sensitivity, and a long-term focus, suggests Dr. Primm. Here's what to look for.

Comprehensiveness. Months or years of drug abuse can leave drug users jobless, friendless, physically ravaged, emotionally troubled, and dually dependent on drugs and alcohol. The most effective treatment programs address a spectrum of needs.

"I call them supermarkets of services—one-stop shopping where clients receive an array of vocational, medical, mental health, spiritual, and other services, all designed to help people stand on their own two feet and take responsibility for their actions," says Dr. Primm.

Cultural sensitivity. When you visit or phone a drug treatment center, ask the director if the program is sensitive to the needs of African-Americans. Then ask for specific examples of this sensitivity. If he seems flustered or speaks only in generalities, consider taking your search elsewhere, advises Dr. Primm.

The need for cultural sensitivity doesn't mean that Whites can't provide excellent services to African-American clients. It also doesn't mean that Afrocentric drug treatment programs, whose Black counselors may use African names, dress in African garb, and encourage clients to focus on their Blackness, are appropriate for everyone. Seek a program that makes you comfortable.

Long-term focus. "Treatment is only 10 percent of the process. The rest of recovery happens once you leave a treatment center. That's why the best programs provide and encourage long-term comprehensive treatment," says Dr. Primm.

Important elements of long-term aftercare include a support network, which should comprise regular group meetings, non-drug-using friends, and a sponsor you can call for support whenever you need it. "If there's no long-term program for African-Americans in your area, why not start your own 12-step support group? No special expertise is needed. The essential component is a group of recovering people dedicated to helping each other," says Majeed.

Know that there's hope. "Not only is living without the use of drugs and alcohol possible, it's also pretty exciting once you get there. There are many gifts and rewards in recovery," says Sonja, who was hospitalized for depression, spent time in a halfway house, and weathered two relapses in her journey to a drug-free life. "Recovery is a healing process. I may still encounter difficulties, but I can and will be able to handle them without using again. I'll be able to face my problems head-on and deal with them appropriately. Today I truly love myself too much to hurt myself by using. I love my new way of life. And for all those who have helped me on this journey, I am truly grateful."

Ear Problems

KEEPING THINGS LOUD AND CLEAR

hen LaToya Summers was ready to move into her first apartment as an 18-year-old college freshman, her mother sat her down at the kitchen table and reminded her what to do if she ever needed help. "You just pick up that phone. I'll always be here for you," she said.

So when LaToya awoke one morning hard of hearing and with a stabbing pain in her left ear that persisted all day—through two history classes, an English seminar, and an afternoon aerobics session—she knew just what to do—call home. "Mama said it sounded like I had an ear infection and that I should see a doctor," says LaToya, a tall, heavyset young woman whose wrists jingle and sparkle with silver bracelets. "When I told her that I thought only babies got ear infections, she said, 'Well, you'll always be my baby!'" recalls LaToya, rolling her eyes.

Baby or not, her mama's advice and diagnosis were right on target. LaToya had a severe ear infection and needed antibiotics, which cleared up her problem and stopped the pain in almost no time. "At this age, I don't always agree with my mother," LaToya says, "but sometimes her help is just what I need."

SOUND COMPLAINTS

Let's look inside two common ear complaints, earache and hearing loss.

Earaches. In adults, earaches usually start when mucus blocks the eustachian tube, which leads from your ear to your throat. Allergies can start the mucus flowing; so can cigarette smoke or a cold. Once the tube is blocked, the warmth and moisture of the inner ear are just what bacteria need to multiply. Stray bacteria from your nose

Henry Thomas, a beefy professional football player, loved to go out and dance with Diane Berry, his childhood sweetheart and the love of his life. But lately he was starting to wonder if Diane felt the same way. Every time Henry suggested that they hit a favorite club and tear up the floor, Diane found an excuse to beg off. She wouldn't even agree to go roller-skating or take in a concert. Finally, he confronted her, and she 'fessed up to her secret.

"For months I had been troubled by this terrible ringing in my ears," says Diane, a slender, attractive flight attendant with a gracious manner. "It sounded like that emergency broadcast system tone that you hear on TV. It was loud and distracting and it never went away." Loud noises—such as house music or live musical performances—only aggravated it. "I never told Henry because I guess I was afraid he'd think I was crazy," Diane admits.

He didn't, and neither did the otolaryngologist (ear, nose, and throat doctor), who diagnosed Diane's condition as tinnitus, a problem in which people hear ringing, buzzing, or roaring in their ears with no known source for the racket.

An estimated 50 million American adults have tinnitus. "It's with you all day and night," says Diane. It ranges from a mere annoyance to a real interference with work and life. Some people describe it as a buzzing or ringing; others hear whistling or

or throat move in to establish a new colony and create an infection in your ear. Pressure changes from the growing bacteria colony can make the eardrum bulge outward, causing even more pain.

Infection isn't the only thing that causes earache. If the joints and muscles of your jaw hurt and it's difficult for you to fully open your mouth, you could also have temporomandibular joint disorder, which can also cause ear pain.

In addition, tumors in the sinuses, mouth, nose, jaw, or even the throat can cause what doctors call referred pain, which means that the discomfort feels like it's in the ear when in reality the tumor and the ear only happen to be served by the same nerves. "I once had a 41-year-old patient who had a tumor that was so far on the back of her tongue that she couldn't see it," recalls Neal Beckford, M.D., an hissing. "Tinnitus can sound like crickets in the evening or the roar of the ocean," says Neal Beckford, M.D., an otolaryngologist and head and neck surgeon in Memphis, Tennessee.

Tinnitus is often a sign of deteriorating hearing, but it can be brought on by an infection, ear wax, medication, or occasionally a tumor. It's also a potential side effect of hundreds of prescription and some nonprescription medicines, including drugs used to treat heart disease and high blood pressure. Tinnitus sometimes has a medical cause—a narrowing of blood vessels or high triglycerides—so it's best to check with your doctor to get a proper diagnosis.

Although there is no cure for tinnitus, there are a few things you can do to turn down the noise. A hearing aid can reduce tinnitus noise by amplifying outside noise and helping to mask the inner noise. Or your doctor can prescribe a tinnitus masker, which looks like a hearing aid but produces either a wide or narrow band of noise that drowns out the noise of tinnitus.

You can also try relaxation techniques. Diane found biofeedback training helped her relax to the point that her tinnitus became more tolerable. If you have tinnitus, don't give up hope. Up to three-fourths of people who have it say that it improves over time.

otolaryngologist (ear, nose, and throat specialist) and head and neck surgeon in private practice in Memphis, Tennessee. "Her only symptom was ear pain."

Hearing loss. Noise damage is the usual cause of hearing loss. Think of standing near the speakers at a rap concert or too close to a pounding jackhammer at a construction site. Noises of this type can damage sensitive structures in your ear. And exposure to any sound loud enough to cause outright pain, such as being within 100 feet of a roaring jet engine, can cause permanent hearing loss.

"Ears are very sensitive," stresses Duane J. Taylor, M.D., lead physician for otolaryngology–head and neck surgery at the Mid-Atlantic Permanente Medical Group in Landover, Maryland. "A lot of musicians, both young and old, suffer high-frequency hearing loss from prolonged exposure to loud music," he says. The louder the noise, the less time it needs to injure your ears. "Twenty years of working in a noisy tool and die plant will cause hearing problems, but so will the split-second explosion of a hand grenade in combat," says Dr. Beckford.

Now Hear This!

Keep your ears in tip-top shape with these simple preventive measures.

Clear the air. Steer clear of cigarette smoke and any allergens—dust, mold, or pollen—that cause havoc with your upper respiratory tract, says Dr. Taylor.

Turn down the volume. "When you wear a personal stereo, the rule of thumb is to keep the volume low enough that bystanders can't hear it," recommends Sandra J. Jones, M.D., an otolaryngologist in private practice in Atlanta.

Plug them up. If you can't control the sound level, protect your ears. If you're exposed to loud noise at work (driving a tractor, doing heavy construction work, or working around noisy equipment, for example) or during recreation (such as hunting), use earplugs, says Dr. Taylor. There are different types available at drugstores. Better still, wear acoustical earmuffs. They muffle loud noises extremely well. You can purchase ear protection at industrial supply shops or hardware stores or ask if your company will provide it.

Be an activist. If your work site is noisy, your employer should offer hearing tests at regular intervals. If your company is unresponsive, talk with the person responsible for safety or contact your local health department or the Occupational Safety and Health Administration (OSHA). (To contact your local OSHA office, dial 1-800-321-OSHA or look in the blue pages of your phone book under U.S. Department of Labor.) Meanwhile, have a doctor check your hearing. If tests show early hearing loss, the doctor will determine the cause, says Dr. Taylor. He'll also tell you how to treat it, which could include using ear protection to keep any damage from getting worse.

Clean it out. Most people's ears are self-cleaning, but some are prone to wax buildup. The ear canal also produces more wax as you age, which is one reason that some older people are hard of hearing. If your ear feels clogged with wax, don't try to loosen or remove it with a cotton swab, hairpin, fingernail, or anything else that could push the wax further into the ear canal and cause serious damage such as hearing loss or dizziness.

If you haven't had past chronic ear infections or ear surgery, you can place two or three drops of mineral oil in your ear at bedtime for three or four days to help soften or loosen the wax. There are also over-the-counter kits with special wax softener drops and a bulb syringe. If you use one of these, read the instructions carefully, says Dr. Taylor. If these methods don't work, see your physician.

Keep the bugs away. Protect your ears from moisture-loving bacteria after swimming or showering by using an eyedropper to insert a few drops of a 50-50 mixture of rubbing alcohol and white vinegar. "The alcohol helps eliminate water from the ear canal," explains Dr. Beckford. "And the vinegar—acetic acid—reduces the pH in the ear, which creates an unfavorable environment for microorganisms."

Easing the Pain

It's difficult to treat ear pain without an accurate diagnosis from a physician, cautions Dr. Beckford. But if you do develop an earache, here are some pain-relief strategies.

Pick a pill. As a first step, an over-the-counter analgesic such as aspirin, acetaminophen, or ibuprofen (Advil, Nuprin) can help relieve ear pain, Dr. Beckford says.

Get steamed. Moist heat can bring relief if the pain is from TMJ syndrome or some other problem unrelated to a middle-ear infection, says Dr. Beckford. "The moist heat increases blood flow into the affected area and helps decrease inflammation," he explains. Try placing a warm, damp washcloth over your ear; repeat for 5 or 10 minutes every two hours.

Let your doctor help. If ear pain is severe and lasts for more than one day, or if it's mild but lasts longer than two weeks, get to a doctor, suggests Dr. Beckford. Don't wait for the pain to go away on its own; it could be a symptom of a serious condition.

Eating Disorders

BREAKING THE CYCLE

ictoria Johnson is one of the first African-American fitness professionals to star in her own collection of workout videos and a national TV show (*Victoria's Body Shop* on the PRIME Sports Network), and run her own company (Metro Fitness in Lake Oswego, Oregon). But her incredible success did not come easily. She's unmistakably a winner who had to triumph over bulimia—a life-threatening binge-and-purge eating disorder—to get where she is today.

"I was the 6th child in a family of 11 children," says Victoria, who is now in her thirties. "My mom and dad were migrant farmworkers who harvested fruit. They couldn't give us much, but they could provide love, an abundance of food, and wonderful times around the dinner table. Mealtimes were the best times in my family.

"By high school, I had learned to feed my desire for food, sometimes gorging myself on half a chocolate cake, hamburgers, ice cream, candy, and more, and I tried to control my weight by taking laxatives following my binges.

"In my freshman year in college, I gained 60 pounds. I was suffering from depression and the stress of trying to fit in, and food, as usual, was my comfort," Victoria says. "That was when I hit my peak weight of 170 pounds at 5 feet 3 inches.

"Later, I began to regularly experience fainting spells, dizziness, and problems sleeping. A trip to the doctor revealed that my pancreas was barely functioning and I was borderline diabetic. I was shocked," she remembers. "After all, I was only 23 years old.

"To deal with my eating disorder, I had to face my loneliness and insecurity. I had to shift my perspective and my lifestyle before I could let go of the excess weight and work on becoming strong and healthy. Now I realize that my experience is shared by many Black women. That's why I decided to tell my story."

Victoria is right: Black women do suffer from eating disorders. Binge eating disorder, which is different from the bulimia that Victoria endured because there is no cycle of purging following the overeating, is the most common type of eating disorder among sisters. People with this disorder eat to excess within short time periods (a 2-hour span, for example). This disorder is not about gorging yourself at Thanksgiving dinner or wolfing down an occasional triple helping of Aunt Etta's sweet potato pie. Women with binge eating disorder regularly feel embarrassed and out of control as they eat large amounts of food at least two days a week for at least six months.

Twice as many Black women as White women over 30 are obese, and binge eating disorder may contribute to these weight-management problems.

It's estimated that the other two major eating disorders, anorexia and bulimia, affect 2 to 18 percent of all American adults. But 90 to 95 percent of those with anorexia and bulimia and 60 percent of those with binge eating disorder are women. And although binge eating is the most widespread eating problem among Black women, anorexia and bulimia are also on the rise among sisters. All three conditions can destroy your health, but they are defined by distinctly different types of behavior, symptoms, and health effects.

People with anorexia eat very little and hide the fact that they don't eat. Some exercise compulsively as well. Even when their bodies become so thin that they appear emaciated to people around them, those with anorexia continue to see themselves as grossly overweight.

People with anorexia generally fall at least 15 percent below their healthiest weight, and some go as low as 60 percent. Women with anorexia stop having their periods because the dramatic weight loss causes their body fat to plummet, disrupting estrogen production. If it leads to heart disease, anorexia can be fatal.

People with bulimia binge and then purge themselves, using laxatives or induced vomiting. They also hide their behavior. They may become rail thin, but it is the complications from the constant vomiting that are more likely to bring their condition to the attention of loved ones and friends. Stomach acids from vomiting can strip the enamel from their teeth. They often become dehydrated, and they may develop arrhythmia (abnormal heartbeat patterns) due to a mineral deficiency caused by purging.

SISTERS AND
FOOD FRUSTRATIONS

"Mystery still shrouds the eating disorders of Black women," says Shiriki Kumanyika, R.D., Ph.D., professor and head of the Department of Human Nutrition and Dietetics at the University of Illinois at Chicago. "People talk about the high prevalence of obesity in African-American women, but there has been very little research done on eating disorders in this group," she explains.

A major study being conducted by several universities and the National Institutes of Health in Bethesda, Maryland, however, confirms many experts' suspicions about Black women and eating disorders. Of the African-American women surveyed, almost 4 percent of study participants reported having binge eating disorder, while only 1 percent reported bulimia, and less than 1 percent had anorexia. Although these figures may seem small, they represent millions of women in the general population.

Still, some folks think that because of cultural factors, Black women are immune to pressures to be thin. In a survey conducted by Dr. Kumanyika, overweight women were asked whether or not they considered their figures attractive. In their responses, only 30 percent of White women said they did, but 70 percent of Black women responded positively.

"The prevalence of anything that relates to purging or starvation may indeed be much lower among Black women," says Dr. Kumanyika, "because we have less concern about thinness."

Our thing is high-fat food. "We're more likely to overeat unhealthy foods because we may learn that pattern from our parents," says Julia A. Boyd, psychotherapist with the Group Health Cooperative in Seattle and author of *In the Company of My Sisters: Black Women and Self-Esteem.*

But this doesn't mean that sisters are immune to the desire to wear a size 5. "We have to live in a lot of worlds, and although our eating behavior is closely related to our community, mainstream culture may also prevail," says Dr. Kumanyika.

Checking Your Food Attitude

No one has to develop an eating disorder. Understanding the roles that food and body image play in your life can help you prevent or manage these conditions. Here's how.

Accept your body. "Generally speaking, we don't have skinny legs and hips," says Victoria. "Our body shapes are beautifully different. We need to work hard on self-love and feeling good about who we are on the inside. When we don't, food becomes too important."

Pass on perfection. Anorexia and bulimia often develop in Black teenage girls or women who are obsessed with meeting mainstream society's unrealistic notions about how women should look or act. Remember that it's what's inside that counts, not some media-generated concept of what a woman should be. Focus on developing realistic professional and personal goals and expectations, says Victoria.

Tend to teens. Eating disorders are especially common during the difficult years that follow puberty. If you have a daughter, make sure that she maintains a balanced, healthy diet, says Dr. Kumanyika. And help her learn to love and appreciate her changing body.

See a therapist. "An eating disorder can be fatal, so you must get help. See a doctor *and* a psychologist, because it is important to treat the root causes of your eating disorder," says Boyd.

Set reasonable goals. Extreme diets are doomed to failure. Your doctor or a nutritionist should help you choose a healthy, realistic weight-management program, whether you are trying to gain weight back or lose it after a bout of binge eating, says Dr. Kumanyika.

Coordinate your care. If you are obese, see your doctor or a dietitian for help in planning a workable weight-loss plan. If you are over 40 or have a chronic illness such as diabetes, have a checkup before starting a diet and exercise program, says Dr. Kumanyika.

Learn all you can. For more information on eating disorders, write to the Eating Disorder Resource Center, 24 East 12th Street. Suite 305, New York, NY 10003 or the Center for Counseling and Health Resources, 611 Main Street, Edmonds, WA 98020.

Eczema

Putting an End to the Itch

or Jeannie Lewis, the arrival of winter means more than getting her woolens out of storage and preparing for the holidays. It means having to put up with an unwelcome visitor: eczema. "Whenever the weather gets cold and the air indoors and out is dry, the skin on my legs becomes dry, itchy, and irritated. Sometimes the itch is so bad that I can't stop myself from scratching until my skin bleeds. I even scratch in my sleep," Jeannie explains.

Like most people with eczema, Jeannie finds that the more she scratches, the larger the affected area seems to become. "I just spend a lot of time hoping for an early spring and that my scars will fade before it's time to switch from tights to sheer hose," laments Jeannie.

How Irritating!

Eczema, also known to physicians as atopic dermatitis, is a chronic skin inflammation for which the cause is unknown. It's especially troublesome because of its intensity. Some people have it for their entire lives and are never sure when the next outbreak will occur or what part of their bodies it will hit. Outbreaks can range from sudden, short-lived dry patches to areas of perpetually crusty, inflamed, unsightly skin.

While African-Americans aren't more prone to eczema than Whites, it's often more troublesome for us. This is because "scratching the irritated skin can lead to dark, discolored patches that are slow to fade," says William Keith, M.D., clinical assistant professor of medicine at Drew Medical School/Martin Luther King, Jr., Hospital and medical director of the Institute for Aesthetic and Cosmetic Dermatology, both in Los Angeles.

Eczema is often triggered by the skin's sensitivity to environmental agents like pet hair, dust, plants, soaps, or wool. Dry air and cold weather can also cause an outbreak, which is why Jeannie suffers each winter. In addition, eczema runs in families. In fact, there's a link among eczema, hay fever, and asthma (which is more common among African-Americans). They're inherited from the same gene, which is why eczema patients may have asthma as well. (Jeannie doesn't have asthma, but her older sister does.) Men and women are equally affected by eczema.

"There's also an emotional component to eczema," explains Dr. Keith. "In people who are prone to eczema, stress or anxiety can excite the nervous system in a way that causes the skin to itch. When you scratch, the rash flares." Jeannie can relate. The worst case of eczema she ever had was around the time she broke off her engagement.

How to Avoid
Rash Behavior

If you are prone to eczema, there are several things Dr. Keith says that you can do to keep it under control.

Stop it before things get ugly. "Most of my African-American patients who come in with eczema do so to treat the skin discoloration that comes from scratching," says Dr. Keith. "Because Black people have brown skin, we often miss the redness that is an early warning sign that our skin is inflamed. If the inflammation or scratching is controlled early, the rash can be prevented. All that scratching stimulates pigment cells and leads to dark patches," he explains.

The solution? At the first sign of itching or inflammation, you can prevent eczema by treating the area with an anti-inflammatory ointment or cream. Look for one percent hydrocortisone preparations at your drugstore. Over-the-counter antihistamines such as diphenhydramine (Benadryl) and pseudoephedrine (Drixoral) can also help you ditch that itch.

Say good-bye to soap. Jeannie finds that her eczema is especially bothersome right after she towels off from a shower. This is probably because soaps contain ingredients that can irritate sensitive skin.

Dr. Keith advises patients with eczema to switch from deodorant soaps to moisturizing cleansers or body washes such as Moisturel Sensitive Skin Cleanser. You'll find them in your drugstore or beauty supply store labeled as "moisturizing" or "nonirritating." Dove soap, which contains a cleansing ingredient that was originally developed to wash the traumatized skin of burn victims, is extremely gentle. The same advice goes for shampoos: Use baby shampoo or other mild types.

Stay out of hot water. Dry skin loves to soak in moisture, but keep the water cool. Not only does hot water make your skin itchier by increasing blood flow to the surface, it also washes away the natural oils that moisturize and protect. Using a mild oil such as Neutrogena body oil can counteract the bath's drying effects, but stay away from scented bath salts and gels.

Learn to lubricate. Keeping your skin moisturized is one of your best defenses against dryness and irritation. Lotions such as Lubriderm or Eucerin are most effective, but even good old petroleum jelly can be used to lock in skin's moisture. Using lotion after your bath or shower is especially important. "Don't towel off. Instead, wring out your washcloth and use that to dry off gently, leaving beads of water on your skin. Then massage in a moisturizer or body oil while your skin is damp, trapping beads of water," advises Dr. Keith.

Change climates carefully. Avoid quick changes in air temperature. Quickly going from a nice, warm room to the cold outdoors, or vice versa, plays havoc with your skin. If possible, spend a brief transition period in a garage or enclosed porch where the temperature is somewhere in between.

Build Fido a doghouse. Sorry, but man's best friends—particularly long-haired breeds—are anything but friendly to those with eczema. Cat dander can also pose a problem. "Consider keeping your pet outdoors, at least until your skin improves," Dr. Keith advises.

Milk it for all it's worth. A compress of cold milk is an effective way to soothe itchy skin. Dampen a gauze pad or a thin piece of cotton with milk and apply it to the itchy area for about 3 minutes. Resoak the cloth and apply at least two more times for 3-minute soaks. Repeat the procedure several times a day, but be sure to rinse your skin in cool water after each application, because the milk can eventually give off a sour smell.

If a large part of your body is affected, Dr. Keith recommends adding milk to your bathwater. For best results, however, you'll need to use a couple of gallons.

Heal with oatmeal. Adding oatmeal to your bathwater is also an effective skin soother. Look for oatmeal-based Aveeno products (soap, bath grains, and lotion) at drugstores. To use regular dry oats, grind about three cups of oats to a powder in a blender. As the bathwater is running, swirl the powder into the warm water to prevent clumping. Get in and soak for 15 minutes.

Give itching the deep freeze. Ice will also help relieve your itch. Jeannie learned just by trial and error that a homemade ice pack did the trick instead of scratching. She puts a few ice cubes in a plastic bag and then wraps the bag in a small towel. Placing this on the itchy area (for a maximum of 10 to 15 minutes) soothes her skin nicely.

Don't stress your skin. Stressful situations can't always be avoided, but you can control how you choose to deal with them. Find ways to relax and stay calm. Meditate, go for a walk, or take long, deep breaths. Avoiding flare-ups of anger or anxiety can help prevent your eczema from flaring up, says Dr. Keith.

Endometriosis

EASING THE AGONY

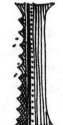**I** was wide awake when my alarm went off. In my frustration, I slammed down the button on the clock harder than usual," says Halima Edwards. "I hadn't slept a wink, and there was no way I was going to the office.

"I dragged myself into the bathroom to look for more painkillers," she continues. "The face I saw in the mirror was not pretty: I had heavy dark circles under my eyes. Although I felt really guilty about calling in sick during tax season because every accountant was desperately needed to keep the company afloat, I knew that I wouldn't be able to do anything constructive that day. So I curled up in bed, popped prescription Motrin, and prayed that the pain would go away. My friends and family didn't understand my monthly bouts of pain, so sometimes things got pretty lonely."

LOTS OF PAIN, NO GAIN

Halima's condition is endometriosis, which commonly causes extreme and often unrelenting pain during a woman's menstrual periods. "Women with the disease often experience pain during intercourse as well as general pelvic pain. There's also a strong association with irregular bleeding and sometimes infertility," explains Zerline Chambers-Kersey, M.D., an obstetrician/gynecologist in private practice in Annandale, Virginia.

And although she feels lonely, Halima has lots of company: According to statistics, approximately five million women in the United States have endometriosis. It affects White and African-American women equally. "Doctors once thought of it as a disorder that affected only White, Type-A women who delayed childbearing until later in life, but that stereotype has not held true," reveals Dr. Chambers-Kersey.

Most women first become aware that something is wrong when their menstrual periods bring pain that over-the-counter medications can not relieve. "When their period nears, women with endometriosis say 'I don't do anything. I can't move. I have to be in bed all day. I can't work. I can't travel,'" says Nancy Roberson, M.D., clinical associate professor of obstetrics and gynecology at the University of Rochester School of Medicine in New York. "This pain gradually worsens and extends until it is no longer confined to their menstrual period."

BEHIND THE SUFFERING

Each month, the glandular tissue that lines the uterus thickens to nurture a developing baby. If you do not become pregnant, the tissue is shed in your monthly menstrual flow.

Endometriosis develops when the glandular tissue from the uterine lining migrates, usually into other parts of the pelvic region. "The misplaced tissues become activated in response to monthly hormonal changes just as uterine (endometrial lining) tissue does, but unlike normal endometrial tissue, the shed tissue is trapped within the pelvis," explains Dr. Chambers-Kersey. These tissues expand and release hormones such as prostaglandins and cause intense pain and scarring of the pelvic organs.

"There are three or four theories about the cause of endometriosis," says Dr. Chambers-Kersey. "Some hypothesize that it may be an autoimmune disease (in which the immune system mistakenly attacks parts of the body as if they were foreign substances). Other experts think that endometriosis is caused by retrograde menstruation, a backup of menstrual flow from the uterine lining back through the fallopian tubes and into the pelvis. Others suspect that it may be a genetic or an inherited disease," she says. If your mother and/or sister has endometriosis, you have a greater chance of developing it also.

Infertility is the other painful aspect of endometriosis—30 to 45 percent of women who are infertile have endometriosis. Although these statistics are scary, many women with endometriosis can become pregnant and carry their babies to term. And in some cases, women who have the disease have no pain or interference with fertility.

TRACKING IT DOWN

Your doctor may do an ultrasound exam after hearing about your history of severe menstrual pain to rule out other medical problems, but the definitive diagnosis is made by direct tissue sampling, says Dr. Chambers-Kersey. This is usually accomplished by a procedure called diagnostic laparoscopy. In this procedure, your doctor makes a tiny incision in your abdomen and inserts a lighted tube called a laparoscope, which allows her to see if there is uterine tissue in unusual places. This procedure requires general anesthesia, but you can usually go home the same day.

STOPPING THE PAIN

Easing endometriosis requires careful medical treatment, supervised by a physician, but Dr. Roberson offers these self-help tips.

Taste relief. Our old friend the low-fat, high-fiber diet, which contains lots of B vitamins and unprocessed complex carbohydrates, such as whole grains, beans, fruits and vegetables, may help. It's also a good idea to avoid caffeine and sugar.

Work it out. "Exercise and a healthy diet do tremendous things," says Dr. Roberson. One study suggests that the earlier in life a woman begins to exercise, the lower her chances of developing endometriosis.

Try an alternative. "I've seen acupuncture work very well for some women," says Dr. Roberson. "It can be an alternative to traditional medication or can be used in conjunction with it." To find an acupuncturist, contact the American Academy of Medical Acupuncture at 5820 Wilshire Boulevard, Suite 500, Los Angeles, CA 90034.

Schedule sex. If sex hurts, watch your calendar and attempt to abstain from intercourse during those times in your menstrual cycle when your symptoms are the worst. If you decide to have intercourse anyway, consider changing your position for comfort, adds Dr. Chambers-Kersey. "Deep thrusting usually causes pain, which is typically worse just before your period."

Bringing Out
the Big Guns

When endometriosis fails to respond to self-help treatments or adjustments in lifestyle, it's time to get tough.

Try pills for pain. Dr. Chambers-Kersey suggests starting with modest over-the-counter pain medications such as ibuprofen (Advil, Nuprin) and working up to prescription drugs only if necessary. "Birth control pills and prescription nonsteroidal anti-inflammatory drugs (NSAIDs) help most women after three or four months of treatment. Once the birth control pills are working, the frequency and dosing of the NSAIDs can be lowered with continued control of the pain," advises Dr. Chambers-Kersey.

Get help from hormones. Prescription hormonal drugs such as leuprolide (Lupron) or nafarelin (Synarel) help to shrink sites of endometriosis in the body and therefore help to reduce pain, says Dr. Roberson. "Birth control pills or Depo-Provera, a progestin, can also be used to help control the pain of endometriosis, but they do not shrink the sites," she says. Dr. Chambers-Kersey adds that these drugs can often bring on a dramatic reduction of the disease's symptoms.

Solve it with surgery. If drug therapy doesn't sufficiently counteract the symptoms of endometriosis, you can ask your doctor about surgery. Dr. Chambers-Kersey explains that laparoscopic surgery using lasers can dissolve or burn away the endometrial tissues. "If this doesn't control the pain, and childbearing has been completed, consider a hysterectomy with removal of the fallopian tubes and ovaries," she says.

Eye Problems

KEEPING A HEALTHY OUTLOOK

nita Beasley left the windy, dusty construction site of the newly completed hospital wing that she had designed. As she walked to her car, she thought about how fortunate the hospital's patients were to have the new facility.

"Suddenly I felt this irritation in my left eye, like a gnat had flown into it," remembers Anita, a 43-year-old architect in Baltimore. Within hours, Anita was in severe pain. "It felt like someone was pushing a needle through my eye," she says, wincing at the memory. "I turned around and headed right back to the hospital," she says.

The ophthalmologist on call examined Anita's eye with a magnifying scope and found the culprit. The wind at the building site had blown a tiny piece of glass into her eye, and it had become embedded in her cornea, the eye's clear, protective covering. The doctor removed the offending sliver, treated the eye with antibiotic, and gave her a patch to protect her eye overnight.

The next day, Anita's pain had been replaced by newfound wisdom. "I never even think about stepping into a construction site without my hard hat, even though it makes a mess out of my short afro, but I have a tendency to take off my safety goggles and lay them to one side when I read blueprints and paperwork. Never again. I've learned my lesson. My eyes are my livelihood," says Anita. "And from now on, I will protect them all the time."

TAKING A LOOK AT EYE DAMAGE

Eyes get poked, scratched, bopped, and bumped all the time. "The eyeball is surrounded by bone, which helps protect it," says Richard Casey, M.D., chief of ophthalmology at Charles R. Drew

University of Medicine and Science, King-Drew Medical Center in Los Angeles. Even so, a blow near the eye—and certainly one to the eyeball itself—can be vision-threatening. "We see lots of black eyes that develop complications like a dislocation of the lens, a detached retina, and bleeding into the eye that can be associated with glaucoma," says Dr. Casey.

Besides problems prompted by injuries, the eye can fall prey to eye infections. One of the most common is conjunctivitis, an inflammation of the thin mucous membrane called the conjunctiva that lines your eyelids and covers the surface of your eyeballs.

Like the mucous membranes in your upper respiratory tract, the conjunctiva is vulnerable to viral or, less commonly, bacterial attack. Irritants and allergens like smog, wind, pollen, makeup, and smoke can also cause conjunctivitis.

In any case, red, scratchy, irritated eyes—the obvious reason that this inflammation is often called pinkeye—are the hallmarks of conjunctivitis, as is a discharge that can range from watery tears to mucus to yellowish or greenish pus. While viral conjunctivitis runs its course within days and allergic conjunctivitis diminishes as the allergens in question are removed, certain types of bacterial conjunctivitis can lead to serious eye damage, such as a severely infected cornea.

Iritis, or inflammation of the iris, the ring of tissue that gives eyes their color, can cause reddened eyes, blurred, hazy vision, and extreme sensitivity to light. "Sometimes light causes such pain that people wear sunglasses indoors," explains Dr. Casey.

Iritis often appears in conjunction with autoimmune diseases such as lupus or rheumatoid arthritis, and it can be a special problem for African-American women because they are more susceptible to these conditions.

"With these diseases, the body mounts an inflammatory response against its own tissues," according to Kevin C. Greenidge, M.D., professor and chairman of the Department of Ophthalmology at the State University of New York Health Science Center in Brooklyn. "In the joints, this inflammation causes arthritis; in the eye, it causes iritis." Other illnesses that are associated with iritis include diabetes, inflammatory illnesses such as ulcerative colitis and inflammatory bowel disease, and infectious diseases such as tuberculosis and syphilis.

Like most mothers, Beverly Jones is always a little fearful when it comes to safeguarding her two toddlers, Malcolm and Rosa. The Detroit homemaker is especially protective of the children's eyes. "I want my kids to experience all the color and texture of a beautiful world," says Beverly as she entertains the laughing children on a playground swing set.

Whether it's your loved ones' eyes or your own, it never hurts to know first-aid. Try the following initial treatments, then see a doctor as soon as possible.

Black eye. Cover the area with a cold compress to limit swelling, advises Richard Casey, M.D., chief of ophthalmology at Charles R. Drew University of Medicine and Science, King-Drew Medical Center in Los Angeles.

Chemical irritation. For injuries from chemicals such as battery acid or hair relaxers, irrigation is the key, says Dr. Casey. Immediately flush out the affected eye with cool, gently running water, holding the eyelids apart with your fingers. Flush the eye for at least 10 minutes, then cover it with gauze or a cloth pad, says Dr. Casey.

Foreign body in the eye. If the object is floating on the white of the eye, remove it gently with the edge of a clean cloth or tissue, advises Kevin C. Greenidge, M.D., professor and chairman of the Department of Ophthalmology at the State University of New York Health Sciences Center in Brooklyn. If you can't see it, seek professional help.

FOCUSING
ON PROTECTION

Fortunately, preventing eye injuries and infections is primarily a matter of common sense. Here are some suggestions from eye specialists.

Treat it like a cold. The infectious form of conjunctivitis is extremely contagious. "If a young child gets it, his whole class can come down with it," says Dr. Casey. If you're near someone who has conjunctivitis, act as if the person has a cold, advises Dr. Greenidge: Wash your hands frequently, especially after touching a towel, doorknob, or other item that the infected person has touched, avoid touching your eyes, and stay out of the range of coughs and sneezes.

Check all your symptoms. Iritis is sneaky. Sometimes it causes no symptoms, and other times physicians focus so much on treating a person's lupus or tuberculosis that they forget to check for the iritis that can accompany it. "If someone in your family is being treated for diabetes or another iritis-associated illness, make sure they get routine eye exams," advises Dr. Casey.

Point it away. Celebrating? Don't cause a tragedy. Place a towel over the champagne cork as you remove the wire net, then keep your hand there as you point the bottle away from people and slowly twist the cork, keeping it under the towel until it is removed. "You'd be amazed at how many devastating eye injuries we see on New Year's Eve," says Dr. Greenidge.

Be careful with contacts. Hard or soft contact lenses—especially lenses made for overnight wear—can predispose you to conjunctivitis or a corneal infection, even if you use them as directed, says Richard S. Baker, M.D., assistant professor of ophthalmology and assistant dean of research at Charles R. Drew University of Medicine and Science in Los Angeles. "If you wear contacts and your eyes get red, irritated, and very sensitive to light, or if you have a decrease in vision, remove the lenses immediately and visit an eye doctor to make sure you don't have conjunctivitis or an eye infection," he advises.

Go with goggles. Whether you're hammering a nail, handling caustic chemicals, or driving in for a layup, wear safety goggles, advises Dr. Casey, who wears goggles even when he's digging in his garden, in case he accidentally flicks microorganism-laden dirt into his face. "I've seen lots of people who have hit a nail, then had it fly back into their eye," he says, "or caught a thumb in the eye during athletics."

SHEDDING LIGHT
ON RELIEF

Before you see a doctor, you can apply a cool compress, such as a washcloth dampened with cold water, to the sore eye to help ease discomfort and clear away any crusty buildup or discharge.

Get to the doctor. If your eyes show the redness and weeping of conjunctivitis, visit a doctor. Like a cold, viral conjunctivitis generally clears up on its own within three or four days. "But also like a cold, a bacterial infection can follow the viral invasion and cause problems you don't need," advises Dr. Casey. Prescription antibiotics specially made for the eyes will limit the damage before things get out of hand. And a cool compress can help reduce swelling, he says.

Watch the red. The redness and irritation of iritis are easy to mistake for conjunctivitis. "I've seen patients who have had iritis for years, and they thought it was pinkeye," says Dr. Casey. But iritis can signal serious illness elsewhere in the body.

"Eyes get red for a reason," says Dr. Casey. "If your eyes are red and you can't associate it with a precipitating reason, like being up all night or spending time in a smoky room, see a physician."

Cool it. If you have iritis, your doctor will probably give you prescription steroid drops or ointment to decrease the inflammation, plus eyedrops for pain. You can also try using a compress. "A cold compress won't treat the illness, but it will help your eye feel better," suggests Dr. Greenidge.

Fatigue
INCREASING YOUR ENERGY LEVEL

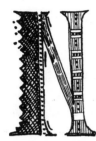ot long after her twins were born, Marlene Smithton began to have a recurring dream. "I'm driving our little import car uphill against this really strong headwind. The exhaust is sputtering, the engine is knocking, and I'm still not getting anywhere," says the 32-year-old homemaker loudly, straining to be heard over the lunchtime laughter of her two-year-olds, Rob and Ellis, who were eating (and playing with) spaghetti and green beans. "Eventually I realized: This dream is my life!"

Marlene and her husband decided that a vacation was in order and called in the reinforcements—his parents—who were only too delighted to babysit while the frazzled couple escaped for a weekend getaway in the nearby Florida Keys. It was just the kind of break that they needed. "We've got great kids, but they demand so much of our energy," Marlene says. Now she and her husband take a weekend break once every few months to refresh their spirits. "It gives our energy levels a real lift, plus the grandparents love having the twins all to themselves. It's a win-win situation," she says.

FACING UP
TO FATIGUE

Whether you earn your living by hauling heavy loads or pushing pencils, being overtired almost all the time has become an increasingly common state for folks in all walks of life. "Fatigue is one of the 10 most common complaints that I see in my practice," says James P. Lewis, M.D., of the Department of Family and Community Medicine at St. Paul-Ramsey Medical Center in St. Paul, Minnesota.

"Lots of African-Americans who come to me feel that they're just dragging through life," adds Elaine Hart-Brothers, M.D., an internist in private practice in Durham, North Carolina. "It's especially difficult for African-American women because we feel we're not supposed to get tired, and we feel guilty when we do."

Some of us may be battling chronic fatigue syndrome (CFS), which doctors define as severe, disabling fatigue that lasts more than six months, along with cluster of symptoms that can include disturbed concentration, impaired short-term memory, disrupted sleep, and muscle pain.

No one really knows what causes CFS, and although there's no cure, there are a variety of methods that doctors use to treat it. It's estimated that between 4 and 10 of every 100,000 American adults have the condition. (For more information on CFS, see page 79.)

The majority of tired people do not have CFS, though. They're just overworked and overextended, and these are problems that can be solved with a few carefully targeted lifestyle changes. The first thing to do is to rule out any physical reason for your fatigue that may be connected to an illness, says Dr. Lewis.

Many of the chronic diseases that disproportionately affect African-Americans, such as diabetes, heart or lung disease, obesity, thyroid disease, kidney or liver ailments, cancer, iron-deficiency anemia, or an immune system disorder like lupus or even HIV infection, can make you feel tired all the time. You should also be aware that the medications that treat some of these and other conditions—blood pressure medications, antihistamines, and even sleeping pills—can be responsible for fatigue, too.

"Your doctor's job is to sift through the many possibilities and decide which ones make the most sense to pursue," says Dr. Lewis. Here's where doctors and patients don't always see eye-to-eye. "Most patients look for a physical ailment," he explains. "But most of the time, fatigue has a strong psychological component."

A psychological component? Sure. Let's face it, none of us can play superman or superwoman for very long without wearing ourselves out. We spend so much time juggling work, home, school, family, and friends that we become walking anxiety machines, fueled by tension and kick-started by caffeine.

"When people are perpetually tense and they can't rest, they naturally become fatigued," says Dr. Lewis. Life in the fast lane also crowds out time for proper sleep, exercise, and nutrition. Too little sleep obviously contributes to fatigue; too little exercise deprives us of a natural energy booster. And while fast food is easy and soul food is comforting, it's hard to get sustainable energy from a diet that's high in fat and low in essential nutrients.

"A diet consisting of foods high in fat and cholesterol could contribute to the development of heart disease and high blood pressure, which in turn might require medications that could make you tired," explains Dr. Lewis. "One thing leads to another, and it all snowballs into fatigue."

Race-related stresses can sap your energy, too. It doesn't matter whether you live in a penthouse suite or a shelter for the homeless. "You can't buy your way out of racism, and dealing with it can run you down," says Dr. Lewis.

STAYING PUMPED

There's a lot you can do to ease fatigue and get energy back into your life.

Tell it to a doctor. "If you feel perpetually wiped out, see a physician," says Dr. Lewis. But don't go to just any doctor. "Ask a friend to recommend a doctor who's supportive, who takes time to be with you without seeming rushed, and who explains things so you can really understand what's going on," he says. It may take several visits before even the best physician can weave together enough information to find out if your fatigue is caused by a physical problem.

Talk about it. This is especially important for guys, who typically keep stress bottled up. "Find a community of friends. Think of it as your 'Waiting to Exhale' group, which can serve as a mutual support group and sounding board," says Dr. Lewis.

Eat right, eat often. If you're worn out, skipping meals or filling up on junk will only make it worse. Your body needs the right stuff to get you back on track. "What you eat is as important as how much you eat," says dietitian Robbin Dunghy, R.D., of suburban Detroit, who recommends four to five daily small meals of whole grains, fresh fruits and vegetables, and lean meats, plus low-fat snacks like air-popped popcorn, rice cakes, and pretzels.

Women should also be sure to eat lots of iron-rich foods, since iron deficiencies can cause fatigue during the childbearing years. Some foods rich in iron include steamed clams, tofu, and lean meat.

Be sure to accompany iron-rich foods with good sources of vitamin C, such as citrus fruits, to help your body absorb the iron, advises Dunghy. You should also try to limit your consumption of coffee, tea, and cola, since caffeine interferes with iron absorption, she says.

Pass on the java. It's not advisable to get into the habit of drinking lots of coffee to get you started or keep you going, says Dr. Hart-Brothers. It's okay to have one or two cups a day, but overdoing it with coffee can irritate your stomach or cause heart palpitations. Plain water is a much better energy booster.

Draw the line. Make the bedroom your sanctuary: Mentally deposit all worldly stresses at the bedroom door. Studying, reading, or watching television in bed is a no-no. Why? Becasue you start to associate the bed with things besides rest. "Beds should be used for two things," says Dr. Lewis. "Sex and sleep."

Just say no (to sleeping pills). "It's far preferable to find the cause of a sleep disturbance and treat that," says Dr. Lewis. Besides, most pills interfere with your natural sleeping patterns, so you may sleep but not feel rested when you wake up.

Move your body. Moderate exercise is relaxing and enjoyable. It builds muscle, strengthens the heart and blood vessels, increases lung capacity, and helps convert convert fat and carbohydrates (the body's sources of fuel) into energy. It's also the perfect daytime prelude for a restful night in dreamland, says Dr. Lewis. Just be sure not to exercise too close to bedtime, he adds, or it could interfere with restful sleep.

Try walking three to five times a week at a comfortable pace, suggests Dr. Hart-Brothers. "And before you set out," she says, "be sure you're wearing comfortable shoes that offer ample support." Walking is not only heart-healthy, it's a great way to relieve mental stress, thereby reducing fatigue.

Nix the nicotine. Nicotine is a stimulant, but smoking has the opposite effect on the body, says Dr. Hart-Brothers. Cigarettes reduce your energy in the short run by diminishing the flow of oxygen to your brain. In the long run, they knock out your immune system and make you prone to exhausting respiratory infections.

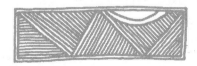

Fibroids

FIGHTING BACK

"very part of my life was controlled by the growths in my uterus," says Deirdre Moore, shaking her head. "From the age of about 37, when I first found out that I had fibroids, until my 40th birthday last year, the pain, bleeding, and hormonal ups and downs just made me miserable most of the time," says the South Carolina public relations executive.

"When I turned 40, I realized that I just wasn't living anymore. I wasn't in a relationship, I had pretty much decided against having a family, and my symptoms were getting worse. I knew it was time to make a change," Deirdre says. "I started by reading everything I could about hysterectomy and recovery so that I could prepare myself to deal with the surgery.

"When I was finally ready, I said my prayers and went to the hospital, and I'm glad I did. Hysterectomies are not the first choice for everyone with fibroids, but because mine were growing and I had chosen not to have children, it was the right choice for me," explains Deirdre, who has only recently regained her trim size-8 figure and incredible energy.

"Now I've got my life back again. I was up and around in a few days after the surgery, and since I opted for a procedure that spared my ovaries, I don't have to face sudden menopause. I was scared out of my wits on the day I went to the hospital, but I now know that I did the right thing. I found a way to reclaim my future and my freedom," she says.

RECOGNIZING A SILENT THREAT

Chances are that you have fibroids, even if you don't know it. More than 50 percent of African-American women of childbearing age have them. The growths are three times more common among us

Fibroid Primer

Fibroids often grow to the size of apples and oranges. Some never get bigger than an apple seed, but others (rarely) grow as large as watermelons. They may grow individually, but they usually appear in clusters. There are also several types, distinguished by where and how they grow.

Intramural. These are the most common type and grow within the wall of the uterus.

Subserous. This type grows outward from the uterine wall into the abdominal cavity.

Submucous. These tumors grow inward from the wall of the uterus, taking up space within it. All fibroids may cause heavy bleeding, but this type is the most likely culprit if your periods are very heavy.

Pendunculated. This type differs from others in that the tumors grow on a stalk that projects either inward into the uterus or outward into the abdominal cavity. This type of fibroid can cause severe abdominal pain if the stalk somehow twists or moves.

than among White women, and they often go undetected because they don't always produce symptoms. When symptoms do arise, however, they are frequently severe and debilitating, requiring medical help.

Fibroids, also called myomas or leiomyomas, are noncancerous growths of smooth muscle tissue on or within the uterus that can cause heavy bleeding, pain, bloating, and other health problems such as endometriosis (excess growth of the uterine lining outside the uterus).

"In African-American women, fibroids are a major cause of infertility and hysterectomy," says Elwyn Grimes, M.D., chairman of the Department of Obstetrics and Gynecology at Meharry Medical College School of Medicine in Nashville, Tennessee.

The good news about fibroids is that they are rarely life-threatening. Only a very small number of fibroid tumors (less than 1 percent) turn out to be cancerous, explains Nancy Roberson, M.D., clinical associate professor of obstetrics and gynecology at the University of Rochester School of Medicine in New York. One of the quick tip-offs that a woman may have a malignancy, however, is that the fibroid will grow far more quickly than normal.

If you have fibroids, understanding the latest treatments can help you avoid years of aggravation and worry and keep you one step ahead of this condition.

CAUSES
AND EFFECTS

Very little is known about the causes, and therefore the prevention, of fibroids. Here's what doctors know so far.

The source. The only known causes agreed upon by physicians and scientists are genetics and high levels of estrogen in the body. Being overweight is a problem because estrogen levels increase as weight increases, and estrogen can cause fibroids to grow. Pregnancy raises estrogen levels, and birth control pills contain estrogen, which is why pregnant women and women on the Pill may find that their fibroids grow very rapidly. Fibroids often decrease in size or even disappear after menopause, when a woman's estrogen production slows down dramatically.

Whether you're heavy or thin, however, you stand a good chance of getting fibroids if your mother, grandmother, or sister had them, because fibroids are hereditary.

Early warnings. Fifty percent of women with fibroids will experience symptoms. Some of the most common problems are extremely heavy menstrual bleeding, abdominal swelling, a sensation of pressure in the abdomen, cramps, painful intercourse, and a frequent need to urinate. In addition, up to 10 percent of infertility cases may be caused by fibroids.

CHOOSING
THE RIGHT TREATMENT

If you are diagnosed with fibroids, the best way to protect your health, and possibly your fertility, is to learn how to treat them.

If you have only small fibroids and don't have any symptoms, working with your doctor to keep a close watch on your progress is a reasonable and healthy option. But be sure to keep your appointments.

"If you skip your follow-up appointments and the next time you come in, your fibroid is the size of a grapefruit, you may have missed the window of opportunity for managing the fibroid without surgery and may end up having to have a hysterectomy," says Dr. Roberson.

"A fibroid that reaches the size of a 12-week pregnancy is the limit," says Dr. Grimes. "If a fibroid grows beyond this size, the possible side effects include infertility or pregnancy complications, anemia, and interference with cancer screening."

If you do need treatment, there are several options available.

Gonadotropin releasing hormone. This is a drug treatment using synthetic hormones called GnRH agonist analogs. They shrink fibroids by causing estrogen levels to drop. These drugs are administered through a nasal spray or injection and can spare the uterus by offering an alternative to hysterectomy. The side effects caused by these medications—similar to the symptoms of menopause—may make treatment with GnRH analogs suitable for only temporarily shrinking fibroids before surgery or menopause.

They may be given, for example, a few weeks before a woman undergoes fibroid-removal surgery in order to shrink them and make the procedure easier and safer. Or, if GnRH analogs are given to a woman who is nearing menopause, they may calm her symptoms until her body's natural drop in estrogen allows her fibroids to shrink to a size that causes little or no symptoms.

Myoma drilling or coagulation. Despite its unusual name, this technique, used by about 20 physicians nationwide, is far less invasive than other surgeries and will spare your uterus. The outpatient procedure involves minimal incisions using a laparoscope (a small tube with a light attached). "We can use this procedure to correct the uterus, not get rid of it," says Leonard Weather, Jr., M.D., director of the Omni Fertility and Laser Institute in New Orleans.

Before the operation is performed, GnRH analog drugs are used to shrink the fibroids. During the surgery, the doctor uses a laparoscope to locate the tumors. Then he punctures them multiple times with a needle so that their blood supply dwindles. Without an ample blood supply, most fibroids will shrink 50 to 70 percent over a period of six weeks.

Myoma drilling or coagulation works best for fibroids that grow from the uterine wall, women near menopause, and women who still wish to have children.

Myomectomy. This is a surgical procedure that requires full anesthesia and hospitalization. This fairly common surgery involves making an incision in the uterus and removing the fibroids while leaving the rest of the uterus intact.

Myomectomy often spares fertility as well. If you elect to have this surgery, select a surgeon who has a great deal of experience with this method of removing fibroids. It is reasonable to expect that he has performed the surgery at least 30 times.

Rollerball endometrial ablation. This procedure sounds like something more likely to be performed on *Star Trek* than in an earth-bound doctor's office, but don't let the name put you off. It is especially helpful for women who have very heavy bleeding. It may allow you to avoid a hysterectomy, but it will not preserve your fertility.

Endometrial ablation is the destruction and removal of the entire uterine lining. During this procedure, the doctor passes a high-frequency electrical current over the wall of the uterus with a surgical device that resembles a tiny paint roller, thus the unusual name.

The procedure can be performed in a half-hour in a doctor's office under mild anesthesia, and patients can return to work the next day. Most have very little or no menstrual bleeding afterward. The method does not bring on premature menopause, however, as the ovaries are not removed. Again, it's smart to find an experienced doctor to perform this relatively new procedure.

Hysterectomy. In the United States, one-third of all hysterectomies are performed for fibroid treatment.

A hysterectomy is major abdominal surgery that involves the complete removal of the uterus. Side effects may include the sudden onset of menopause (if the ovaries are also removed) and a higher risk for heart disease, since it causes a drop in estrogen (estrogen is what gives women a natural advantage over heart disease).

Large or fast-growing fibroids that cause intense symptoms almost always require surgery. But remember that your fibroids may become less severe with the onset of menopause, when your hormone levels drop. If your doctor recommends the surgery, be sure to get a second opinion. Ask about the less invasive therapies listed above before you make your decision.

Fibromyalgia

Tracking an Elusive Illness

ne summer morning, Janie Wells, a nurse's aide at a convalescent home, was lifting a patient out of bed when she felt a stabbing pain in her lower back. "I didn't think much of it, you know," recalls Janie, a heavyset woman whose chestnut-brown braids frame dimpled cheeks. "I know I'm only 34, but in my line of work, aches and pains are just an occupational hazard. I often move hospital beds, push wheelchairs, and do other physical labor."

At first her doctor thought it was a herniated disk. But over the next few weeks, something odd happened. The pain and tenderness migrated, first to Janie's upper back, then to her arms.

The doctor was stumped. "He did a bunch of tests and finally he shrugged his shoulders and said he thought I was imagining it," says Janie.

His response sounded crazy to Janie, so she got a second opinion, and a third, and a fourth, until she found a rheumatologist (a physician who specializes in muscle, tendon, and joint disorders). Although she had to travel a fair distance from her Queens, New York, home, it was well worth the trip, because he recognized her chameleon-like symptoms and said, "I think you may have fibromyalgia."

Since that summer two years ago, Janie has had small triumphs and disappointing setbacks. The pain hasn't disappeared, but she has discovered that she can keep it "75 percent under control" by adhering faithfully to her physical therapy program of walking and relaxation exercises. "It's no fun being in pain, especially when you have a six-year-old to keep up with," she says. "But I'm really proud that I've gotten to this point."

Figuring Out
the Fibromyalgia Mystery

Fibromyalgia is a common but poorly understood illness that affects the muscles, ligaments, and tendons. We don't know what causes the pain of fibromyalgia, but we do know what may trigger it: stresses such as illness, physical or emotional trauma, or hormonal changes.

The most common symptoms of fibromyalgia are widespread pain and fatigue. People describe the pain as burning, radiating, aching, gnawing, cramping, or even stabbing. And some degree of that pain, which can be severe, is usually constant. The pain can migrate, but it settles in any of 18 specific areas in the neck, back, arms, thighs, and knees. The presence and pattern of these tender points are what distinguish fibromyalgia from other pain disorders.

"This is a particularly difficult disease for people whose work involves repetitive motion," explains Judith R. Lee-Sigler, M.D., assistant professor of medicine at the University of Illinois College of Medicine at Urbana-Champaign and staff physiatrist (a physician who specializes in physical medicine and rehabilitation as well as muscle, tendon, and joint disorders) at Carle Clinic Association in Urbana. Movement causes significantly more pain in a person with fibromyalgia than in a healthy person. And it takes much longer for the person with fibromyalgia to bounce back. "If you're healthy and you decide to paint your house, you feel sore but functional afterward," says Dr. Lee-Sigler. "If you have fibromyalgia and you paint your house, you feel incapacitated for a long time."

The fatigue from fibromyalgia can be even more debilitating than the pain. The condition disrupts deep sleep, so people can wake up exhausted despite having a full night's sleep. In fact, the fatigue is sometimes mistaken for chronic fatigue syndrome. "People with fibromyalgia who once took pride in being able to work two jobs suddenly find that they have a hard time managing one," says L. Anita Cone, M.D., associate physician at Georgia Spine and Sports Physicians in Marietta. "By the end of the day, they're just worn out."

Changes in mood, such as feeling blue or down, as well as migraine and tension headaches, abdominal pain and bloating, constipation alternating with diarrhea, and urgent or frequent urination are also commonly associated with fibromyalgia.

With all of these general symptoms, many of which are

common to other disorders, fibromyalgia is frequently misdiagnosed. In addition, it cannot be detected through an x-ray or a laboratory test, and many doctors have not been trained to recognize it. As a result, many people undergo repeated and complicated evaluations before they are correctly diagnosed.

Gender plays a role, too. Nine out of 10 fibromyalgia patients are women, who are the least likely to be listened to by many physicians. "Lots of women go from doctor to doctor being told that there's nothing physically wrong with them," says Margarita Hanser Gardiner, M.D., assistant professor of medicine at the Medical College of Pennsylvania and Hahnemann University in Philadelphia.

"Many people with fibromyalgia are told that something is wrong with their heads," adds Dr. Lee-Sigler, who recalls one patient who saw no fewer than 15 physicians before finding one who recognized her fibromyalgia.

Working on Relief

Fibromyalgia can be managed. "Everyone who has fibromyalgia can be helped if they're willing to help themselves," says Dr. Cone. "People who work at it may ache, sometimes every day, but they're functional, they perceive their pain as less intense, and they're happier."

How do you fight back against such an elusive disorder? Well, most illnesses have an Achilles heel, and fibromyalgia has at least five. They include good medical care, deep sleep, relaxation, exercise, and emotional support.

Find the right doctor. Many doctors are unlikely to recognize fibromyalgia when they see it. "Patients are often told 'There's nothing we can do for you' or 'You'll have to live with this,' when in fact the doctor just doesn't understand what's wrong," says Dr. Lee-Sigler. If you feel you're getting the runaround, talk with a rheumatologist or a physiatrist, she suggests.

Ask if the doctor treats fibromyalgia, advises Dr. Cone. "If so, there's a good chance he or she will be receptive to considering this diagnosis in your case."

But note: You should see your family doctor before you pursue a specialist, advises Dr. Gardiner. "Your pain and fatigue could be caused by many things besides fibromyalgia," she says. You will want to rule out these other conditions before you visit a specialist.

Sleep it off. Low doses of tricyclic antidepressant medications such as amitriptyline (Elavil), nortriptyline (Pamelor), and doxepin (Sinequan) even out the sleep disturbances associated with fibromyalgia and help reduce the pain. People with fibromyalgia tend to have low levels of serotonin, so some may respond to serotonin uptake inhibitors such as fluoxetine hydrochloride (Prozac) and sertraline hydrochloride (Zoloft).

If you have been diagnosed with fibromyalgia and have trouble sleeping, ask your doctor about getting a prescription. "Although these medications are also antidepressants, patients with fibromyalgia are not necessarily depressed and usually respond to lower doses than the doses needed to treat depression," explains Dr. Gardiner.

Take five. "Many people with fibromyalgia are Type-A perfectionists," says Dr. Lee-Sigler. The ability to relax is an important part of fibromyalgia management. She suggests that you listen to a meditation tape, learn and practice biofeedback, do yoga, take a warm bath, or sip a cup of soothing herbal tea or warm milk before bed.

Break a sweat—carefully. "People with fibromyalgia often say the pain worsens when they're sedentary, gets better when they're moderately active, and gets worse when they're vigorously active," says Dr. Gardiner. For safe, moderate exercise, she suggests walking, swimming, biking, or low-impact aerobics.

"Exercising in a heated pool is great, too, especially if other low-stress options are still too hard on the body," says Dr. Cone. She suggests aquatic exercises with a buddy or in a group sponsored by your local YMCA or Arthritis Foundation.

"Don't worry about meeting a target heart rate, and don't be hard on yourself if you can only exercise in small doses," Dr. Lee-Sigler says.

Get support. "Support is extremely important, because people with fibromyalgia so often feel depressed and isolated," says Dr. Cone. "After being told 'You're just a whiner' or 'You're weak,' it's great to find people who can affirm you and talk about shared experiences." To find a support group near you, call your local arthritis chapter or the National Arthritis Foundation at 1-800-283-7800.

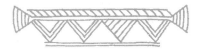

Flesh Moles

CLEARING UP YOUR COMPLEXION

hen Rhonda Burton, 34, first noticed the raised, dark bumps that were beginning to appear on her face, they made her think of some of the great times she had spent down South with her Grandma Ella.

"As a little girl, I had often climbed into Grandma Ella's lap and asked, 'Nana, why do you have spots?'" Rhonda says. "My grandma would laugh and say that those spots were 'little bits of wisdom' she'd earned from living so long. Well, those little bits of wisdom later appeared on my daddy. Then they began cropping up across my forehead and the small area of skin beneath my right eye.

"Warm memories aside, I couldn't help but worry about whether those bumps would lead to cancer or grow until they distorted my features. Finally, when two moles in the cluster under my eye fused together into one large, raised bump on a little stalk, I made a beeline for a dermatologist," Rhonda says. The doctor gave her an explanation and suggested some ways to reclaim her once-smooth skin.

A BLEMISH ON BEAUTIFUL BROWN SKIN

These raised, molelike bumps are actually called dermatosis papulosa nigra (DPN), according to Carla E. Herriford, M.D., a dermatologist in private practice in Los Angeles. More than half of all Black people develop these harmless growths, which are generally round or oval and flesh-colored or darker. They can also appear in people of other races. Like the largest one in the cluster under Rhonda's eye, they are sometimes attached to the skin by a little stalk.

Many folks start noticing these moles in their early thirties, and they are common in middle-aged and older people. Although they tend to affect men and women in equal numbers, women are more likely to seek a doctor's advice about removing them for cosmetic reasons, says Dr. Herriford. The cause of this skin condition remains unknown, but Rhonda's dermatologist explained that these moles tend to run in families.

Although these moles are harmless, any mark or growth on the skin that changes in appearance over time needs to be checked by a
· physician to rule out skin cancer.

MOLE
CONTROL

"There is no way to prevent dermatosis papulosa nigra," says dermatologist Susan C. Taylor, M.D., of Society Hill Dermatology in Philadelphia, "but these small growths can be concealed cosmetically or removed surgically." Years ago, before many Black people could afford to see specialists, the home remedy—tying off the growths with thread until they withered and fell off—was all we had. Because this practice can cause scarring and infection, however, it isn't advised, says Dr. Herriford. Here's what you should do instead.

Take cover. Under makeup, that is. Moles that don't protrude too far above the skin's surface can be effectively minimized with a concealer stick that matches your skin tone. (It's a common misconception that concealer should be lighter.) Dermablend, available at department stores, boutiques, skin-care clinics, and some pharmacies, makes a smudgeproof body cover that can be used on the chest area, says Dr. Herriford.

Zap them. Your doctor can use a technique called electrodesiccation (sometimes done under local anesthetic) in which a mild electric current is applied to the mole, drying it out. "A week to 10 days later, it falls off," says Dr. Herriford.

Get clipped. To remove stalk-type moles, Dr. Taylor prefers simply cutting them off with surgical scissors under local anesthetic in her office. "Patients tend to have fewer problems with scarring or discoloration this way, but *do not* try to cut the growths off yourself," she says. Although it's a myth that doing so can cause a person to bleed to death, as some of us may have heard, it can lead to infection or other problems, not to mention pain.

Choose the right doc. If you're considering having moles removed, consult a dermatologist; skin specialists are trained to prevent scarring, keloids, and discoloration. Ask friends or family members if they know someone who has had a flesh mole removed and find out how satisfied they were with the physician. "Personal referrals are extra insurance that you have chosen the right doctor," says Dr. Herriford.

Get the facts. And speaking of insurance, it's also a good idea to find out ahead of time whether your medical insurance will cover the cost of treatment. "Many plans provide limited access to specialists and limited payment for cosmetic procedures, although they will usually pay for removal of these moles if they have become painful, infected, or uncomfortable," says Dr. Herriford.

Food Poisoning

SETTLING STOMACH DISTRESS

haking his head in near disbelief at the memory of his cousin Tony's wedding, Eric Simmons recalled the events of that weekend. "The reception was on a Saturday," he explains, "and by Sunday, I was the only one left on my feet. They found out exactly what caused it, though—the curried goat. I heard that it tasted pretty good, but it was on the buffet table a little too long." The next day, wedding guests were dropping like flies. "I suppose that was the baddest goat that ever lived," Eric says with a smile. "It fought on beyond the grave. I'm thankful that I didn't have a taste for it that day."

Most of the people who were at Tony's wedding spent the rest of the weekend fighting diarrhea and stomach pain. Unfortunately, their bout with food poisoning became more memorable than the wedding itself.

REASONS TO BEWARE

Although many people think of it as rare, almost all of us have lived through the everyday food poisoning that doctors call gastroenteritis. The Centers for Disease Control and Prevention (CDC) in Atlanta estimates that somewhere between 6 and 80 million cases of food poisoning occur annually in the United States. The range is so broad because only a small percentage of cases are actually reported. The good news is that "the illness—and the accompanying vomiting, diarrhea, and abdominal cramps—are rarely life-threatening. It usually runs its course in 24 to 48 hours and disappears a day to two afterward," explains Victor Scott, M.D., chief of gastroenterology at Howard University Hospital in Washington, D.C. Your body will generally heal itself with a little time and a lot of liquids. For children and the elderly, however, the dehydration caused by unchecked diarrhea and vomiting can be fatal.

When to Call the Doctor

Generally, food poisoning is mild, lasts only a day or two, and has no lasting effects. In some cases, however, such as in small children and people over 65, it can be dangerous and should be evaluated by a physician. You should also see a doctor if you have any of the following problems.

• Your symptoms do not improve after two days.
• You are unable to hold down water or other fluids after 24 to 48 hours.
• You run a fever.
• You begin to pass bloody stools.

If you think that you are immune because you are always careful about where and what you eat, you are at least partially right. But for the most part, you can be exposed to the bacteria that cause food poisoning just about anywhere—even in your own kitchen. Social settings, however, like church suppers, family picnics, and poor Tony's wedding—gatherings where food is handled by several people and left out for hours so it's accessible to guests—pose a much higher risk.

While you're filling in friends and family on the latest news, foodborne bugs are busy breeding and awaiting their chance to disturb the peace in your intestinal tract. Virtually any food can cause food poisoning, but there are several high-risk habits that can greatly increase your chances of getting sick.

One of the most common problems is leaving prepared food out for long periods. Even if Mama always left the food out on Sundays until absolutely everyone had their chance at seconds, letting food sit at room temperature for more than an hour is one of the most common ways to turn a delicious dinner into a ticket to days and nights in the bathroom.

Certain favorites like dishes made with shellfish such as shrimp and foods made with eggs or mayonnaise (potato salad, for example) should be handled with extra caution, says Dr. Scott. People also often fail to realize that even foods like fresh-cut fruits and vegetables or beverages like iced tea can be trouble if they are left unrefrigerated for long periods of time.

THE
SOURCE

Two of the most common troublemakers in cases of food poisoning are salmonella and *Staphylococcus aureus* bacteria. The CDC says that certain strains of *Escherichia coli* bacteria have also been implicated in the fatal poisoning of children in the Pacific Northwest who ate undercooked fast-food hamburgers in the early 1990s.

Bacteria are not the only source of foodborne illnesses. According to Dr. Scott, "the culprits in cases of food poisoning are often viruses, particularly a bug called the Norwalk Agent, which is known to run amok among people in enclosed spaces like cruise ships."

Whether viruses or bacteria, these unwelcome bugs cause you misery either by invading the lining of your intestine after being ingested with food or by releasing a toxin that damages the intestinal lining. Your body fights back by producing a watery discharge to flush the bug or the toxin out; for you, that means diarrhea. Other organisms produce poisons that may trigger vomiting.

HELPING
YOUR BODY HEAL

Diarrhea, as uncomfortable as it is, is nature's way of ridding your body of poisons and offending organisms, "so just ride it out if you can," says Dr. Scott. Children, the elderly, or people with weakened immune systems, however, are at high risk for dehydration and should get quick medical attention if they are stricken with diarrhea.

For healthy young and middle-aged adults, the trick to feeling better is giving your body a chance to recover. On day one, slowly sip cool (not cold) water first, then follow that with clear fluids such as apple juice or weak tea, says Dr. Scott. Don't eat solid food until the diarrhea slows down. Then slowly start with bland, soft foods such as soft-boiled egg whites, white rice, or cereals. By the next day, you should be able to eat a fairly normal diet.

Try to avoid taking over-the-counter (OTC) or other medications unless your doctor specifically recommends it. Most OTC preparations can lead to a more prolonged illness, and antibiotics can actually make you a food poisoning carrier who feels well but harbors the organism and can pass it along to other people. "The one exception," says Dr. Scott, "might be medications such as Pepto-Bismol that contain the

While most types of food poisoning are nonfatal, botulism holds a special danger for children and adults of all ages. This toxin is rare but is most often found in improperly canned or packaged foods that are not kept at the proper temperature. It is so powerful that 1 gram has the potential to kill more than 100,000 people.

The best way to protect yourself is to realize that botulism toxins are not visible to the naked eye. Be suspicious of any damaged container or can, especially if it contains an oil-packed food, says Victor Scott, M.D., chief of gastroenterology at Howard University Hospital in Washington, D.C. Steer clear of cans that are swollen, dented, punctured, or more than two years old. The contents may be deadly. Your rule should be: When in doubt, throw it out.

It's also important to remember that you cannot eliminate botulism toxins by cooking the food. In addition, less than a spoonful can kill, so don't try the "I'll just dip my finger in and taste it test," either. And here's a special warning for parents: Raw honey can cause botulism poisoning in children under one year of age, even if the honey in question has no effect on adults. To be safe, some experts suggest not giving honey to infants.

The first symptoms of botulism are usually nausea, vomiting, and the inability to speak or swallow, followed by muscle weakness, difficulty keeping your eyelids open, paralysis, and then death. The minute any symptom occurs, go to the emergency room, says Dr. Scott.

active ingredient bismuth subsalicylate, which binds itself to the offending organism in your intestinal tract and actually helps to carry it out of the body." For adults, a little baking soda and water solution (¼ teaspoon of baking soda mixed into an 8-ounce glass of water) will also help to settle your stomach and replace some of the sodium your body loses when you have diarrhea, says Dr. Scott. He also recommends a number of oral rehydration solutions, such as Pedia Lyte, which are available at drugstores. They contain sugar and electrolytes in just the right concentrations to stimulate the reabsorption of fluids.

EATING
BY THE RULES

A little bit of care can go a long way in cutting your risk of food poisoning. Try these simple steps.

Cook food thoroughly, but avoid overcooking. Most bacteria are killed by sustained high heat. Insert a meat thermometer and cook beef to an internal temperature of 160°F, pork to 160°, and chicken to 180° (sorry, no red or pink juices allowed), says Bettye Nowlin, R.D., a spokesperson for the American Dietetic Association. When heating leftover food in the microwave, reheat thoroughly to the original cooking temperature before eating.

Keep the fridge cool. Keep your refrigerator at 40°F and your freezer at 0°, says Nowlin. Store meats in the freezer and thaw them in the refrigerator (not on the counter) with a plate under them to keep juices from dripping onto other foods. If meat is not going to be used in one to two days, it should be frozen promptly after purchase.

Make picnics quick. Keep cold foods cold and hot foods hot. Serve the food, cover it, and whisk it back to a fridge or an ice-cold cooler as soon as possible. The cooler should be well-insulated and tightly sealed, says Nowlin. To be safe, don't serve egg dishes, seafood, custard, cream pies, or potato salad if there's no refrigeration handy.

Keep your hands clean. Be compulsive about washing your hands before and after handling food, after visiting the bathroom, and after handling meat, says Nowlin.

Take extra care with kitchen tools. Wash them with hot, soapy water and rinse cutting boards and counters well, says Nowlin. Cutting boards should be made of plastic, not wood, because plastic cutting boards have a nonporous surface and are easier to clean.

Be extra careful about fish and shellfish. Shellfish can harbor invisible poisons from naturally occurring organisms such as algae, according to the Food and Drug Administration. Raw clams and oysters are dangerous delicacies at any time of the year. They may harbor food poisoning–causing bacteria and viruses, but cooking will destroy these organisms. And raw fish can be home to several types of parasites.

Foot Problems

SOOTHING YOUR SOLES

"I am the worst, do you hear me?" says Jeanette Johnson, fiddling with her shoulder-length braids. "Almost nothing can give me the strength to resist a hot pair of kicks, and if you don't believe me, you should have heard the argument I was having with myself—in the middle of Macy's shoe department—last Saturday afternoon.

" 'You really don't need those dark burgundy suede pumps, but they match that new dress, and they would add some flavor to that pantsuit you bought at a sample sale a few weeks ago,' I told myself.

"There was only one pair of shoes left, and the price was right—50 percent off after two markdowns. One small, or actually large, problem: The shoes were just a teensy bit snug. To tell the truth, they were tight, but don't you know, I bought them anyway," says Jeanette.

DOGGING YOUR FEET

The cost of buying shoes solely on the basis of looks, with no regard for comfort, is high in terms of both dollars and foot pain. First of all, those too-tight, fly-looking shoes are going to spend more time in the box than on your feet because you can barely stand to walk in them. Then, if you do manage to squeeze them on fairly often, you could end up with corns, calluses, and toe jams—not the funky kind but the kind that can cause bulging bunions or cramped hammertoes.

It's worth it to your feet to buy shoes for comfort, says podiatrist Dennis E. Castillo, D.P.M., clinical assistant professor of surgery at the State University of New York Health Science Center in Brooklyn, whose private practice overflows with patients who have ailments that could have been avoided by staying out of ill-fitting shoes.

He also says that far too many African-Americans endure unnecessary pain and complications simply because they don't take preventive steps to take care of their feet. Not only that, they avoid the doctor's office when there's a problem. "We tend to wait a really long time to seek medical attention," says Dr. Castillo.

"We tend to use pain as a primary symptom, and when the pain is severe, it's a little late in the game," says William H. Rutherford, D.P.M., clinical instructor at Howard University College of Medicine and chief of the podiatry section at Howard University Hospital in Washington, D.C. Both Dr. Castillo and Dr. Rutherford recommend that everyone visit a podiatrist at least twice a year.

With regular checkups, they say, a podiatrist can spot potential problems and take corrective action. Things like corns, bunions, calluses, and plantar pain on the bottom of the foot are manifestations of underlying problems such as improper gait, bony deformities, foot imbalance, and improperly fitting shoes, Dr. Rutherford explains.

"We can't change the way you walk," he says, "but we can compensate for the imbalance." Sometimes that compensation is as simple as recommending the right shoe for the right activity. In other cases, you may need orthotics (customized inserts for your shoes).

Adrienne Dawson, who spends a lot of time on her feet as a customer service representative at a post office in lower Manhattan, says that unlike some women, she has a foot fetish, not a shoe fetish. "I have nice toes, nice feet, and I keep them that way. I make an effort to buy good-looking shoes that are also comfortable. And that means they have to fit," she says. And she could care less about salon pedicures. Instead, she is one of those rare people who visits a podiatrist as often as she does a dentist.

An ingrown toenail prompted her first visit to the family podiatrist nearly a dozen years ago when she was pregnant. "I've been hooked ever since. I just like the pampering," she explains, passionately describing the whirlpool and other treatment that she gets during her regular visits. "It relaxes me, and I just feel so good afterward."

When, despite her best efforts, she developed a small lump on her left baby toe, she paid visit to her podiatrist. He removed the hard, calloused layer of skin (a corn) to give her temporary relief from the pain. "He said that the hard skin will come back, but with regular treatments

If you decide to treat yourself to a professional pedicure, visit a reputable nail salon, says William H. Rutherford, D.P.M., clinical instructor at Howard University College of Medicine and chief of the podiatry section at Howard University Hospital in Washington, D.C. And keep these tips in mind.

• Make sure that the equipment is sterile. It's the law, so don't be afraid to ask.

• Have your toenails cut straight across and no shorter than the edge of the toe.

• Be sure the operator uses only a pumice stone or a coarse emery board to remove dead skin. Razors can cause cuts and infections and should not be used.

I can function without much discomfort," says Adrienne. A corn keeps coming back because, as the muscles of the foot and ankle try to adapt to imbalances in foot structure, there's pressure on certain parts of the foot, which causes pain, explains Dr. Castillo.

Adrienne did not want to follow in the troubled footsteps of fellow patients that she sees in her podiatrist's waiting room, like the woman who had to have surgery to remove a heel spur (a painful bony growth under her heel) because of chronic pain.

"The heel spur itself is not as common as one would think. Most of the time people come in with plantar fasciitis," says Dr. Rutherford. This painful condition is caused by inflammation of the band of tissue known as the fascia that connects the heel to the ball of the foot.

Plantar fasciitis can be the result of running or jumping on hard surfaces, wearing improper or poorly constructed shoes, or being overweight. Treatment can include stretching exercises, orthotics, taping or strapping the foot, physical therapy, oral and/or injected anti-inflammatory medications, and as a last resort, surgery, says Dr. Rutherford.

More than 43 million people have foot problems, according to the American Podiatric Medical Association. Here are some common problems and some tips for handling them, as well as some ways to prevent them in the first place.

Bunions: Coping with a Curved Joint

Bunions occur when the big toe angles toward the other toes and a bump forms on the large joint of the big toe. It's officially called hallux valgus.

A bunion can rub against your shoe, causing pain and swelling. Although the bone structure that predisposes people to bunions tends to run in families, women get them four to five times more often than men do, mainly from wearing tight, high-heeled shoes. Hammertoe, which makes a toe curl down, often occurs in response to a bunion, as the adjoining toe or toes try to get out of its way. Although it usually occurs at the second toe, it can also affect other toes. Here's what to do about bunions.

Shield it. Many bunions are eased, although not corrected, by comfortable shoes or bunion shields that you can buy at drugstores. For extra comfort, you can cut a hole in your old shoes to wear around the house.

Consider surgery. If walking or wearing shoes is too painful, corrective surgery to reduce the size of the protrusion or straighten the toe may be necessary, says Dr. Rutherford.

Corns and Calluses: Softening Tough Bumps

If your shoes chafe, layers of hard or soft dead skin build up on the toes and between the toes. The result is a corn. Here's how to relieve the pain.

Keep toes loose. Wear shoes that fit. There should be room at the toe of the shoe for your toes to move. If the shoes don't feel comfortable in the store, they aren't going to feel better after you buy them. The style of shoes—heels, slip-ons, slingbacks, or lace-ups—is your decision. Just make sure that they fit, says Dr. Rutherford.

File away. You can treat hard corns yourself by rubbing a pumice stone or podiatry file over them. You may also use nonmedicated corn pads unless you have diabetes or poor circulation. Be wary of using over-the-counter corn-dissolving acids, though. "They cause problems because they burn the good skin along with the bad," Dr. Castillo says. Consult your doctor in cases of severe pain, infection, or malformed feet.

All people with diabetes should be examined by a podiatrist regularly," emphasizes William H. Rutherford, D.P.M., clinical instructor at Howard University College of Medicine and chief of the podiatry section at Howard University Hospital in Washington, D.C.

Statistics bear out his point: According to the American Diabetes Association, African-Americans are twice as likely as Whites to have diabetes, and the more than two million of us who have it also tend to have more serious complications, including amputation of toes, feet, or limbs. Several years before Ella Fitzgerald's death in 1996, for example, both of her legs were amputated because of diabetes.

"A lot of people with diabetes are not sure how to recognize foot problems," Dr. Rutherford says. One major problem is that African-Americans who have limited access to medical care may be ill-informed about diabetes and its side effects. Another is that people with diabetes may not even know that they are developing sores on their feet because of poor circulation and neuropathy, or loss of sensation.

"Neuropathy causes what I call a short-circuiting of the nervous system—the electrical system of the body, so to speak," Dr.

FENDING FOR YOUR FEET

Most foot problems can be prevented with a little tender loving care and better-fitting shoes. Here's what podiatrists recommend.

Go low. "I can't wear 3-inch heels any more," Adrienne says. "I only buy shoes with heels under 2 inches. High heels are like sliding boards, and my toes come out on the losing end." Over a lifetime, they cause women to have four times as many foot problems as men, according to the American Podiatric Medical Association. Wearing shoes with very high heels can also cause back pain, adds Dr. Castillo.

If you walk to work, which is not a bad idea, wear flats or sneakers and change into your dress or work shoes after you arrive, says Dr. Rutherford.

Rutherford explains. People with diabetes may have no sense of how tight is too tight when it comes to their shoes and may overlook a blister, puncture wound, or ulcer. "People with diabetes don't always feel pain or notice injury until days or weeks later, when the symptom becomes a crisis situation," Dr. Rutherford says. "They should check their feet daily for redness, swelling, blisters, or anything that does not appear normal, even though there is no pain."

Unfortunately, many people regard foot problems in the same way they do a cavity: "If it doesn't hurt, how bad can it be?"

"That's why the amputation rate is so high," says podiatrist Dennis E. Castillo, D.P.M., clinical assistant professor of surgery at the State University of New York Health Science Center in Brooklyn. One patient told him that she had switched from a size 8 to a size 7 shoes because they felt more comfortable. In reality, it took dropping down a size for her to feel the shoes at all.

"I tell my patients, 'If you have diabetes, I don't want you touching your feet,' " Dr. Castillo says. That includes not trimming toenails, Dr. Rutherford adds. Both podiatrists see their patients with diabetes bimonthly, monthly, or more often if they have serious foot problems.

Avoid the point. You don't have pointy feet, but unfortunately, many women's shoes are designed as if you did. Use your best judgment in choosing the style of shoes that best fits your feet, says Dr. Rutherford.

Dismiss the digits. A shoe size ain't nothin' but a number; ignore it. Buy the size you really need based on fit, and make sure there's a half-inch of wiggle room between your big toe and the tip of the shoe, says Dr. Rutherford.

In a survey conducted by the American Orthopaedic Foot and Ankle Society, 88 percent of the nearly 400 women polled were wearing tight shoes at the time.

Say "I don't know" when a salesclerk asks for your shoe size, Dr. Rutherford suggests. Have your foot measured to get the proper fit.

"You get your glasses changed every year or two," he points out. "Your feet change, too. Why continue to buy a 7½ B when your foot may be an 8 B or C." Dr. Castillo also recommends that you stand when having your foot measured. "When you stand up, your foot splays and you get the proper width. Proper width is just as important as proper length," he says.

Be fashionably late. Buy shoes later in the day when your feet have undergone their natural changes, Dr. Rutherford says.

Free your feet. Wear sandals when it's warm outside, and if you don't have diabetes, go barefoot indoors, says Dr. Castillo.

Take a load off. Feet need rest and relaxation just like other parts of the body. Treat them to an occasional warm soak and foot exercises, says Dr. Castillo. If you have diabetes, test the water for a comfortable temperature with your hand, not your feet or toes, which may not have full sensitivity, he adds.

Get the right gear. If you run, walk, play tennis, or engage in any other fitness activity that puts extra pressure on your feet, be sure to invest in a well-constructed, properly fitted pair of shoes designed for your type of activity, says Dr. Castillo. Cross-training shoes are a good choice for people who participate in a variety of aerobic workouts. The cushioning and support will keep your feet healthy while the rest of you gets in shape.

Be conservative. If your feet don't hurt but you hate the way they look in sandals, you probably shouldn't undergo surgery, says Dr. Rutherford.

"Surgery is just one form of treatment," he explains. "It's not recommended for everyone. It's not a cure-all, but it does work, and it can be very effective and rewarding."

"I take the careful approach," Dr. Castillo says. "I only consider surgery if the deformity is painful or the person can no longer find comfortable shoes to wear."

Fungal Infections
FIGHTING A COMMON PROBLEM

ames Barber had athlete's foot, and the brother had it bad. "I took one look at his feet," his wife, Robyn, teases, "and I almost said 'I don't!'"

Throughout his freshman year in college, James had innocently worn a pair of cloth-lined vinyl slippers into the communal shower. The constant moisture ("Those slippers never did dry out," he recalls) practically invited fungus. And so for the next 17 years, James endured a nightly ritual: rubbing and scratching the itchy, peeling skin between his toes.

Nonprescription powders and creams slowed the infection down, but none of them were strong enough to cure such a deep fungal onslaught. One day James decided his poor dogs were worth a trip to the doctor, who prescribed an oral medicine that eliminates fungal infections from the inside out. Two months later, James had brand-new feet.

"I remember thinking, gee, my toes look weird," says James, a tall, muscular systems engineer with skin the color of coffee beans. "It had been so long since they were healthy that I didn't recognize them!"

FUNGUS AMONG US

Meet some members of the tinea family. They're not big, but they sure are bad. *Tinea* is the scientific group name for the fungal infections known as jock itch (*Tinea cruris*), athlete's foot (*Tinea pedis*), ringworm of the scalp (*Tinea capitis*), and nail fungus (*Tinea unguium*). "These fungi aren't dangerous or life-threatening, which is good, because they're awfully hard to avoid," says James P. Lewis, M.D., of the Department of Family and Community Medicine at St. Paul-Ramsey Medical Center in St. Paul, Minnesota. Guys think they can sidestep athlete's foot by staying away from locker rooms, but fungi are all around us.

A fungus raises a ruckus when it penetrates the skin and takes up residence, typically causing mild to severe itching, irritation, skin rash, and pain. Each type has distinctive characteristics, depending on the area of the body that's affected.

Jock itch. This marks the crotch with a ring of inflamed skin that can become infected. It tends to flare during the summer months.

Athlete's foot. This usually affects the areas between the toes and can spread to the soles of the feet, causing itching, peeling, cracking, whitening, or inflammation.

Ringworm of the scalp. More common in children, ringworm causes a flaky, itchy bald patch and telltale black dots (the remnants of broken hairs) on the scalp.

Fungal infections of the nails. These cause toenails and occasionally fingernails to become thick and lusterless or soft and powdery. The nail can also become discolored (yellow or white, or for deeply pigmented folks, black to gray). Debris collects under the nails, possibly separating the nail from the underlying tissue.

An estimated 70 percent of the population gets some sort of fungal infection at least once in their lives. Athletes (and those of us who regularly visit the local gym) are at special risk because they come in contact with floor tiles, used towels, and other surfaces that can harbor fungi.

The infection can be spread directly, by person-to-person contact, or indirectly, when an uninfected person comes in contact with or handles an object touched by an infected person. Scalp ringworm is commonly spread through person-to-person contact, but children occasionally pick up the fungus from dogs and cats.

"There's a very high incidence of scalp ringworm among African-American children," says Patricia Treadwell, M.D., associate professor of dermatology and pediatrics at Indiana University School of Medicine in Indianapolis, although experts aren't sure why.

"One contributor may be African-American hairstyling," suggests Rebat M. Halder, M.D., professor and chair of the Department of Dermatology at Howard University College of Medicine in Washington, D.C. "Braids or cornrows expose more of the scalp to air and fungus, and pomades may work like glue to hold the fungus close to the skin."

TAMING
THE TINEA

Here's how to lay out the unwelcome mat for tinea infections, plus some sure-fire tips for what to do when our little fungal friends decide they want to kick up their heels and stay a while.

Be like the Sahara. Fungi are plants, and plants thrive in moisture. So one time-tested way to discourage tinea from getting under your skin is to stay bone dry. Dry yourself thoroughly after bathing, advises Dr. Lewis. "Blow-drying your toes after a shower is a good way to make them inhospitable to athlete's foot fungus," he says.

He also advises against going barefoot in public facilities such as gym locker rooms and bathrooms. Fungi can even be found in carpet.

It's better to wear sandals than shoes because sandals let air circulate and evaporate perspiration on your feet. "And if you can get away with periodically removing your shoes and socks at work, do it," Dr. Lewis says.

Another way to avoid unwanted fungus is to never wear another person's shoes or socks. "And if you have any old athletic shoes, toss them," says Dr. Lewis. He also suggests using an antifungal powder or spray in your shoes every week.

Cozy up to cotton. Cotton is a natural fiber that's much more skin-friendly than synthetics, which suffocate your skin. "Wear cotton socks if you have athlete's foot and cotton underwear if you have jock itch," Dr. Lewis suggests.

Hang loose. Wear loose-fitting clothes. They not only let fungus-friendly moisture evaporate, they also prevent skin chafing and irritation that can give fungus a green light into your nether zones, says Dr. Lewis.

Don't spread it around. Tinea infections are more contagious than a yawn. The fungus has even caused epidemics among African-American schoolchildren. Prevent its spread by isolating it. "If you've got a fungus, don't share anything that touches your infected area with an uninfected person," advises Dr. Halder. That means hats, hair ornaments, combs, hairbrushes, hair curlers, towels, shoes, and pillows.

Be on the lookout. Scalp ringworm is often mistaken for something else—even dandruff. "Children don't usually get dandruff," says Dr. Halder. "If an African-American child has scaling of the scalp, you should suspect ringworm and see a doctor without delay."

Ply it with powder. "Over-the-counter antifungal powders work well against most fungal infections of the skin," says Dr. Lewis. For jock itch and occasional athlete's foot, try tolnaftate (Tinactin Powder Aerosol), miconazole nitrate (Micatin), or undecylenic acid (Desenex).

For chronic athlete's foot, ringworm of the scalp, or other deep-seated fungal infections, you need stronger medicine. Your doctor can prescribe the oral antifungal medicine griseofulvin (Grisactin).

Griseofulvin may clear up fingernail infections if the medicine is taken until the nail is completely regrown and all infected material is gone, a process that typically takes 6 to 12 months. It is less effective for toenail fungus. Ask your doctor if this medication is right for you.

Can the cornstarch. "Stay away from powders containing cornstarch," advises Dr. Halder. Because bacteria thrive on cornstarch, the fungal infection may not get worse, but a bacterial infection can develop on top of the fungal infection.

Cream it. For ringworm or other fungal infections that cause inflammation, irritation, or itching, Dr. Lewis recommends a combination treatment: an over-the-counter antifungal medicine like clotrimazole (Lotrimin AF) plus an over-the-counter 0.5 or 1 percent hydrocortisone cream like Cortaid.

"The steroid cream may help reduce the inflammation, but you have to use it with the antifungal," he says. "Steroids, when used alone, suppress the immune system and can actually make the fungal infection worse." He also notes the importance of continuing the antifungal cream for five to seven days after the inflammation clears to be sure that any residual fungi are killed. When the irritation disappears, discontinue the steroid cream.

Call a professional. "If a fungal infection persists for more than two weeks after you start treating it, or if it gets worse, see a doctor," advises Dr. Lewis. You may need a prescription treatment, or it may not be a fungal infection at all.

Gallbladder Disease

SKIPPING THE STONES

his doesn't feel like indigestion," Arlene McDonald kept thinking as her husband rushed her to the emergency room of Phelps Memorial Hospital in suburban North Tarrytown, New York. For weeks she had felt nauseated and bloated after meals, but tonight was the worst, and she had terrible pain. "Oh, I thought I was dying for sure," the spry grandmother remembers. "It felt like a knife was pushing right through me."

Then, a half-mile from the hospital, the excruciating pain suddenly vanished. Arlene was relieved but mystified until a doctor at the hospital explained that she had probably had a gallstone attack. "He told me that the best thing I could do to prevent a recurrence was to eat a lower-fat diet and lose some of this weight," she says.

"When I retired from my job as a school librarian a few years ago, I really began to pack on the pounds. I guess I really didn't notice until the doctor pointed it out," Arlene explains. Gradually, she changed her diet and started walking on the treadmill at the local Y. In a few months, she had lost nearly 25 pounds. That was five years ago. Since then, it's been so far, so good. "I haven't had pain since that night," she says proudly.

A GALLING PROBLEM

After you polish off the last of the pound cake or feast on one (or even two) chicken burritos from your favorite Mexican place, you probably forget all about it. Well, your gallbladder doesn't: It has the tough job of helping you digest all the fat you consumed.

Tucked beneath your liver, the gallbladder is a sac about the size and shape of a small pear. Its job is to store bile, a brownish liquid that breaks fat into small droplets that can be absorbed by the small intestine. "The effect is just like using dish detergent on a greasy frying pan," says Victor Scott, M.D., chief of gastroenterology at Howard University Hospital in Washington, D.C.

Bile trickles from the liver, where it's made, into the gallbladder. When the body calls on the bile to break up fat, the bile is expelled from the gallbladder through a tube called the cystic duct, which leads into the small intestine through another tube, the bile duct.

Bile is rich in cholesterol and compounds known as bile salts. In a normal, healthy gallbladder, these two bile ingredients coexist in balance, and no gallstones form. But when bile is too rich in cholesterol or too deficient in bile salts, small, solid particles may form. As additional cholesterol (and sometimes other substances) coat the particles, they grow to become gallstones, which typically range in size from as small as a grain of sand to as large as a marble and can be smooth or have sharp edges.

If you happen to develop gallstones, you can take some comfort in the fact that you are certainly not alone. About 25 million Americans—8 to 10 percent of the population—have them at any given time. And you can have them without knowing it. In fact, most people with gallstones experience no symptoms at all.

Women experience more gallstone problems than men do because being overweight, using oral contraceptives, or having had more than one child increases a woman's risk. And as a rule, you're more likely to develop gallstones as you grow older. But elderly African-Americans have fewer problems than most older people. "For some reason, Black men in general develop gallstone problems less often than White men do, and the risk for Black women actually declines with age," says Anthony Kalloo, M.D., director of gastrointestinal endoscopy at Johns Hopkins University School of Medicine in Baltimore.

What happens when gallstones cause problems? Usually the trouble spot is the cystic duct (the tube leaving the gallbladder). As stones flow with bile out of the gallbladder, they can get stuck in the duct, causing intense cramping pain in the right or center of the upper abdomen. The pain usually begins 20 or 30 minutes after meals and subsides after several hours.

The pain is often accompanied by bloating, belching, nausea, and vomiting. If the stone moves back into the gallbladder or passes through the bile duct into the small intestine, the pain can disappear.

If, however, it stays lodged in either the cystic duct or the bile duct, the stone can cause inflammation or infection, which requires immediate medical treatment, including antibiotics and often surgical removal of the gallbladder.

GAINING
THE ADVANTAGE

Here's what the experts recommend to treat gallstones and/or prevent a recurrence.

Ditch the fat. Gallstone woes aren't always avoidable, says Dr. Kalloo, but it helps to keep your fat and cholesterol intake low and to maintain a reasonable body weight. "We find that people whose weight fluctuates a great deal are at higher risk of forming gallstones," he says.

So steer clear of quick-weight-loss schemes. Even if you do lose weight on a fad diet, you're more likely to gain it back and repeat the cycle in the future, he says. Maintaining a nutritionally balanced, low-fat diet also helps reduce the frequency and perhaps even the severity of gallstone attacks.

Know the symptoms. If you experience intense cramping pain in your abdomen that doesn't respond to antacids or over-the-counter acid-reducing medicines as such as ranitidine (Zantac), cimetidine (Tagamet), or famotidine (Pepcid), you know it's time to see your doctor, advises Dr. Scott. "If they start to cause pain, it'll probably only get worse," he says. And if you have a chronic illness like diabetes or heart disease and you experience gallbladder symptoms, see your doctor without delay.

Pop a pill. Prescription medications containing bile salts such as ursodoxycholic acid (Actigall) can dissolve gallstones gradually over many months. These medicines are recommended for people who have small stones composed solely of cholesterol. The drugs can cause side effects such as diarrhea but can offer an alternative for those who aren't good candidates for surgery. They work temporarily for about 30 to 40 percent of gallstone patients. "Once you stop taking the medicine, the gallstones will come back," says Dr. Scott.

Try high-tech moves. Ultra-high-frequency sound waves can shatter gallstones without surgery. This procedure, called shock wave lithotripsy, works best on gallstones smaller than ¾ inch in diameter and in patients who have no more than two stones. "Most people have multiple gallstones—some can have hundreds—and many are larger than ¾ inch," says Dr. Kalloo.

Don't rule out surgery. Removal of the gallbladder, a relatively common procedure called cholecystectomy, offers permanent relief from gallstones. The surgeon uses a narrow instrument called a laparoscope that allows him to perform the operation without making a large incision. Additional small incisions may be needed to accommodate other instruments that are used to tie off the ducts and blood vessels. Compared to older surgical techniques, laparoscopic removal of the gallbladder offers sizable advantages.

"Patients tolerate the procedure well, and they're usually discharged the next day or even the same day as the surgery. Many find that they can return to work as soon as the third day after surgery," says Dr. Kalloo.

What's it like to live without a gallbladder? "Most people do just fine," says Dr. Scott. You may experience some diarrhea and find that you have more frequent bowel movements than before. That's because the now-steady drip of bile salts into the small intestine acts as a laxative, but there are no lasting side effects.

Glaucoma

Saving Your Sight

When it's baseball season in Baltimore, and the summer skies turn an iridescent blue, many young brothers live to catch an Orioles game. But 39-year-old George Brown doesn't watch as much as listen. His eyes no longer follow the expert moves of his favorite players because he has glaucoma. "He can see hand motion with one eye, but he's legally blind," explains his physician, Eve Higginbotham, M.D., professor and chair of the Department of Ophthalmology at the University of Maryland School of Medicine in Baltimore.

George is hoping that laser surgery—which has at least a 50 percent success rate in cases like his—will slow the loss of his sight.

KNOWING THE RISKS

You don't have to bet your sight against these odds, though. Once you understand glaucoma, you can understand why early diagnosis and treatment are so important.

Glaucoma isn't nearly as common as conditions like high blood pressure or cancer, but it's the leading cause of blindness in African-Americans. In the general population, among people 40 to 65, 1 person in 1,000 has glaucoma, and the rate increases to 1 in 500 in people older than 65. But the disease shows up earlier and more often in African-Americans.

When researchers at Johns Hopkins University School of Public Health in Baltimore surveyed one East Baltimore neighborhood, they found that Blacks were four times more likely to have glaucoma than Whites. The peak age for glaucoma development in Blacks can be as early as the midthirties, whereas those in the general population don't get it until their midfifties.

But as George Brown can tell you, glaucoma can rob you of your sight long before midlife. "I've seen entire families with glaucoma," says John P. Mitchell, M.D., assistant professor of clinical ophthalmology at Columbia University College of Physicians and Surgeons in New York City. "In one case, a 40-year-old mother had it, and so did her 16-year-old daughter."

People of African descent run a higher-than-average risk of developing glaucoma because "the disease is common in West Africa, where many of our ancestors originated," explains Dr. Mitchell. You're also at higher risk if glaucoma runs in your family, if you're over age 40, or if you're nearsighted or farsighted.

What's glaucoma about? Think of it as a miniature plumbing problem. Special cells inside your eye constantly produce a clear, watery fluid called the aqueous humor. Normally the excess fluid reenters the bloodstream through a tiny drainage channel in the front of the eye. The problems start when, for reasons that are not clear, the drain becomes clogged and fluid slowly collects inside the eye. As the pressure builds, it damages the delicate optic nerve, eventually causing loss of peripheral vision and potential blindness.

SAFEGUARDING YOUR VISION

The best way to deal with this sight-robber is to catch it before it has a chance to do significant damage. Here's what experts recommend.

Don't wait for warning signs. There are no early symptoms of glaucoma. "You can be feeling fine and seeing fine and have advanced glaucoma," cautions Dr. Higginbotham. So it takes a doctor's exam to detect glaucoma in time to prevent damage to your eyes. "The earlier glaucoma is diagnosed, the more likely we can keep you seeing until you're 100 years old," she says.

Use the best defense. If you're an African-American over age 35, the American Academy of Ophthalmology recommends having your eyes checked once every two years (once a year if glaucoma runs in your family), even if your vision seems fine. If you're 18 to 35, you should have an eye exam every three to five years.

Make no mistake. Many people assume that they're being tested for glaucoma when they are examined for glasses. Not necessarily. To check for glaucoma, your ophthalmologist or optometrist should do three things: test your peripheral vision, scope your optic nerve for damage, and measure the pressure inside your eye. "After an eye exam, ask your eye-care provider, 'Did you test for glaucoma?'" advises Dr. Mitchell.

Hang tough with treatments. Glaucoma can't be cured; once optic nerve fibers die, they can't be brought back to life. But the disease can be treated with medication that either reduces the production of fluid in the eye or opens the drain for it. Diligent use of prescribed eyedrops can prevent the need for laser surgery, which stretches open the drainage channel.

Don't drop the drops. "Many patients don't take prescription eyedrops seriously. They put them in the same class as over-the-counter preparations like Murine or Visine. They think strong medicine has to be in pill form," says Dr. Higginbotham.

"Eyedrops don't help you feel better because glaucoma does not cause pain, so many patients stop using them regularly," explains Richard Bensinger, M.D., spokesperson for the American Academy of Ophthalmology. But eyedrops can save your vision years down the road. So if your doctor prescribes them, use them—even if you can't feel (or see) instant relief.

Ask about Xalatan. Latanoprost solution (Xalatan) is a new type of eyedrops for glaucoma that has fewer side effects and is more effective than some current medications, explains Dr. Higginbotham. Ask your doctor if it's right for you.

Gum Disease

HOLDING ON TO YOUR TEETH

was getting ready for my twentieth high school reunion a while ago," Esther Robinson says. "I took a glance at the mirror and thought, 'Not bad for a sister pushing 40.' I was dressed to kill, and I thought I looked fantastic.

"But then, as I was completing my makeup with a fierce shade of berry lipstick, I looked at my teeth. Somehow my grin seemed different—older—than the one in my yearbook. 'Could I really be getting a bit longer in the tooth?' I wondered.

"I went to the dentist a week later and found out that I really was. He told me that because of improper dental care and oral hygiene, my gums were receding and my teeth were starting to loosen," Esther says, shaking her head. She had ignored an earlier warning sign—bleeding gums while brushing—and now she had periodontitis, or advanced gum disease.

WHY YOU ARE AT RISK

Many of us—especially those who haven't had a cavity since high school—figure we're in the clear as far as oral health is concerned. In fact, when it comes to taking care of our teeth and gums, we may be headed for a failing grade. Periodontitis, which tends to appear in the midthirties, is the leading cause of tooth loss in people over 35. Three out of four adults—even those who believe they are careful about brushing—have some form of it. The incidence of gum disease tends tend to be slightly higher in Blacks than in Whites, and the problem is usually related to improper oral hygiene, diet, and access to quality dental care.

A greater proportion of African-Americans live in poverty and have limited access to dentists, explains Chester Aikens, D.D.S., past president of the National Dental Association, an organization of Black dentists.

This is not to say that the more fortunate among us have nothing to worry about. "I come for checkups twice a year!" protested Esther to her dentist. But did she brush three times a day? The hygienist pressed her. "Well, not at bedtime," Esther admitted sheepishly. What about flossing? "Only after I have ribs or corn on the cob," she replied.

Gum disease is a sneaky enemy that approaches with little warning. Invading bacteria, which attack our teeth and gums and cause tartar buildup and decay if left unchecked, can cause our teeth to loosen and eventually fall out. "Some of us are more susceptible to the effects of bacteria than others, because of heredity or hormone changes during menstruation, pregnancy, and possibly menopause," says Dr. Aikens.

"Medications for the treatment of epilepsy, depression, heart disease, and allergies can put you at even greater risk because they can often cause gums to enlarge, furthering periodontal disease," he explains. Diseases like AIDS and diabetes (which affects 1 in 10 Blacks) also weaken your ability to fight invading bacteria.

THE PLAQUE ATTACK

As bacteria live, reproduce, and die on your gums, they leave behind a filmy substance called plaque (pronounced *plack*) on your teeth. Plaque then puts you at risk for tooth decay and other dental woes. Over time, plaque builds up and may harden into a rocky deposit called tartar. That's the stuff that the hygienist takes a pickax to while your fingers are digging grooves into the arms of the dental chair.

When your healthy gums become irritated by plaque and tartar, you have an early stage of gum disease called gingivitis. If plaque and tartar are allowed to continue to build up between the gums and teeth and gradually burrow deeper and deeper beneath the gum line, eventually they'll work their way into the very bone in which your teeth are anchored. This advanced stage of gum disease (by now it's actually a bone disease) is called periodontitis. If left untreated, it will undermine a tooth's support structure so completely that the tooth will get wobbly and finally drop out. Bring on the mashed potatoes.

Generally, a commitment to oral hygiene and regular dental checkups—our best protection against gum disease as well as tooth decay, bad breath, discolored teeth, and a host of other oral problems—is easy and affordable. But when it comes to oral hygiene, many African-Americans are dental delinquents. About a third of us don't go for checkups on a regular basis, compared to less than a quarter of Whites. And when we do make appointments, it's often for emergencies, like pulling a tooth or other oral surgery. "African-Americans, particularly those who are economically disadvantaged and have less access to dentists, sometimes don't have a clear enough understanding of the value of preventive care. Therefore, less emphasis is placed on doing those things that will lead to good oral health," says Dr. Aikens.

What can you do about it? Your toothbrush and dental floss are your first lines of defense against gum disease. Your dental hygienist is also a vital ally: Twice-yearly cleanings to get rid of the plaque you're missing at home are a must. Between visits, here's what you should do to hold on to your teeth as well as keep your smile bright, your breath fresh, and your mouth cavity-free.

Brush—and don't rush. "At a minimum, be sure to brush after breakfast and before you go to bed at night," says Hazel Harper, D.D.S., assistant professor of community dentistry at Howard University College of Dentistry in Washington, D.C., and president-elect of the National Dental Association. Brushing after every meal is ideal.

The correct method of brushing, says Dr. Harper, begins with holding the brush properly. Hold the handle in your palm and extend your thumb to act as a support. This grasp tilts the brush at an angle, so the bristles can clean under the gums as well as reaching the tooth surfaces. Vibrate the brush gently back and forth, covering only three teeth at a time. Then, with a flick of your wrist, roll the brush against the sides of your teeth to sweep debris and bacteria away from the gum line. Finish up by brushing the chewing surfaces of your teeth and your tongue to sweep away bad breath, Dr. Harper says.

How long should you brush? Most people spend less than a minute, but to do it right, it will take you more like three or four minutes.

Floss daily. A toothbrush can't clean between your teeth and under your gum line. That's where floss fits in: It can slip into every crevice. Dr. Harper advises taking an 18-inch-long piece of floss and wrapping it around both index fingers. Guiding the floss between your thumbs, use 1 to 1½ inches and gently insert it between two teeth. Curve the floss into a *C* shape against each tooth and gently slide it against the root of the tooth under the gum line until you feel resistance. Hold the floss against the tooth and gently scrape the side, moving the floss away from the gum. Slightly rewrap the floss around your fingers so that a new section of floss is being used and move on to the next tooth.

Snuff out tobacco. Smoking steals calcium from bone and suppresses the immune system. It also decreases blood supply to the mouth, which interferes with the healing process. Although Esther had tried to quit smoking before, the thought of a toothless future (not to mention bad breath and stained teeth) got her to give up her smokes for good. And if you use chewing tobacco, you should know that it can cause dental problems and oral cancer.

Dash to the dentist. Go for routine care every six months, Dr. Aikens says. If your gums look inflamed or bleed when you brush, have your dentist take a look even sooner. If you are pregnant, schedule a couple of visits before your last trimester, when you shouldn't lie flat for a dental cleaning.

Dine on "C" foods. Vitamin C helps keep your gums healthy, so make sure that you have at least five servings of foods such as citrus fruits, tomatoes, strawberries, green and red peppers, and broccoli daily, suggests Dr. Harper.

Stock up on calcium. Some studies indicate that strong bones equal strong teeth. Dr. Harper says that you should eat plenty of calcium-rich foods such as low-fat yogurt, low-fat cheese, and canned salmon (with the bones). Your goal should be at least 1,000 milligrams of calcium a day.

Say cheese for dessert. Studies show that cheese, of all things, might help reduce cavity-causing bacteria if you can't brush your teeth right after a meal. Stick to hard, aged, low-fat varieties.

Hair Damage and Loss

PROTECTING YOUR CROWNING GLORY

uanita Procope was the type of woman whose hair was always fly. She'd check out the latest styles and head straight to the salon, where she was permed, colored, weaved, braided, or bleached to perfection. "I admit that I have always loved getting a new 'do. Lots of sisters love new clothes—I love new hair. It's sort of like trying on a new personality every now and then," she says.

The problem is that years of styling and profiling left 36-year-old Juanita with hair loss on the front, sides, and back of her head. "I was shocked," she explains. "My hair had always been healthy, and I thought of baldness as something that happened to guys."

Now she has dropped the dyes and perms for a loose weave that she hopes will allow her hair to grow back to its former glory. "The urge to at least change the color is almost overwhelming, but I've learned my lesson. I'm going to give this head a rest," she says.

THE ROOT
OF THE PROBLEM

What many of us think of as hair care—lots of dutiful visits to the stylist, having perms and color—actually adds up to hair damage. When it comes to hairstyling, many African-Americans have elevated simple good grooming to an art form. Whether our hair is fried, dyed, and laid to the side, gelled or marcelled, faded or braided, getting our heads together is part obsession and part self-expression. The thing is, hooking up our look takes its toll on our hair in terms of breakage or loss.

Since everyone's head is different, it's hard to predict how we'll respond to a certain product or process. But some types of hair loss and most types of breakage can be avoided or minimized.

As was the case with Juanita, chemical treatments are often responsible for hair breakage. "Anything chemical that permanently changes the color or texture of the hair weakens it and can cause damage," says Greta F. Clarke, M.D., a dermatologist in private practice in Berkeley, California.

"Relaxers, especially, can strip away the hair's cuticle (outer layer), causing a loss of elasticity that can cause strands to snap off during styling," says William Keith, M.D., clinical assistant professor of medicine at Drew Medical School/Martin Luther King, Jr., Hospital and medical director of the Institute for Aesthetic and Cosmetic Dermatology, both in Los Angeles. Too much styling, especially with heated appliances, can exacerbate the problem.

HEADING OFF TROUBLE

To hold onto your length and prevent damage, try the following tips.

Take it easy with touchups. Talk to your stylist about the possibility of spacing retouches further apart to minimize use of relaxer or dye. "This is especially important with relaxers," says Dr. Keith, "because you want to relax the new growth only, and allowing it to grow out about an inch makes application easier." He recommends retouching every 8 to 10 weeks for medium-textured hair, every 8 weeks for coarse hair, and every 12 weeks for fine hair.

Pick the proper product for your hair type. Consult with your stylist or dermatologist to determine which products will work best for you. For instance, Dr. Keith generally recommends no-lye relaxer for fine hair because it is a bit less harsh. Switching brands of chemical treatment may also cause adverse chemical reactions and breakage, so try to stick with the same brand each time you relax or color.

Select a simple style. If your hair is brittle or otherwise damaged, give it a rest from the overmanipulation that fancier styles require, says Faith Brown, instructor at Empire Beauty School and owner of Classic Hair Designs in Allentown, Pennsylvania.

Trim hair regularly. Regular haircuts eliminate damaged ends, which can catch on combs or brushes and lead to pulled and broken hairs, says Brown.

Take the heat off. Heat styling robs hair of moisture and re-

Baldness can be the result of hereditary pot luck. If you're genetically predisposed, you may lose more hair than is normally replaced by Nature. The result is a condition called androgenetic alopecia, or simple male pattern baldness.

Contrary to popular belief, the tendency toward baldness isn't passed down only on your mother's side, says Greta F. Clarke, M.D., a dermatologist in private practice in Berkeley, California. And while there's no cure for pattern baldness right now, there are some remedies that work for some men.

Reach for Rogaine. The drug minoxidil, marketed under the brand name Rogaine, may help hair grow back. "Rogaine's effectiveness varies widely among individual users," says dermatologist Susan C. Taylor, M.D., of Society Hill Dermatology in Philadelphia. Between 20 and 40 percent of users experience varying degrees of hair regrowth while using the drug. In 90 percent of the cases, Rogaine helps to prevent further hair loss but doesn't necessarily replace lost hair. Dr. Taylor also notes that the regrowth may either be similar to the hair that fell out or be baby-fine fuzz.

"Remember, it's much more effective when treatment is started in the early stages of hair loss, when you have slight thinning as opposed to completely bald spots. And if you use it and

siliency. Keep blow drying and hot curling to a minimum. If you press your hair, don't do so more than once a week, and use a warm—not hot—comb. "If you insist on having your hair bone straight, it's likely to thin out as the years go by," says Dr. Keith.

Condition often. Dr. Keith recommends using a deep conditioner once every two weeks and putting extra on the ends. You should use an instant conditioner after all other shampoos and use a leave-in conditioner after a relaxer, says Brown.

Loosen up. Thinning hair at the temples or hairline is often the tip-off that too-tight braids, rollers, or ponytails are causing hair loss, says Brown. Since having hair pulled out in this fashion often causes permanent damage to the follicle and inhibits regrowth, preventing this problem by loosening up those locks is essential. "If the style causes any discomfort, it's too tight," warns Dr. Clarke.

get results, you need to keep using it for the rest of your life to sustain the benefit," says Dr. Taylor.

Even though Rogaine is now available without a prescription, it's a smart idea to consult your doctor prior to using it. Minoxidil has side effects just like other drugs. It can be absorbed into the bloodstream and cause your heart rate to speed up, and people who have uncontrolled high blood pressure may find that the use of Rogaine could cause their blood pressure to fall quickly and result in dizziness or fainting.

Check out hair transplants. If a hair transplant is performed by a well-trained physician who is experienced in doing the procedure, a natural-looking effect can be created. However, transplanted hair is subject to the same natural thinning process as the rest of your hair. Basically, a hair transplant may buy you some time, but it probably won't guarantee you a full head of hair for a lifetime, says Dr. Taylor.

Other men opt for nonsurgical, or cosmetic, hair replacement, in which synthetic hair is bonded or glued to the scalp. If you decide to go this route, however, you should never allow synthetic hair to be attached to your scalp with needles, says Dr. Taylor.

Switch styles. Rotating hairstyles now and then will prevent prolonged stress on any one area, says Brown. If your braids ran in one direction the last time, for example, have them rebraided in a different direction, she advises.

Get to the source. If you've tried everything and still have thinning hair or bald spots, see your doctor. Your condition could be linked to an underlying medical condition such as lupus or a thyroid disorder. Proper management of the disease can bring improvement of the hair loss, says dermatologist Susan C. Taylor, M.D., of Society Hill Dermatology in Philadelphia.

Headache

OUTSMARTING THAT NAGGING PAIN

ometimes it seems like I spent three months of my life lying motionless in the dark on my mother's couch," says Theresa Harper, a Boston physician. "I'm not some high-maintenance diva who demands pampering, it's just that at that point in time, I was getting awful headaches almost every evening," she explains.

"The worst headache I experienced occurred one Thursday after a terrible day at the clinic. That day, every single patient showed up for his or her appointment, which is absolutely unheard of. I was glad they kept their appointments, but as a result, I was stressed-out and beside myself before noon," she says.

And the day got worse. As she was driving home from work, Theresa's car stalled during rush hour on one of Boston's busiest streets. That's when the familiar ache began, directly behind her right eye. She realized that the headaches were coming more frequently, and drugstore painkillers no longer seemed to ease the pain.

"I had a Bible study class that night, but I could hardly function. I remember thinking, 'How ironic, I'm a doctor, but I can't get rid of my own headaches.' On the way home from class, I stopped off at my mother's for a visit, and she could see the pain in my eyes.

"'I know you're the doctor in the family,' my mother said, 'but I don't like all these headaches you've been having. I want you to call a doctor tomorrow—someone who specializes in headache treatment.' As usual, my mom was interfering—and right," says Theresa.

Theresa's doctor explained that stress was her problem. He prescribed weekly massages to ease her stress and muscle tension. Within three weeks the headaches were gone for good.

WHAT
A PAIN!

Headaches are common—88 percent of women and 69 percent of men get them at one time or another. "Headaches are one of the main reasons that people make visits to neurologists," says Calvin B. Wheeler, M.D., clinical instructor in the Department of Neurology and Pediatrics at the University of California, San Francisco, School of Medicine and child neurologist and assistant physician-in-chief at Kaiser Permanente Medical Center in Fremont, California. Half of the general population gets at least one headache a month, and 5 percent get them daily. Women also experience headaches more frequently than men because of their fluctuating estrogen levels.

The three most common types are tension, migraine, and cluster headaches.

Tension headaches, despite their name, aren't always caused by emotional tension but rather result from painful contractions in the muscles of the neck, head, face, or shoulders. When a tension headache takes hold, it feels as if a rubber band were being tightened around your head.

Migraine and cluster headaches are called vascular headaches. Doctors suspect that insufficient levels of a neurochemical called serotonin triggers them by causing blood vessels in or around the brain to constrict. This reduces blood flow to the brain and causes nausea, dizziness, and altered vision, which are the early warning signs that let you know that a migraine is on its way. Following constriction, the blood vessels dilate, or expand, and press against adjoining structures. This pressure is the cause of typical migraine pain—a throbbing headache on one side of the head that can last for hours or even days.

Migraines are generally thought to be the most painful type of vascular headaches, but cluster headaches can also cause intense agony. Unlike migraines, cluster headaches usually go away within an hour, only to return soon after. The headaches strike in clusters at predictable intervals as often as several times a day over a three- to eight-week period, then taper off for a while.

Cluster headaches tend to primarily affect men from 20 to 40 years old and often cause tearing from the eyes, nasal discharge, and pain on one side of the head, says LaFayette Singleton, M.D., assistant professor of neurology at the University of Chicago School of

Medicine. They also affect heavy smokers and drinkers more often than other folks.

Just how bad can headache pain actually be? "When we asked our patients to rate their headache pain on a scale of 1 to 10," Dr. Wheeler recounts, "about 18 percent said their headaches were mild and usually didn't interfere with functioning, 23 percent said their pain was moderate and impaired their activities somewhat, and 9 percent said that their headaches were severely disabling and stopped them from working, cleaning house, or pursuing their hobbies."

If your head hurts, you may have your mom and dad to thank for it. To a certain extent, you inherit a tendency toward headaches, says Dr. Wheeler, because some people's blood vessels and brain membranes are genetically different from others.'

Although people sometimes worry that a severe headache means that they may be having a stroke or brain hemorrhage, a headache is usually just a headache, promises Dr. Wheeler. But see a doctor if you have changes in sensation in any area of your body, such as numbness and heaviness in the arms, face, or legs, accompanied by a headache on one side of your head, says Shawna Nesbitt, M.D., assistant professor of internal medicine at the University of Michigan School of Medicine at Ann Arbor. These signs could indicate a stroke, although people who get migraines may have similar symptoms.

If you have high blood pressure and you get a headache that you feel is the worst you've ever had, see your doctor right away. You could have bleeding in the brain due to uncontrolled high blood pressure. This is called a subarachnoid hemorrhage, and it is a little more common in Blacks than in Whites, says Dr. Wheeler. The pain is often intense, steady, and deep and may be worse in the neck.

STOPPING IT
BEFORE IT STARTS

Your head doesn't have to hurt. Here are some strategies for giving headaches the boot.

Bust that stress. Stress probably causes more headaches than just about any other trigger. If you think something or someone is making your head hurt, you are probably right. Do everything you can to eliminate tension in your life and ease tightness in your neck and

If you find that you are getting headaches two or three times a week or more, if they're getting stronger, or if they come with a fever, nausea, or coughing, see your doctor. Your headaches could be a symptom of a serious health problem, or you may need more than drugstore remedies to eliminate the pain.

"There are two types of headache medication, abortive and preventive," says Calvin B. Wheeler, M.D., clinical instructor in neurology and pediatrics at the University of California, San Francisco, School of Medicine and child neurologist and assistant physician-in-chief at Kaiser Permanente Medical Center in Fremont, California.

Abortive medications, which stop the pain after it's begun, are used for headaches that occur twice a month or less and are not completely debilitating. These include oral nonsteroidal anti-inflammatory drugs such as ibuprofen (Advil, Nuprin), naproxen (Aleve), and aspirin that you can buy over the counter. If your headaches are really severe, your doctor may give you a prescription for a combination medication such as isometheptene, dichloralphenazone, and acetaminophen (Midrin); acetaminophen and codeine (Tylenol with Codeine No. 3); butalbital, aspirin, and caffeine (Fiorinal); oxycodone and aspirin (Percodan); or hydrocodone and acetaminophen (Percocet).

Preventive medications are generally used when headaches occur frequently (two to three times a week) or are so debilitating that a person is out of commission for days, says Dr. Wheeler. They include valproic acid (Depakene), propranolol (Novopranol or Propranolol), and amitriptyline (Elavil), among others. These drugs must be used daily—perhaps as often as three or four times a day—to be effective, says Dr. Wheeler. They are often used until a person has been headache-free for six months to a year.

shoulder muscles. A heating pad, ice packs, or nighttime neck and shoulder massage can make all the difference, says Dr. Wheeler.

Watch what you eat. Foods can definitely contribute to

headaches. A class of food chemicals called tyramines are powerful blood vessel tighteners and are found in red wine, fresh bread, beer, and cheese. There are also many other triggers, such as monosodium glutamate (MSG), which is found not only in Asian cuisine but also in frozen foods, lunchmeats, and many other processed foods. MSG must be listed on food labels, so read them carefully if you suspect that you're sensitive to MSG. Some experts recommend that you keep a headache diary to help pin down your food triggers.

TURNING OFF
THE PAIN

Even if you are unsuccessful at keeping headaches away, you can probably eliminate the pain. Here are a few tried-and-true tactics.

Ask for feedback. If you have recurrent headaches, ask your doctor for a referral to a biofeedback specialist, who can show you how to train yourself to control neck and shoulder tension by getting auditory or visual feedback from a special biofeedback device, says Dr. Singleton. Once you learn, you can easily stop tension—and pain—at home or work.

Get rest. You need sleep to handle stress, so try to stick to a regular sleep schedule, says Dr. Wheeler.

Eat well. Hunger can trigger headaches in some people. If you find that's true for you, eat small, frequent meals throughout the day.

Cut the coffee. Limit your caffeine intake to avoid painful caffeine withdrawal headaches, says Dr. Wheeler. Switch to decaf or herbal tea.

Ice it. Pressing a cold pack to your head is worth a try, since a cold compress may help relieve painful throbbing by constricting arteries in the scalp, says Dr. Wheeler.

Reach for a painkiller. Taking aspirin or other over-the-counter analgesics such as ibuprofen (Advil, Nuprin) or naproxen (Aleve) as soon as you feel a headache starting may help relieve pain. But don't overdo it, says Dr. Wheeler. Over time, constantly taking analgesics can cause rebound headaches. This effect is usually caused by the caffeine in analgesics.

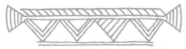

Heartburn

PUTTING OUT THE FIRE

lat on his back on a hospital gurney, Donnie Wilkerson was sure he was going to die. "I had heard a public service announcement on TV that said that severe, burning chest pain was a key sign of a heart attack," says the burly, 39-year-old insurance company manager. "The pain in my chest was so severe that it brought tears to my eyes, so I got myself to a hospital as quickly as possible."

No wonder the nurses looked so concerned as they attached electrodes from the EKG machine to Donnie's perspiration-slick chest.

The doctor told Donnie that there was good news and bad news. "The good news was that my heart was fine. The pain was probably heartburn," he says. "The bad news was that the awful burn wasn't going to cool off as long as I was almost 60 pounds overweight.

"I'd never been one to diet," Donnie says. "I ate what I had a taste for and lived with the consequences, but this heartburn had to go." Since he was reluctant to change his diet, he decided to try exercise instead. On his daily commute between his Staten Island, New York, home and his Manhattan office, he left the subway one stop before his destination and walked briskly the rest of the way. He later gave in and combined his new exercise routine with a low-fat, high-fiber diet. Over the course of 15 months, Donnie lost 53 pounds and every last trace of heartburn.

UNDERSTANDING A BURNING ISSUE

Heartburn is so common that most folks don't give it a second thought. But maybe they should. "Heartburn isn't normal," says William Emikola Richardson, M.D., medical director and president of the Atlanta Clinic of Preventive Medicine. "If you have it, something is wrong." (The pain of heartburn has been known to mimic that of a myocardial infarction, or heart attack. If you ever suspect that you may be experiencing a heart attack, get to the emergency room as soon as possible to check out the possibility.)

Heartburn, also known as acid indigestion or dyspepsia, happens when harshly acidic stomach juices splash against the lower esophagus. Acid normally doesn't bother the stomach, which is lined with a protective layer of mucus, but the esophagus is mucus-free. Its sole protector is a tough little ring of muscle called the lower esophageal sphincter, which acts like a bottlecap on the stomach. When the sphincter fails to do its job by closing properly, stomach acids can wash against the exposed esophagus and cause that familiar burning sensation that most of us expect after too many french fries or an overdose of pepperoni pizza.

"Anything that increases pressure on your stomach and stresses your lower esophageal sphincter can set you up for heartburn," says gastroenterologist Joanne A. Peebles Wilson, M.D., professor of medicine and associate chief of gastroenterology at Duke University Medical Center in Durham, North Carolina. "Obesity or pregnancy can do that."

Certain foods can also cause trouble by relaxing the esophageal sphincter. Alcohol, fatty foods, chocolate, caffeine, and mint all loosen this crucial muscle. "So when you end a meal with a rich chocolate dessert, an after-dinner drink, and a mint, you're really setting yourself up for heartburn," says Victor Scott, M.D., chief of gastroenterology at Howard University Hospital in Washington, D.C.

Large meals can also bring on the burn, because a full-to-the-brim stomach brings acid-washed food in close contact with the esophageal opening. A stuffed stomach also takes longer to empty, especially when the meal was rich in slow-digesting fat.

Finally, there's a condition called a hiatal hernia that is associated with heartburn but usually causes only mild discomfort. The esophagus passes through a small opening in the diaphragm (the muscular partition that separates the chest from the abdomen) as it meets the stomach. If this opening is weak, a pocket can form in the stomach where acid-washed food can reach the lower esophagus. Hiatal hernias are extremely common in both Blacks and Whites, and the incidence increases with age.

If you're a heartburn sufferer, you can take a little comfort from knowing that this misery doesn't single out African-Americans. In fact, we're less likely than Whites to develop a serious consequence of heartburn—esophageal cancer. Repeated exposure to stomach acid, or chronic heartburn, can injure esophageal tissue, potentially causing a full-blown ulcer. When that injured tissue heals, it's more likely to become malignant.

"Cancer of the lower esophagus is most common in White male smokers," says Dr. Scott. "But it's one of the fastest-growing cancers in the United States in terms of the number of new cases, and African-Americans should do everything they can to avoid damage to the esophagus."

Dousing
the Flames

Handling heartburn is a three-stage process that begins with making lifestyle changes. If those don't work, try medication, says Dr. Scott. Surgery is a last, and rare, resort. Remember, however, that you may not be able to wipe out heartburn entirely. "You don't cure this condition," says Dr. Scott. "You control it." Try these tips from the experts to keep your digestive tract cool and calm.

Slim down. If you're overweight, decreasing your girth can reduce the upward pressure on your stomach. It really does help, says Dr. Scott.

Banish your belt. Girdles and belts only increase the pressure on your stomach contents, says Dr. Scott. You'll be more comfortable without them.

Digest before you rest. Give yourself 2 to 3 hours after eating before you do the gardening, go to sleep, or engage in any other activity that causes you to bend over or lie down, advises Dr. Scott. It takes at least 2 hours for food to move through your stomach, and until it does, stooping, lying down, or bending over gives acid a better opportunity to creep into your esophagus.

Make meals smaller. Avoid eating large meals, suggests Dr. Wilson. Smaller, low-fat meals often prevent heartburn because the stomach empties of food, and thus acid, more quickly.

Keep your lungs clear. The nicotine in cigarette smoke relaxes the lower esophageal sphincter, Dr. Scott points out. Cigarette smoke also stimulates stomach acid production.

Go easy on the nightcaps. This advice actually applies to drinking at any time of day. Alcohol opens the acid faucet in your stomach and relaxes the lower esophageal sphincter, says Dr. Richardson.

Chew it up. Try chewing gum. "It increases the flow of saliva, which is a natural buffer against stomach acid," says Dr. Wilson. For the same reason, he says, you should also be sure to chew your food thoroughly, as well-chewed food is easier to digest.

Know your food rules. Try drinking a beverage 15 minutes before you eat the rest of the meal, then have fruit as your first course, suggests Dr. Richardson. "The liquid will pass through your stomach quickly, as will the fruit, which will allow the stomach to digest the main portion of the meal unimpeded," he says. "Drinking beverages along with the meal only dilutes your stomach juices. And eating easily digested foods such as fruit along with more slowly digested foods like starches or protein interferes with the natural passage of foods through your stomach."

Go tropical. Papaya extracts and the digestive enzymes lipase, amylase, and protease, all available at natural food stores, can help prevent heartburn by aiding digestion, says Dr. Richardson. Be sure to take them with meals. One caution, however: "Don't take protease if you have an ulcer," he says. "It digests protein, which is what stomach muscle is made of, so it will make your ulcer worse."

Neutralize it. Over-the-counter antacids like Tums and Rolaids neutralize stomach acid. As a preventive, try taking them at least an hour before meals and at bedtime. "These medicines give immediate but temporary relief," says Dr. Scott. Alternatively, you could try an acid-blocker like cimetidine (Tagamet), ranitidine (Zantac), or famotidine (Pepcid), which inhibits secretion of stomach acid.

In severe cases, your doctor can prescribe a proton pump medicine such as omeprazole (Prilosec), which actually stops acid production entirely. Proton pump inhibitors don't seem to hurt digestion, although we don't know much about their long-term effects, says Dr. Scott.

Consider going under the knife. A surgeon can correct a hiatal hernia that isn't helped by lifestyle changes or medicines. New laparoscopic techniques make surgery an option more frequently than ever before, although it's still relatively uncommon. "Surgery is an extreme remedy for heartburn, but it may be appropriate for severe heartburn or for young people whose recourse otherwise would be years of medication," says Dr. Scott.

Tip your bed upward. When you raise the head of your bed up to 8 inches, gravity becomes a nighttime ally and helps keep stomach acid where it belongs. Solid wooden blocks securely placed under the headboard posts should do the trick.

Heart Disease

Steering Clear of a Killer

arold Perkins was walking up one of San Francisco's steepest hills on the way to a coffee house when he felt a burning sensation in his chest. "At first I thought 'Is this what an ulcer feels like?'" recalls Harold, a theatrical producer and former dancer in his late forties who is still trim at 6 feet 1 inch and 180 pounds. "I was worried sick about a stage production I was having a hard time financing, so I just thought that the stress had done a number on my stomach."

The burning persisted during a dress rehearsal later that day. "It seemed to flare up when I was doing something strenuous, like helping the stage crew move some scenery," he remembers. About 4:00 in the afternoon, after a particularly intense bout of burning chest pain, Harold decided he'd had enough. "I just suddenly felt that I was dealing with something more than an ulcer," he says.

Harold stopped the rehearsal and asked his director to drive him to a hospital. There doctors discovered that Harold had high blood pressure and a related condition called left ventricular hypertrophy, or LVH, in which one of the chambers of the heart is enlarged. LVH often leads to angina, a type of chest pain that is associated with heart disease and is a signal that the heart isn't getting enough oxygen.

"When the doctor asked me how long I'd had high blood pressure, I told her it was news to me," says Harold, recalling his surprise. "It was a little embarrassing."

But when the doctor explained that his out-of-control blood pressure could have led to an enlarged heart, which could cause sudden death, Harold realized that things could have been much worse. "When I heard that, I decided to change my lifestyle, make it back to the doctor's office for every appointment, and worry a little more about my health and a lot less about the theater," he says.

The Heart
of the Matter

The term *heart disease* refers to an entire family of cardiovascular conditions. Occasional problems such as infections of the inner lining of the heart membrane (endocarditis), disturbances in the heart's rhythm (arrhythmias), malfunctions of the heart valves (such as mitral valve prolapse), and inherited defects in the structure of the heart (congenital heart defects) are also part of the family tree.

The most worrisome conditions are diseases such as atherosclerosis (see page 33), which develops when the blood vessels that feed the heart become narrowed or clogged by fatty deposits. If the blood supply to the heart is restricted, it can cause angina. Complete blockage of these blood vessels can cause a heart attack.

Angina can also be a warning sign of other indications of heart disease, including LVH, the condition that caused Harold's chest pain. In time, LVH can cause the left ventricle to grow so large that it no longer operates efficiently or in unison with the heart's other three chambers. Eventually, if your high blood pressure and heart condition are not treated, your heart just shuts down.

At least one in four African-Americans has high blood pressure, and more than 10 percent of those who have high blood pressure also have LVH, the first sign of serious heart involvement. By treating high blood pressure, however, you can usually prevent and even reverse LVH.

Understanding
Your Risks

As recently as the 1940s, doctors mistakenly believed that heart disease was as unusual in African-Americans as membership in the local country club. The real deal is that heart disease kills more Americans of all races—954,000 each year—than any other disease. And African-Americans are especially prone to developing this killer. "We've got more heart disease than any other population group in the country," explains Edward Cooper, M.D., professor emeritus of medicine at the University of Pennsylvania Medical Center in Philadelphia and the first African-American president of the American Heart Association (AHA). Compared to the rates among Whites, Blacks' death rates from heart disease are 46 percent higher for men and an incredible 69 percent higher for women.

For Gwen Walker, learning was a way of life. But like countless other Black women, this Cincinnati-based educator didn't know a thing about the source of the dull ache in the center of her chest.

"It was the end of the academic quarter, and I thought it might be nerves—or indigestion," recalls the youthful-looking 65-year-old. When emergency room doctors found that she had suffered a heart attack and recommended bypass surgery to open a blocked artery, "I was shocked," Gwen remembers. "And scared."

Scared enough to give her lifestyle a thorough makeover. Gwen quit smoking and watched her cholesterol level plunge 40 points in two months. She also gave up her favorite food—double cheeseburgers—and started to concentrate on enjoying low-fat, low-cholesterol dishes. And she's been burning up the exercise machines at a local cardiac rehabilitation unit. "Before the heart attack, I thought being on my feet all day was enough exercise," Gwen says. But now? "They ask us to make 36 return visits to exercise after a heart attack or surgery. I just celebrated my 500th visit."

Unlike Gwen, many Black women don't get a second chance. The heart disease death rate for African-American women is 69 percent higher than that for White women. What's to blame? In addition to obesity, diabetes, and high blood pressure, we can point a finger at the unique stresses that African-American

Why do we have so many cardiovascular problems? Mostly because we also have higher rates of high blood pressure, diabetes, inactivity, and obesity.

Let's start with high blood pressure. This condition literally wears down your heart because it forces the heart to work extra hard to pump blood. The strain also damages the inner lining of the slender coronary arteries that feed the heart muscle and causes the heart to enlarge.

Over time, this bruised lining attracts cholesterol and debris from the bloodstream, which combine to form fatty deposits that can gradually narrow the arteries and reduce the blood supply to an area of the heart. Eventually the coronary arteries can become completely blocked, women are under because of our sex, race, and income, says Cheryl R. Martin, M.D., assistant clinical professor of cardiovascular medicine at the Medical College of Wisconsin in Milwaukee. "And stress aggravates all other risk factors."

Then, too, African-American women often fail to recognize the symptoms of heart disease and don't get to the hospital in time to get help. When White men experience chest pain, for example, research shows that they most often proceed quickly to an emergency room, mention a suspected heart attack, and receive immediate—and often lifesaving—care.

"If African-American women complain about chest pain at all, they're most likely to tell a friend or family member, 'Oh, I don't feel quite right today. I think I'll lie down for a while.' If they get to the hospital, it's often many hours later, too late for clot-busting drugs to help their hearts. When a nurse asks, the women may say 'I don't feel good' instead of mentioning chest pain, so doctors aren't as quick to presume a heart problem," Dr. Martin says.

If you're an African-American woman, take Dr. Martin's advice about heart disease. Learn the symptoms, be very clear when explaining them to your doctor, and don't be afraid to ask for help.

damaging or killing the part of the heart muscle fed by the affected arteries. If the infarct—the affected area of the heart—is small, people usually recover. If it's large, the result can be a fatal heart attack. Sudden death can result when either a large or a small area of the heart is damaged, but it occurs more commonly with damage to a large area.

The next thing to watch out for is diabetes, which is almost twice as common in Blacks as in Whites. Diabetes is often accompanied by high blood levels of cholesterol, the fat that clogs your arteries. Nearly half of all Black men and slightly more than half of Black women have cholesterol levels that are above the safe level of 200 milligrams per deciliter, primarily because they eat too much fat, says Dr. Cooper.

Robin Drummond, R.D., a dietitian affiliated with the Heartbeats Life Center, a community-based cardiovascular health center at the Medical Center of Louisiana in New Orleans, can offer a very simple, though painful, explanation of what a rich, fatty diet can do to your heart.

Drummond, a Louisiana native, recalls meals from her childhood: platters of stewed chicken with gravy, beans flavored with bacon drippings, and fruit pies and cobblers with crusts made with shortening. "I would remove the skin from my chicken," she remembers, "and my dad would say, 'Don't throw food away. I'll eat it.'" Drummond lost her father to heart disease when he was only 56, a tragedy that helped convince her to become a dietitian; she now works with heart patients.

Lack of exercise is another major risk factor for heart disease among Blacks. A majority of brothers (63 percent) and sisters (68 percent) are not physically active. Being sedentary lowers blood levels of HDL (high-density lipoprotein) or "good" cholesterol and elevates levels of LDL (low-density lipoprotein) cholesterol, the "bad" type. Exercise is especially beneficial because it elevates HDL cholesterol.

An inactive lifestyle can also lead to obesity, which is particularly common among African-American women (more than 40 percent are obese). Obesity opens another Pandora's box. If you're overweight, you risk at least three other conditions associated with heart disease—high blood pressure, high blood cholesterol, and diabetes, all of which can lead to thickening and hardening of the coronary arteries. "Black people just don't realize how much being overweight can set off a whole cycle of health problems," says Dr. Cooper.

BEATING THE ODDS

Since the conditions mentioned above have such an impact on our increased tendency toward heart disease, you need to deal with all of them in order to lower your risks. Here's what experts recommend.

Reshape your plate. You just can't overestimate the importance of a low-fat, low-sodium diet in preventing heart disease. "Scale back on fast foods and high-sodium foods, including processed, cured, and smoked meats, cheeses, seasoning salts, condiments, salted snacks, pickled products, and canned soups, vegetables, and meats. And try using herbs, spices, and lemon juice as flavor enhancers instead of salt," Drummond suggests. (Check with your doctor, though, before using a salt substitute containing potassium chloride. It may cause medical problems especially if you have kidney disease.)

Forget about eating anything fried. Bake, broil, grill, sauté, or poach meats and seafood and eat lots of fresh fruits and vegetables. Use food nutrition labels to track your daily sodium and fat intake. For healthy individuals, the Daily Value of 2,400 milligrams of sodium is a reasonable amount, and you should keep your fat intake below the 30 percent of calories recommended by the AHA. "People feel better when they eat differently," says Drummond. "It's easier to breathe and you have more energy once you lose weight and lower your blood pressure."

Shake a leg. "It doesn't take much physical activity to benefit your heart," says Dr. Cooper.

"At least 30 minutes a day three times a week will do. You can accumulate it in lots of ways—riding an exercise bike, walking around the block, or running around the yard with your dog," says Keith C. Ferdinand, M.D., medical director of the Heartbeats Life Center.

No ifs, ands, or butts. Smoking can affect your blood by increasing LDL cholesterol and decreasing HDL. It also hardens the arteries and makes your blood thick as well as increasing the tendency to develop clots. This all adds up to an increased chance of heart disease, so kick the habit.

Quitting smoking takes serious willpower. Only one in five smokers who try to quit do so successfully. But give it a go—it's definitely worth it. After one year of abstinence, you'll slash your risk of smoking-related heart disease by 50 percent.

Acupuncture, hypnotism, or a support group might help some people cope with the cravings and withdrawal symptoms most smokers experience when trying to kick the habit, according to the American Medical Association. You can also purchase nicotine gum or nicotine patches over the counter. They work by letting you gradually reduce the amount of nicotine in your body.

Make it a family affair. Because heart disease runs in families, so should prevention. "If your lifestyle and eating habits are hurting your heart, chances are your kids may have the same health problems when they reach your age," says Drummond. Help ensure their healthy future by making sure the entire family eats sensibly and gets plenty of exercise.

Capitalize on a capsule. Vitamin E is a heart protector: It seems to prevent LDL cholesterol from stopping up your arteries. Since it's tough to get this vitamin in a healthy diet (it exists only in fats), try a supplement that supplies 400 international units daily, says Dr. Ferdinand.

Know the warning signs. You can greatly increase your chances of a full recovery from angina or a heart attack by receiving quick medical attention, so learn to read your body for warning signs.

The signs of angina are chest pain or a burning sensation, with or without shortness of breath, that occurs when there are increased demands on your heart, such as during cold weather or after a physically or emotionally stressful encounter.

The classic sign of heart attack is severe chest pain. But many heart attack sufferers don't experience what Dr. Ferdinand calls the "Fred Sanford syndrome." Instead you may experience sudden arm, neck, or jaw pain, chest tightness, sweating, nausea, vomiting, or what seems like heartburn.

If you have any of these symptoms, have someone take you to the emergency room immediately, advises Dr. Ferdinand. "Sometimes people with these symptoms wait 6 to 7 hours to see a doctor," he says. "The more time they spend treating themselves at home, the less time we have to save their hearts."

Hemorrhoids

EASING THE IRRITATION

When Horace Griffin took a job hoisting luggage for the Greyhound Bus Company, he figured it would be a great way to make it through those lean undergraduate years. And it was: The extra cash was right on time. But the extra strain on his torso left him with an unexpected and uncomfortable souvenir: hemorrhoids. "They're like a burning, itching paper cut," says the well-muscled Horace, now 35 and a young professor of religion. "The pain isn't severe most of the time, but it's always there, waiting to flare up from the least irritation."

Happily, Horace is living proof that you can't keep a good man down. He's discovered that watching his diet does wonders for his hemorrhoid pain. The Florida native restricts his one hard-to-resist down-home favorite—fried chicken dinners—to once a month. Otherwise he enjoys high-fiber treats like fruit salad, bran muffins, and bowls of steaming oatmeal. "All that fiber helps me be regular, and I have less straining," he says.

VEINS
UNDER PRESSURE

Here's a quiz. If every American with hemorrhoidal veins suddenly moved to Canada, how many of us would be left on United States soil? 100 million? 200 million?

The correct answer is zero. Technically speaking, we've all got them. These veins lie just beneath the mucous membrane that lines the anus and the lower part of the rectum. "Everyone has hemorrhoidal veins," says Adam M. Robinson, Jr., M.D., a colorectal surgeon and Force Surgeon for Commander Naval Surface Force, U.S. Atlantic Fleet, in Norfolk, Virginia. "But not everyone's veins bleed, itch, or cause pain."

Hemorrhoidal veins become uncomfortable and irritated when we persistently strain to have bowel movements or subject our bodies to other froms of physical exertion or prolonged sitting. All that pressure leaves the veins swollen, twisted, and vulnerable to rupture from an irritation such as passing a hard stool, scratching, or wiping too hard with toilet tissue. These irritations can cause bleeding and pain, two classic signs of hemorrhoids. The problem only worsens when painful defecation causes us to shy away from the bathroom. When stool remains in the rectum long enough for additional water to be absorbed from it, it becomes drier, harder, and only more painful to pass.

Sometimes hemorrhoids protrude from the anus, where they can itch and leak mucus. If these prolapsed hemorrhoids happen to contain a blood clot, the pain can be memorable. They hurt like the devil, notes Dr. Robinson.

Hemorrhoids also afflict people who habitually endure pressure on the rectal area. The strain from the weight of an unborn child, for example, is one reason that nearly 60 percent of hemorrhoid sufferers are female. Hemorrhoids are also more common in weight lifters and in taxi drivers, pilots, and others whose work requires that they sit for long periods of time.

So we're talking big numbers here—an estimated 10.4 million hemorrhoid sufferers nationwide. African-Americans aren't affected any more frequently than Whites are, although a predisposition to hemorrhoids can be inherited.

SMOOTHING
THE WAY

Hemorrhoids aren't inevitable. Here are a few tips for keeping them out of your life.

Fill up on fiber. If you're hemorrhoid-free, fiber will help you stay that way. If you're not, fiber can help make life much more comfortable. Set your sights on 30 to 35 grams of fiber a day, including five half-cup servings of fruits and vegetables, suggests Wayne B. Tuckson, M.D., assistant professor of surgery at the University of Louisville in Kentucky.

Wash them away. "Water is the single best laxative there is," says Dr. Tuckson, because it prevents stools from drying out. Go for drinking six to eight glasses of the wet stuff each day, he suggests.

Take care of business—quickly. Sitting on the toilet for a long time allows gravity to stretch the anal canal, possibly contributing to hemorrhoids. "The bathroom is not the place to read *War and Peace*," says Dr. Tuckson.

Obey the urge. Most people get the strongest urge to move their bowels 30 minutes after breakfast, "but whenever you get the feeling, act on it," says Dr. Tuckson.

HEALING THE HURT

Hemorrhoids are quite responsive to treatment, often without surgery. First, though, you need to be sure of what you're dealing with.

Don't be fooled. "Only about 35 to 50 percent of patients who come to me for treatment of hemorrhoids actually have them," says Debra Ford, M.D., assistant professor and chief of the Division of Colon and Rectal Surgery at Howard University Hospital in Washington, D.C., and the first board-certified female African-American colorectal surgeon. "So a doctor shouldn't just take your word for it and give you a hemorrhoid cream."

Other possible diagnoses include an anal infection, an anal tear, or anal dermatitis. Colorectal cancer also has many of the same symptoms as hemorrhoids. "Treatment (and health risks) differs for each, so you should visit your doctor for a definitive diagnosis," says Dr. Ford.

Get what you pay for. "The first time a doctor evaluates you for hemorrhoids, she should take a thorough history and perform a digital rectal exam with a gloved finger," Dr. Ford says. Then the doctor should visually examine the tissues of your anus and rectum. "In proper hands, the entire examination takes less than 5 minutes," she says. But be sure you get the complete exam.

Interview the doc. Rectal exams can be embarrassing and a bit intimidating. So sit down with the doctor prior to the exam and ask what kind of exam he plans to do, suggests Dr. Ford. "The doctor should explain everything beforehand," she says. "If he says, 'Oh, don't worry about it,' you should seek another opinion."

Stick with psyllium. Psyllium is the active ingredient in Metamucil, Fiberall, Serutan, and some other nonprescription bulk laxatives. It gives stools bulk and softens them, making them easier to pass. "Three or four weeks of psyllium can mitigate or even reverse hemorrhoids," says Dr. Robinson. Take it only when you need it.

One disadvantage of psyllium laxatives, however, is that you don't get the nutrients that are offered by fruits and vegetables, so don't slack off on your diet while getting your fiber from these laxatives.

Go OTC. Over-the-counter medicines containing hydrocortisone can decrease the size of inflamed hemorrhoids. "Creams are better than suppositories, which the rectal muscles tend to pull inside the body beyond the actual site of the hemorrhoid," says Dr. Ford. Foams are also better, but they are available only by prescription.

Soak to soothe. "Sitting in a warm bath several times a day can bring blessed relief from hemorrhoid pain," says Dr. Robinson.

One size doesn't fit all. There are many medical approaches to handling hemorrhoids. For moderate to severe cases, a doctor may tie off the hemorrhoid with a tiny rubber band (it falls off within a few days) or remove it surgically. But mild cases should respond well to conservative medical treatment.

Lighten your load. Any extra weight that you may be carrying can also put unwanted pressure down below. Try to slim down to help prevent or treat hemorrhoid problems.

Hepatitis

GUARDING AGAINST INFECTION

 orraine Conroy, a veteran automotive safety inspector with an office wall full of commendations, admits that she's obsessed with doing things right. She has to be. She knows that other people's lives depend on her work. "My crew calls me 'White Gloves,' because they know that I'll send a car back in a heartbeat if there's the slightest risk of danger," says the stocky, 42-year-old Californian, her voice reflecting professional pride and motherly concern.

The same goes at home. When Lorraine was still a teenager, her best friend, Denice, came down with what appeared at first to be the flu, except that it didn't go away or get better. "Girlfriend was achy and feverish and sick to her stomach for over five weeks," remembers Lorraine.

"One day she called me, and in this weak, dragged-out voice, she said she felt so bad that she just wanted to die." Lorraine took her to the doctor, who told Denice that she was in the grip of a nasty case of hepatitis B—a sexually transmitted disease (STD) that Lorraine hadn't even heard of before.

That's when Lorraine decided that she was going to be - ultracareful when she became sexually active. "Thanks to that experience, I was practicing safe sex before it was even called safe sex," says Lorraine with a knowing nod. "I think anyone who says condoms can't be exciting is really missing out," she says. "The sex is still great, and believe me, the peace of mind is even better."

THE ABCs
OF HEPATITIS

Although some types of the disease can be sexually transmitted, hepatitis, unlike AIDS, gets almost no headlines. It infects more than 1,000 Americans a day, even though there's a vaccine for the most common types that can stop it in its tracks, and it's increasingly prevalent among young African-Americans. Hepatitis is an infectious disease of the liver that's dangerous and even life-threatening, but it's 100 percent preventable.

Hepatitis is caused by any one of several strains of viruses, each responsible for a different form of the disease. There's hepatitis A, hepatitis B, and others, all the way to hepatitis E. Among this alphabet soup of microorganisms, hepatitis A, B, and C are the most important and most common.

The hepatitis A virus, found in fecal matter, makes people sick when poor personal hygiene or sewage-contaminated water or food brings the virus to the mouth. The disease is common in nonindustrialized nations that have poor sanitation systems.

"This is the virus that hits you when you go to Mexico and have something tasty, and the next thing you know, you're sick as a dog," says Celia J. Maxwell, M.D., an infectious disease specialist at Howard University in Washington, D.C. Hepatitis A can also be found in day care centers, nursing homes, and other institutions where people come in contact with body secretions and excretions.

Hepatitis A feels like the flu. You lose your appetite and feel nauseated, achy, weak, and feverish. The illness usually clears up by itself in two to eight weeks, but it can be so debilitating that weeks or months may pass before you feel fully energized. "If you have any of these symptoms for more than a week, see your physician," says Dr. Maxwell.

THE PATH
TO INFECTION

Hepatitis B and C are even more serious health threats. Each year brings an estimated 410,000 new cases of these diseases. The C form is particularly dangerous, causing 8,000 to 10,000 deaths annually.

Hepatitis B and C can cause a variety of liver disorders that can bring on flulike symptoms or fatal liver failure. Like hepatitis A, hepatitis B and C usually clear up without treatment within eight weeks or so. Again, you should see your doctor if any of these symptoms persist, according to Dr. Maxwell.

During the 6 to 12 weeks or more between the time you're infected and the time you first notice symptoms, you can still infect someone else. In fact, some people with hepatitis B, and to a greater extent, C, can become carriers of the disease without having any outward symptoms. There are a staggering one million chronic carriers of hepatitis B and more than three million chronic carriers of hepatitis C in the United States.

If you're a carrier of the common B virus, one of the most serious risks, aside from unknowingly infecting your sex partner(s) or your children, is the threat of liver cancer. "It's like having a splinter in your liver for years," explains Dr. Maxwell. The chronic presence of the virus in the bloodstream can cause hepatocellular carcinoma, an ominous liver cancer that's usually unresponsive to chemotherapy or radiation. It's estimated that carriers of the B virus are about 340 times more likely to develop liver cancer than noncarriers.

Like the AIDS virus, hepatitis B and C viruses live in blood and body fluids and are spread by intimate contact. That means vaginal or anal intercourse, needle-sharing by intravenous drug users, accidental needle sticks—an occupational hazard for health care workers—and occasionally blood transfusions (although routine screening of donated blood has greatly decreased this risk). "Unnecessary blood transfusions should be avoided," says Jessie L. Sherrod, M.D., pediatric infectious disease specialist at King-Drew Medical Center in Los Angeles and a member of the Advisory Committee on Immunization Practices at the Centers for Disease Control and Prevention (CDC) in Atlanta. And as with HIV, infected mothers can pass hepatitis B to their infants during childbirth. There is one difference, though: It's a lot easier to spread hepatitis than AIDS.

"When it comes to ease of transmission, the AIDS virus is a wimp compared to the hepatitis virus," says Dr. Maxwell, which is another reason not to be complacent about this disease.

The CDC recommends that infants be immunized against hepatitis B at birth because, although infants rarely get the virus, they are at greatest risk for developing cancerous liver tumors. "The peak age group for hepatitis is 15- to 39-year-olds, and most young adults get it through sexual intercourse," explains Winston S. Price, M.D., National Medical Association trustee and assistant professor of pediatrics at the State University of New York Health Science Center in Brooklyn. "We immunize children because that way, we can reduce the potential reservoir of the virus."

But universal immunization of infants with the hepatitis B vaccine didn't begin in some states until the mid-1990s, so most American children, adolescents, and adults have never received the vaccine. That's especially true for African-Americans and other people of color, says Dr. Maxwell. "We may not seek immunizations, because preventing a disease that could happen sometime in the future isn't as immediate as our daily concerns," he explains.

There's another reason that hepatitis poses a greater risk to African-Americans than to Whites. "African-Americans are at higher risk for most infectious diseases because the crowded conditions in which many lower-income people live are ideal for the transmission of viruses," says Dr. Sherrod.

But hepatitis can be stopped by protecting yourself from exposure to blood and body fluids, practicing good hygiene, and being careful.

PLAYING IT SAFE

For the best protection, get immunized against hepatitis B; if you're traveling, get immunized for A. You'll cut your chances of contracting B and C if you avoid exposure to blood, semen, and vaginal fluids, says Dr. Sherrod. Here are some other precautions.

Don't leave home without it. If you're planning international travel to a destination with questionable sanitation systems, ask your doctor for a blood test to see if you're immune to hepatitis A, Dr. Sherrod advises. As with many other viruses, if you've had hepatitis A once, chances are your body is immune to later encounters with the virus. If you are not immune, she says, you should get a hepatitis A vaccination by requesting it from your doctor.

Stick with bottled water. When traveling in Africa, Asia (except Japan), the Mediterranean, the Middle East, Central and South America, eastern Europe, Mexico, and parts of the Caribbean, stay away from tap water or freshly drawn spring water. It's the best way to avoid hepatitis A. Drink only bottled water and avoid beverages containing ice, says Dr. Sherrod. While you're traveling, steer clear of dairy products, fresh fruits and vegetables (which may be washed in contaminated water), custards, pastries, and raw shellfish, too.

Wash your hands. Use soap and very warm water after you use the bathroom, change a diaper, or come in contact with restroom faucets and doorknobs. "Be especially careful at day care centers, nursing homes, and other institutions," says Dr. Sherrod.

Vaccinate the kids. "Obstetricians are required to screen mothers for hepatitis B. If the mother tests positive, she'll need to receive hepatitis B immunoglobulin and a hepatitis vaccine so she won't pass on the infection to her baby," says Dr. Price. Even if you test negative, your infant should receive the hepatitis B immunization to protect against future infection, he says.

The American Academy of Pediatrics advises three doses of the hepatitis B vaccine: the first dose within the first two months of life, the second dose one to two months later, and the third three to four months after the second.

Protect teens, too. "Lots of kids come down with hepatitis even though they have no history of intravenous drug use, needle sticks, or blood transfusions. They get it through unsafe sex, tattooing, sharing razors and toothbrushes, or exposure to individuals who are chronic carriers," says Dr. Price. "If your child wasn't immunized as an infant, immunize her as a teen."

Let your Uncle foot the bill. Uncle Sam, that is. The hepatitis B vaccine series is pricey—from about $100 to $175 for all three shots, depending on where you live. Fortunately, it is now available at no cost to children under age 18 who qualify under the federal Vaccines for Children Program. Check with your pediatrician or your local health department.

If you're at risk, roll up your sleeve. "Many city health departments also offer the hepatitis B vaccine at a reduced rate if you live with someone has hepatitis B, if you're a health care worker, if you engage in high-risk homosexual or heterosexual behavior, if you're on dialysis, or if you're an intravenous drug user," says Dr. Price. "No one should feel they can't afford this vaccine."

Be safe, not sorry. Safe sex is the only way to go, says Dr. Price. "Any technique that protects you against AIDS will also protect you against hepatitis B and C," he says. "That means using condoms for intercourse and dental dams or condoms for oral contact."

High Blood Pressure

KEEPING IT DOWN

axine Washington calls it her conversion experience—the day she became a believer in a brand new kind of living. In 1991, the summer after her father died unexpectedly from a massive stroke, Maxine's doctor warned her that her blood pressure was also creeping into the danger zone. He suggested eating a little less and exercising a little more.

Maxine swore off fried foods and joined an Afro-jazz dance club, but temptation was always just around the corner. "My best friend was always dropping by, trying to get me to go out for ice cream with her," recalls the Georgia landscape designer, throwing up her sun-darkened arms. "I would tell her, 'Girl, you'd better get out of my house with all those fat grams!' But I'm an ice cream lover, too, and it was a humid summer, so it was tough."

Resisting calories got a lot easier after her next doctor's visit. Not only had 12 weeks of Maxine's new regimen dropped 15 unnecessary pounds from her 5-foot, 7-inch frame, but her blood pressure had fallen into the normal range. "I couldn't believe losing a little weight would make such a difference in my blood pressure," she says. "You know, I love my girlfriend (and my ice cream), but now I listen to my doctor first."

UNSOLVED MYSTERIES

Experts say that it's the number one health problem facing African-American adults, and with good reason. The damage wrought by high blood pressure (hypertension) is so profound that it defies easy description. A staggering array of the diseases that harm African-Americans—stroke, heart attack, kidney failure, atherosclerosis (hardening of the arteries), and kidney disease—have a connection with high blood pressure.

"Most African-Americans realize that high blood pressure is bad, according to various surveys, but many of us don't appreciate how pervasive it is," says cardiologist Edward Cooper, M.D., professor emeritus of medicine at the University of Pennsylvania Medical Center in Philadelphia and the first African-American president of the American Heart Association. "Compared to Whites, hypertension in African-Americans is almost twice as prevalent, more severe, and more likely to be untreated, and it begins earlier in life," he says.

The odd thing is that no one is really sure where all this high blood pressure in Blacks comes from. One theory suggests that the meager provisions given to slaves during their passage to America may have promoted the survival of those who were best able to retain sodium (and therefore resist dehydration). If our genes are indeed programmed to retain salt, it makes sense that we would be more salt-sensitive and more prone to high blood pressure.

"If you assume that genetics set the stage, lifestyle factors complete the picture," says Elijah Saunders, M.D., associate professor of medicine and head of the Division of Hypertension at the University of Maryland School of Medicine in Baltimore.

What lifestyle factors are we talking about? Eating too much salt and fat, being overweight, exercising too little, and drinking too much alcohol all can have a detrimental effect on your blood pressure.

Salt-rich diets make the body retain water so that it can dilute the excess sodium to safe levels, and the extra fluid in the bloodstream increases blood pressure. Fatty foods contribute to atherosclerosis, a major cause of high blood pressure. Every extra pound of body fat that you put on your frame taxes your heart and increases your chances for high blood pressure. When you're inactive, your blood pressure–regulating mechanisms don't work as they should, and small arteries can begin to shut down, making the heart work overtime.

Stress can increase your blood pressure, too. You may be fully aware of your stress level when the boss yells at you, but you may experience more subtle forms of stress because of racism. "Racism leads African-Americans to take on nontraditional habits and values that can hurt blood pressure," says Jules P. Harrell, Ph.D., professor of psychology at Howard University in Washington, D.C. In other words, the self-destructive behaviors we sometimes engage in—drinking too much, failing to exercise, and eating junk food—aren't true to our culture. A lot of it comes from racism-induced anxiety, depression, and anger, all mental states that can raise blood pressure, says Dr. Harrell.

Blood pressure is measured with two numbers. The first number, systolic, is a measure of the pressure when the heart beats, that is, when the muscle contracts to squeeze blood out through the arteries. The second number is diastolic, which measures the pressure when the muscle is relaxed, allowing blood to flow back into the heart.

If your blood pressure reading is 110/75, it means that your systolic pressure is 110 and your diastolic pressure is 75. It also means that your blood pressure is in the normal range. But normal blood pressure for one person is not the same as normal blood pressure for another. Your age, for instance, will make a difference (blood pressure tends to rise slightly with age), and so will your state of mind when you have the test (anxiety tends to raise blood pressure). Because of the various factors involved, be sure to discuss your blood pressure reading with your doctor.

Here's how the numbers shake down: For systolic, normal is 135 or lower, borderline is 135 to 140, and high is 140 or above; for diastolic, normal is 85 or lower, borderline is 85 to 90, and high is 90 or above.

Blood pressure tends to be higher in older adults. Before age 55, high blood pressure is more likely to affect men than women, but by age 75, women catch up and surpass men in high blood pressure risk. And even kids aren't immune. "From adolescence on, African-American youngsters tend to have higher blood pressure than their White peers," says Dr. Cooper.

RELEASING THE PRESSURE

"We can't change genetics, but we can change our environment," says Dr. Saunders. That means that not only can we lower high blood pressure, we can also prevent it—just by changing how we live. "I can help you control hypertension with less medicine or maybe no medicine, but only if you change your lifestyle," says Dr. Saunders. Here are some smart strategies.

Start them off right. Introduce your kids to heart-healthy habits from day one, advises Dr. Saunders. "Use salt sparingly, so they don't learn to crave salty foods. Encourage children to be physically active. And don't let them eat in front of the TV. It's too easy to eat lots of calories without being aware of it," he says.

Set a good example. "What's good for kids is good for the rest of us, too," says Dr. Saunders. A balanced and varied low-fat, high-fiber diet plus plenty of heart-pumping physical activity is the best present you can give your cardiovascular system.

Get cuffed. High blood pressure as a rule is initially unnoticeable and painless. You won't know you have it unless you have it checked. Have your pressure monitored at least once a year if it's normal and at least once every few months if you already have high blood pressure, Dr. Cooper suggests. "If I had my druthers," he says, "I'd make sure every household had a blood pressure cuff just like they have a thermometer. They are relatively inexpensive and are available at most pharmacies." Visit your doctor regularly for a blood pressure check or be alert for free screenings that hospitals sometimes offer.

Minimize your middle. Lose 20 pounds and you'll shave an average of 10 points from your systolic reading and 8 points from your diastolic reading, according to one study. "And if you're already taking blood pressure medicine, weight loss can make the drugs more effective," says Dr. Saunders.

Walk this way. If you have mild high blood pressure, walking just 20 to 60 minutes a day three to five days a week can help lower both your diastolic and systolic blood pressure by 10 points, according to the American College of Sports Medicine. Of course, other aerobic exercise, such as swimming, jogging, or step aerobics, will do the trick, too.

Give your menu a makeover. Did you know that the average fast-food burger and a bag of fries can contain half of the recommended daily limit of 2,400 milligrams of sodium? It's true. Keep your sodium intake in the safe zone by keeping your eye on the salt content of foods. Read labels and watch for excess salt in canned and other processed foods.

Munch your minerals. Calcium and potassium are about the most heart-friendly minerals you'll ever meet, explains Dr. Cooper. "Calcium and potassium work hand in hand with a low-sodium diet to lower blood pressure," he says. Plus, they come packaged in terrific-tasting foods. Calcium is abundant in low-fat yogurt, skim milk, and other dairy products and in broccoli, collards, and turnip and mustard greens. Aim for at least 1,000 milligrams a day—the amount in about 3½ cups of skim milk.

You should try to get 3,500 milligrams of potassium daily. The mineral is found in fruits such as raisins (544 milligrams per half-cup), cantaloupe (494 milligrams per cup), and bananas (449 milligrams in one banana) as well as vegetables like baked potatoes (1,137 milligrams in one potato with skin) and lima beans (484 milligrams per half-cup).

Douse the butts. Smoking doesn't cause high blood pressure, but if you already have it, smoking can make its complications worse. So say good-bye to the cigarettes, says Dr. Cooper.

Do decaf. A study at the University of California at Los Angeles found that healthy young men with normal blood pressure who drank three cups of coffee a day had a 6-point increase in their diastolic and systolic blood pressure. The researchers found that even after 12 hours without caffeine, that morning cup of coffee elevated their blood pressure. "If you have high blood pressure and you drink coffee, it's probably not a bad idea to switch to decaf until you can bring your pressure under control," says Dr. Saunders. "However, more studies are needed to be certain of the role of caffeine in high blood pressure."

Learn to relax. According to one study of elderly African-Americans with high blood pressure, meditation lowered systolic readings by up to 10 points and diastolic by up to 6 points, while progressive muscle relaxation (methodically tensing and releasing the major muscle groups of the body) lowered readings by 4 and 3 points respectively. "Every African-American should learn relaxation techniques that work for them," says Dr. Harrell. You can enjoy relaxing with music, dance, tai chi, or whatever works.

Know your meds. Success rates for treating high blood pressure with medication are lower for Blacks than for Whites. "You can't always try the same strategies as you do with White patients and expect them to work," explains Dr. Saunders. The usual doses of two types of medications, beta-blockers and most ACE inhibitors, for example, often don't work as well in African-Americans as they do in Whites. If your drug treatment isn't working, talk to your doctor about alternatives. What does work?

In the past, diuretics have been considered the first line of defense for Black patients with hypertension, according to Dr. Saunders. These drugs reduce blood pressure by ridding the body of excess fluid and salt through the urine and thus reducing the volume of blood that must be pumped through the arteries. Although relatively inexpensive, diuretics can sometimes cause unpleasant side effects such as raising cholesterol and sugar levels, lowering levels of beneficial potassium, and making it difficult for some men to achieve and maintain erections. Now diuretics are often prescribed in small doses or in combination with other drugs.

Long-acting calcium channel blockers help relax and widen the blood vessels, thus lowering blood pressure and reducing the amount of work the heart has to do. They are quite effective in lowering high blood pressure in Blacks and generally cause fewer side effects than diuretics, although they are more costly.

ACE inhibitors and beta-blockers help prevent the production of enzymes that constrict blood vessels. "In the past, we felt that ACE inhibitors and beta-blockers weren't very useful for African-Americans," says Dr. Saunders. "But now understanding of the best way to use these medications has been improved. In some cases, we now recommend taking higher amounts of the medication than usually prescribed, restricting dietary salt, or adding a low dose of a diuretic to get the best effect of an ACE inhibitor or beta-blocker in Black patients."

Don't be fooled. There's a myth going around that no matter how high your blood pressure is, once it is under control, you can toss your blood pressure medicine.

It's not true. "If you have stage 1 (mild) hypertension (a reading of 159 over 99 or lower) and you lower it into the safe range with medications plus weight loss, a low-sodium diet, and exercise, you can often decrease or discontinue your blood pressure medicine," says Keith C. Ferdinand, M.D., medical director at Heartbeats Life Center at the Medical Center of Louisiana in New Orleans. "But with more severe hypertension, make sure you talk with your doctor. You may need to stay on the medicine for life."

For more information, call the National Heart, Lung, and Blood Institute at 1-800-575-WELL.

HIV/AIDS

LIVING SMART AND SAFE

Belynda Dunn does not look like she is wrestling with a deadly disease. Her carefully styled hair is thick and glossy; her smooth, brown skin is something any woman would envy; and her classic "sister body" does an impressive job of filling out her red and black pants suit. But Belynda has AIDS, and like most African-American women with the disease, it caught her completely by surprise.

"About 10 years ago, the man I was engaged to marry suddenly left town without a word," she explains. "When I later discovered that he died of AIDS, I was shocked."

Belynda believes that the stigma and denial surrounding AIDS in the Black community played a large part in her fiance's lack of awareness about his condition and safe sex. "I didn't know that he was an intravenous drug user, but I have no doubt that he loved me and tried to do his best," says Belynda. "But this was 1986, when AIDS was really treated as this shameful, gay disease."

At first, Belynda was devastated by the discovery that she was infected with HIV. "I fell apart. I lost my home and my friends." She did not get back on her feet until she turned to the church. "The church supported me and helped me find a home," Belynda recalls. Gradually, she embraced the reality of taking control of her health care, getting her life back on track, and amazingly, finding the strength to help others.

"I knew I couldn't be the only one who had this story to tell," Belynda says, "so I felt I had to be there for other people." Today, the 46-year-old activist is the African-American Program Manager for the AIDS Action Committee of Massachusetts. "I speak out in churches, community centers—anywhere people will listen. I ask them to find compassion and passion in their hearts to let go of the denial and help those of us living with HIV and AIDS."

Understanding an Epidemic

AIDS is caused by the human immunodeficiency virus (HIV), which is carried in infected blood, semen, or vaginal fluids. The most common means of contracting HIV is engaging in unprotected sex. You can also get it by sharing HIV-infected needles. HIV can also be passed through transfusions of HIV-contaminated blood, platelets, or plasma.

Upon entering the body, HIV infiltrates the immune system, settling in the white blood cells. The virus then uses the cells' reproductive machinery to reproduce itself. As the white blood cells die off, the new HIV particles are released into the bloodstream to infect other white blood cells. This depletion of white blood cells weakens an infected person's immune system, eventually impairing its ability to resist a wide range of infections and certain cancers.

Many people have no symptoms when they are first infected with HIV, even though an immune-system war rages within them. They often remain symptom-free for months or years, although 75 percent of infected people do have at least some symptoms within 10 years of infection.

The most common initial symptom is swollen lymph glands. Additional symptoms that follow include fatigue, chills, fever, night sweats, a dry cough, sudden weight loss, chronic diarrhea, and thrush (yeast) infections of the mouth and esophagus. These symptoms may last for a prolonged period of time or they could rapidly give way to AIDS.

No one knows how AIDS started. "But rather than spending our energy speculating on how it began, we need to focus on the problem at hand—preventing and curing the disease," says Wayne L. Greaves, M.D., associate professor of medicine at Howard University Hospital in Washington, D.C.

We could start by acknowledging that the problem really does exist. Although HIV/AIDS hits African-Americans particularly hard (it's currently the leading cause of death among African-American men and women ages 25 to 44), Black AIDS experts say that their attempts to broach the subject are often greeted by silence. "We don't want to accept ownership, so we deny AIDS," explains Dr. Greaves. But there's also reluctance to talk about the gay men, intravenous drug users, and partners of HIV-positive men and women who are our neighbors, fellow church-goers, family, and friends and who are at very high risk for contracting the disease.

"We in the African-American community have to embrace this disease in order to beat it," emphasizes Wilbert Jordan, M.D., director of the Oasis Clinic at King-Drew Medical Center in Los Angeles. "And that means embracing those who have it."

GUARDING AGAINST INFECTION

The risk of contracting AIDS can be dramatically reduced with careful changes in lifestyle. Here's how to stay healthy.

Consider abstinence. It almost goes without saying that the best protection against contracting HIV through sex is to abstain from sex altogether, says Dr. Jordan. While this may seem unrealistic for most sexually active adults, it is an option that concerned parents, teachers, and counselors should discuss with preteens and teens. Talk with them and help them understand the risks of rushing into adult behavior, he urges.

Don't take chances. Know what's risky and what's not, and avoid risky behavior, advises Dr. Jordan. Consider this: When he asks his HIV-positive patients how many drinks it would take for them to have unprotected sex with an attractive stranger, the response from women and men alike, on average, is three. Social situations that involve alcohol are especially dangerous because we tend to do things under the influence of alcohol that we normally wouldn't do. "We need to think more highly of ourselves than to allow a little alcohol to expose us to such a potent disease," he says.

Know yourself. Sometimes sexual behavior is driven more by a painful past than by hormones. "I'll tell a promiscuous adult that I think they were sexually abused as a child, and they'll say, 'How did you know?' " says Dr. Jordan. If your past may be influencing your unhealthy sex habits, get counseling or therapy, he says.

Keep a condom handy. Lubricated latex condoms protect best because latex is particularly strong and the lubrication prevents rips, acting as a barrier against HIV. "The overwhelming risk for women is from having unprotected sex. But remember, with the exception of the female condom (which is made from polyurethane and is also safe),

What's wrong with this picture?

Deanna Lynn considered herself smart, sophisticated, and definitely in control of her life. That's why she thought nothing of it when Tray—a guy she'd been keeping her eye on for a long time—suggested that they spend some private time together.

They had the kind of evening that most people dream about—the champagne was cold, the mood was hot, and the company was spectacular. The next morning, Deanna was very pleased with herself for remembering to have natural condoms on hand.

Well, this scenario may be steamy, but it isn't safe. It violates most of the three cardinal rules of safe sex, according to Wayne L. Greaves, M.D., associate professor of medicine at Howard University Hospital in Washington, D.C.

1. Avoid sex with strangers (or people you barely know) and with people who may have had multiple sex partners. Monogamous sex is always safer. Remember, monogamous doesn't just mean having one partner, because that partner could have had sex with lots of people. It means having sex with one partner whose only sexual contact is with you.

2. Use a latex condom every time you have intercourse. The AIDS virus can slip right through the lambskin or "natural" condoms (which Deanna used), which are made from sheep intestines.

3. Use a condom on the penis for both intercourse and oral sex and a dental dam (a thin sheet of latex that fits over the entire vaginal opening) during vaginal oral sex. Dental dams can be purchased at condom specialty stores or near the condom section in some drugstores. Actually, while it's unlikely that you can get HIV through oral sex, it's best to avoid it unless you're sure your partner is HIV-free.

the responsibility for the use of male condoms falls on men," says Janet L. Mitchell, M.D., chairperson of the Department of Obstetrics and Gynecology at Interfaith Medical Center in Brooklyn.

Take the test. Before you have unprotected sex—that is, without a condom—make sure you are both disease-free.

Ask any physician or health department for an HIV blood test for you and your partner. There are home tests available over the counter that cost about $40 at drugstores. Or for home delivery of a test kit within 7 to 10 days, call Confide at 1-800-THE-TEST or Home Access at 1-800-HIV-TEST. Packages are delivered discreetly.

No matter what the outcome of your first test, you should be retested three to six months later. "Wait until you get two negative results before you have unprotected sex," advises Dr. Mitchell. If you test positive, seek a doctor's care immediately and be sure to notify your partner, she advises.

Know your blood supply. Sterilization and testing for HIV have virtually eliminated the risk of contracting AIDS through a blood transfusion in this country. But that's not true in many parts of the world. Of course, it's unlikely that you'll need a blood transfusion while traveling, but if you do, it's important to know if the blood supply is safe before you consent to receive one. If it isn't and you feel even remotely well enough to travel, you might consider returning to the United States for treatment, says Dr. Jordan.

Don't share syringes. Because AIDS is transmitted through the blood, you can easily contract the disease by injecting yourself with a needle that was previously used by another person, says Dr. Greaves.

COPING WITH AIDS

A new generation of AIDS medications shows exciting promise for stopping HIV dead in its tracks. These drugs, approved by the Food and Drug Administration, are called protease inhibitors. They disrupt the functioning of an enzyme that HIV needs to complete its life cycle. Three protease inhibitors are currently available: saquinavir-mesylate (Invirase), indinavir-sulfate (Crixivan), and ritonavir (Norvir).

In combination with low doses of azidothymidine (AZT), a drug that reduces the occurrence of opportunistic infections, protease inhibitors drastically reduce HIV levels in infected people. "If we can start treatment in an HIV-positive person before the immune system is destroyed, these medicines can actually mean the difference between progressing to AIDS and remaining symptom-free," says Dr. Greaves.

The long-term effects of these drugs are unknown. And treatment is expensive—on the order of $10,000 per year—although the medicines are available through some state-funded AIDS programs as long as you are financially eligible. Depending on the type of insurance you have, your insurance might cover some or all of the treatment.

If you're HIV-infected or you have AIDS, here's some self-care advice.

Take charge. "Don't sit back and wait for things to happen," says Dr. Mitchell. Take control. "I tell my patients, 'You can live with this disease or you can die with this disease. If you take care of yourself by reducing stress in your life, improving your diet, and exercising, you can do well,'" he says.

Go with combination therapy. The latest research shows that conventional medicines are more effective in combination than they are alone. "So if your doctor is prescribing a single antiviral drug, you should ask why he is not using combination therapy. It's important to know what's going on, and there may be a reason why your doctor is giving you this treatment," says Dr. Mitchell.

Protect your baby with AZT. If you're pregnant, get tested for HIV, recommends the American College of Obstetricians and Gynecologists and the Centers for Disease Control and Prevention in Atlanta. By doing so, you might help protect the health of your unborn baby. If you're HIV-infected and you do nothing, you have a 25 percent chance of passing the virus to your child. But if you take AZT during pregnancy, the risk of transmission falls to just 8 percent, explains Dr. Mitchell.

Find a respectful doctor. People with AIDS often differ racially and culturally in their approach to living with the disease. "African-Americans are more reluctant than Whites to accept Western drug therapies for AIDS, and women are more reluctant than men," says Dr. Mitchell. Find a physician who appreciates these differences and who's willing to put your needs first, she advises.

"Alternatives such as herbal therapies and macrobiotics have not been scientifically proven, but doctors should respect their patients' autonomy enough to allow therapies that the patient feels most comfortable with," says Dr. Mitchell.

Offering Support

By now, too many of us know someone who has been diagnosed with HIV/AIDS. Here are some ways to be supportive.

Be empathetic. That doesn't mean being nosy or doing things that they can do for themselves, says Dr. Greaves. "Just be accessible. Tell the person, 'If you want to talk, I'm here,'" he says.

Learn to say "I love you." Love and support are critical for people struggling with a deadly disease. "You don't have to condone the circumstances that brought someone to the AIDS ward," says Dr. Jordan. "Just support them." AIDS is not a curse; it's a disease.

For up-to-the-minute information about HIV and AIDS, phone the National AIDS Hotline at 1-800-342-AIDS, 24 hours a day, seven days a week. You can receive confidential doctor and/or resource referrals as well as basic information. The hotline also accepts requests for printed HIV/AIDS information, which is delivered in discreet packaging.

You may also contact the Black Leadership Commission on AIDS at 1-800-573-2522 (in New York, 212-614-0023).

Impotence

BECOMING YOURSELF AGAIN

oseph Mills was frustrated. He was 45 years young, still trim and looking good, but he was already cornered by a man's most private embarrassment: dwindling erections. After several months, Joe mustered the courage to visit the Male Dysfunction Clinic at Johns Hopkins Hospital in Baltimore in search of an answer. And the answer he got was quite a surprise.

"We gave Joe a thorough physical and reviewed his medical history and use of medications," recalls clinic director Arthur L. Burnett, M.D. "The only possible cause I could think of was the fact that he was a chain smoker, so I suggested he get some help and kick that habit." Joe dropped the cigarettes cold turkey. "The next time I saw him, he was delighted," says Dr. Burnett. "He had cut out smoking, and sure enough, his erections were returning to normal."

IT'S NOT ALL
IN YOUR HEAD

Impotence, the word used to describe the inability to achieve or sustain a satisfactory erection, is really a misnomer. It doesn't mean that you're powerless or that you've lost your sex drive. You don't lose your ability to ejaculate. And, believe it or not, you don't lose the pleasure of orgasms. Men can experience all three of these without having erections, says Dr. Burnett. That's why you hear less talk of impotence these days and more about erectile dysfunction, a term that's clinically accurate.

Upward of 30 million American men have difficulty with erections to different degrees, according to estimates. But only 1 percent of them seek medical care. It can be embarrassing to talk about such a private concern in a urologist's office, so many men may deal with this in many different ways.

But surely one reason that erectile dysfunction rarely comes up is misinformation. For years, urologists pinned erection difficulties on emotional or psychological problems like stress, overwork, or depression. Many men believed that their bedroom frustrations were all in their heads. That's not so today. "We think 80 to 90 percent of all erectile dysfunction is caused by medical problems," says Kevin L. Billups, M.D., assistant professor in the Department of Urologic Surgery and director of the National Institute for Men's Health at the University of Minnesota in Minneapolis. The major players are vascular diseases such as atherosclerosis, diabetes, and high blood pressure, which damage blood vessels.

What do blood vessels have to do with erections? Everything. Erections occur when blood flows through the arteries into the spongy tissues of the penis. When the veins that drain these tissues squeeze tight, the blood is temporarily prevented from flowing out again, and the result is an erection.

But that's just part of the picture. Blood flow is governed by the squeezing or relaxing of the muscles that wrap around the blood vessels in the penis like insulation on a wire. Those muscles in turn are controlled by nerve impulses from the brain. So any illness that clogs blood vessels, damages nerves, or impairs the brain can eventually show up as trouble between the sheets.

That's also why Blacks have more erectile dysfunction than Whites: We have higher rates of diabetes, cardiovascular disease, and other illnesses that we don't commonly associate with sexual function. What's more, many of the medications used to treat these and other illnesses—diuretics, antidepressants, male hormones, and others—can wilt erections.

Smoking, which causes blood vessels throughout your body to constrict, reduces the amount of blood that can fuel an erection. Moderate to heavy alcohol consumption or any type of drug abuse can bring on erectile problems as well.

RISING
TO THE OCCASION

It is possible to keep your distance from conditions that predispose guys to erection frustrations. Here's what Marc Lowe, M.D., chief of urology at the Group Health Cooperative of Puget Sound (central division) in Seattle recommends.

Chill way out. If you're a Black man who's not under some kind of stress, congratulations: You're probably the only one. Stress can dramatically reduce your ability to develop an erection, so create your own stress-reduction routine. Take a walk after work. Pick up a book or a magazine. Put on a soothing CD. Shoot some hoops. Get out to the driving range. Do anything that will cut you some slack.

Use it or lose it. Research shows that men who stay sexually active keep the machinery lubricated. So go ahead, indulge (safely, with condoms, of course).

Go lean. Who needs clogged penile arteries? A diet low in saturated fat and cholesterol helps ensure a nice strong blood flow where it counts.

Work up a sweat. Routine physical exercise does two things, explains Dr. Lowe. "Moderate exercise improves your libido (sex drive), and it may help keep your blood vessels healthy."

Cycle gently. Injury to your perianal region (the area near your anus and testicles) can damage nerves and blood vessels that feed the penis. One culprit is too many miles on a hard bicycle saddle. If you feel numbness or discomfort while biking, stand up or take a break, advises Dr. Lowe.

BRINGING THEM BACK

What if you're already having a problem? Remember three things, says Dr. Billups. "First of all, erection problems are extremely common, so don't feel like you're the only one. Second, the problem is probably medical, not psychological. In other words, it's not your fault. Third, and the best news of all: We can correct it in 95 percent of our patients." Here's the lowdown on getting yourself back on track.

Ask for help. You'll want to see a urologist. Ask how many patients he has seen for impotence and how long he has treated the condition, advises Dr. Billups. If the doctor sounds inexperienced or insensitive, try someone else. "Sad to say, some physicians, and even some urologists, don't treat erectile dysfunction as a serious matter," he cautions.

Expect a thorough exam. Your doctor should take a detailed medical history, give you a physical, ask you questions about the frequency and quality of your erections, note any medications you're taking, and perhaps take a blood sample to measure the amount of testosterone in your system, Dr. Billups explains.

Don't rule out therapy. If your body is in good working condition, your emotions may be the key. "If your doctor recommends psychological counseling, don't be embarrassed," says Dr. Lowe. "Many patients respond extremely well to counseling," he says. "Try to find a therapist who specializes in treating sexual dysfunction."

Boost those hormones. If your sex drive isn't what it used to be, and a blood test shows that you have low testosterone levels, your doctor may prescribe testosterone therapy using injections or patches. "I use it with some patients," says Dr. Billups. "About 25 percent of the men with low testosterone have better erections after therapy."

Needle yourself. This one sounds cruel and unusual, but it offers hope for the not-too-needle-squeamish. You learn to self-inject medicines into your penis before sex that produce an erection that lasts 30 minutes to an hour. These drugs work by relaxing your blood vessels so that the blood can rush into your penis. "You use a very thin needle, and the actual injection doesn't hurt very much," reassures Dr. Billups. "The major disadvantage is lost spontaneity."

Pump it up. There are vacuum devices available that work like this: You slip your flaccid penis into a plastic cylinder that is attached to a lightweight vacuum pump. You squeeze the handle of the pump, which reduces air pressure inside the cylinder and creates an erection by drawing blood into the penis. Then you remove the device and place a band at the base of your penis to keep the blood where you want it. "It's minimally invasive," says Dr. Billups. "Many older couples like this device."

Plant an implant. Another treatment option involves surgically implanting a mechanical device, of which there are two basic kinds. With the semirigid type, bendable rods are surgically implanted into the penis. You bend them up when you're ready for action.

Inflatable implants use a hydraulic device that allows you to pump up an erection when you need it and deflate it when you don't. "The implants are inconspicuous. If you had 10 men in a shower, you couldn't tell which one had the implant," says Dr. Billups. "And men and their partners who have them like them. Implant procedures still have the highest patient and partner satisfaction rate of the different treatment options," he says.

Incontinence

HOLDING YOUR WATER

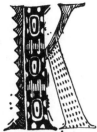

Karen Scott dropped into the overstuffed chair in the vending area of the YWCA. Her copper-colored, muscular body was clad in black Spandex. She paused to pull back her thick brown hair and towel off her neck. She seemed to need to settle in for a minute before talking about the health problem that caught her by surprise about a year ago. "Give me a minute, girl," she pleaded between swigs of spring water. "That step class was live!"

Then she was ready to explain. "You know I had to stop doing aerobics for a while, and that wasn't easy, because I'm hooked on it. In fact, I used to be an aerobics instructor, and I had no problems doing vigorous workouts. But after I had my second child, I had to run to the bathroom after or even during a 60-minute class. On some days, I'd leak urine just from jumping up and down. It made me so self-conscious, I finally stopped teaching and working out.

"I thought about seeing a doctor, but I just kept putting it off because it was so embarrassing, and it made me feel so old. . . . I mean, this is a problem my mother should be having. I'm only 34," Karen says with a laugh.

Karen did eventually visit her gynecologist, who suggested she try special exercises designed to strengthen her pelvic-floor muscles. "Exercise is my thing. Once I understood that it was the answer, I was on my way. Now I've been doing them for a while, and I'm much better. I may even go back to teaching class," she says.

AGE ISN'T THE ISSUE

Karen's reluctance to talk about her problem with her doctor is not surprising when you consider that most people think of urinary incontinence (lack of bladder control) as a condition of old age. "In fact, urinary incontinence affects half of all women under 45 at some time in their lives," says Carol Bennett, M.D., associate professor of urology at the University of California at Los Angeles School of Medicine.

Although both men and women are susceptible to incontinence, women are twice as likely as men to experience it. Men have thicker muscles to hold the urethra shut. They also don't have to deal with the physical stresses of childbirth: The fetus can put added pressure on the bladder of a mother-to-be, and the trauma of vaginal delivery can weaken the muscles that open and close the urethra.

People with incontinence may leak urine, as Kate did, during high-impact activities such as aerobics, but for many the most distressing aspect is the fact that you can lose bladder control even during less strenuous everyday activities such as picking up your children, laughing, or even sneezing.

Understanding incontinence is simple. Think of it this way. Kids love to play with water balloons on hot summer days. If they tie the necks of the balloons tightly, they can toss them around with abandon. But what happens if they don't tie off the balloon after filling it with water? The pressure of the water against the neck of the balloon means that someone is going to get wet.

This is basically what happens to your bladder when you begin to have a problem with incontinence. The sphincter muscles at the neck of your bladder, like the loosely tied neck of a balloon, no longer stay closed tightly. Sometimes the pelvic muscles, which surround the sphincter muscles, are to blame. If you strengthen the pelvic muscles, you can correct your incontinence.

There are four types of incontinence: stress, urge, mixed, and overflow. Stress incontinence is the result of increased pressure within the abdomen that forces urine to leak from the bladder without warning. It can occur anytime your bladder is jostled—by coughing, laughing, or doing aerobics, for example. Urge incontinence is different: You do get a warning, but not a sufficient one. You feel that you have to go right away. Before you can get to the bathroom, you leak.

Actually, many people with incontinence have both urge and stress incontinence, a condition that is appropriately called mixed incontinence.

Although it's true that more men and women tend to develop

incontinence as they age, it isn't age itself but any one of a number of medical conditions that sets you up for incontinence. It can result from having had multiple vaginal or bladder surgeries or from an enlarged prostate that interferes with urine flow. Having a hysterectomy, for example, may elevate your risk. "The high rate of hysterectomy among Black women makes this an important risk factor for us. And as Kate learned, multiple pregnancies can also put you at risk. But there is no magic number of children that will cause the problem," says Dr. Bennett.

Overflow incontinence is another type of incontinence that is of particular concern for African-Americans because of their increased risk of diabetes. Diabetes causes neuropathy, or nerve complications. As a result of nerve damage to the bladder, it doesn't always empty efficiently. Instead, it fills up like a bucket and spills over, causing overflow incontinence.

Other medical conditions that can cause incontinence include Parkinson's disease and stroke, but these conditions tend to affect people who are older than 40.

"If you notice a problem with incontinence, make sure you see your doctor, gynecologist, or urologist," says Dr. Bennett. Most people don't have to live with this inconvenient and embarrassing problem. Eighty percent of people who are incontinent see improvement within 3 to 12 weeks of using simple self-help techniques. If these don't work, your doctor may be able to evaluate you and if necessary, prescribe drugs that increase your control by calming and relaxing the bladder's involuntary contractions.

STRATEGIES
FOR STAYING DRY

Whatever the cause and whatever type of incontinence you have, your bothersome bladder can probably be trained. Here's what urologists and gynecologists suggest.

Lose pounds. "Overweight women should lose weight to prevent stress incontinence," says Dr. Bennett. Extra weight places increased abdominal pressure on the neck of the bladder and causes leakage.

Tune in, turn off. Biofeedback machines give you feedback on your ability to control certain bodily functions. The feedback can take the form of visual or auditory cues, such as lights of different colors or beeps at different pitches. For a referral to a biofeedback specialist, call the National Association for Continence at 1-800-BLADDER. Once you receive training, you should be able to better control your bladder, says Dr. Bennett.

Tap into Kegels. Kegel exercises can tighten the pelvic-floor muscles around the bladder to prevent leakage from stress incontinence. Kate's doctor prescribed these exercises for her, and they worked. They can be effective for both men and women.

To make sure you are performing Kegels properly and contracting the right muscles, do this exercise while you are on the toilet. Try to stop your urine flow midstream by contracting the muscles in your pelvic area, then start it again by releasing the muscles. Once you get a feel for this exercise, you can perform the contractions anywhere, without the help of the urine flow. But Kegels won't tighten your pelvic muscles unless you commit to doing them repeatedly. Try doing 20 to 25 Kegels at a time, holding the contractions for 20 to 25 seconds each. Repeat the exercises three times a day, says Dr. Bennett.

Control the urge. If you have urge incontinence, try adopting a schedule. The goal is to urinate when you decide to, not when your bladder wants you to. The next time you have the urge, try not to go to the bathroom right away. The more you practice, the easier it may be to wait. Lengthen the time between urges at a pace that's comfortable for you, says Dr. Bennett. If you can't control your urge, see your doctor for further evaluation.

Check your meds. Some medications can increase your risk for incontinence. Many older people take diuretics, for example, to help eliminate excess water. If you have incontinence and are taking medications, talk to your doctor about whether they could be causing the problem.

Infertility

MAKING A MIRACLE HAPPEN

evar and Stephanie Cozart Burton have truly been blessed. His career is thriving as a result of his highly acclaimed work in the role of Lt. Cmdr. Geordi LaForge on the TV series *Star Trek: The Next Generation* and the big-screen hit, *Star Trek: First Contact*. She is in demand as one of the most successful makeup artists in film and television. But there's lots more good news in their lives. "We know that we have been very fortunate," says Levar, referring to their personal triumph over infertility.

"My problems started years before we were married," says Stephanie. "Doctors had already told me I had at least one blocked fallopian tube, but the cause was never determined."

"So although we knew that Stephanie might be infertile when we were married," says Levar, "we were determined to attempt to have a biological child."

"It really was difficult. One doctor ignored my health problem. He told me to go home, relax, and just have unprotected sex for six months," says Stephanie. "Another doctor ended a consultation by drawing a picture of my fallopian tubes on a piece of paper, scribbling over them with his pen, and then saying: 'See this? These are your tubes. You'll never conceive.'"

Then the couple met Richard Marrs, M.D., of Los Angeles. "He went about solving our problem as if he were doing God's work," says Levar. Dr. Marrs was able to bypass Stephanie's blocked fallopian tubes by harvesting eggs directly from her ovaries. The eggs were then fertilized in vitro (in a glass dish in a laboratory) and implanted in her uterus.

Even though only 21 percent of in vitro implants result in full-term pregnancies, the Burtons' faith, perseverance, and strong commitment to their nine-year relationship paid off: Stephanie conceived on her first try, at age 39. Their daughter, Michaela, is now 2.

Understanding
Infertility

About 1 in 10 couples, Black and White, have problems conceiving. "There is this myth that Black people don't have infertility problems. But after 20 years of working with infertile couples, I can tell you that some of my most difficult cases have been Black couples," says Elwyn Grimes, M.D., chairman of the Department of Obstetrics and Gynecology at Meharry Medical College School of Medicine in Nashville, Tennessee.

Infertility is generally defined as the inability to conceive after one year of intercourse without a contraceptive, explains Ervin E. Jones, M.D., Ph.D., associate professor of obstetrics and gynecology at Yale University School of Medicine and clinic chief of the Yale In-Vitro Fertilization Programs.

There are four main categories of infertility: fallopian tube disease, ovulation disorders, cervical problems, and the male factor.

Fallopian tube disease. Doctors also call this tubal disease, and it is a main cause of infertility. Tubal disease can be caused by any number of conditions, including sexually transmitted diseases (STDs), endometriosis (in which the lining of the uterus grows outside the uterine cavity), and pelvic surgery. In some cases, like Stephanie's, the cause is undetermined.

Another example of fallopian tube disease is pelvic inflammatory disease (PID). This generalized infection of the pelvic area is usually caused by STDs such as gonorrhea or chlamydia that have been left untreated. Twelve percent of women who have one bout with PID become infertile, two bouts make 25 percent of women infertile, and half of the women who have three bouts will be unable to conceive.

Ovulation disorders. About 25 percent of infertile women have problems with ovulation, says Vivian Lewis, M.D., an obstetrician and gynecologist and director of the Reproductive Endocrinology Unit at the University of Rochester Medical Center in New York. These are disorders that prevent viable eggs from being released from the ovary. Ovulation problems may be due to many causes, ranging from changes in weight to hormonal imbalances. Obesity can contribute to ovulation problems because the extra fat tissue disrupts the body's hormonal balance.

Another condition, known as polycystic ovaries, is very common in African-American women. Cysts form on the ovaries due to a hormonal imbalance and cause a cessation of ovulation.

Cervical problems. In women who are infertile because of cervical problems, sperm cells can't penetrate the cervical mucus and gain entry to the fallopian tubes, where fertilization occurs. Cervical problems may be caused by any of a number of infections or by damage to the cervix from any previous surgery or traumatic childbirth.

The male factor. This odd phrase is modern medicine's way of saying that the source of infertility frequently rests with men and that women have no monopoly on conception difficulties. In 40 to 50 percent of all infertile couples, the problem is due to something involving the man.

There is a whole range of potential problems, but the most frequent is low sperm count or low sperm motility, says Dr. Jones. This means that the man produces sperm that are too few in number or too sluggish to reach the fallopian tube and fertilize the egg.

Many men are resistant to the idea that they may have a problem, says Dr. Lewis. Many African-American couples run into trouble because there is a misconception that fertility has to do with sexual potency. "Men make the mistake of linking their sperm count to their manhood. This type of thinking could keep men from seeking help that could bring children into their lives," says Levar.

Then there is the issue of a woman's age at the time she attempts to conceive. A woman's ability to conceive and sustain a pregnancy to delivery is affected by age, explains Dr. Jones. Women are most fertile between the ages of 18 and 25. Because of subtle hormonal changes, reproductive function starts to diminish prior to age 35, when estrogen levels begin to fall, but not every 35-year-old or 40-year-old is the same.

There is also evidence that the eggs of older women are less likely to be fertilized and develop. In men, the progression is much slower and very gradual, with no substantial loss of sperm production even into their seventies.

Infertility takes a heavy emotional toll, says Sherry Molock, Ph.D., associate professor in the clinical psychology program at Howard University in Washington, D.C. "It is really important to realize that you are a couple and that infertility is not either person's fault," she says.

CULTIVATING
FERTILE GROUND

Many cases of infertility can be prevented with simple precautions and regular medical care. If having children is a goal for you, protect your fertility with these steps.

Limit your sexual partners. From a preventive perspective, eliminating exposure to STDs by limiting the number of sexual partners you have and using condoms is important, says Dr. Jones. "One of the saddest things I deal with is young women with chlamydia infections that have destroyed their fallopian tubes. You know those patients will come back in five years after trying unsuccessfully to conceive," he says.

Forgo cigarettes and alcohol. There is reasonably strong evidence that smoking has an adverse effect on fertility, and certainly more-than-moderate alcohol consumption (moderate consumption is no more than one drink a day for women and two a day for men) affects it, says Dr. Jones. Studies also show that smoking can affect sperm quality as well as ovarian function, so if your partner is a smoker, ask him to kick the habit.

Have annual pelvic exams. Regular gynecological exams are essential after you become sexually active because many diseases can be detected and dealt with early, before they threaten your fertility, says Dr. Jones.

Plan carefully. Try not to wait too long to become pregnant. Women who are older than 40 often have a more difficult time conceiving, says Dr. Jones.

TRYING
TO CONCEIVE

If you believe that you are having trouble getting pregnant, there are steps you can take to make sure you get the best care.

Keep tabs on your fertility. A woman is most fertile around the time of ovulation, which is usually the midpoint of her menstrual cycle, explains Dr. Lewis. The most efficient way to determine ovulation is to buy a urine-testing, or ovulation predictor, kit at the drugstore. It measures increases in luteinizing hormone, which increases just before an egg is released. You can also check your temperature for the slight increase just after ovulation, but this may not be as reliable as the urine test. "The temperature charts are only helpful in determining that ovulation has already occurred," says Dr. Lewis.

Insist on answers. After your doctor maps out a treatment plan, always ask these questions, suggests Dr. Lewis: How likely is it that the treatment will succeed? What are the short- and long-term side effects? What alternatives are there?

Get the right kind of help. The couple should see a reproductive endocrinologist, a specialist in infertility, advises Dr. Jones. "What's most important is that you don't wait until you are in your late thirties before seeking care. Seek care very early, within one year unless there is a known problem, and make sure your doctor at least performs a basic workup to investigate the four major factors of infertility before even thinking about putting you on fertility drugs," says Dr. Jones.

Understand the options. Disorders of ovulation are often treated by regulating ovulation with prescription drugs. But it takes considerable expertise to manage these drugs, which carry the risks of multiple gestation (producing many fetuses, not all of which may be carried safely to term).

Ovarian hyperstimulation syndrome, a condition in which the ovaries become enlarged and estrogen levels rise, is another dangerous risk of some fertility drugs. Some preliminary research also suggests that fertility drugs may slightly increase your risk of developing ovarian cancer. Make sure that you have a doctor and pharmacist who stay up to date on the latest research and who can help explain the side effects and administration of the drugs, says Dr. Jones.

If blocked fallopian tubes are causing the trouble, doctors can often surgically open the tubes and remove scarring. In some cases, like the Burtons', in vitro fertilization is another approach.

Don't forget your partner. There may be any number of causes for male infertility, Dr. Jones says. The best care for this problem is a team approach, with an infertility specialist and a urologist working together, because many of the things that result in low sperm production are caused by a obstruction of the ejaculatory system, he says.

Talk to each other. Keeping the lines of communication open is vital, adds Dr. Molock. Infertility can be so stressful that it puts a strain on your relationship. Women want to talk about their feelings and men want to do something, not talk, so there is often conflict. Consider seeking counseling, suggests Dr. Molock.

Accept help. The Burtons' story may sound like a miracle, but there is hope for infertile couples who want biological children. RE-SOLVE is a nationwide organization that provides infertility education, financial counseling, and emotional support. To get more information or to find a group in your area, write to RESOLVE, 1310 Broadway, Department GM, Somerville, MA 02144-1731.

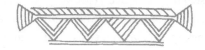

Inflammatory Bowel Disease

TAMING A TROUBLED TRACT

hicago native Diane Morgan, 23, will probably never forget her first business trip, but not because of its success. She tells of emerging from her hotel bathroom in a state of shock. "I had experienced diarrhea before, especially before a big presentation," says Diane, a stout, outspoken accountant with a flair for designer fashions. "But bloody diarrhea? I was scared out of my wits."

Diane rushed to her family physician, who sent her to a gastroenterologist after learning of her symptoms. The tests performed by the specialist revealed an illness that Diane had never heard of. "When the doctor said I had ulcerative colitis, the first thing I thought was, 'Mom was right. I do worry too much,'" she says with a chuckle. "Then I learned that this isn't an ulcer you get just from obsessing over stuff."

Diane's doctor treated her condition by giving her three months of steroid treatment and suggesting that she learn how to manage anxiety and stress a little better. That was several years ago, and the bloody diarrhea hasn't returned. "Which is great," Diane says, reaching for a photo of her grinning toddler. "It's wonderful to be able to focus on more enjoyable priorities, like being a good mom."

BELLIES UNDER FIRE

There are many conditions that cause inflammation of the bowel, but when doctors talk about inflammatory bowel disease (IBD) they are usually referring to ulcerative colitis or Crohn's disease. Both cause inflammation of the gastrointestinal tract, typically resulting in diarrhea, severe abdominal pain, fever, and loss of appetite. "Inflammatory bowel disease can be very mild or it can be life-threatening," explains Victor Scott, M.D., chief of gastroenterology at Howard University Hospital in Washington, D.C.

So what distinguishes one illness from the other?

Location, for one thing. Ulcerative colitis and Crohn's disease can resemble each other when only the colon and large intestine are involved. The difference is that Crohn's disease can involve any portion of the gastrointestinal tract, from the mouth to the anus. Ulcerative colitis, on the other hand, causes inflammation of just the colon or large intestine.

Then there's the issue of penetration. Ulcerative colitis affects only the lining of the colon or large intestine, causing ulcers and bleeding—just as a stomach ulcer does—which shows up as bloody diarrhea. That's what happened with Diane. Danger arises when the entire colon is involved: The bowel may become very dilated, or expanded, resulting in a condition called toxic megacolon. This is an emergency situation that can cause perforation or rupture of the bowel and lead to death if not treated appropriately, says Sadye B. Curry, M.D., gastroenterologist and associate professor of medicine at Howard University College of Medicine in Washington, D.C.

Crohn's disease, on the other hand, can affect the entire thickness of the intestinal wall, sometimes causing fistulas, or abnormal passages, that spill stool into the nearby organs such as the bladder or vagina or into the abdominal cavity, causing an infection called an abscess, which is marked by fever and abdominal pain.

IBD can be misdiagnosed, since a symptom as nonspecific as bloody diarrhea can be caused by anything from a bacterial infection to AIDS. Dr. Curry tells of a 10-year-old girl who came to the hospital with weight loss, fever, and anemia that had been diagnosed as anorexia nervosa, an eating disorder. "The child's mother fortunately refused to believe the doctor's diagnosis," says Dr. Curry. "Instead of keeping her daughter in psychiatric care, she asked us to give a second opinion." As it turned out, the child had Crohn's disease.

In Search of a Cause

There are lots of clues to the source of IBD, including the possibility of viruses and bacteria, but nobody knows for sure. "People may have a genetic predisposition," says gastroenterologist Joanne A.

Peebles Wilson, M.D., professor of medicine and associate chief of gastroenterology at Duke University Medical Center in Durham, North Carolina. For instance, if one family member has ulcerative colitis, there's a 10 to 15 percent chance that another family member will have it, too.

People are typically in their twenties when they show the first signs of IBD, although 200,000 of the estimated two million Americans with IBD are children. Females are two to five times more likely to be affected than males, and Whites are five times more likely to be affected than Blacks.

In fact, many years ago, some physicians believed that African-Americans didn't get Crohn's disease at all. "Crohn's was believed to be associated with a certain personality type—people who were smart and aggressive," explains Dr. Curry. "Folks saw us as shiftless and lazy. They probably thought we didn't fit the profile of a Crohn's patient, so they figured we didn't get the disease." Nowadays, most doctors know better.

KEEPING YOUR STOMACH CALM

Living with IBD can feel like riding a roller coaster blindfolded, because its course is unpredictable. Some people experience a single attack in their twenties, then go months or years without symptoms. Others are affected much more frequently, some almost constantly.

"These diseases are serious," says Dr. Curry, "but in most cases they can be controlled." Here's how.

Go easy on the fiber. For once, here's cautionary advice on dietary fiber. High-fiber foods don't cause IBD to flare up, but they can worsen diarrhea once an attack is under way. The inflammation of Crohn's disease can be so severe that the intestines become narrowed, or in severe cases obstructed or blocked. In such cases, the bulkiness of fiber can compound the problem. In the case of ulcerative colitis, fiber can worsen the diarrhea associated with it. "If a patient is having an attack, restricting fruits and vegetables and whole grains may help ease the symptoms," says Dr. Curry.

Ditch the diary products. Lactose intolerance, the body's inability to break down lactose, or milk sugar, is common among African-Americans, says Dr. Curry. It causes digestive problems and can aggravate IBD. Limiting dairy products or using an enzyme supplement containing the protein lactase (Lactaid) will help you digest lactose.

Scale down stress. Major stresses—like losing a loved one or being fired from your job—and sometimes even day-to-day aggravations can precipitate an IBD flare-up.

"One of my patients had attacks of ulcerative colitis each Christmas season because he found it was stressful to be with his family," recalls Dr. Scott. Stress-relievers like meditation, regular exercise, and vacations can help, says Dr. Curry. So can joining a local IBD support group. Contact the Crohn's and Colitis Foundation of America at 1-800-932-2423 for information on support groups and doctors in your area.

Take advantage of medication. Prescription medicines that reduce swollen tissues can help reduce the inflammation associated with IBD. "We use steroids as a first line of therapy to reduce the swelling of moderate or severe cases," says Dr. Curry. "Then we use aspirin-like prescription drugs for mild to moderate inflammation and to maintain remission of the disease."

Ask about surgery. If medications can't control the pain and other symptoms, surgery can be an option, but only in some cases.

"Surgery is much better suited for ulcerative colitis," says Dr. Scott. For one thing, the disease is confined to the colon, which you can lose and continue to live a healthy, normal life. "In addition, once a surgeon removes any inflamed colon, the disease is gone forever. This is not the case with Crohn's disease, which tends to recur later in formerly healthy tissue. Half of all Crohn's patients who have surgery experience a return of symptoms within five years," says Dr. Scott. An extended period of a disease-free, medication-free life may be psychologically beneficial, however.

Be your own advocate. "Occasionally when I ask a Black patient about surgery they've obviously had, by virtue of the abdominal scar I see during an unrelated examination, I'm amazed at the number of patients who don't know what the doctor did," says Dr. Curry. Take responsibility for your own care, she advises. "Read, read, read, and ask questions," she says. The more you know, the more you can ask pertinent questions and get the first-rate treatment you deserve.

Inhibited Sexual Desire

TURNING UP THE HEAT

ev Carson heard the front door open and thought, "Oh, no, he's home." She checked the clock and caught sight of her reflection in the dresser mirror. She was sprawled across the bed in her favorite old flannel nightgown, with raggedy slippers on her feet and rollers and a scarf on her head—and Troy was coming through the door.

"I was worn out," Bev says. "I had been working overtime to try to keep from being next on the corporate hit list of lawyers being laid off, so I didn't move as Troy came in. I closed my eyes and pretended to be asleep."

But Troy knew better. And even in that granny getup, Bev still looked good to him. He sat down next to her, planted a kiss on her forehead, and wrapped his arms around her. When she pulled away, Troy nuzzled her neck and murmured to her, "Come on, sweetheart," as he rolled onto the bed next to her.

"I pushed him away and said, 'I'm not playing games, Troy! I'm tired and I've got a lot of things on my mind,'" Bev continues, looking a little sheepish. "I looked at Troy as his face twisted with anger. Then he shouted at me, 'Yeah, I know, I know—everything but me!' He jumped off the bed and slammed out of the room. A few minutes later, I heard his car leave, and although I was sorry that we had argued, a part of me was relieved that I wouldn't have to worry about having sex." Then, figuring that she probably wouldn't sleep anyway, Bev decided that she might as well work on some of those new tax files, so she reached for her glasses on the night table.

That argument was just a repeat performance of one that the couple had been having for weeks—he was hurt, she was angry, and nobody was getting anywhere.

TIRED
AND TURNED OFF

Troy and Bev's ongoing battle is not unusual. Their problem is played out night after night in bedrooms all over America. But it doesn't have to be that way.

Bev loves her husband, and Troy has no desire to leave his wife, but inhibited sexual desire, or ISD, can wreak havoc on a marriage if it is not carefully understood and addressed. ISD is more than just the occasional desire to pass up sex for a favorite TV show or a good book. It's the sort of indifference to lovemaking that makes some men and women go for six months to a year or longer without wanting to have sex, masturbate, or even fantasize about sex.

"Most causes of ISD are psychological, not physical," says Marlene F. Watson, Ph.D., a couple and family therapist in private practice in Philadelphia. Physical problems can be at the root of ISD, however, especially if a man is experiencing erectile dysfunction or someone is struggling with a chronic disease. A simple discussion with your doctor can help determine whether you are dealing with physical or psychological concerns.

The emotional issues are tougher to tackle. As with all men and women, ISD in African-Americans sometimes has to do with stress, overwork, or unresolved conflict in a relationship. "But many of the African-American women in their thirties and forties that I see in my practice lose their sexual desire as a result of disappointment in a relationship—if there has been infidelity, for example," says Dr. Watson.

ISD is not rare; it's the most common issue for couples who seek help from sex therapists. And while some couples go on for years not discussing the problem or pretending that it's not an issue, it can harm a relationship. A lack of sexual intimacy can strain a marriage for several reasons, says Dr. Watson. First, it is frequently not a mutual condition: One partner may no longer want sex, like Bev, while the other partner feels angry, frustrated, and rejected, like Troy. When that happens, spouses may be more likely to argue and consider infidelity or even divorce. The other issue is that sex helps a couple achieve and maintain intimacy. Avoiding sex may just become a way of avoiding being close and connected, says Dr. Watson.

How It Begins

The common pattern is one in which one partner, like Bev, gets involved in other activities that keep him or her chronically busy, unavailable, or tired. Another scenario is the one in which the man is overly controlling and the woman subtly rebels by losing her sexual desire, explains Dr. Watson.

"If you permit someone to stifle and control you, you lose your power in a relationship. After this happens, many women feel that sex is the one place that they still have power," says D. Kim Singleton, Ph.D., a clinical psychologist in private practice in Washington, D.C.

Depression also interferes with the ability to enjoy the good things in life, such as laughter, food, friendship—and sex. "One way in which depression often manifests itself is through ISD," says Dr. Watson. But Black men and women sometimes don't acknowledge the extent of the depression they may be feeling, so they are unlikely to make this connection and seek treatment.

As many parents know, children have a way of changing a couple's sex life as well. When women become mothers, the physical recovery from childbirth and the demands of caring for a newborn can lead to fatigue and disinterest, but interest in sex typically returns after two to three months, says Dr. Watson. If it doesn't, seek help.

"Men can have ISD just as women do, but women talk about it a bit more," says Dr. Watson. "Men tend to hide, make excuses, or avoid the issue by indulging in compulsive behaviors such as workaholism."

As difficult as it can be to build and maintain a happy, fulfilling relationship, "ISD is not inevitable," says Dr. Watson.

Keeping the Love Lines Open

ISD is easier to prevent than it is to cure, so here are a few tips for keeping the bedroom blahs at bay.

Talk to each other. Marital conflicts that are unresolved in the living room will resurface in the bedroom, so it's important to communicate, says Dr. Singleton. One useful technique for positive communication is to talk about your feelings rather than your partner's disappointing actions. If you say "I feel abandoned when you forget our plans to visit my family" or "I feel hurt when you flirt with other women," for example, you will create fewer defensive reactions from your partner than if you say, "You're always ducking my family" or "You're always drooling at other women," says Dr. Singleton.

Spice it up. Try something new in the bedroom, says Dr. Singleton. You don't have to swing from the chandelier, but pick a new position or test drive a little unusual foreplay to keep things interesting.

BRINGING BACK
THE PASSION

If you suspect that ISD has taken over your sex life anyway, you can still warm things up again.

Go to a pro. It may be a little difficult to get yourself to do it, but it's well worth the trip. Talking to a marriage counselor or sex therapist who specializes in ISD is really the most important step toward getting things back on track. "Because of the complexity of the problem, I recommend that couples who face ISD seek treatment," advises Dr. Watson.

"But don't choose just any sex therapist. Choose someone who understands relationship dynamics," she says. Look in your local telephone directory under Marriage and Family Therapists for a therapist who is certified by the American Association for Marriage and Family Therapy (AAMFT). The longer ISD continues, the worse it gets, so seek help.

In conjunction with help from a professional, try these self-help suggestions for a sexual reawakening, suggests Dr. Watson.

Make time to make love. First, find time in your life for sex. Stop obsessing about the car payments, your next promotion, or the 10 pounds you gained—relax, get loose, and let yourself think about sex and sensuality. Indulge in sexual thoughts and fantasies and pay attention to sexual urges when you feel aroused.

Seek some carnal knowledge. There are lots of books written just for couples who want to keep the heat in their relationship. Pick up some self-help books on the subject and read them together. Dr. Watson recommends *For Each Other*, by Lonnie Barbach. Or you might try reading a little erotica together; look for *The Hand I Fan With* by Tina M. Ansa, she says.

Rate it *X*. If you are both comfortable with the idea, you might watch an erotic film or two. Visual cues often help jog the sensual memory.

Warm up with massage. Set aside time to give each other a massage. As you massage, focus on your feelings when you give and when you receive. This will facilitate sexual communication between you and your partner and get you thinking about yourselves romantically again.

Check your medication. Health problems can sometimes cause trouble in the bedroom. Since African-Americans have high rates of high blood pressure, you should know that blood pressure medication can lower your sex drive. The popular antidepressant fluoxetine hydrochloride (Prozac) can also turn people off sexually, and diabetes may also cause erectile dysfunction in men.

If you are taking medications, especially blood pressure medications, and you notice a difference in your sex drive, be sure to talk to your doctor, because your medications can be changed or adjusted, says Dr. Watson. But never stop taking medications without your doctor's approval.

Shape up. Research shows that people who get regular aerobic exercise have healthier sex drives, so if you find yourself disinterested in sex and you're not getting any exercise, get up and get moving.

Handle things with care. Try to have compassion for your partner, even if you feel rejected or you think he or she is unreasonably angry. Be especially careful about slinging hurtful words and accusations at a time in your relationship when nerves are already raw. Try to be patient and work things out with an open heart and mind.

Insomnia

Getting a Good Night's Sleep

nsomnia? It just runs in my family," Malcolm Jefferson used to tell himself. That's when it almost ran him over. After one particularly restless night, Malcolm was driving his two toddlers down a Milwaukee freeway on the way to day care when he nearly plowed into a school bus. "I was so tired that I fell dead asleep going 45 miles an hour," remembers the dapper, 35-year-old pediatrician, who sports a Kente bow tie with his white coat. "I was so shaken up that I went home to my wife and said, 'You've got help me.'"

Malcolm's wife helped by encouraging him to inventory the issues that were making sleep so elusive. She had to use three sheets of paper, he recalls. "It was a huge list, everything from too much coffee to worrying about my patients to getting to bed at a different time every night." Once it was all written down, Malcolm started modifying the problems he could control. Just two nights later, he was like a bear in hibernation. "The only problem we have now is my snoring," Malcolm admits sheepishly. "My wife says she created a monster."

In Search of Sleep

Insomnia—persistent difficulty in falling asleep or staying asleep—is extremely common, affecting some 20 percent of the population. One reason that it is so widespread is that literally dozens of things can cause it.

Do you have a physical symptom or complaint? In some cases, insomnia can result from an underlying health problem such as heart disease, depression, emphysema, or the chronic pain of arthritis or backache.

Are you wrestling with an emotional disorder? "Fully half of all cases of insomnia are caused by some sort of psychiatric disturbance," says James P. Lewis, M.D., of the Department of Family and Community Medicine at St. Paul-Ramsey Medical Center in St. Paul, Minnesota. Both depression and anxiety disorders can disrupt a good night's sleep. So can a condition called psychophysiologic insomnia, where you become conditioned to be aroused, rather than sleepy, in your bedroom. "People with this form of insomnia typically think of their problems when they go to bed, so they associate their bedrooms with frustration and anxiety," explains Dr. Lewis. "Often they can sleep in a hotel or on a plane, just not in their beds."

Are you on medication? Bronchodilators, prescription amphetamines, diuretics, thyroid hormone, and even over-the-counter or prescription sedatives can cause drug-induced insomnia. "Medicines that help you fall asleep do so at the expense of REM sleep, the period of deep sleep that helps you feel rested in the morning," says Mark Yerby, M.D., associate clinical professor of neurology and public health at Oregon Health Sciences University in Portland. "That's why long-term use of sleeping medicine isn't a good idea."

Along the same lines, nicotine—and of course, caffeine—can keep you walking the floors at night. And did you know that alcohol is bad news, too? "Alcohol may help you fall asleep, but it causes a rebound effect that excites your brain, so it's harder to stay asleep," explains Dr. Yerby.

If your job forces you to work shifts that change periodically, you already know how difficult it can be to adjust to new sleep patterns. In fact, some say that the rhythm of modern life itself—especially late-night studying, partying, or television-watching—is enough to leave us staring at the ceiling at 3:00 A.M. (a condition called night-owl insomnia, by the way).

"Our ancestors went to bed early and got up early. That's consistent with what we know about melatonin, a brain chemical and sedative that's produced in larger amounts at night," explains William Emikola Richardson, M.D., medical director and president of the Atlanta Clinic of Preventive Medicine. "If you don't stick to this rhythm, you can get less and less sleep at night, causing fatigue during the day."

SUCCESSFUL, DRUG-FREE SNOOZING

Insomnia poses a special challenge for African-Americans. "We're sometimes dealing with racism, the need to work multiple jobs, all sorts of stresses," says Dr. Richardson. "We have to be experts at sleep enhancement." Fortunately, it's easy to rise to the occasion. Check with your doctor if you're concerned about any of the issues mentioned above. Then try these suggestions.

Skip the brainwork. Late-night phone conversations, television-watching, and even reading can be too brain-stimulating for a restful night's sleep. Try something a little more relaxing, such as meditation, prayer, yoga, or stretching, suggests Dr. Richardson. Deep breathing is a terrific relaxer, he says. Inhale for four counts through your nose, hold for two counts, then exhale through your nose or mouth. "Try it for a few minutes before bedtime," he suggests.

Practice good "sleep hygiene." Try establishing habits that help you sleep, like keeping a regular bedtime, avoiding naps, and relaxing with a nonstressful activity 30 to 60 minutes before you go to bed.

"It's also important to reserve your bedroom for sleep and sex," says Dr. Lewis. "No reading, no TV, and especially no paying bills." Go to bed when you're ready to sleep, he suggests. "If you can't get to sleep after 30 minutes, get up and do something else until you're sleepy."

Sip yourself to sleep. A cup of herbal tea can help you put the day's worries safely behind you. "Valerian root, hops, skullcap, and passionflower are nonaddictive and have no known side effects," says Dr. Richardson. They are all available at natural food stores.

Cut out caffeine. Caffeine can really sneak up on you. It is found in chocolate and sodas as well as coffee, and many people become more sensitive to its jittery stimulation as they grow older. "Some are so sensitive that the tiny amount of caffeine in decaffeinated coffee is too much," says Dr. Richardson. If you are overdoing it, cut back slowly to avoid the headache pain that can come from abrupt withdrawal. If you drink four cups a day, try three cups a day for a week, then two, and so on until you're off completely, he recommends.

Get moving. "Regular exercise can help restore your energy during the day and help you sleep better at night," reminds Dr. Yerby. But don't work out too close to bedtime, as the adrenaline rush can keep you up. Try to do your activities before 6:00 P.M.

Irritable Bowel Syndrome

CALMING YOUR COLON

he knew she had a killer schedule, but Deborah Woods was confident that she could handle it. What she didn't know was that her colon couldn't.

Deborah was living life at 100 miles an hour as an overworked medical resident in Washington, D.C., when she began to feel abdominal pains. Three weeks later, when she consulted Victor Scott, M.D., chief of gastroenterology at Howard University Hospital in Washington, Deborah was in severe pain and experiencing alternating bouts of diarrhea and constipation. "When I asked about her lifestyle, everything was rushed," says Dr. Scott. "She skipped breakfast, she ate poorly when she did eat, she worked hard, and she put in terribly long hours."

After Dr. Scott excluded other potential causes, Deborah's busy lifestyle combined with her stomach problems led him to diagnose irritable bowel syndrome. A gradual switch to high-fiber foods, some downtime to relax each day, and plenty of fluids have thus far kept her colon functioning properly. "She's fine now," says Dr. Scott. Now if she could only do something about that schedule.

EMOTIONAL OVERLOAD

Five out of every 10 people who see a doctor for abdominal complaints will be diagnosed with irritable bowel syndrome (IBS), a condition that afflicts at least 10 to 15 percent of all American adults. According to Wayne B. Tuckson, M.D., assistant professor of surgery at the University of Louisville in Kentucky, IBS can affect anyone. "IBS is probably no more prevalent in African-Americans than it is in Whites," says Dr. Tuckson. "Anyone who leads a stressful lifestyle and has poor dietary habits is at risk."

Unfortunately, since symptoms are often varied and nonspecific, spotting the cause can be difficult. A diagnosis of IBS is usually made only after other possibilities have been ruled out. "With IBS, there's nothing structurally wrong with the bowel," explains Dr. Scott. "It just doesn't function properly."

A specific cause isn't clear, but IBS does seem to be related to overly sensitive nerves in the intestines. In a normal digestive system, muscles periodically contract to rhythmically push semidigested food through the small intestine and colon. With IBS (also called spastic colon), the nerves that control those muscles are unusually sensitive to stimuli like stress, anxiety, hormones, and certain foods or food ingredients. When the nerves are overstimulated, they can turn smooth intestinal contractions into uncoordinated spasms.

The results are chronic diarrhea or constipation or both, sometimes alternating from day to day. "Constipation is especially common among IBS patients who eat diets that are low in fiber," says Dr. Tuckson. "With the reduced bulk, the colon only compacts the stool without moving it downstream."

What else does IBS cause? None of it is pleasant: abdominal gurgling and rumbling, bloating and gas, mucus mixed with stool, and the feeling that your rectum is never completely empty. IBS can be troubling enough to make you feel pretty nervous about straying too far from a lavatory.

The fact that a definite cause is unknown and that those affected tend to be anxious might encourage some doctors to erroneously tell IBS sufferers that it's all in their heads. But, says Dr. Tuckson, "IBS is for real and should be considered a psychosomatic illness." While this diagnosis implies that the bodily symptoms reflect a psychological state, "the discomfort is very real," says Dr. Tuckson.

While we don't know what actually causes IBS, we do know what triggers episodes once IBS is present: stressful, anxiety-provoking life events, either large, such as divorce or the loss of a loved one, or small, such as a confrontation with the landlord or anxiety over grades. That helps explain why young adults are at high risk. "Many older adults have learned more successful ways of managing stress," says Dr. Tuckson.

Certain foods are bad news for some people with IBS. Dairy products often spell digestive trouble for African-Americans due to our higher incidence of lactose intolerance. Other culprits may include caffeine, alcohol, the artificial sweetener sorbitol, beans, spicy or fatty foods, corn, wheat, monosodium glutamate (MSG), and occasionally high-fiber items such as bran or bulking laxatives containing psyllium (such as Metamucil), says Dr. Tuckson.

If psyllium is a problem, he says, try Citrucel. It contains methylcellulose, which behaves differently in the gut and won't cause gas as psyllium can. You can also use an enzyme product like Beano if beans, grains, or other high-fiber foods cause you distress. "You can add a few drops to every meal, if you need to," says Dr. Tuckson.

RELIEVING STOMACH STRESS

Life often isn't easy for people with IBS, but here are some ways to smooth things out.

Learn to relax. Lots of folks with IBS just don't know how to relax, plain and simple. "Rest, recreation, and exercise are all good bets," suggests Dr. Scott. "A warm cup of soothing herbal tea works wonders," adds Dr. Tuckson, who has IBS.

Not sure what tensions trigger your IBS attacks? "Try keeping a journal to help you understand connections between your IBS symptoms and the stressful situations that may cause them," says Dr. Scott. Then begin to use stress relievers like taking brisk walks or practicing deep breathing on a regular basis, he suggests.

Mind your menu. Eat thoughtfully, not haphazardly, says Dr. Scott. "Many of my IBS patients have very little for breakfast, eat a big meal at the end of the day, and then go right to bed," he says. "In addition, there's usually not enough fiber or fluid in their diets."

A regular, high-fiber diet will do a lot to help maintain normal bowel function, agrees Dr. Tuckson. Try for five servings of fruits or vegetables each day for a total of 35 grams of fiber, he recommends. "Substitute one food for another to build up your fiber intake. Have raisin bran instead of sausage and eggs, for instance, and a sandwich on whole-wheat bread instead of white," says Dr. Tuckson.

Keep a food diary. If you've got IBS, practically any food or food ingredient can come back to haunt you. It's not always easy to make the connection between eating a specific food and suffering the consequences later. Keeping a record of the things you consumed before an IBS flare-up will help you make sense of it all, suggests Dr. Scott.

Watch your cycle. The workings of the gastrointestinal tract respond to the hormonal ebb and flow of the menstrual cycle, which can affect IBS. Women can help their doctors get an accurate diagnosis by noting where they are in their cycle when they experience IBS episodes, suggests Dr. Tuckson.

Call in reinforcements. See a doctor to have your symptoms diagnosed, and don't be shy. A detailed history and meticulous physical exam are important, because some IBS symptoms can resemble those of colon cancer, inflammatory bowel disease (ulcerative colitis and Crohn's disease), or other illnesses. "If someone has an abrupt change in bowel habits, blood in their stool, weight loss, or fever, we must exclude other conditions before treating the symptoms as IBS," says Dr. Tuckson.

Experts generally advise using as few medications as possible for IBS. In certain cases, however, your doctor may recommend prescription drugs. Antispasmodics such as dicyclomine hydrochloride (Bentyl) or hyoscyamine sulfate (Levsin) can ease painful cramping. To relieve diarrhea that's not accompanied by cramping, ask your doctor about diphenoxylate hydrochloride (Lomotil). Constipation that isn't relieved by over-the-counter bulking agents such as Citrucel may be helped by the prescription drug metaclopromide (Reglan).

Keloids

KEEPING YOUR SKIN SCAR-FREE

anessa Brown's trip to Bermuda was everything she'd imagined it would be—and unfortunately, a little bit more.

"While taking in the scenery on a moped," she recalls, "I went into a skid and fell hard onto a gravel-topped driveway. I got a nasty gash on my shoulder, and when it healed, I had a dark, raised scar," recalls the 28-year-old advertising agency executive.

"As soon as I got home," she says, "I began searching the local Yellow Pages for a dermatologist who could get rid of the scar—and tell me how to avoid getting them in the future."

A PARTICULAR PROBLEM
FOR OUR SKIN

Like many African-Americans, Vanessa has skin that is particularly prone to keloids, which are smooth, thick, elevated scars that develop after the skin is traumatized by a cut, burn, or other injury. In some cases, even vaccinations or insect bites can cause a keloid scar. The unsightly and sometimes painful protrusions can appear almost anywhere on the body and are frequently seen on the shoulders and chest. They can also form on the arms (after a fraternity "branding," for instance) or on the lower abdomen (following a cesarean section). "One of my burn patients developed keloids on her head, breasts, arms, trunk, and the soles of her feet," recalls James E. C. Norris, M.D., a New York plastic surgeon formerly with the Harlem Hospital Burn Center.

Doctors have yet to discover why Blacks, as well as other people with dark complexions, are so prone to this dermatological nuisance. But they do know several ways to smooth the scars once they form— or better yet, to keep them from forming in the first place.

SAVING
YOUR SKIN

Keloids tend to run in families. If you're aware that you may be prone to keloids, it's best to try to prevent any trauma to the skin that can develop into a scar. Of course, as Vanessa found out, accidents do happen. But in many cases, keloids can be prevented by taking precautions as simple as wearing protective gear while in-line skating, for instance, or not having your ears pierced. If you do get a cut or scrape, don't interfere with the healing process, says Dr. Norris. Protect it and let it heal naturally. If you are prone to keloids, Dr. Norris advises seeing a doctor if you have an injury.

Here are Dr. Norris's additional tips for protecting your skin.

Make it the real thing. "Avoid costume jewelry—especially earrings—if you are keloid-prone." Allergic reactions to nickel alloy or other alloys can cause inflammation and sores and eventually lead to keloids. "I treated one young lady whose pierced ears gave her no trouble for years until her boyfriend gave her some imitation gold earrings. The resulting irritation left her with keloids," recalls Dr. Norris, who recommends that his patients wear 14- or 18-karat gold jewelry.

Shelve the Schick. "Avoid the razor. Black men's tightly curled hair is prone to razor bumps. If the bump develops into a keloid, it can be very hard to treat," says Dr. Norris. Men prone to razor bumps or keloids should consider removing hair with a depilatory cream or telling the barber to use clippers—not a razor—to give them a skin-friendly shave.

Increase the peace. "So many of our youth are involved in violence. As a result, a lot of the younger keloid patients I see have been injured in fights or attacks," explains Dr. Norris.

Share your family history. If you're planning to have surgery and you know keloids run in your family, tell your surgeon. The doctor can help prevent keloids from forming by injecting an anti-inflammatory steroid medicine at the incision site during or following your operation.

TREATING
KELOID SCARS

Developing a keloid doesn't mean that you have to be scarred for life. The first and most important step is to find a doctor who knows the score. Treating keloids is tricky and takes time. "No two patients respond exactly the same way to keloid treatment," says Dr. Norris. "In fact, sometimes two keloids on the same person respond differently, depending on their location." So find a dermatologist or plastic surgeon who seems knowledgeable and committed to finding the right solution for you. "It's okay to ask the doctor, 'How comfortable do you feel treating this?'" advises Dr. Norris. "In my experience, most doctors who feel uneasy will opt out and refer a patient to someone with more expertise in treating keloids.

"Keloids are often easier to treat with medication while they're still evolving. It is possible to treat older or more elevated keloids with medication, but some may require surgery," says Dr. Norris. There is no standard treatment for keloids, so approaches vary from doctor to doctor. In Vanessa's case, her dermatologist prescribed a special adhesive tape impregnated with a steroid medication. After showering, Vanessa applies the bandage to the affected area at home. She visits her doctor regularly to monitor the treatment's progress and to check for any adverse reactions to the drug or the tape.

If keloids develop on your earlobes after you've had your ears pierced, your doctor might give you disks resembling earrings that have springs inside to compress the affected area, reducing keloid formation. "This pressure device is particularly effective immediately after surgery or if the keloid is in the early stage of development," says Dr. Norris.

If your keloid is elevated but fairly small, a steroid injection from your physician can help flatten it. Wearing a special patchlike tape impregnated with steroids, as Vanessa does, can shrink the scar tissue further. X-ray treatment also seems to retard the growth of the cells that produce keloid tissue, although the radiation risk makes this a poor choice for children. Doctors can remove large keloids surgically with a scalpel or laser, then follow the surgery with a steroid injection.

When administering a steroid injection, a skilled doctor will be careful to isolate the keloided area and avoid injecting the drug into normal tissue. This will prevent the normal tissue from becoming thin, weak, or streaked in appearance. Be sure to have the site monitored carefully during follow-up exams.

Kidney Ailments

FILTERING OUT DISEASE

ouis Jefferson, a hard-working, good-natured security guard was being treated for a minor ailment at a walk-in health center near his Boston home when his blood test results came back abnormal. Three months later, Louis was on dialysis. At age 38, he had irreversible kidney failure.

"I had been warned about my high blood pressure 10 years before," says Louis, "but I didn't take it seriously because I was feeling okay."

Louis contacted his siblings to warn them that they, too, might be at risk. "Each of my brothers had healthy kidneys except one—my younger brother, whose blood test showed an abnormality similar to mine," says Louis. But for him, the outcome was far more favorable. "The doctors caught it early. He should be fine," says Louis. "Kidney failure was devastating for me. But some good came out of the situation—I saved my baby brother."

YOUR BODY'S PURIFICATION SYSTEM

As daily concerns go, kidneys don't exactly rank high on the list. Yet healthy kidneys can mean the difference between a shattering illness and a long and vigorous life.

Kidneys are miniature filtration factories: Their job is to filter wastes from your blood. With over one million tiny filtering units, these two bean-shaped organs purify all the blood in the human body. Red blood cells are too large to penetrate these filters, so they're returned to circulation, but the liquid waste products squeeze through. As the waste passes through long tubes called nephrons, many of the useful substances such as glucose, water, salts, and amino acids are reabsorbed into the body. The concentrated liquid that is left—now called urine—flows to the bladder for excretion.

Your body's entire blood supply circulates through the kidneys about twice every 5 minutes, 24 hours a day. The system runs like clockwork, at least until something like high blood pressure comes along. High blood pressure is a principal reason that a disproportionate number of African-Americans suffer from end-stage renal disease, a shutdown of the kidneys that requires kidney transplantation or dialysis. While African-Americans make up only 12 percent of the U.S. population, we account for 32 percent of people with this disease.

Why is high blood pressure so devastating to the kidneys? One reason is that it can speed up the process of atherosclerosis, the thickening and hardening of the arteries that feed the kidneys their oxygen-rich blood supply. The thicker the arteries get, the less blood flows through. Eventually you have oxygen-deprived kidneys, which develop scar tissue, begin to shrink, and lose their ability to function.

But high blood pressure isn't the only thing that can wear out the kidneys. Being overweight, smoking cigarettes, and drinking too much alcohol all can hurt. Diabetes or a diet too rich in fatty foods can eventually clog kidney blood vessels as well. Lupus, a disease that is common in African-American women, can also cause kidney damage.

Bacterial infections, among them kidney infections, may also lead to progressive kidney damage. This is particularly important for African-Americans, many of whom may have sickle cell disease. Kidney infections are a major cause of death for people with this disease. The sickle cells clog the small arteries in the kidneys, eventually leading to damage to the kidney filters that allows vital blood proteins to leak into the urine.

However you get there, kidney failure is a devastating health crisis. You lose your appetite, become nauseated, and feel weak and fatigued. It's also difficult to concentrate. "Many patients tell me they can't read a newspaper," says Clinton D. Brown, M.D., director of the ambulatory dialysis unit and the hypolipidemia clinic and assistant professor of medicine at the State University of New York Health Science Center in Brooklyn. "That's because chemicals toxic to the nervous system have built up in their blood, and the impaired kidneys can't flush them out." Without prompt medical intervention, kidney failure can quickly become fatal.

Kidney failure is deadly serious, but it's just one of many things that can go wrong with your kidneys. You can also develop stones and tumors. With one exception—polycystic kidney disease, in which fluid-filled pouches develop in the kidneys—African-Americans are more prone than Whites to all major kidney disorders. Our high rates of high blood pressure and other kidney-wounding diseases is a major reason, but not the only one.

"There's also some evidence that our kidneys have a different anatomical structure than those of Whites," says Henry T. Smith, M.D., chief of the Division of Internal Medicine at Hennepin Faculty Associates and director of the Hypertension Clinic at Hennepin County Medical Center in Minneapolis. "Our renal (kidney) arteries are smaller, for example, in patients with high blood pressure." And, as with so many diseases, "we often come for medical care late, when the disease is already advanced," explains Keith Norris, M.D., vice-chairman of the Department of Medicine at Charles R. Drew University of Medicine and Science, King-Drew Medical Center in Los Angeles.

The bottom line? If treating your kidneys with kid gloves isn't on your to-do list, maybe it should be.

KIDNEY CARE

Kidney disease gives few warning signs. There is no pain in the early stages. In fact, many people with kidney disease often have no decline in urine output, or the decline is so slight that they do not notice it. The kidneys frequently continue to make urine, although they are unable to excrete the waste products from the body. "Often it is not until you lose 75 or even 90 percent of your kidney function that your kidneys stop producing as much urine as they should. Thus, in many ways, kidney failure is similar to high blood pressure in that they are both often 'silent' until the disease has progressed pretty far," says Dr. Norris.

That's why preventing kidney disease should start early. In addition to keeping high blood pressure and diabetes under control, here's what the experts advise.

Know your folks. If you know your family tree, you'll be tipped off to illnesses that could place you at high risk for kidney disease.

"Look for a family history of three things: high blood pressure, diabetes, or kidney disease," advises Dr. Norris.

Get tested. There are no standard guidelines for how often you should be screened for kidney disease, although the National Kidney Foundation recommends that it be done at your regular yearly checkup. "Everyone should have a urinalysis (which is the same as a 'dip-stick' urine test) as part of a routine doctor's checkup," advises Dr. Norris. If you're at high risk, he says that you should have your doctor do two additional tests: a blood test to measure serum creatinine, a blood chemical that is elevated in kidney disease, and a microscopic examination of the urine.

If the results of one or more of these tests are abnormal, then depending on what the abnormality is, you may need to be followed more closely or you may need a more detailed evaluation, including a timed urine test, in which your urine is collected for 24 hours. Your doctor may refer you to a kidney specialist for a more detailed discussion of the test results and their implications, says Dr. Norris.

Watch those painkillers. Over-the-counter nonsteroidal anti-inflammatory drugs like ibuprofen (Advil, Nuprin) and naproxen (Aleve), if taken several times a day for several years, can cause kidney damage even in people who have healthy kidney function to begin with. "Up to 10 percent of all kidney damage is caused by these medicines," Dr. Norris says. "If you have a family history of kidney problems, avoid these drugs. Even if you don't have a family history, take the warning label seriously and use them in moderation."

Ask about anemia. People with failing kidneys often develop anemia. That's because healthy kidneys produce a hormone called erythropoietin, which stimulates bone marrow to produce red blood cells. As erythropoietin levels decline, the risk of anemia increases, and with it such uncomfortable symptoms as water retention, fatigue, and shortness of breath.

Dr. Brown's preliminary research with small numbers of kidney failure patients suggests that erythropoietin supplementation, as prescribed by a doctor, may benefit people in the early stages of kidney disease. "Patients feel so much better, and it may delay having to go on dialysis," he says.

Be proactive about transplants. One-third of all kidney failure patients who are on waiting lists for transplants are African-

Americans. And the demand for donated kidneys far exceeds the supply.

Everyone who has kidney failure is entitled to an evaluation for a kidney transplant, yet African-Americans tend to receive transplants less often than Whites. "This is frequently because we are not as close a match to the transplant as the White patient, and it is primarily White patients who donate organs," says Dr. Norris. "If more Blacks were to donate transplants, then hopefully we would have more close matches." It is important that African-Americans know that transplants are available. It is even more important for African-Americans with healthy kidneys to consider being organ donors, says Dr. Brown.

Pay attention to pain. Kidney disease is usually painless. But if you experience severe pain in your lower back, along with with fever, chills, and possibly nausea and vomiting, you could be fighting a kidney infection or a bladder infection, which can occur when the bacteria that lead to kidney infection get trapped in the urethra. "Bed rest, doctor-prescribed antibiotics, over-the-counter pain relievers, and plenty of fluids—at least 2 quarts a day—will usually get rid of an infection; sometimes, however, hospitalization may be necessary," says Dr. Smith.

If you're a woman, you can help prevent kidney infections by wiping from front to back after a bowel movement to keep fecal bacteria from invading the urethra, suggests Dr. Smith. Other preventive measures include urinating after intercourse, drinking eight glasses of water per day, and wearing underwear with a cotton crotch. If you're a man over age 50, you should have an annual prostate exam, which will detect prostate enlargement. An enlarged prostate promotes bladder and kidney infections by preventing the bladder from fully emptying, says Dr. Smith.

Lactose Intolerance

MAKING FRIENDS WITH MILK

ngela Martin just loves food. "I guess that's why I became a registered dietitian—at least that way I'm duty-bound to keep things healthy. Otherwise, I'd be as big as a house," she says. "But these days, I just can't eat everything."

Angela discovered her new culinary limitations in New Orleans, of all places, when she traveled to a convention with a group of other Black dietitians. Although she was at a business conference, she had a great time sampling the incredible food that the city is known for. When the last day of the conference came, she happily tried dishes at the Healthy Foods Fair. "After two days of crawfish and gumbo, I figured it was time to get back on track," Angela explains with a smile.

She went from booth to booth, tasting low-fat, high-nutrient versions of everything from soup to nuts, and it seemed that almost every other booth had its own healthful variation on ice cream or frozen yogurt. She lost count of how many she'd tried. "Then I got a cramp. Shortly after, the gas and bloating arrived. A few hours later, I had diarrhea. At first I thought it was just the spicy food, but after a day or two, I was still having trouble with dairy products." At the age of 40, after years of eating dairy products, Angela had developed lactose intolerance.

THE DAIRY BLUES

Roughly 50 million Americans have lactose intolerance. And African-Americans are more likely to develop it than Whites, explains Bettye Nowlin, R.D., a spokesperson for the American Dietetic Association. Three-quarters of African-Americans are lactose-intolerant, as are more than 80 percent of Asians, 79 percent of Native Americans, and 51 percent of Hispanics—but only 21 percent of Whites.

"Lactose intolerance is the inability or decreased ability to digest lactose, or milk sugar, which is found not only in milk, cheese, butter, margarine, ice cream, and other dairy products but also in goodies such as cakes, cream soups, and sauces," says Barbara Dixon, R.D., a dietitian in Baton Rouge, Louisiana, and author of *Good Health for African-American Kids*.

Lactose intolerance occurs when there is a deficiency of a specific enzyme, called lactase, in your small intestine. When you have an adequate amount of lactase, it gets busy breaking down lactose in the intestine into a form that your body is able to digest and use. If your body does not produce enough lactase, you are likely to experience the stomach cramping, bloating, and diarrhea that so annoyed Angela.

For some people, symptoms of lactose intolerance may occur early in life, whereas for others, it may not develop until early adulthood or middle age.

ANNOYING, NOT THREATENING

"Lactose intolerance is a pretty common disorder, and it's fairly benign," says Patricia Holsey, M.D., a family practitioner with the Henry Ford Medical Center in Royal Oak, Michigan. "If you suspect that you have lactose intolerance, try eliminating all dairy products for a week, then reintroduce them one at a time. When your symptoms emerge, you should have a pretty good idea of how much dairy you can tolerate before your stomach rebels. But if you experience severe cramps, severe abdominal pain, bloating, and diarrhea," she adds, "you should get in touch with your doctor to be certain that you do in fact have lactose intolerance, not a more serious health condition."

Sometimes a doctor will administer a test to measure the hydrogen concentration in your breath. Bacteria that feed off lactose when it is not digested break apart the lactose molecules and produce hydrogen. If you are lactose-intolerant, the level of hydrogen in your respiratory system increases.

THE QUESTION
OF CALCIUM

Dairy products are rich sources of calcium, which is important in maintaining proper nutrition and preventing and fighting osteoporosis, a disease characterized by a decrease in bone strength. Pregnant and breastfeeding women in particular need extra calcium to help nourish a healthy baby while protecting their bones.

How can you get enough calcium (the Daily Value is 1,000 milligrams) if you can't drink milk? "There is a lot of hype that we must drink our milk, but the big question is, can everyone drink milk?" asks Dixon. "The answer, of course, is no. There are other good sources of calcium, so it doesn't make sense to press milk on people who can't tolerate it," she says.

Dark leafy vegetables such as collard greens and kale are traditional African-American foods that supply a wealth of calcium without the lactose problem of dairy products. Broccoli, tofu, kidney beans, sesame seeds, almonds, sardines (with bones), canned salmon (with bones), and fortified instant oatmeal are also rich calcium sources. "And for those who are not eating calcium or calcium-rich foods, a registered dietitian can assist you in suggesting a calcium supplement," says Dixon.

CALMING
YOUR TUMMY

Dr. Holsey points out that treatment for lactose intolerance couldn't be easier: simple avoidance. Most people learn the amount of dairy they can tolerate, and that's all they eat. Try these tips if you have a problem with lactose intolerance.

Know your limits. "Many people can prevent or minimize lactose intolerance simply by including only small amounts of dairy in their diets," says Dixon. Others can build up their tolerance (with the guidance of a dietitian) by gradually increasing the amount of milk and dairy products they consume.

Obviously, try to avoid or minimize dairy consumption. "Some people can tolerate small portions without problems; only large amounts within a short period give them symptoms," says Dr. Holsey.

Check the supermarket. You can now find a variety of dairy products that have been specially formulated for the lactose-intolerant. You might also try Lactaid (lactase enzyme that can be added to foods) as well Lactaid milk, which is lactose-free, says Dr. Holsey.

Read the fine print. Look at food labels carefully, because milk is present not only in dairy products; it is added to many processed foods. You should look for ingredients such as freeze-dried acidophilus, calcium caseinate, casein lactose, whey, nonfat milk, milk solids, and buttermilk, advises Dixon.

Indulge in culture. Yogurt that is labeled as containing live cultures can be safely eaten. Although yogurt is high in lactose, the bacteria in live cultures break down and release the lactose, thus preventing symptoms. But if you buy frozen yogurt, you must buy the lactose-free variety, because when yogurt is frozen, the cultures are killed, advises Nowlin. You can also try sweet acidophilus milk, which contains the necessary bacteria.

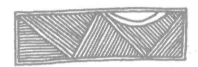

Lupus

HEALING WHEN YOUR BODY'S OFF-BALANCE

ebbie Simon is 5 feet 11 inches and weighs 122 pounds, so why does she keep a size 24 dress in her closet? "To remind me," she says, "so I continue to take good care of myself.

"Nine years ago, I was 30 years old and always on the go," says the black-haired, hazel-eyed media executive. "I combined a full-time job with a fledgling broadcast career and a busy social life." She did, that is, until the day her energy deserted her. "At some point, I began to feel extremely tired for no discernible reason. I started calling in sick so much that my boss demanded a doctor's statement."

Her first doctor took one look at the swollen lymph nodes in her neck and hospitalized her. "I thought I had cancer, and my doctor never told me I didn't," says Debbie. But countless vials of blood, biopsies, and exploratory surgeries later, Debbie's doctors were still ordering new tests for everything from leukemia to AIDS. In the meantime, the fatigue, anxiety, and even night sweats continued, while rashes began to mark her light brown complexion.

Unfortunately, during this time she had a miscarriage. "I wanted children, and it wasn't until after the miscarriage that my internist figured out why it happened and why I had all those other problems. He figured out that I had lupus."

Debbie was treated with prednisone, a prescription steroid that tamed her worst symptoms but created others. "I ballooned from 120 pounds to 250 pounds, a size 24, seemingly overnight. My hair thinned and my face swelled up.

"I knew I needed emotional support. Eventually, I redis-covered my faith in God, and from that moment I began to improve. I felt less anxiety, had fewer symptoms, and lost weight. I also completed treatment. Today I feel healthy, happy, energetic—and normal."

A Disease
That Seeks Out Sisters

Lupus is the hallmark of a malfunctioning immune system. It occurs when the immune system, which is designed to protect you from disease, turns on you and attacks the tissues in your body instead.

Lupus can happen to just about anyone, but it does most of its damage to women, especially African-American women. About 1 in every 250 Black women develops the disease, while the figure for White women is about 1 in 400. In total, between 1.4 and 2 million people in the United States have been diagnosed with lupus.

"Lupus affects women 10 times more often than men," says Patricia A. Fraser, M.D., a rheumatologist and assistant professor of medicine at Harvard Medical School. It most often strikes women in their childbearing years—between the ages of 15 and 45. Some theories suggest that hormones produced by the ovaries increase a woman's susceptibility.

There's also no explanation for why lupus is so common, and so serious, in Black women. "Some of the risk may be inherited," says Dr. Fraser. "We do know that if one twin has lupus, the other is more likely to have it. Even in families where there are no twins, if one family member has lupus, their immediate relatives are more likely to have lupus than people in the general population."

Doctors also suspect that the disease is brought on by a combination of inherited factors and environmental exposure, says Dr. Fraser. "The environmental exposure may include a viral infection, but we haven't yet been able to identify a specific virus," she says.

Debbie has the most common type of lupus, systemic lupus erythematosus (SLE). With SLE, nothing in the body is safe or sacred, since the immune system may target the connective tissue of any organ or joint in the body. The attack usually results in severe inflammation or damage to joints, skin, and vital organs such as the lungs, kidneys, heart, and brain.

Common symptoms of the disease include fatigue, arthritis pain, fever, hair loss, and muscle weakness and tenderness. Women with lupus are also prone to Raynaud's disease, a circulatory ailment that affects the hands and feet. Some people have a limited form of the disease called discoid lupus erythematosus (DLE), which involves only the skin and scalp.

The best known symptom of SLE is a red, raised, butterfly-shaped rash across the bridge of the nose. When SLE was first discovered in the 1800s, the rash pattern reminded early physicians of the facial markings of a wolf, thus the name *lupus*, which is the Latin word for "wolf."

Although there is no known cause for most cases of SLE, adverse reactions to certain medications may mimic some of its symptoms. These drugs include high doses of hydralazine (Alazine), used for high blood pressure; procainamide (Pronestyl), which is used to regulate heart rhythm; and isoniazid (INH), which is a treatment for tuberculosis. "Drug-induced lupus is not more common in African-Americans," says Dr. Fraser.

UNDERSTANDING THE SYMPTOMS

One of the most difficult aspects of dealing with lupus is the unpredictability of the outbreaks. The disease can be mild, moderate, or very severe. Lupus may also erupt for months or years, go into complete remission, and then erupt again for no clear reason.

The stress of dealing with symptoms like Debbie's fatigue can also make it difficult for some people with lupus to pursue normal lives. Most women, like Debbie, also experience some hair loss. It may be permanent if they have DLE, but women with SLE find that it may wax and wane with episodes of the disease, says Dr. Fraser.

People with lupus often have photosensitivity, which means that they cannot tolerate the sun. Even driving a car on a sunny day or going outside briefly can result in a rash on sun-exposed areas or dizziness and headaches, says Dr. Fraser.

Because it can strike any area of the body, other symptoms of lupus include mouth and nose sores, unexplained fevers, enlarged lymph glands, and arthritis in the small joints, particularly of the fingers and wrists. The inflammation of the body's tissues is often worst when you first get up in the morning, and your joints may feel hot and swollen. You may even have chest pains and shortness of breath, says Dr. Fraser.

"Accurately reading symptoms and getting prompt care can be even more critical for African-American women because we not only

Is It Lupus?

Getting an accurate diagnosis of lupus can be a struggle. If you are an African-American woman of childbearing age and you're not feeling well, see your doctor, especially if you have a mild fever, joint pain, achiness, chronic fatigue, or weight loss," says Margaret A. Fountain, M.D., an arthritis specialist in private practice and the health editor for a local television station in Baltimore.

If your doctor suspects that lupus is your problem, see a rheumatologist. The Lupus Foundation of America can help you find one, and they can also give you information about local chapters of the foundation as well as support groups. Call them at 1-800-558-0121 for more information.

The rheumatologist will take a complete medical history and conduct a top-to-toe physical exam, including a thorough check of the mucous membranes in your mouth and a search for rashes. He may test you for the presence of specific proteins like antinuclear antibodies (ANA) and possibly antiphospholipid antibodies to confirm a diagnosis of lupus. Nearly 95 percent of people with lupus have a positive ANA test, and 20 to 50 percent test positive for anti-phospholipids.

develop lupus more often, we die of it more often than any other group," says Margaret A. Fountain, M.D., an arthritis specialist in private practice and the health editor for a local television station in Baltimore. One study, for example, found that many of us not only have lupus but also high blood pressure that leads to kidney problems, including chronic renal (kidney) failure. Because chronic renal failure is the leading cause of death in people with lupus, regular monitoring and contact with a physician are critical, says Dr. Fountain.

PUTTING YOUR BODY
BACK ON TRACK

There are no known preventive measures for lupus, but it can be successfully treated. "Many people with lupus lead normal lives," says

Dr. Fraser. The best way to help yourself is to learn to recognize the things that trigger eruptions and work with your physician to determine the medications that work best for you.

Address stress. There is some evidence that stress may make lupus worse, so avoid it as much as you can. Dr. Fraser recommends that lupus sufferers try meditation, prayer, or relaxation exercises. And don't forget aerobic exercise as a stress-buster. It releases endorphins, the brain chemicals that heighten your mood and relieve tension. A moderately vigorous workout three times a week will also help to soothe some of the joint aches that lupus often brings.

Don't scrimp on care. Lupus is chronic and ongoing, and many of the more serious problems like kidney disease, heart disease, anemia, and blood vessel inflammation may develop without warning. Make sure you get high-quality, consistent care and build a good relationship with your doctor. See your doctor at least every three to six months, says Dr. Fountain. "If you have any of the more serious problems, more frequent visits may be necessary."

Make a pregnancy plan. As Debbie discovered, pregnancy holds special risks for women with lupus. It may make the disease worse, and there is an increased chance of pregnancy complications. Nearly 15 percent of lupus pregnancies end in miscarriage, and women with lupus are three times more likely to deliver prematurely than other women. It's impossible to control all of these factors, but you and your doctor should discuss when it's best for you to conceive, based on your symptoms and overall health, says Dr. Fountain.

Be wary of wonder drugs. There is no cure for lupus, and if there were, you probably wouldn't find it in the classified ad section of a magazine. Be conservative and careful about your treatment choices. Lupus is a multi-billion-dollar business for charlatans, says Dr. Fountain.

Become a diet detective. Some anecdotal evidence suggests that lupus episodes can be triggered by reactions to certain foods. "But there have been only a few controlled studies with lupus and food, and nothing conclusive has been found, so we haven't been able to definitely say that any specific food affects lupus," says Dr. Fraser. For your own safety, pay close attention to how your body responds to foods, and if you think you're having a reaction, cut that food out of your diet.

Eat well. The question of whether the antioxidant vitamins C and E and beta-carotene are helpful to people with lupus has not yet been answered. The best approach is to make sure that you get as many of these nutrients as possible from your diet, says Dr. Fraser. Cantaloupe, spinach, and mangoes are good sources of beta-carotene. For vitamin C, try either fruits or fruit juices like orange and pineapple and vegetables like brussels sprouts, broccoli, and cauliflower. Get vitamin E from sunflower seeds, vegetable oils, and wheat germ.

Be sun-shy. In addition to being a way to protect your beautiful brown skin, protecting yourself from the sun is an important part of preventing lupus eruptions. Avoid the sun when possible. If you must be outside, wear a hat and use sunscreen with an SPF (sun protection factor) of at least 15 on all exposed body parts—it's critical, says Dr. Fraser.

Check out complementary medicine. Some anecdotal and medical evidence suggests that lupus symptoms may respond to some alternative complementary health treatments. Some studies conducted on acupuncture and arthritis (which often comes with lupus), for example, show a reduction in pain and inflammation without drugs. Similar studies suggest that Chinese herbal treatments show some promise as well, notes Dr. Fountain. For the best results, try to find a rheumatologist who will include alternative, well-studied, safe treatments in your care plan if you would like to try them. But never stop taking your standard medications without the approval of your doctor.

Protect your immune system. Anything that taxes your immune system can bring on lupus symptoms, so avoid alcohol, tobacco, chronic stress, and caffeine and get plenty of rest, says Dr. Fountain.

Know what to expect from treatment. Doctors usually prescribe prescription nonsteroidal anti-inflammatory drugs such as naproxen (Anaprox) for pain and joint inflammation. They also occasionally prescribe steroids such as prednisone (Deltasone) to reduce severe joint problems. Hydroxychloroquine (Plaquenil), a drug that is commonly used for malaria, also works very well against arthritis pain and some rashes associated with lupus, says Dr. Fountain.

Lyme Disease

FIGURING OUT THE BEST PROTECTION

onnie Perkins, an eternal skeptic who hated to go to the doctor, was not about to jump in the car and go running to his physician when his wise and patient wife, Elaine, noticed an unusual rash on his thigh.

"It could be a tick bite," Elaine remembers telling him as they sat down to breakfast that morning. "We're right here in Hartford, and we both know the state of Connecticut is one of the most deer tick–infested parts of the country. You also did an awful lot of yard work this week."

"I told her that it would take more than a little rash to get me into a doctor's office," Lonnie says. At that point, Elaine figured she'd said as much as she could, so she let him be.

"But a few days later," Lonnie continues, "I was pretty frightened." His "little rash" had disappeared from his thigh, only to reappear on his belly. "It was spreading everywhere," he says.

Lonnie couldn't get to the doctor fast enough. When he returned from his appointment later that afternoon with a diagnosis of Lyme disease, he had a prescription for an antibiotic and a bouquet of red roses for his wife.

"He told me he was sorry he doubted me," Elaine laughs, "and hugged me, saying, 'Where would I be without you?' I told him that we shouldn't even think about that."

LEARNING ABOUT LYME

It's America's most common bugborne ailment, affecting an estimated 9,000 people annually, according to the Centers for Disease Control and Prevention in Atlanta. But don't be surprised if it doesn't strike a familiar chord. "This disease is not all that commonly reported among African-Americans and is probably underreported," says Andrew D. McBride, M.D., director of health for the city of Stamford, Connecticut.

Lyme disease is caused by *Borrelia burgdorferi*, a type of bacteria that normally live in white-footed mice. When hungry deer ticks feed on the mice, they pick up the bacteria. And when infected ticks bite you, they transmit the bacteria to you.

Once the bacteria enter your skin, they incubate for a while, anywhere from three days to a month. Then they can spread to other parts of your body, typically causing what appears to be a case of the flu: fatigue, listlessness, chills, fever, headache, stiff neck, and muscle aches. These symptoms often come and go, although the malaise and fatigue may stick around for weeks. If it's not treated, Lyme disease can cause heart problems, meningitis, a type of facial paralysis known as Bell's palsy, or chronic arthritis.

In fact, it was a 1975 outbreak of what appeared to be juvenile rheumatoid arthritis in Lyme, Connecticut, that first led health officials to discover *B. burgdorferi*—and give it a new name.

UNSIGHTLY SIGNS

How do you know if you have Lyme disease? The first sign may be a tick bite, a reddened, raised circle that usually doesn't itch. "Sometimes there's a hole—like a pore—in the middle of the area," says Nadu Tuakli, M.D., a family practitioner in Columbia, Maryland. Many people develop the signature of Lyme disease, a distinctive red bull's-eye rash that spreads from the bite outward in concentric rings, occasionally to a diameter of 3 inches or more.

Sometimes the rash migrates from one part of the body to another. "The rash is one reason that Lyme disease is underdiagnosed in African-Americans," says Dr. McBride. "It's often difficult to identify on a patient who has dark skin. In addition, many physicians just don't think of Lyme disease when they see a Black patient."

Black patients don't think to mention the possibility of Lyme disease to their doctors, either. Most of us don't know much about the disease, because outside of rural areas, the prime territory for the illness is wooded suburbs where there are lots of deer, but few of us.

But since we hunt, fish, garden, hike, and work outdoors like everyone else, we need to know how to avoid Lyme disease. And even city dwellers can contract Lyme disease if they spend weekends in the country or send their kids to camp. And does your pet roam an area that is frequented by deer? Deer ticks love warm-blooded animals and will hop on as your dog or cat trots by. Your pet can then bring the ticks home to you.

DON'T GET TICKED

Can you outsmart Lyme disease? Sure you can. Here's how.

Tread with care. For starters, avoid backyard bushes during tick season (May through October in many places), advises Dr. McBride. Lyme disease has been reported in nearly every state, but the hot spots are the Northeast, the Midwest, and along the Pacific coast. In populated portions of these areas, the most likely place to find ticks is in bushes that lie between suburban lawns and surrounding woods. "Deer ticks avoid hot summer lawns, which can dry them out. And in the deep woods, the animals they're looking for are too scattered," explains Dr. McBride.

Dress the part. If you spend time in the woods or tall grass during tick season, wear long-sleeved shirts and long pants, and tuck your pants inside your socks or boots to make it hard for a tick to reach your skin, advises Dr. McBride. Wear light-colored clothing to make ticks more visible, he says.

"Hats are important, especially for children, because bushes and grasses are often taller than their heads, and the scalp is one of the hardest places to spot a deer tick," says Lois V. Melchior, M.D., a family practitioner and member of Dimensions Affiliated Physicians in Hyattsville, Maryland.

Be unpopular . . . with bugs, that is. Before you hit the great outdoors, apply an insect repellent containing DEET to your clothes, arms, legs, and head, advises Dr. McBride. Be sure to read the precautions printed on the product labels, he warns. Or spray your clothes, carpeting, bedding, and furniture with the pesticide permethrin found in a prodcut called A-200. Be cautious with this repellent, however: Avoid contact with your skin, don't inhale the vapors, and be sure to read the warning label carefully, advises Dr. McBride.

"If you're looking for a bug repellent that doesn't smell like, well, bug repellent, try Skin So Soft by Avon," suggests Dr. Tuakli. The skin moisturizer has natural repellent qualities.

Protect your pet. Use a pet shampoo that repels ticks (not all flea products do, says Dr. McBride). Use tick-repelling sprays before you release your pet for outdoor exploring, and inspect your four-legged friend for ticks upon its return.

Leave your clothes behind. When you return to your home after a trip to the woods, leave your clothes in your garage or mud room for laundering, advises Dr. Tuakli. "That helps separate you from any ticks you may be carrying before they have a chance to bite you," she says.

Pull it off. Scrutinize your skin carefully after an outdoor sojourn. The deer tick you're looking for is tiny—about the size of a poppyseed. You probably won't be able to feel it when it bites. If you see a deer tick on your body, cleanse the area with mild soap and water, advises Dr. Melchior. "Don't use alcohol: It tends to disintegrate the tick, which makes it hard to remove in one piece," she says. Using a magnifying glass, grasp the tick with pointed tweezers as close to the skin as possible and gently pull straight out, she says. If you're able to remove the entire tick, it is helpful to save the specimen and have your family physician identify it.

IF YOU ARE BITTEN

In the event that you don't successfully repel this unwelcome bug, here's what to do.

Watch for symptoms. If you live in Lyme territory and you notice symptoms, see your doctor right away. "Some doctors in high-risk regions treat for Lyme disease as soon as they know someone's been bitten, without waiting for symptoms to develop," says Dr. McBride. "But certainly, if you notice symptoms, you should seek a doctor's care immediately. This is a disease you want to treat early."

Go with antibiotics. It's easy for your doctor to treat Lyme disease. He'll prescribe a two- to four-week course of antibiotics, which usually rids you of the problem.

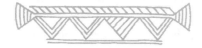

Lymphoma
RECLAIMING GOOD HEALTH

hen Mickey Anderson recalls her last weeks of law school, she admits she took a big risk. By trying to stay focused on final exams, she had to deny how lousy she felt.

"I had been feeling feverish, and the glands in my neck were swollen," says Mickey, an outgoing, silver-tongued legal aid lawyer whose friends say she reminds them of a very thin version of Oprah. "It felt like the flu—except it was April instead of flu season, and the symptoms dragged on for weeks with no improvement."

Her exams safely behind her, Mickey finally made it to a doctor near her Fairfax, Virginia, home, only to hear a startling diagnosis: She had Hodgkins' disease, a cancer of the lymph system.

"The sound of the word *cancer* alone was pretty ominous," says Mickey, lowering her eyes to the mug of chamomile tea in her hands. "When my doctor told me the odds were good with aggressive treatment, I told him to do what he needed to do."

It's been nearly two years since Mickey, now 34, finished the chemotherapy treatment that rendered her cancer-free. Her hair has grown back, and the intermittent nausea brought on by her treatments is now a distant memory. "Enduring the side effects of chemotherapy was nothing compared to what I almost lost," she says.

LEARNING TO RECOGNIZE IT

Lymphoma, or cancer of the lymph nodes, targets the body's infection-fighting immune system, which consists of the lymph nodes, the small vessels that link them, and the spleen (a large gland-like organ located in your upper abdomen). The lymph system helps trap and destroy bacteria and other foreign substances. You can often tell that your body is battling an infection because affected lymph nodes become swollen.

Roughly 60,000 Americans were diagnosed with lymphoma in 1996. While anyone is susceptible, the disease is rarer among African-Americans and women.

There are 16 different types of lymphoma, which are classified according to the type of immune system cell they attack. The two main categories are Hodgkin's disease and non-Hodgkin's lymphoma; non-Hodgkin's lymphoma is seven times more frequent than Hodgkin's disease. In either case, the most common symptom is one or more swollen glands, usually in the neck, armpit, or groin. People also have fevers, lose their appetite, lose weight, and generally feel ill. Night sweats are also common. "It's not unusual to wake up with the bed literally drenched in sweat," says Otis W. Brawley, M.D., director of the Office of Special Populations at the National Cancer Institute in Bethesda, Maryland.

Hodgkin's disease—the easier of the two lymphomas to cure—is most common among young adults (ages 15 to 34) and seniors (age 60 and older). Non-Hodgkin's lymphoma occurs at any age, but the incidence increases with age. The key to recovering from all types of lymphoma, however, is early detection, says Dr. Brawley. Learning to read the disease's often subtle symptoms is an important part of maintaining your health.

After the initial symptoms appear, the course of the disease depends on how quickly the lymph node tumors grow and how many of the dozens of lymph nodes throughout the body are involved. Sometimes the disease progresses with amazing speed. In other cases, tumors grow so slowly that they pose little immediate health risk. "Many people with slow-growing tumors don't even realize something's wrong with them for years," says Ellsworth Grant, M.D., an oncologist in private practice in Pasadena, California. "If they're feeling reasonably well and few lymph nodes are involved, they often live happily for 10 years without the disease bothering them."

The causes of lymphoma aren't entirely clear, although researchers know that it has connections with other illnesses. One particularly aggressive form of non-Hodgkin's lymphoma, for example, is called

Burkitt's lymphoma and typically affects teens; it may stem from exposure to the Epstein-Barr virus, which causes mononucleosis, sometimes called the kissing disease. (Most people who have the Epstein-Barr virus, however, do not get Burkitt's lymphoma.) Lymphomas are also common in people whose immune systems are compromised, such as AIDS patients, organ transplant recipients, and people with rheumatological diseases such as rheumatoid arthritis or lupus. "In fact, the first hint of the AIDS epidemic was that lots of men in San Francisco were developing and dying of lymphoma," says Dr. Brawley.

Researchers say that if someone in your family has lymphoma, you may be at higher risk for the disease. People with lymphoma are also prone to develop other cancers later in life.

LIVING
THROUGH IT

Since we don't know what causes lymphoma, we can't do much to prevent it. We can treat it, however. Unlike other cancers, lymphoma tumors can't be removed. "The tumors are like gooey little popcorn balls," explains Dr. Brawley. "If you try to remove them, you can inadvertently leave a piece behind, and they may grow back."

So physicians use other approaches. Depending on the type of lymphoma, the number of affected lymph nodes, and other factors, doctors may use radiation, chemotherapy with cancer-fighting medications, or a bone-marrow transplant. These measures can be extremely effective. Dr. Grant recalls a 20-year-old patient in an intensive care unit who was so ill from lymphoma that she needed a respirator to breathe for her. "She looked terrible. She was dying before our eyes," he says. Five days after chemotherapy treatment began, the young woman was well enough to walk around her hospital room. "It was one of the most amazing things I have seen in medicine," he says.

Ironically, it's the aggressive tumors that yield such spectacular cures. "Chemotherapy kills rapidly growing cells. In fact, it's the death of the rapidly growing cells that produce hair and line the digestive tract that cause the hair loss and diarrhea that often comes with chemotherapy," explains Dr. Brawley. "We can cure lymphomas of all types, but the slow-growing tumors are the hardest to handle."

Here's advice from the experts.

Get to a doctor quickly. Lymphoma is one of the more curable cancers, but early detection is still important, stresses Dr. Grant. "The less disease you have and the smaller your lymph nodes are, the greater the chance of a cure," he says. "If you feel a firm, rubbery lymph node somewhere on your body and you have not recently had a cold or an infection near that node, have it checked out by your physician."

Try to relax. It's natural to be anxious if you discover swollen lymph nodes, but they're very common. They can signal something as innocuous as a reaction to deodorant. "All swollen lymph nodes don't need a biopsy, and all aren't cancer," assures Myra E. Rose, M.D., associate professor of clinical medicine at Morehouse School of Medicine in Atlanta.

Get the details. If a biopsy indicates that you have lymphoma, ask your physician exactly what type you have and how advanced it is, advises Dr. Rose. "Find out what the treatment will be, how long it will take, whether it can cure, and what you can expect," she suggests. "If you know what your goals are, it helps you make it through the treatment."

Don't hold back. If you're on chemotherapy, keep your doctor closely apprised of the state of your health. "I ask my patients not to assume anything," says Dr. Rose. "If they're not feeling up to par, I want to know about it. They may think they just have a cold that's going around, but their symptoms could be a side effect of chemotherapy or a sign that the cancer is spreading."

Hang in there. As Mickey learned, living through cancer treatment can be tough, but continuing to live a full life can be the reward. Medications can help. "Our medications for nausea and vomiting are much better than they were even five years ago," says Dr. Grant. And if you're concerned about hair loss, remember that nothing is forever. "We can't guarantee the color or texture," he says. "But if you had hair to begin with, it'll grow back once therapy stops."

Stay positive. Cancer treatment is no party, "but a great mental attitude really helps," says Dr. Grant. "Lots of successful cancer patients find the ability to reach deep down within to keep their spirits up and to remain calm, which I think may even help their bodies fight the cancer."

Menopause

EMBRACING AND MANAGING CHANGE

udy Washington, the night editor of a major newspaper in Chicago, remembers an upsetting night: "It was 9:50, and I was about to miss my 10 o'clock deadline. The phone rang, and I snatched it up impatiently. It was the composing room foreman, asking about some stories that he said he needed. I was sweating.

"I felt like I had one nerve left, and this pot-bellied, cigar-smoking little troll was working it. I insisted that I had sent down everything for the front page," she says, "but the truth was that I could barely remember what the stories were about. I was almost trembling with anger and anxiety as I hung up.

"I told myself, 'Get a grip, girl. You've been doing this job for years; surely you can handle it tonight.' I lifted my hair off the back of my neck, trying to get cool, and I noticed how dry and fragile it seemed. Surely this was more than a reaction to a new perm. And for the hundredth time, I wondered, 'Why doesn't anyone else seem to feel the heat in here?'"

She was only 43, but she had been feeling tired and unable to concentrate. To top it off, she was having cramps, a signal that her period was arriving unexpectedly. "Suddenly, it was all too much," she says. "I abandoned the mess on my desk for the refuge of the women's room. I began to cry as I looked at my blemished chin, dry hair, and perspiration-streaked face. 'What's happening to me?' I wondered. 'This has gone far enough. Tomorrow I'm going to see my doctor.'"

HORMONE ALERT

What was happening to Judy was menopause, or more specifically, perimenopause, the four- to six-year span before the actual end of menstrual periods. As Judy discovered when she talked with her doctor, menopause is not a tragedy but a natural transition that can be made less uncomfortable with herbal remedies or, if necessary, with medication.

"The problem is, many women don't recognize it when it appears," says Zerline Chambers-Kersey, M.D., an obstetrician and gynecologist in private practice in Annandale, Virginia. "When a woman's ovaries produce less estrogen, she experiences symptoms of estrogen deficiency." These can include hot flashes, sleep disorders, fatigue, mental confusion, menstrual irregularities, genital changes, and dry hair, skin, and nails. "She may feel like she's on an emotional roller coaster," says Dr. Chambers-Kersey. "But she still has her period and can become pregnant, so she may not realize what is happening to her."

You don't actually reach menopause until your menstrual period has stopped for a year, which typically happens at about age 51, but the process can begin anywhere between the ages of 40 and 60, or even younger. One percent of women under 40 enter menopause each year.

"It's likely that your pattern will follow your mother's," says Dr. Chambers-Kersey. If you want to get a better idea of how near you are to menopause, ask your doctor for a test that measures the amount of follicle-stimulating hormone (FSH) in your bloodstream. The levels go up before menopause because your body produces extra FSH in an effort to release an egg. If your doctor tells you that your levels are high, you may be going into menopause.

CULTURAL HEALING

"Most women experience some physical changes with the onset of menopause," says Nancy Roberson, M.D., clinical associate professor of obstetrics and gynecology at the University of Rochester School of Medicine in New York. "But," observes Julia A. Boyd, a psychotherapist with the Group Health Cooperative in Seattle and author of *In the Company of My Sisters: Black Women and Self-Esteem*, "I don't see a lot of African-American women having psychological trouble with this issue. I wonder if we, as Black women, place the same negative emphasis on aging that Whites place on it. I haven't noticed it to be a focus for us."

"Black women tend to have fewer symptoms, and they don't

bother us as much because we ignore them, and the next thing you know, we're done with it," adds Dr. Chambers-Kersey.

Although menopause is frequently feared as an official end to fertility and therefore the end of sexual attractiveness, it is more properly viewed as a beginning, says D. Kim Singleton, Ph.D., a clinical psychologist in private practice in Washington, D.C. "Our attitude toward menopause is related to our attitude toward aging in this society, which views menopause as a disease. If we free ourselves from this viewpoint, we realize that we are free from pregnancy, free from periods, and free to express our libido without fear. The hot flashes and other symptoms can all be controlled," she says.

MASTERING MENOPAUSE

Your journey into menopause is involuntary, but you can—and should—jump into the driver's seat and take control. Here's what the experts say about relieving symptoms and protecting your health.

Get in shape. "Keeping fit through diet, exercise, and stress control is really important. Women are socialized to take care of everybody else, but make sure you take care of yourself," says psychologist Nsenga Warfield-Coppock, Ph.D., assistant visiting professor at Catholic University of America in Washington, D.C.

Doing a half-hour of weight-bearing aerobic exercise three times a week maintains bone density and lowers cholesterol levels. "It also boosts your psyche through the release of mood-altering chemicals called endorphins," adds Dr. Warfield-Coppock.

Eat for vitality. Try a diet that contains less than 20 percent of calories from fat, restricts meat, and is rich in a variety of fruits, vegetables, and whole grains, says Dr. Chambers-Kersey.

Make sure to include at least one 3- to 4-ounce serving a day of a soy food such as tofu, she recommends. Soy foods contain small amounts of natural chemical compounds called phytoestrogens, which are plant hormones that are thought to weakly mimic the action of estrogen. And eat more whole grains and flaxseed, which also contain these natural chemicals.

Deal with stress. "It is very important to reduce your stress level. Find a stress-reducer that works for you, whether it's prayer,

(continued on page 296)

Hormone replacement therapy (HRT) is currently the most advanced and effective treatment for the symptoms of menopause. The HRT strategy is simple: It replaces the estrogen (and in some cases, progesterone and testosterone) that your body has stopped producing with medications in the form of pills, patches, or creams. "HRT protects against heart disease (lowering your risk by 50 percent) and prevents stroke, two major killers of African-American women," says Nancy Roberson, M.D., clinical associate professor of obstetrics and gynecology at the University of Rochester School of Medicine in New York.

	Estrogen Cream *(Estrace, Premarin)*	*Estrogen Patch* *(Climara, Estraderm)*	*Estrogen Pills* *(Premarin)*
Benefits	Eases vaginal dryness; reduces hot flashes and osteoporosis risk; can be used by smokers	Eases vaginal dryness; reduces hot flashes and osteoporosis risk; can be used by smokers	Reduces osteoporosis and heart disease risk; eases hot flashes, night sweats, and vaginal dryness
Risks	No heart disease protection	No heart disease protection	Increases blood pressure; estrogen alone increases risk of uterine cancer from 1 in 1,000 to as high as 1 in 100; may increase breast cancer risk after 5–15 years

But HRT is controversial, and some doctors feel that its risks outweigh its benefits. Some studies based on long-term use of estrogen alone show a 30 percent higher risk of breast cancer and up to a tenfold greater risk of uterine cancer. Estrogen can also activate fibroids and aggravate fibrocystic breast disease. There are many individual factors to consider, so be sure to discuss HRT in great detail with your physician.

Since not all HRT prescriptions are the same and each therapy offers its own benefits and risks, here's the information you need to make an informed decision.

Estrogen-Progesterone Combination (Premphase, Prempro)	Estrogen-Testosterone Combination (Estartest, Premarin with Methyltestosterone)	Oral Contraceptives (various Ortho-Novum formulations)
Significantly reduces risk of endometrial cancer	Restores libido; relieves hot flashes; may increase bone density	Provide estrogen for women who undergo early menopause
Added progesterone weakens estrogen's heart disease protection	Can cause acne, facial hair growth, lowered voice, clitoral enlargement; can lower "good" cholesterol, linked to increased risk of heart disease	May raise breast cancer risk for some women

meditation, or playing volleyball," advises Dr. Warfield-Coppock.

De-fat your diet. A *Prevention* magazine survey showed that eating a low-fat diet is a big factor in helping women have a positive experience with menopause. Reduced fat intake can also help keep your weight down, which may prevent early menopause, says Dr. Chambers-Kersey.

Don't let cigarettes clock you. "Smokers enter menopause three to five years earlier than nonsmokers because smoke metabolizes estradiol, a chemical that acts like an anti-estrogen and hastens menopause," says Dr. Chambers-Kersey. So stop smoking and you will be more likely to avoid early menopause, plus you'll have fewer symptoms.

Ditto for alcohol. Alcohol can bring on hot flashes. Watch your reaction to cocktails and give them up if they make you flush.

Bone up on calcium. Estrogen loss promotes bone thinning, or osteoporosis. Arthritis also tends to worsen after menopause, but taking in at least the Daily Value of 1,000 milligrams of calcium before menopause protects you from both conditions. The National Institutes of Health recommends even more calcium—along the lines of 1,500 milligrams daily—for postmenopausal women who are not using hormone replacement therapy (HRT) and for women over 65. A diet that includes low-fat milk and yogurt, sardines and canned salmon (both with bones), and turnip, mustard, and collard greens will beef up your bones and can help save you from the ravages of osteoporosis and osteoarthritis.

Use Nature's secrets. Dong-quai, blue and black cohosh, sarsaparilla, wild yam root, and other herbs that contain mild plant hormones may ease your symptoms, as can evening primrose oil. Be sure to ask your doctor's advice before taking them, however.

Work on heart health. Postmenopausal estrogen depletion raises a woman's heart disease risk 300 percent by age 65, so have your lipid levels checked as you near your fifties. Lipid analysis gives you the numbers on your total cholesterol—the "good" high-density lipoproteins, the "bad" low-density lipoproteins, and triglycerides. If any of these numbers are in the danger area, you should consider HRT and discuss its pros and cons with your doctor.

Practice sex therapy. The loss of estrogen causes the vaginal walls to thin and the vagina to become drier. These changes can make intercourse uncomfortable. A sensitive partner can help solve this problem simply by extending foreplay. Studies suggest that women who remain sexually active have less dryness and thinning, says Dr. Chambers-Kersey.

Your doctor can also prescribe estrogen creams to reverse dryness. Two types, Dienestrol and Premarin, are inserted directly into the vagina with an applicator, just like some spermicides. Or you can easily supply the needed moisture with an over-the-counter water-based lubricant such as K-Y Jelly, Replens, or Astroglide, suggests Dr. Chambers-Kersey.

Menstrual Irregularities
GETTING A HANDLE ON YOUR CYCLE

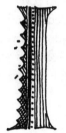

I began to get really frustrated with my periods when they started to become heavier and erratic," says Pat Lawson, an Illinois home-maker. "I'm only 35, so I thought it was a little soon for menopause. I was just sure that I'd developed fibroids, since almost every other Black woman I knew already had them."

Even though she was afraid of finding out what was going on, Pat did an excellent job of taking charge of her situation. Over a period of three months, she kept a careful diary of the ups and downs of her menstrual cycle and her aches and pains, and she took it with her when she went to her gynecologist.

"My doctor was wonderful," Pat recalls. "He checked me from top to toe and then happily delivered the news that I was absolutely fine. He explained that the changes in my cycle were perfectly normal and due to the fact that our periods naturally become heavier as we age."

Pat initially felt bad about running to the doctor for nothing, but he assured that sharing her concerns with him was the best thing she could do and that keeping a diary actually made it easier for him to make a diagnosis.

UNDERSTANDING THE UNEXPECTED

As Pat discovered, there are many things that can change the course of your menstrual cycle. Some are indications of serious health problems, and others are a natural part of growing older. "There are very few women whose bodies operate with clockwork precision, and most women have pain or very heavy or very light flows at some time or another. But for 25 percent of women, bad cramps, spotting, or missed periods become a regular pattern," says Alise Jones Bailey, M.D., an obstetrician and gynecologist with Buckhead Women's Medical Group in Atlanta.

On average, women lose about 3 tablespoons of blood with their menstrual flow each month. Changes in flow can be caused by many diseases and conditions, from the benign to the serious.

Fibroids, noncancerous uterine growths that are quite common in African-American women, can cause a very heavy flow. So can pelvic inflammatory disease, a pelvic infection that often develops when sexually transmitted diseases (STDs) go untreated. Endometriosis, a condition in which tissue from the uterine lining wanders from the uterus and attaches itself to other organs, can also cause heavy bleeding. Uterine hyperplasia (abnormal thickening of the uterine lining), polyps (small noncancerous growths on the lining of the uterus), cancers of the uterus, cervix, and vagina, and blood-clotting disorders are all likely to cause excess bleeding, says Dr. Bailey.

If you are like Pat, your menstrual flow may become heavier as you age because your uterus keeps growing until you reach your midthirties. This means that at 35, you have slightly more uterine tissue available to produce your period than you did at 21.

The menstrual problems listed below rarely amount to more than monthly aggravation, but check with your doctor to be sure that your problem is not masking a more serious condition.

Spotting. After the age of 30, women are more likely to make too little of the hormone progesterone. This creates a hormone imbalance that can lead to spotting, which results when the uterine lining releases small amounts of blood between periods. It can be normal for some women, especially around the time that they ovulate and sometimes when they are pregnant, but it also occurs in women who have polyps, fibroids, or cancer. Women who take the Pill or contract chlamydia, an STD, may also experience spotting.

Cessation of periods. When your periods stop for 90 days or more and you're not yet experiencing menopause, doctors call it amenorrhea. "When it comes to having regular cycles, even exercise can be too much of a good thing," says Dr. Bailey. Overexercise can cause a complete absence of periods; some avid exercisers experience amenorrhea because their hormone levels are altered when their body fat drops below 10 percent. For the same reason, women with extreme anorexia or bulimia can experience amenorrhea.

Severe cramps. Dysmenorrhea is the medical term for the severe pain that many women experience each month. One in 10 women has cramps bad enough to incapacitate her each month for anywhere from an hour to three days.

During menstruation, hormones called prostaglandins are released, triggering the uterine contractions that we feel as cramps. Cramps are a fairly common problem, but women should remember that serious conditions, such as fibroids or endometriosis, can cause cramping pain, says Dr. Bailey. An ectopic, or tubal, pregnancy can also cause very painful periods, and this medical emergency can be fatal if not diagnosed in time.

Visit your gynecologist to make sure your cramps are just a normal part of your menstrual cycle. If they aren't related to an underlying medical problem, you'll be relieved to know that they may subside or at least improve by the time you reach 30 or after you have a baby, according to Dr. Bailey.

Irregular or infrequent periods. This condition is sometimes called oligomenorrhea. If your menstrual cycle is shorter than 21 days or longer than 35 days, you may have this condition. Medications, emotional upset, disease, and stress can all alter your cycle temporarily, says Dr. Bailey. Birth control methods such as the IUD and the Pill may disrupt your cycle as well.

Dr. Bailey also points out that any kind of steroid-based medication, including some medications for asthma and lupus, can cause changes in your periods.

MONITORING
FOR PREVENTION

You can't always prevent menstrual pain and irregularity, but you can identify small problems before they balloon into big ones.

Seek regular care. An annual pelvic exam and Pap smear are essential. They will allow your doctor to identify a potentially serious problem before it gets out of control, says Yvonne Thornton, M.D., director of perinatal diagnostic testing at Morristown Memorial Hospital in New Jersey.

Pay attention. You know best what is normal for you. If you perceive increased pain, depression, irritability, irregularity, spotting, breast tenderness, or changes in flow or cycle length, pay attention to them and, as Pat did, record them and share them with your doctor.

There are steps you can take to manage difficult or changing menstrual periods, says Dr. Bailey.

Use the calendar. Keep track of your periods, because women often don't realize that their cycle is changing. Your gynecologist needs to know when your last few periods began and ended, what changes you have seen, and for how long. If you simply get into the habit of making notes on the calendar every month, you'll be able to give your doctor detailed information.

Go natural. Some herbs may actually reduce the levels of prostaglandins, the natural hormones that cause cramping, without side effects. Talk to your doctor about trying evening primrose oil, meadowsweet, or feverfew.

Get moving. Exercise helps relieve menstrual cramps and bloating, although it has no effect on abnormal bleeding. It encourages the brain to produce endorphins, pain-dulling chemicals that elevate your mood and help reduce irritability.

Seek relief. For cramps, the occasional use of over-the-counter nonsteroidal anti-inflammatory drugs such as aspirin and ibuprofen (Advil, Nuprin) can help, says Dr. Bailey. Don't go overboard, though, as frequent use of these medications is known to cause stomach trouble. If menstrual pain or irregularity persists for more than two months, you should consult a doctor.

Consider the Pill. If you are otherwise healthy, a nonsmoker, and under 35, birth control pills can help regulate your cycle. Ask your gynecologist if this is the right option for you.

Migraines

ENDING THE PAIN

ara Powers, a 28-year-old graduate student at New York University in Greenwich Village, says, "I'm still learning what triggers my migraines, but I think I've found a home remedy that works for me. At least it nipped one in the bud the last time I tried it.

"Last semester, I had been working late night after night, and I had just turned in my thesis on the work of Jean Toomer. I was a mess—dark circles under my eyes, dreadlocks sticking out every which way—so I came home after class and collapsed in my favorite chair," she recalls. "But Gayle, my roommate, walked in and said, 'Oh, no, you don't. We're going to get you out of here to celebrate tonight. Let's hit the road.'

"I was thankful for the opportunity to relax, so I got myself together and we went uptown to her brother's for a party," says Lara. "Well, her brother and his friends were cool, but the house was filled with smoke. Then somebody handed me a glass of red wine, and Gayle insisted on making a toast to my success. I really appreciated the support in that room, but I was just too tired to party, so I made my excuses, told Gayle to hang out, and left to go home.

"Just as I settled into a cab, I began to see small flashing lights, the sure sign that I was on the fast track to a migraine. The stress, smoke, red wine, and exhaustion had done a number on me. As soon as I got home, I tried my secret weapon. I put in earplugs to block out all sound, grabbed a can of cola, went into my bedroom, and turned down the lights. After drinking all of the soda quickly, I lay down and closed my eyes. Believe it or not, the migraine failed to take hold. The next morning I was pain-free," she says with a smile.

"I'd heard about the cure from a girlfriend, who had learned about it from her doctor," Lara explains. "I have no idea why it works, but it does the trick for me."

The Birth
of a Migraine

Eighteen percent of women (almost one in every five) and 6 percent of men experience migraines, pulsing or throbbing headaches that typically occur on one side of the head and are often accompanied by nausea and a heightened sensitivity to light and noise. Migraines bear almost no relationship to everyday tension headaches when it comes to pain. They can be debilitating, preventing some people from carrying on with their lives.

A migraine is a type of vascular headache, which means that it is caused by activity in the blood vessels in the brain. Doctors now think that migraines have to do with brain excitability, explains Calvin B. Wheeler, M.D., clinical instructor in the Department of Neurology and Pediatrics at the University of California, San Francisco, School of Medicine and child neurologist and assistant physician-in-chief at Kaiser Permanente Medical Center in Fremont, California. In people with migraines, the brain tissue gives off an electrical impulse, almost like a seizure, and this causes changes in the blood vessels that in turn affect the blood flow and the amount of oxygen that reaches the brain.

Serotonin, an important chemical messenger in the brain, is also involved. When serotonin levels drop, blood vessel walls constrict, or narrow, and this temporarily reduces the amount of blood that can flow to the brain. The reduced blood flow causes the altered vision, nausea, and dizziness that create the migraine aura, an early warning sign that one of these headaches is on the way. You may experience visual changes such as flashing lights or scintillating scotomata, a line that suddenly cuts through your field of vision. Some people say that it can split the print on a page like a bolt of lightning.

Scientists don't yet understand how the fluctuating chemical levels trigger headaches, but one theory holds that when serotonin levels fall, levels of the body's pain-causing chemicals, notably one called substance P, rise.

After they constrict, the brain's blood vessels dilate, or expand, and then the real trouble begins. The swollen blood vessels press against adjoining structures, causing migraine pain that can last for hours or even days.

Once the migraine begins, some visual changes may persist. Or you may even temporarily lose part of your vision, says Dr. Wheeler.

Any part can be lost, but people often complain of tunnel vision, which means loss of peripheral vision, he adds.

During a migraine attack, if you feel clumsy or have temporary weakness in your hands or arms or if you have pain that you would describe as the worst headache of your life, see a doctor right away to rule out the possibility of stroke or hemorrhage, says Dr. Wheeler.

As with other types of headache, women are especially susceptible to migraines, says LaFayette Singleton, M.D., assistant professor of neurology at the University of Chicago School of Medicine. Some 60 percent of women find that their migraines are worse around their menstrual periods, when estrogen production rises in preparation for menstruation. Women who take birth control pills or hormone replacement therapy also have a slightly increased chance of developing migraines or having migraines that are more severe. "These headaches are probably also due to changing estrogen levels, because they tend to begin during the week when the woman is off the Pill," says Dr. Wheeler.

Heredity and stress can also make you migraine-prone, and even children are not immune: A study in Scotland found that 11 percent of children get migraines.

Poorly Understood but Preventable

The trick to avoiding migraines is to figure out what triggers them for you.

Know and heal thyself. To some extent, you must become your own headache detective, says Dr. Wheeler. Look for precipitating factors, such as foods or environmental conditions. High-fat foods such as pork, avocado, peanut butter, and sour cream are potent triggers for lots of folks. Beans, peas in the pod, and large amounts of raw garlic and onions also turn on the pain for some people, says Dr. Singleton.

Cheese, chocolate, and processed meats that contain chemicals called tyramines are also high on the list. And alcohol, especially red wine and champagne, which contain tyramine, is almost sure to set them off.

Watch scent sensations. Your environment can also give you a splitting headache. The smells of strong perfumes, fresh paint, and cigarette smoke are common troublemakers for people who get migraines. Interestingly, menthol cigarette smoke is a worse trigger than nonmenthol, says Dr. Wheeler.

Don't go to extremes. Long car trips, high altitudes, temperature changes, ice cream, bright lights, and excessive exercise can all put a person who is migraine-prone out of circulation for a while, says Dr. Singleton. Even a rapid drop in atmospheric pressure can trigger migraines, which means that people with migraines can often predict rain as well as the weatherman.

Get enough calcium and vitamin D. A report from Mount Sinai Medical Center in New York City indicates that a few women found migraine relief after their doctors prescribed 1,200 milligrams of calcium and 1,200 to 1,600 international units of a special type of vitamin D supplements. But don't stock up on vitamin D on your own, as it can be toxic. Ask for your doctor's advice.

Protect your immune system. Stress, poor sleeping and eating habits, and general neglect of your health can also make it easy for migraines to get the best of you. Dr. Singleton points out that stress is a factor in all types of headaches, especially migraines. He recommends that you try any type of relaxation therapy that works for you, including biofeedback, relaxation therapy, or massage. Getting adequate sleep, exercise, and proper nutrition can also help you reduce stress levels and stay healthy, he says.

Try the Wheeler technique. If you catch it early enough, you can stop a migraine in its tracks, says Dr. Wheeler. If you feel the telltale pain beginning as Lara did, Dr. Wheeler suggests that you drink a full 12 ounces of cola rapidly, then sit quietly in a dark room with an ice pack or cold compress on the area of pain. Your migraine will often go away in 10 to 15 minutes. This works best for people who normally don't drink too much caffeine, probably because the sudden jolt of caffeine in the cola short-circuits the headache.

KILLING THE PAIN

As anyone who gets migraines will tell you, when you have one, the only thing you can think of is pain relief. Painkillers have to be used carefully, however, to ease your discomfort and not make the pain worse, says Dr. Wheeler.

Take care with OTCs. Over-the-counter medications should not be taken more often than once or twice weekly because they can encourage rebound headaches, says Dr. Wheeler. Rebound headaches occur when the medication wears off and the headache returns with a vengeance. Besides, oral medications don't work well for many people with migraines because the nausea that often accompanies the headache interferes with the absorption of the medication in the stomach, he adds.

Go for the big guns. The prescription drug ergotamine (Cafergot, Ercaf) will often stop migraine pain, but it can make the accompanying nausea even worse. On the other hand, sumatriptan (Imitrex), which is available by injection or orally from your doctor, helps stop migraine in its tracks. The drug helps the brain absorb serotonin, which lowers the pain level. And it often works without side effects, says Dr. Wheeler.

Motion Sickness

STEADYING YOUR STOMACH

ate Newton sighed with pleasure as the sightseeing boat began its hour-long tour of Marina del Rey, California. "These deep-blue waters put me in mind of the islands," she says with a smile. "But they also remind me of something less pleasant—the only time I was ever seasick," she recalls with a grimace.

"When I lived in St. Croix, my home was a houseboat," recalls Kate. "I was sure that nothing could make me seasick. Then one evening, I set sail to Buck Island with some friends. The sunset was beautiful, but we didn't enjoy it for long.

"After eating barbecue and curries and drinking champagne, everyone was seasick—including me. I couldn't understand why I got sick this one time, and then it occurred to me. I lived on a big houseboat, but I had never been on a small sailboat." Now she takes a motion sickness pill as a precaution before she boards any type of ship.

MIXED MESSAGES IN MOTION

Whether it's carsickness, airsickness, or that ominously queasy feeling you get on a boat, motion sickness can rock your world. At some point, 90 percent of all Americans, Black and White, feel green. "Men and women are affected equally," says Victor Scott, M.D., chief of gastroenterology at Howard University Hospital in Washington, D.C. But for women who are premenstrual or pregnant, hormone levels may make it even more likely that they'll lose their lunch in the lurch.

Motion sickness begins innocently enough with yawning, drowsiness, perhaps a mild headache, and a dry mouth. These are quickly followed by cold sweats, belching, disorientation, flatulence, a sensitivity to strong smells, anxiety, apathy, and even depression. And then, of course, there's the nausea and vomiting.

It's the activity in your slightly confused inner ear that brings on all the trouble. Your inner ear plays a key role in keeping your balance, sort of like a biological compass that keeps you oriented. Your eyes and some of your joints also have these internal compasses, and they are all meant to work together—while you're walking on dry land.

When you are being passively moved by the gentle sway of a land, air, or water vehicle, these compasses can get contradictory messages, explains Dr. Scott. "The illusion of self-induced motion does the damage," he says. The body is fooled into thinking it is active, when actually it is being moved passively by the boat, car, plane, or train. This illusion somehow then fools the body's sense of equilibrium, and this in turn stimulates the brain's vomiting center.

Traveling Easy

You can lose the illusion, however. These few simple preventive steps may save you from hours of misery.

Spice things up. Many people find that ginger helps to keep their stomachs calm, and some medical studies show it can be more effective than Dramamine and other drugs at keeping motion sickness at bay. "Take two capsules of ground ginger root 20 minutes before the trip starts," suggests Kathy Williamson, N.D., a naturopathic physician in private practice in Los Angeles. "Chew on ginger root, eat gingersnaps or ginger candy, or drink ginger beer," she adds.

Keep your eyes front and center. "If you're prone to seasickness, fix your eyes on the horizon. This will bring some stability to your sensations," advises Dr. Scott.

Always face forward when traveling by train or bus and choose the window seat on planes. You want your eyes, ears, and knees to perceive the same bump or swerve at the same time, so don't cut off your line of vision to windows because the lack of visual clues will make matters worse.

Leave your book at home. Do yourself a favor and put that magazine down. When you read while riding, your eyes sweep the page in a left-to-right motion, while your inner ear rides a roller coaster of dips and bumps. All this makes your stomach feel as if it's been left behind, says Dr. Scott.

Steer clear of smoke. Avoid cigarette smoke and perfume or cologne while traveling. Strong odors can encourage motion sickness.

Snack as you go. "Eat a small, low-fat, easily digestible snack every 2 hours or so," Dr. Scott advises. A study of diet and airsickness at the Center for Aerospace Sciences in North Dakota suggested that eating a carbohydrate-rich snack just before a trip may discourage motion sickness.

Stay liquid. "Drink plenty of fluids, but not alcohol," suggests Dr. Scott. As Kate and her friends discovered, alcohol can predispose you to motion sickness.

Go electric. "At Digestive Disease Week, a conference for 10,000 doctors in San Francisco, I saw a device that straps around the wrist like a wristwatch and produces electrical stimulation of an acupressure point," says Dr. Scott. If you want to try it, you'll need a prescription from your doctor. It's called the ReliefBand, and it's made by Maven Laboratories in Citrus Heights, California.

In the Eye of the Storm

If self-help measures fail to solve your problem, there are other treatment options for mild to serious cases of motion sickness.

Try punctures or pressure. "Acupuncture works well for some people. But you can also try a simple acupressure technique whenever you start feeling queasy. Simply press the nei-kuan point in your wrist," says Dr. Williamson. To find this point, find the crease of skin where your wrist joins your hand. The nei-kuan point is three finger widths below this point. Place your index finger between the tendons you feel there and press until you begin to feel better.

Take medications early. Dramamine, Bonine, and other over-the-counter motion sickness drugs are most effective when taken an hour before you start traveling, says Dr. Scott. Promethazine (Phenergan), a prescription drug, is also highly effective.

But beware: All of these medications can make you drowsy or dizzy. They are not the best option if you're getting behind the wheel or planning to drink alcohol. Pregnant women and seniors should check with their doctors before using any prescription or over-the-counter motion sickness drug.

Nutrition

Eating to Win

bout three weeks into my new eating plan, the change really caught me by surprise," says Sheila Thomas. "Ever since I was a teenager, you had to practically tilt the mattress and dump me on the floor to get me out of bed," she says, laughing. "Then one morning I got up an hour before the alarm, turned on my favorite morning DJ, and hit the shower. When I stepped out of the bathroom, raring to go, and it was only 6:45, I said to myself, 'Check this out! Nap used to be my middle name, and now all of sudden I'm Miss Morning Person.'"

Sheila was into staying in shape, so she had always found a way to get to the gym for occasional workouts. But the source of her new-found energy was her diet. "A trainer who I was sort of . . . well, really flirting with at my gym noticed that I would do things like work out and then eat a candy bar on my way out the door. My motto was, 'If I'm not fat, what's the difference? I'm only 32,'" says the Milwaukee-based administrative assistant. "He said the difference would eventually show up in my cholesterol levels, and even if the sugar and fat I consumed didn't fatten me up, it would tire me out.

"I didn't get a date, but he gave me a copy of a healthy eating plan that laid out all the basics of good nutrition," she says. "And I've got to say, the difference is really something. It was hard limiting sweets, especially, but I feel great, and I dropped a couple of pounds in the bargain."

You Are What You Eat

Eating right (along with getting exercise) is the best preventive medicine known to man. Almost every chronic disease that African-Americans struggle with has a risk factor that's connected to the way many of us eat. Few of us are in danger of starving, but we can still do a lot of serious damage if we choose the wrong foods. The human body is a machine, and just like a sleek, finely tuned car, it needs the right grade and quality of fuel to ensure that it keeps running in top-notch condition.

The basics are simple. Carbohydrate, protein, and fat are the three nutrients that provide the energy you need for everything from breathing to running a marathon. Along with these energy-providing nutrients, vitamins, minerals, and water play a role in every bodily function and process.

We are very fortunate because we live in a time when nutritional deficiencies, as measured by minimum needs, are rare. Our problem is more a result of riches—an overabundance of high-fat, high-sugar, high-salt goodies. Yet even considering the fact that we are not in danger of overall deficiency, there are some nutrients to which you need to pay particular attention to ensure that you get the critical minimum.

Folate, for example, is a B vitamin that is extremely important for women during their childbearing years, because deficiencies at the time of conception and very early in pregnancy can result in serious birth defects. Folate also helps ward off cervical cancer. But if you don't eat a balanced diet, it's hard to get the Daily Value of 400 micrograms.

The National Cancer Institute encourages all Americans to strive for five, which means eating a minimum of five half-cup servings of fruits and vegetables daily. The five-a-day strategy is also part of the Food Guide Pyramid, established by the U.S. Department of Agriculture (USDA). The USDA bases its recommendations on what it calls the leader nutrients in fruits and vegetables, such as vitamins C and A. Here's how it works.

The basics. The base of the pyramid is plant-based and includes the foods that should be the foundation of your diet. These are minimally processed breads, cereals, rice, and pasta. The USDA recommends eating 6 to 11 servings of these foods each day, with the smallest number of servings for people who consume about 1,600 calories day, such as sedentary women, and the highest number for people who consume about 2,800 calories a day, such as active men. A serving is 1 slice of bread, 1 ounce of ready-to-eat cereal, or ½ cup of cooked cereal, rice, or pasta.

Level two. Vegetables and fruits are at the next level of the pyramid. Eating a variety of them helps you get your daily quota of vitamin C, beta-carotene, and folate and other B vitamins. Aim for three to five servings of vegetables and two to four servings of fruits a day. This way, you'll easily meet your five-a-day goal, and you'll get extra protection against both minor illnesses and chronic diseases. A serving is 1 cup of raw, leafy vegetables; ½ cup of other vegetables (cooked or chopped raw); 1 medium apple, banana, or orange; ½ cup of chopped cooked or canned fruit; ¾ cup of vegetable or fruit juice; or ¼ cup of dried fruit.

Level three. The milk group and the meat and bean group are at level three, which means you should eat them in much smaller amounts than the grains, vegetables, and fruits.

From the milk group, you need only two servings of milk, yogurt, or cheese a day unless you're pregnant or a young person between the ages of 13 and 25, in which case you need three servings. A serving is a cup of milk or yogurt, 1½ ounces of natural cheese, or 2 ounces of processed cheese.

You only need two or three servings a day from the meat and bean group, which is the section of the pyramid that includes protein. This food group also includes dry beans or legumes and nuts, which are nonanimal sources of protein, as well as eggs. African-Americans need to increase their consumption of these nonanimal protein sources and reduce their consumption of meat.

Selections from the milk and meat groups should be lean and low-fat, since excess dietary fat is linked to a host of health problems. Eat lean beef or poultry and low-fat yogurt and drink skim or low-fat (1 percent) milk, for example. And remember, a serving of meat is 3 ounces, which is about the size of a deck of cards.

At the top. Finally, there is the group of foods comprised of fats, oils, and sweets. As you probably already know, fats are seldom lacking in American diets, especially African-American diets. Since keeping fat to a minimum is essential if you want to avoid being overweight and developing high cholesterol, which leads to heart disease, high blood pressure, and loads of other problems, and the amount of fat you need is easily supplied by meat and dairy foods, there's no need to seek out fats and oils. (The Daily Value for total fat for someone eating 2,000 calories a day is no more than 65 grams. Of that, 20 grams or less should be saturated fat.)

As for sweets, some nutrition experts recommend that you get only 10 percent of your calories from sugar. Food labels list both added sugar and naturally occurring sugar. You can tell that a food is high in sugar if the first or second ingredient on a label is corn syrup, high-fructose corn syrup, sugar, honey, or some other form of sugar.

What about Soul Food?

Our favorite foods receive a bad rap because we include too much fat, sugar, and salt in our traditional recipes. But that doesn't mean that you have to give up collard greens and sweet potatoes to be healthy. We need to remember that the basics of the typical African-American diet are good. "We have always enjoyed fresh vegetables, fish, and chicken, but unfortunately, we add fat to them," says Lillie R. Williams, R.D., Ph.D., chairperson of the Department of Nutritional Sciences at Howard University in Washington, D.C.

In fact, most cultures where sisters are stirring the pots produce foods that are packed with fiber, vitamins, and other goodies. The hot peppers and yams of Africa, the seafood and fish stews of the Caribbean, and the black-eyed peas, rice, and cornbread of the American South are some of the healthiest foods around, particularly if you keep things lean.

Getting the Nutrition Advantage

Here are a few basic concepts for high-powered eating.

Keep it green. Focus on a vegetable-based diet of whole, minimally processed fresh foods. Add whole grains such as breads, cereals, and rice, seasonal fresh fruits, and dried beans to that dietary foundation, says Dr. Williams.

Get real. When it comes to 10 daily servings of fruit and vegetables (5 of each), Dr. Williams points out that Blacks need to understand that sweetened, fruit-flavored drinks do not count as a fruit.

"African-Americans tend to cook vegetables to death and often rely on processed foods, such as lunchmeats, frozen meals, and packaged macaroni and cheese, leaving out good sources of vegetables and fruits. We need to go back to basics and use our current knowledge to eat the way we did years ago—wholesome fruits and vegetables, high-fiber beans and peas, and brown bread," says Rovenia Brock, Ph.D., nutritionist and health correspondent for Black Entertainment Television (BET) News.

Trim the fat. Fat occurs naturally in meat and dairy products, and we eat way too much meat, says Lauren Swann, R.D., president of Concept Nutrition Consulting in Bensalem, Pennsylvania. Since you don't need extra helpings of oil and animal fat in your diet, take a close look at your cooking methods.

Broil, grill, or steam food. Let sauces, soups, and gravies cool and skim the fat off the top before reheating and eating. Use vegetable oil sprays instead of bottled oil, margarine, or butter. Try low-fat cheeses, milk, and ice cream. And taste some of the new fat-free snack foods and desserts, says Swann.

But remember that fat-free does not mean calorie-free—you still have to eat in moderation. In particular, watch your intake of fat-free snack foods. And read the labels, says Swann. Olean, the nonabsorbed fat, has been associated with causing diarrhea in some people.

Eat fewer sweets. Sugar, which Swann believes African-Americans eat to excess, can erode your teeth and contribute to other heath problems, such as obesity. Try cutting back on the number of "lumps" in your coffee or tea, sweetening baked goods with fruit juice instead of sugar, and eating low-sugar desserts such as stewed or baked fruit, fresh fruit cup, or fruit canned in its own juice.

Learn the rules. Follow the Food Guide Pyramid and read food labels. If you normally eat about 2,000 calories a day, try to limit fat to less than 65 grams, cholesterol to less than 300 miligrams, and sodium to less than 2,400 milligrams. You should also try to get at least 25 grams of dietary fiber daily.

Osteoarthritis

Boning Up on Joint Protection

or years, I'd had minor pains in my fingers," recalls Gayle Worthy, a Cleveland-based mental health therapist with two children. "Later, my knees hurt, especially when I used stairs, but the pain came and went. As soon as I'd decide to go to the doctor, it would disappear. Then one day my knees hurt so badly that I fell and needed help getting up. That got me to the doctor's office fast.

"First I was diagnosed with carpal tunnel syndrome, but it turned out that I had osteoarthritis in my knees and my hands. Now I keep it under control with over-the-counter pain relievers, heat, and moderate exercise. I'm much better than I was two years ago," says Gayle with a sigh of relief.

While Gayle's story may seem pretty typical, here's a surprising fact: She's 34, and not only did she play varsity volleyball in college, she is still slim, muscular, and in incredible shape.

Age Is Not the Issue

Despite the usual image of arthritis as a disease of the elderly, the average age of someone who has it is 47. Most people with arthritis have the type called osteoarthritis, a condition that can appear as early as your teen years.

Osteoarthritis is not age-related, says Margaret A. Fountain, M.D., an arthritis specialist in private practice and the health editor for a local television station in Baltimore. But it is gender-related—women make up the overwhelming proportion of people with arthritis. Osteoarthritis affects about 16 million people (12 percent of the U.S. population), almost 12 million of whom are women. Arthritis is also diverse: 40 million Americans suffer from over 100 forms of arthritis. Osteoarthritis and rheumatoid arthritis are the most widespread types.

Osteoarthritis, also known as degenerative joint disease, results when the cartilage that cushions the bones in your joints erodes from the wear and tear of daily activities, whether it's working with a jackhammer, carrying around 30 pounds of extra body weight, or playing varsity volleyball.

Figuring Out the Risk

No one knows why two to four times as many women are affected by arthritis, but some research suggests that estrogen may have something to do with it. The confusion lies in the fact that experts disagree about its connection. Research in Taiwan has implicated estrogen as a cause of arthritic changes in the joints, but Dr. Fountain believes that estrogen may be protective, and some medical studies support her viewpoint. She points out that a woman's arthritis accelerates after menopause, when estrogen levels decline. Here are some of the factors that are known to put you at risk for osteoarthritis.

Hysterectomy. Estrogen levels decline abruptly after a hysterectomy, says Dr. Fountain. A woman who has a hysterectomy at 25 can develop arthritis that's just like her 60-year-old mother's by the time she reaches 30. Since large numbers of Black women have hysterectomies before age 50 because of fibroids, we have an increased risk.

Genetics. Arthritis runs in many families.

Congenital malformations. If your bones are improperly aligned or shaped, even in very minor ways, you can put an unusual amount of stress on a weight-bearing joint, which encourages osteoarthritis. You can't change your bone and ligament structure, says Dr. Fountain, but you can lose weight to minimize this effect.

Overdoing it. Both injury and excessive exercise encourage osteoarthritis, so work and play with care. Athletes—both amateurs and professionals—can tear ligaments as a result of bad form and overuse. At work, accidents and repetitive motion injury can also encourage osteoarthritis.

Carrying a heavy load. The risk and severity of osteoarthritis increase as your weight increases because of the extra stress on your joints.

GETTING
RELIEF

If you think you have osteoarthritis, here are Dr. Fountain's recommendations on how to cope.

Don't suffer in silence. The first time you experience joint pain or swelling, whether it's in your fingers, knees, ankles, or hips, visit your doctor. Pain that starts your day and eases with rest could be caused by osteoarthritis. The earlier the condition is detected and treated, the less damage it will do to your joints over time.

Exercise with care. Moving arthritis-stiffened joints is definitely the best way to ease the pain and increase your mobility, but too much exercise can make the problem worse. Pay attention to your body's pain signals and use proper technique to minimize stress on your weight-bearing joints. And always warm up and stretch gently before getting started and cool down afterward. Your doctor or a personal trainer can help you develop a workout that's easy on your joints.

Stay light on your feet. Try to keep your weight under control. Overweight people are at greater risk for osteoarthritis, so talk to your doctor about a diet and exercise program if you need to shed some pounds.

Try a little heat. Heat gives you relief by helping to loosen the muscles, ligaments, and tendons that surround a joint. All the parts of a joint operate more smoothly when warm.

Heat from a warm shower or bath or moist heat like a hot water bottle is best. Try it twice a day for 10 to 15 minutes each time.

Then cool it down. Sometimes it helps to follow the 10 to 15 minutes of heat with 10 to 15 minutes of cold. Use a regular ice pack or wrap the ice tightly in a cloth, since applying ice directly could damage your skin. The hot and cold combination should be especially helpful when your pain is severe.

Give your joints a break. When joints are very inflamed, the best thing for them is rest. Balance activity and inactivity for the best results. Lie down or put your feet up for 20 to 30 minutes a few times a day. And always try to get a good night's sleep (at least 8 hours).

Don't dog your feet. Ill-fitting shoes can put extra pain and strain on already inflamed ankles and knees. Try to wear shoes that provide both comfort and good support.

Try an alternative. A few studies have shown that acupuncture is very effective for relieving arthritis pain. It is also free of side effects, since it does not involve the use of any medication. Contact the American Academy of Medical Acupuncture at 5820 Wilshire Boulevard, Suite 500, Los Angeles, CA 90036 for a recommendation for an acupuncturist anywhere in the United States.

Medicate the pain. Over-the-counter painkillers such as ibuprofen (Advil, Nuprin) and aspirin work very well for arthritis pain. Don't mix different types of painkillers, though.

"You may buy your painkillers at the pharmacy, but ask the pharmacist or doctor for advice before you combine medications or exceed recommended dosages. You should also let your pharmacist or doctor know if you are taking drugs for other conditions before deciding to take pain medications," says Dr. Fountain.

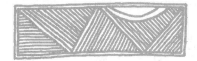

Osteoporosis

REDUCING YOUR RISKS

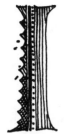"I thought black women didn't get osteoporosis," Dana Johnson, the pastor's secretary, remarked to her dinner companions at the fellowship dinner of the Minnesota First Methodist Church.

The reason for her comment was that earlier that day, almost the whole congregation had witnessed Sister Perkins's misery as she cried out and fell back into her pew when she tried to rise after services. Her small, wizened face was contorted with pain as her distraught daughter held her hand and waited for the ambulance. A few hours later, when her daughter called the rectory from the hospital to say that her mother was resting comfortably, she told the pastor that her mother had broken her hip simply by trying to stand up. The doctor said that her bones had been severely weakened by osteoporosis, which was not surprising in a woman of 74.

"I asked Dana to look around her," says April Cheatham, one of the few nurses in the congregation. "I told her that I see cases at the hospital every day." And when Dana surveyed the room, she saw that many of the older women were stooped and moving gingerly.

"When I asked Dana if she had ever stopped to think how many women are on the shut-in list because they've broken their hips," April continues, "she commented that she never wanted to get like that. I told her that she needed to start taking care of herself now, before she goes through menopause. I've been taking calcium supplements, working out, and eating with my bones in mind for as long as I can remember, and my doctor says my bone scan shows I'm in good shape, even though I'm 65."

Setting the Stage
for a Tough Break

"There is a progressive increase in bone density up until your twenties, but from the midtwenties or midthirties, we all lose bone at a rate of 0.5 to 1 percent a year," says Linda Bradley, M.D., a staff gynecologist at the Cleveland Clinic Foundation in Ohio. The slow loss of bone may result in the stooped, shortened stature and thin, porous, fragile bones that characterize osteoporosis. "For many women, though, osteoporosis is viewed as an event, like a fracture, rather than a lifelong process," she says.

This disease typically affects women in their fifties who have gone through menopause. "But the process of bone loss begins to occur in the early thirties. Women can lose 1 percent of bone mass yearly, with an accelerated loss of 1.5 to 3 percent yearly during menopause. Women with osteoporosis have no symptoms until a fracture occurs," explains Dr. Bradley.

"Approximately 25 million Americans suffer from osteoporosis," she says. Eighty percent of those who have osteoporosis are women, and we break our hips two to three times more often than men. And, although osteoporosis rates are much lower among African-American women, we still have to protect ourselves from the disease.

Certain conditions put a woman of any race at greater risk, including a family history of osteoporosis, greater height, endometriosis (inflammation of the lining of the uterus), irregular periods, a bout with an eating disorder that produces amenorrhea (absence of menstruation), excessive alcohol consumption, smoking, or too much thyroid medication, says Dr. Bradley.

Boosting
Your Bones

The good news about osteoporosis is that it can be prevented if you are willing to work at building strong bones early in life. Here are some steps to take.

Count on calcium. Getting adequate calcium is the best way to fight osteoporosis. According to the National Institutes of Health, before menopause, you should consume the Daily Value (DV) of 1,000 milligrams of calcium. After menopause, if you're using hormone replacement therapy (HRT), you should continue to get the DV; if you're not using HRT or you're over 65, you should aim for 1,500 milligrams. Pregnant women should have at least 1,200 milligrams to protect themselves and their babies.

"Children often obtain ample calcium from milk, but for many adults, the high fat content coupled with lactose intolerance makes other sources of calcium far more nutritionally attractive," says Barbara Dixon, R.D., a dietitian in Baton Rouge, Louisiana, and author of *Good Health for African-American Kids.*

"Sardines, tuna, salmon, tofu, almonds, and instant oatmeal are very good sources of calcium without the saturated fat found in many dairy products," says Dixon. Green vegetables such as collard greens and broccoli will also boost your calcium levels. And you should also reduce your intake of coffee, soda, and tea because caffeine can increase the excretion of calcium from your body.

You can supplement your calcium intake with antacids, calcium citrate drinks like calcium-fortified orange juice, or vitamins, but they are not all created equal. "Citrucel, a fiber supplement, is a good source of calcium because it can be taken without food and is well-absorbed by the body. Some people may experience gas or constipation with additional calcium," says Dr. Bradley.

"If you choose to take an actual calcium vitamin supplement, you should check the fine print on the label to see how much elemental calcium you'll absorb from each pill and how quickly the pill will dissolve in your stomach. If calcium in pills won't be absorbed from the stomach within 30 minutes, the body won't use much of it. Look for the statement, 'This calcium supplement has met a 30-minute dissolution standard as per USP standards,' " advises Dr. Bradley. Or try a little home chemistry: Fill a tall glass with vinegar, drop a pill in, and stir vigorously. If the pill dissolves in the glass within 30 minutes, your supplement will dissolve in your stomach within 30 minutes.

Get plenty of D. Calcium can't do its job of building and maintaining bone without adequate vitamin D. "Because our skins make vitamin D when exposed to sunlight, people who don't get enough sunlight and women who don't eat a balanced diet may not get enough vitamin D," says Dr. Bradley.

For women who need to take a supplement, Dr. Bradley suggests multivitamins that contain vitamin D. "There are also calcium

A bone-density test is a valuable yet simple tool for testing the strength of your bones. "Currently, less than 10 percent of all women who have osteoporosis are being treated," says Linda Bradley, M.D., a staff gynecologist at the Cleveland Clinic Foundation in Ohio. "Even with a patient's history and symptoms, osteoporosis may not be detected without diagnostic testing. Therefore, many women would benefit from bone-density testing." Here's what you need to know about this test.

When: Have a baseline test at menopause and then as often as your doctor recommends. If you are at high risk because of a family history of osteoporosis or a personal history of an overactive thyroid or if you regularly take medications such as steroids (prednisone) or blood thinners (warfarin), consider having the baseline test done in your forties and then as often as your doctor recommends, says Dr. Bradley. "Low bone mass is the single most accurate predictor of future fracture risk."

How it's done: There are a few different tests. The most common, called dual energy x-ray absorptiometry (DEXA), shows if you have a potentially serious amount of bone loss. As you lie on a table, a technician takes x-rays of common fracture sites—your hip, spine, and wrist. A computer evaluates the image to determine your bone strength. The amount of radiation exposure you'll receive is less than that from a chest x-ray.

Cost: $75 to $250. Check with your insurance carrier to see if it's covered.

pills that contain vitamin D, but be careful to take no more than 400 international units of vitamin D a day, because it can be toxic in large doses," warns Zerline Chambers-Kersey, M.D., an obstetrician and gynecologist in private practice in Annandale, Virginia.

Learn to lift. Besides getting enough calcium throughout your life, doing weight-bearing exercises such as walking, stair climbing, weight lifting, and aerobics will build bone mass, says Dr. Bradley. And it's never too late. "In early life, weight-bearing exercise builds bones, and later in life, it preserves bone. Older women should see a physical therapist for formal instruction because some exercises help, but others increase the risk of fractures," she says.

"Also, the elderly should make their homes as 'fracture-proof' as possible. Many accidents like falls, slips, and mishaps occur in the bathroom or kitchen. Make sure you have slip-proof rugs in the bathroom and handrails and mats in the bathtub. Slippers or house shoes with nonskid soles are essential," she says. "Many physical therapists can make additional recommendations to enhance safety in your home."

Forget the butts. Smoking steals bone, so do yourself a favor and stop smoking now. Smokers have a higher risk of osteoporosis.

TREATING
WEAKENED BONES

There are several treatment choices for women who develop osteoporosis. Here are your options.

Consider prescription solutions. "There are several prescription medications approved for osteoporosis. Calcitriol (Rocaltrol) is a pill that you take once a day. Calcitonin (Calcimar) is a drug that you inject into a muscle three to five times per week, or you can use the convenient calcitonin nasal spray (Miacalcin)," says Dr. Bradley. The only other prescription medication approved for the treatment of osteoporosis is the newest, alendronate (Fosamax), a pill that you take with water in the morning at least 30 minutes before eating or drinking anything else. Talk with your doctor to determine the best drug treatment for you.

Check out HRT. By replacing diminishing levels of estrogen, hormone replacement therapy (HRT) helps prevent the dramatic bone loss that occurs during menopause. "In my opinion, every woman, including every African-American woman, should absolutely think about HRT before menopause and discuss its pros and cons with her doctor even earlier," says Dr. Bradley.

"The major concern with HRT is that 10 years of treatment may increase a woman's risk of breast cancer, but this is an extremely controversial area. Neither the doctors nor the studies have reached a consensus about whether or not HRT increases the risk," she says.

Ovarian Cancer

SURVIVING AGAINST THE ODDS

welve women of different ages, sizes, and colors are seated on metal folding chairs in the meeting room of a Manhattan-based cancer support group. Rashida Cochran, a 28-year-old bicycle messenger with a trim, red natural, opens the day's session by saying, "After my surgery, they told me that they thought they had gotten all the cancer, but I couldn't really consider myself cured for five years. That was four and a half years ago, and so far, so good.

"I've kept up my healthy lifestyle. I eat a high-fiber, low-fat diet and work out three times a week—staying in good enough shape to dodge New York City cabbies—and I've tried to relieve my stress. I meditate and pray, and coming here helps immensely. It's comforting to know that I'm not the only one going through this."

"I really should start working out, too," says Janet Miller, shifting uncomfortably in her chair and wondering why the group can't find wider seats for mature posteriors like hers. "I need to lose weight, and heaven knows I've got enough stress. I start my second round of chemotherapy tomorrow, and my doctor says that they couldn't remove all the cancer."

"What sort of cancer do you have?" asks Rashida.

"Ovarian," Janet, who's 63, replies.

"So do I," answers Rashida. "I think we're the only ones in the group. Please give me a call if you need anything or just want to talk."

AN ILLNESS THAT IS
POORLY UNDERSTOOD

Rashida and Janet needed to join together and offer each other a little sisterly support, because ovarian cancer is a relatively rare cancer in the general population, and it's rarer still in African-American women, says Otis W. Brawley, M.D., director of the Office of Special Populations at the National Cancer Institute in Bethesda, Maryland. About 16 of every 100,000 White women in the United States get ovarian cancer, but only 10 of every 100,000 Black women develop it. The five-year survival rate for White and Black women is similar: 44 percent for Whites and 38 percent for Blacks.

If ovarian cancer is caught before it spreads, as Rashida's was, the cure rate is high: 90 percent. Unfortunately, only 23 percent of White women and 20 percent of Black women are diagnosed at that early stage. The other kind of ovarian cancer, called regional and distant, which Janet has, is very rarely cured, says Dr. Brawley.

To help understand the risks, consider that over her life span, a woman's chance of developing breast cancer averages 1 in 8. The odds of developing ovarian cancer are only 1 in 53 for White women and 1 in 90 for Black women, but the risk increases with age. Almost three-fourths of all women who get ovarian cancer are over 50, and more than half of Black women are 61 or older, says Dr. Brawley.

Some young women like Rashida, who get the disease during their childbearing years, tend to develop a slow-growing form that can be arrested before it spreads.

"There have been many advances in treatment, and that can increase the number of cures and increase the life spans of many patients," says Edward W. Savage, Jr., M.D., medical director and chief of gynecology at the King-Drew Medical Center in Los Angeles and professor of obstetrics and gynecology at the medical center and the University of California at Los Angeles.

The catch is that while the key to curing ovarian cancer is early detection, it is almost impossible to diagnose in its early stages. The primary symptoms feel like common stomach or menstrual problems. Women may try over-the-counter remedies for some time before seeking professional help. Then, when they do see a physician, they may be treated for an ulcer, a hiatal hernia, or gastritis, since the symptoms can masquerade as these conditions, says Dr. Savage. There is no simple test for detecting ovarian cancer, he explains.

The mystery of ovarian cancer doesn't stop with the problem of early detection. Scientists are unsure about what causes it. It may be that a carcinogen (cancer-causing substance) finds its way to the ovaries through the vagina.

Another theory suggests that ovarian cancer may be caused by the wear and tear that the monthly menstrual cycle places on the ovaries. Each month during ovulation, a mature egg literally bursts through the wall of the ovary, then the ovarian tissue repairs itself.

UNDERSTANDING YOUR RISK PROFILE

It is possible to prevent ovarian cancer, but first you need to understand your personal odds of developing the disease.

Women who have a first-degree relative—that is, mother, daughter, or sister—with ovarian cancer have a 1-in-20 chance of developing it themselves. Women with two such relatives have a 1-in-14 (or 7 percent) chance.

About 3 percent of women who have two or more family members with ovarian cancer have a hereditary ovarian cancer syndrome, which means that they are at higher-than-average risk. These rare women have a defect in a gene that has been identified as causing either breast or ovarian cancer or both. They have an 8-in-10 chance of getting one or both diseases. But this gene defect is present in only 5 to 7 percent of women with ovarian cancer.

GETTING THE BEST PROTECTION

Preventing ovarian cancer is not an exact science, but there are steps you can take to stay healthy.

Don't dust. We're not talking housecleaning here. A study of more than 400 women at Harvard Medical School found that women who used talcum powder on their genital area on a daily basis for many years were three times more likely to get ovarian cancer than women who did not. While this doesn't mean that there is a definite correlation between talcum powder and ovarian cancer, according to Dr. Brawley, you may want to forgo using your favorite powder below the waist until there is more conclusive evidence.

Know your history. The best indication of risk is your family history, says Dr. Savage. Talk to your family members and find out whether any of your relatives has had the disease.

Consider the Pill. Some data suggest that women who take birth control pills for at least four years at some time before menopause have half the ovarian cancer rate of women who don't take it. This may be because the pill cuts down the number of times that you ovulate in a lifetime.

Give birth. Women who do not have children have twice the risk of ovarian cancer of women who have two or three, explains Dr. Savage, perhaps because pregnancy suspends ovulation for long periods of time.

Breastfeed. If you choose to have children and breastfeed for a lifetime total of one to two years, notes Dr. Savage, you can reduce your risk of ovarian cancer by one-third.

Go carrot crazy. An Ohio State University study of over 200 women found that those whose diets were high in foods containing beta-carotene had a reduced risk of ovarian cancer. Crunching carrots is an easy, natural way to get lots of beta-carotene, but sweet potatoes, kale, and turnip greens are also good sources of this nutrient.

Tie it up. If you are sure that you don't want any more children or you're not interested in getting pregnant at all, consider having your fallopian tubes tied as a form of birth control. A Harvard Medical School study of more than 120,000 nurses found that women who had their tubes tied reduced their risk of ovarian cancer by 67 percent, although no one is sure why.

Think twice about ovary removal. According to a panel of experts at the National Institutes of Health (NIH) in Bethesda, Maryland, the risk for a woman with one close relative who had ovarian cancer is probably not high enough to warrant the removal of her ovaries. But for women who come from a family with hereditary ovarian cancer syndrome, the NIH panel believes that the risk is high enough to recommend removal of the ovaries as a preventive measure after childbearing is completed or by age 35.

Although removing your ovaries sounds like a good way to prevent ovarian cancer, particularly in women who have a hereditary syndrome, it does not reduce the risk of ovarian-related cancers that might grow elsewhere in the abdominal cavity.

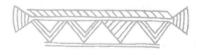

Painful Intercourse

SEXUAL HEALING

lthea Jackson can't remember every single time it happened, but the day she recalls most clearly was marked by the fact that she was fighting off a terrible cold. "I was lying in bed one morning, blowing my nose every 5 minutes and popping cold pills. I had on my sexiest burgundy silk pajamas, but I still felt stuffed-up and unattractive," explains the 37-year-old graphic designer.

And to make matters worse, the cold pills—or the cold—had left her constipated. "I told my husband, Ron, 'I'm sorry about the auto show, but I feel too bad to even get out of bed, so go with your buddy Edgar,'" she says.

But Ron was having none of it, she recalls. "He told me, 'That's all right, baby, I'm right where I want to be.'"

"Cute as he is, I could have wrung his neck," says Althea, "I just wanted to roll over and go back to sleep. But sometimes in a marriage you have to try to push yourself a little, so I hung in there," she says.

Cold or no cold, Ron not only wanted to hang out, he wanted to make love. Althea gave in, thinking that it might take her mind off her sinuses.

"But a few minutes later, when he asked me for the third time what was wrong, I knew I really had a problem. The sex really hurt—it was horribly painful, and I had no idea why," says Althea.

ALL PAIN, NO GAIN

Although it may seem surprising, Althea has plenty of company. Experts at Northwestern University in Chicago estimate that up to 50 percent of all sexually active American women, Black and White, will experience painful sexual intercourse at some point in their lives.

Painful intercourse comes in many forms and from many causes, including fibroids, endometriosis, pelvic infections, pelvic inflammatory disease, hemorrhoids, surgical scar tissue, yeast infections, sexually transmitted diseases (STDs), and a lack of vaginal lubrication, says Zerline Chambers-Kersey, M.D., an obstetrician and gynecologist in private practice in Annandale, Virginia.

Some women have pain only with deep thrusting or certain positions. Others experience pain, sometimes severe, as soon as their partner attempts to penetrate the vagina. Whatever the type, many women assume that the pain is normal or inevitable and don't try to find help.

African-American women are more likely than others to ignore their bodies' painful messages, says Dr. Chambers-Kersey. "We are socialized to care for others but not ourselves, and we develop a habit of ignoring our body's messages. But sex shouldn't hurt, and if you have this problem, you can be helped—if you talk to your doctor," she says.

WHY DOES IT HURT?

Before you can ease the agony of painful intercourse and get things back to normal, you and your doctor need to identify the source of your discomfort. Here are some common causes.

Vaginal dryness. Your problem may be too little lubrication, especially if you're over 30. Estrogen helps to promote the natural moisture of the vagina, and if your estrogen levels drop for any reason, your vagina may be so dry that the friction of sex is painful. Dryness can also be caused by menopausal changes that occur with age. As your ovaries produce less estrogen, your vagina produces less lubrication, which can make having intercourse rough and uncomfortable.

Also, if you take antihistamines for a cold or allergies, as Althea did, you may find that they can dry mucus secretions throughout your body, including your vagina.

Fluctuating hormones. Hormonal imbalances, caused by illness or by medications like antidepressants, blood pressure medications, or anti-cancer drugs, may result in less estrogen and/or less lubrication. If you are having trouble with painful intercourse and you are taking any of these types of medications, consult your doctor to see if these drugs could be the cause of your problem, says Dr. Chambers-Kersey.

An impatient partner. As you mature, you need more time to become aroused and lubricated, so a woman in her thirties and forties may need more foreplay. Your partner may not be taking enough time to arouse you.

Constipation. If there is stool resting in your colon during intercourse, your vaginal walls may be painfully squeezed between the man's penis on one side and the hardened stool on the other. This was part of Althea's problem.

Uterine problems. The presence of fibroids or endometriosis can cause similar pain if thrusts of the penis put pressure on the involved tissues during intercourse. Since Black women are prone to fibroids, they may experience painful intercourse as a result.

Structural problems. If your uterus is tipped backward as a result of natural causes, surgery, or pelvic scarring, intercourse can be painful. Some women may also have unusually short vaginas, which can also lead to pain.

Episiotomy scarring. During childbirth, the obstetrician may do an episiotomy, a vertical cut in the vagina to help accommodate the baby's head. The scar tissue that forms later may be very sensitive and make intercourse painful.

STDs or infections. Painful intercourse may be a warning sign that you have an STD or a bad vaginal infection. Both conditions can irritate the vaginal opening and make sex painful.

Vaginismus. Sometimes a woman's anxiety about sex can trigger a dramatic physical reaction: The muscles of her pelvic floor spasm and her vaginal opening closes, making sex excruciatingly painful, if not impossible.

Psychological factors. Sometimes there's a strong mental and emotional component to painful intercourse, says D. Kim Singleton, Ph.D., a clinical psychologist in private practice in Washington, D.C. Your painful physical response to intercourse may be psychologically associated with traumatic or forced penetration earlier in life.

"I've been in private practice 12 years, primarily with African-American women, and the only association I've found is with past trauma such as child abuse, rape, or psychological or physical abuse.

I would treat painful intercourse as a medical condition in addition to psychological counseling," says Dr. Chambers-Kersey.

KEEPING
PAIN AWAY

To keep uncomfortable intercourse from putting a crimp in your love life, Dr. Chambers-Kersey offers these suggestions.

Guard against infections. If you suspect that you have an STD or an infection, see your doctor and have it treated immediately. And always use a condom unless you're in a long-standing, mutually monogamous relationship.

Stay regular. Eat high-fiber foods, including lots of fresh fruits and vegetables, and drink plenty of water to avoid constipation.

Try something new. If you feel discomfort during sex, try a new position. When the woman is on top or a couple lies side by side, the woman can control the depth, angle, and frequency of thrusting and possibly eliminate the pain.

Jazz up the foreplay. If your partner isn't providing the type or length of foreplay that you need to become well-lubricated, the solution is simple. Extend the foreplay or talk with your partner about your needs before you get in a romantic situation.

Slow down after pregnancy. Let your episiotomy heal and don't go for the gold the second your doctor gives you the green light. Approach sex gradually. When you do have sex, the process should be slow, with no deep thrusting.

EASING
THE ACHE

If you're having painful intercourse, here are some steps you can take to make things comfortable again.

Get a little help. If vaginal dryness is the problem, a vaginal lubricant such as Replens, K-Y Jelly, or Astroglide can help provide moisture. If painful intercourse is due to menopausal dryness and tissue changes, hormone replacement therapy (HRT) can help. Talk to your doctor about trying estrogen-containing creams such as Premarin, which are inserted into the vagina, or pills such as estradiol (Estrace). You can also ask your doctor about Estraderm and Climara, which provide a continuous supply of estrogen through a skin patch.

Relax those muscles. Vaginismus can be treated. Doctors use a technique called vaginal dilation to help women with vaginismus say good-bye to their pain. They show women how to dilate, or open, their vaginas by inserting their own fingers. Eventually, they can accept penetration without pain.

Consider counseling. When a physical exam reveals no source for your problem, consider a second opinion. If your doctor can't find a physical explanation, find a therapist who makes you comfortable and try to gain a better understanding of your feelings about sex and how they may have developed, says Dr. Chambers-Kersey.

Pelvic Inflammatory Disease

SAFEGUARDING YOUR FERTILITY

enata James sat up in bed and ran her long fingers through her shoulder-length braids. They came away damp. She was having miserable, cramplike pains and she felt feverish and achy—again.

"This had been going on all summer," Renata recalls, "but that day my stomach felt particularly hot and tender. I swung my legs out of bed, pulled on a robe, and walked into the bathroom, making a mental note to call the doctor as soon as I got to the office. I still felt lousy after my shower, but I was determined to make it through the day.

"My husband, Marcus, was downstairs leafing through the *Wall Street Journal*. When I refused the bagel he'd toasted for me, he looked puzzled. Then, while pouring some coffee, I doubled over in pain. It had never been this bad before."

Marcus asked what was wrong, and Renata replied that she was okay. "I told her that I didn't believe she was okay and that I was going to call her office. Then I was going to make sure that she went to the doctor," he says.

Later that day, when the doctor delivered her diagnosis, Renata didn't know whether to feel reassured or worried. "I was glad it wasn't cancer or a tubal pregnancy. But I asked the doctor, 'What's PID and why do I have to go into the hospital?' The doctor told me that a lot of women ask that question, and then she explained," says Renata.

WHAT IS PID, EXACTLY?

Many women are unfamiliar with pelvic inflammatory disease (PID) because the term is a catch-all phrase for a group of conditions.

"PID actually means a general inflammation of the female

pelvic organs," says Zerline Chambers-Kersey, M.D., an obstetrician and gynecologist in private practice in Annandale, Virginia. But in order to fully define a specific individual's condition, you need to explain it in terms of where the inflammation is located. The term *salpingitis* means an infection has inflamed the fallopian tubes. *Endometritis* is an inflammation affecting the uterine lining. Women can also develop an endometritis-salpingitis combination. If untreated, all of these inflammations can blossom into peritonitis, a life-threatening inflammation of the lower pelvic region—the uterus, fallopian tubes, and bowels.

"PID is usually caused by a sexually transmitted disease (STD). Up to 80 percent of PID sufferers harbor the organisms that cause gonorrhea," says Dr. Chambers-Kersey. When an STD like gonorrhea is left untreated and becomes more severe, it spreads from the lower genital tract to the upper reproductive area and uterus. Once the STD organism enters the uterus, a rampant infection develops.

"All women are at risk, and African-American women are not more prone to PID than other women, although in the past some doctors have associated PID with women in lower socioeconomic classes and therefore with us," says Dr. Chambers-Kersey.

In addition to the intense pain and fever that sent Renata to the doctor, one in every four women with PID also experiences serious effects such as ectopic pregnancy or permanent infertility caused by scar tissue blocking the fallopian tubes.

Your odds of becoming infertile due to PID also increase if you have repeated bouts with the disease. One in eight women who have had PID once will be infertile, as will one in four women who have had it twice and half of the women who have had it three or more times.

PID is particularly dangerous because it's very tough to diagnose, and it can live in the body for a long time without giving you any sign that you are sick. "Initially, you may not have any symptoms, but if it's true PID, you eventually will. It may also help to know that PID's chief symptoms are often mistaken for appendicitis," explains Dr. Chambers-Kersey.

African-American women may be slow to get a diagnosis because we are likely to try to ignore chronic pain rather than go to a doctor. First, we must learn to pay attention to abdominal pain. "Because of the way African-American women are socialized, we develop the habit of carrying on as if everything were fine when it's not. We have a habit of ignoring the body's messages," says Lorraine Bonner, M.D., a founding member of On-Call Physicians Medical Group at Summit Medical Center in Oakland, California.

Prevention Strategies

"PID is so common today because unprotected sex is so common today," says Dr. Chambers-Kersey. If you have an active sex life, here are the ways to protect yourself against the disease.

Get to know him first. Find out your partner's sexual history before you sleep together. Ask him the tough questions, such as: "Have you had multiple partners?" "Do you wear a condom?" and "Have you ever had or been tested for STDs?" And be aware that the answers may not be 100 percent reliable. To be on the safe side, ask him to be tested for gonorrhea and chlamydia.

Count on condoms. "Condoms are essential for protection against STDs and PID, so insist on them," says Dr. Bonner. Other barrier methods such as the diaphragm are better than nothing, but they don't offer the protection of a condom.

Get tested—often. "You should be tested for gonorrhea and chlamydia at the time of your regular physical or pelvic exam. If you have discharge and irritation around the time of your period, realize that this could spell PID," says Dr. Chambers-Kersey.

Don't douche. Douching may kill off the helpful bacteria that compete with the disease-causing kind, which can leave your body more vulnerable to infection.

Dump the butts. Although it's not clear why, research shows that smokers, especially women who light up more than ten times a day, are at greater risk for PID.

Be careful with contraception. The Pill increases your chance of contracting chlamydia, but it decreases the chance that chlamydia will move into your uterus and cause PID. Also, you are at a slightly higher risk for infections that can lead to PID just after an IUD is inserted. "Your personal PID risks should be part of your birth control discussions with your doctor," says Dr. Chambers-Kersey.

Get quick care. "Don't self-treat. See a doctor right away if you have pain or discharge. Any delay in getting antibiotics will give an infection more time to cause trouble in your system," says Dr. Chambers-Kersey.

Stick with the treatment. Your doctor will prescribe antibiotics, based on the source of infection. For chlamydia, a woman needs at least 10 to 14 days of oral antibiotics, says Dr. Chambers-Kersey. But if the infection is more extensive—if you have a fever or a tender belly or if tests show an abscess—hospitalization is called for, she explains. If, like Renata, you need to be hospitalized, you'll probably receive intravenous antibiotics for a week to 10 days, followed by oral medication.

Prompt treatment will help prevent the fertility problems that can be caused by PID. "If you are treated promptly and thoroughly for PID, you should heal with no problems," says Dr. Chambers-Kersey.

Post-traumatic Stress Disorder

OVERCOMING A PAINFUL PAST

atrina Landry, a plump, giggly fifth-grader, was the pride of her close-knit neighborhood in New Orleans. She was a straight-A student who was popular with everyone.

But then folks started noticing a change in Katrina. The normally gregarious youngster became sullen and began to complain of nightmares.

"It got so bad that she would barely lift her head and make eye contact with you," says Katrina's art teacher, Gina Richards. By the end of her first semester of school that year, Katrina's once-shining report card was blotted with Ds and Fs.

"At first," says Katrina's mother, Donna, "I was shocked and confused by her behavior. Then I remembered that several years back, Katrina was sexually abused by an uncle. At the time, I comforted her, and I took her to a psychiatrist.

"I think that therapy was one of the things that helped her become as well-adjusted as she was," Donna says. "I couldn't understand why she was going downhill now, years later."

The answer emerged after Katrina spent a few months in a second round of therapy. Now that she was almost a teenager, Katrina understood what it meant to have lost her virginity as a little girl. "Since she was only six when she was abused, she didn't really comprehend what she had lost," Donna says.

"When kids at school began to whisper about boyfriends and going out, she figured out that she had been robbed of the chance to make that decision for herself. She began to feel betrayed by adults, and she felt rage and a loss of power over her life," says Donna. After another period of intense therapy, Katrina is back to her old self. She's relaxed around people, and she's bringing home terrific grades.

TRAGEDY THAT
REFUSES TO FADE

Post-traumatic stress disorder (PTSD) is the name of the condition that overwhemed Katrina, and it may be one of the most underappreciated serious illnesses in America, especially among African-Americans. It affects Black Americans of all ages, incomes, and genders, often leaving in its wake depression, alcoholism, drug abuse, domestic violence, sexual assault, homicide, and suicide. Yet few of us even understand how it works or develops.

PTSD first became news after the Vietnam war, when returning veterans had difficulty readjusting to civilian life because of the traumas they had experienced while on the battlefield. Years later, psychologists identified PTSD in rape victims. Since then, researchers have realized that PTSD can affect people who survive any of a broad spectrum of traumas, from fires to hurricanes, drive-by shootings to plane crashes, sexual abuse to spousal battering. In other words, PTSD can follow any event that produces horror, helplessness, or fear.

The shock of such stressors can be so severe that witnesses or victims will either consciously or unconsciously push all memory of the actual event out of their minds. And if they do remember it, they may detach themselves from it emotionally. "Inner-city children who have seen people shot often talk about it with no emotion," says Terence Killebrew, Ph.D., a clinical psychologist at the Manhattan Vet Center in New York City.

But whether or not the memory is conscious or unconscious, the slightest trigger—a certain smell, a particular sound—can unleash horrifying nightmares and memories of the original trauma months or even years later. "The more you are able to avoid the stimuli associated with the trauma, the more time is likely to pass after the event before you experience PTSD symptoms," explains Dr. Killebrew.

The impact of these resurrected images can lead people to extreme behaviors. Children who have experienced trauma may cry incessantly or act out in inappropriate ways. Adults with PTSD may use alcohol or other drugs to try to deaden their distress. Some adults become workaholics in their quest to avoid thinking about the trauma. Some withdraw from friends and family and become despondent because they believe that no one understands their pain.

"Once your life has been threatened, you develop a sense of hypervigilance. You are overly sensitive to what's going on around you and develop a sense of mistrust," says Dr. Killebrew. Some people with PTSD go days without sleeping. "They sit up at night watching movies because when they close their eyes, they see the traumatic events again. Some avoid crowds because they no longer trust people. After a traumatic event, suddenly you feel that life is very precarious," he explains.

WHEN IT'S
CLOSE TO HOME

African-Americans don't always recognize PTSD because we tend to overlook such behavior. "Our culture is much more accepting of aberrant behavior. We see a lot of people who are struggling, and when we do, we're apt to say, 'Oh, he's just going through his thing,'" says Dr. Killebrew.

"When people are surly, cranky, bold, or irritable, Black people lump them into one category and call them crazy," explains Carl Bell, M.D., president and chief executive officer of Chicago's Community Mental Health Council, professor of clinical psychiatry at the University of Illinois School of Medicine, and clinical professor of public health at the University of Illinois School of Public Health. "But a person who hears a loud noise and jumps 3 feet in the air because they once saw a friend killed by gunfire isn't crazy, they're in touch with an ugly kind of reality." In any case, you can't help if you just dismiss the behavior. That person needs support and help.

"We used to think that only victims of violence had stress-related disorders," says Dr. Bell. "Now we know that merely witnessing violence can bring them on." You don't even have to be an eyewitness. "Sometimes family members, upon learning about the trauma that their child or significant other went through, may begin to experience the symptoms of PTSD," says Dr. Killebrew.

Nor does the stressful event have to be gruesome. "A child who's sent to a series of foster homes because his mother is hooked on crack can experience post-traumatic stress, too. How would you feel if you were separated from your mother as an eight-year-old?" says Dr. Bell.

By the same token, not everyone who experiences trauma develops PTSD. "About one-third of all trauma witnesses develop post-traumatic symptoms," says Dr. Bell. That's where factors like race and poverty come in. African-American Vietnam veterans, for example, have twice the rate of PTSD that White vets do, Dr. Bell points out. "It's not because Black soldiers were exposed to more trauma during the war but because our community has more family dissolution, more maternal separation from children, and more death and disability, all of which seem to heighten vulnerability to PTSD," he says.

INTERVENTION
EQUALS PREVENTION

Loving, caring support is the best medicine for someone who's struggling with post-traumatic stress. Patient, empathetic counseling by a mental health professional can help victims of all ages cope with a variety of trauma-related feelings.

Family support is extremely important, too, but it's rare. "After someone has experienced trauma, many families blame the person for being weak-willed if they don't snap right back to being normal," says Dr. Killebrew. "Let people go through whatever they have to go through and encourage them to get professional help."

How do we ultimately pull the plug on PTSD? We can start by stopping the violence in our communities. And that begins with our children. "Violence is a learned behavior. It can be unlearned if the environment is conducive to teaching alternative ways to resolve disputes," says Rodney Hammond, Ph.D., director of the Division of Violence Prevention at the Centers for Disease Control and Prevention in Atlanta.

Here are some ways to prevent youthful violence and help yourself or other adults cope with PTSD, says Dr. Hammond.

Teach life skills. "It's important for youth to learn positive social behavior and anger management. Start a violence-prevention program in your community," advises Dr. Hammond. Some children see assault as the only way to feel worthy when they're angry or frustrated. "Good violence-prevention programs do four things: They show kids that their behavior is influenced by their feelings; they affirm children's feelings; they teach kids that they can choose how they respond to their feelings; and they show kids that they have an option of settling disputes by talking them out," he says. Pastors, parents, and teachers can work together to build programs in their neighborhoods.

Give them the words. Use vignettes as teaching tools, Dr. Hammond suggests. For example, you might talk to your kids about the best way to react if a friend borrows a jacket and returns it in poor condition.

"We tell kids that the best thing to do is to talk to the person one-on-one, away from a crowd so it doesn't incite violence, and say, 'We've been friends for a long time. When you took my jacket and messed it up, it made me feel that you didn't respect me.' Talking it out may be hard for kids at first. But eventually it will help them develop a positive sense of self and an amazing feeling of satisfaction," he says.

Join the neighborhood crime watch. "These programs decrease the chances that children will be exposed to violence," says Dr. Hammond.

Set an example. "Agree with your kids on what the household rules are, and be consistent," Dr. Hammond suggests. And discipline children by praising them for appropriate behavior and verbally disapproving of inappropriate behavior.

Turn off the TV. Read or play games with kids instead. The violence children see on TV matters because it is presented as if it occurs without pain or consequence, explains Dr. Hammond. That can predispose children to act violently without feeling.

Insulate yourself. If you think you may have PTSD, be on the lookout for these signs of trouble, says Dr. Bell.

▲ Adults with PTSD often relive the initial trauma that triggered their problem through nightmares, flashbacks, or intrusive thoughts or images of the event. This is a symptom that says it's time to get help.

▲ The second most common sign of PTSD is "numbing," an emotional detachment from people and things and persistent avoidance of the stimuli associated with the trauma. You distance yourself from family or friends and avoid thoughts, feelings, or places that may remind you of the trauma.

"People may lose a sense of the future and stop going to work or school. They just give up because they feel that bad things will happen to them no matter what they do," says Dr. Bell.

▲ The third sign is hyperarousal. "People with PTSD are like a guitar string that's strung too tightly," says Dr. Bell. They're irritable, jumpy, and unable to concentrate. They also suffer constant fight-or-flight reactions, which means that their blood pressure can shoot up, their hearts may beat fast, or they may sweat for no reason. Their bodies are on constant alert.

Find help. If these symptoms last more than one month, see a mental health professional for an evaluation, says Dr. Killebrew. Many types of professionals—nurses, social workers, psychologists, and psychiatrists—can diagnose PTSD. The treatment (talk therapy or drug-assisted therapy) depends on the severity of the condition. The sooner you get help, the better your recovery will be, adds Dr. Killebrew.

Give yourself a little TLC. There's lots you can do to ease PTSD while being treated. Dr. Bell's prescription is to avoid alcohol, get moderate exercise, cultivate healthy interpersonal relationships, and educate yourself about PTSD so you can be an active participant in your healing. And learn to laugh. Humor is a great stress reliever.

Show your love. We don't have good data on what makes people resilient in the face of trauma. "It could be that the one-third of the assaulted population that experiences PTSD had maternal bonding problems so that in the face of extreme distress, they can't retreat to warm memories of being hugged," says Dr. Bell.

"No one can stop PTSD," agrees Dr. Killebrew. "But we can at least fortify our family and friends when we show them genuine support and love," he says.

Pregnancy

Making Healthy Babies

efore I drift off to sleep each night, I faithfully record my unborn daughter's 'kick counts,'" says Tula Tucker. "Things have changed a lot since my first child was born more than two decades ago." Back then, Tula's obstetrician said nothing about counting all of those tiny movements within a specified period of time to monitor her baby's well-being. But that's not the only thing that's changed about Tula in recent years.

"I'm in better shape now than I was before," Tula says, comparing her two pregnancies, which are an incredible 25 years apart. "I ran until I was three months pregnant." Although the Newark, New Jersey, grandmother looks much younger than her 45 years, she causes more than a few mouths to drop at the sight of her round stomach and prematurely gray hair.

"But I've been feeling excellent. The doctors are really amazed at me," she says. And for those inquiring minds who wonder whether she had any help from modern medicine, the answer is a resounding no. She conceived the old-fashioned way. "This is my egg, and my husband's sperm, and we can't wait to meet this baby," she says.

Early Care Is Key

Counting kicks is just one of many things that moms-to-be can do to ensure a healthy start for their little bundles of joy. "At 28 weeks, for example, a fetus may kick 20 times in 30 minutes. A dramatic falloff from that number might be a sign of fetal distress," says Jennifer Y. Greene, M.D., an obstetrician and gynecologist in private practice in Akron, Ohio.

"We're beginning to focus on both ends of the pregnancy more

(continued on page 346)

To have a successful pregnancy, you can benefit from good nutrition from before conception until delivery, and beyond if you are breastfeeding. Make sure your diet is as healthy as possible to help prevent certain complications and guard against low birthweight and infant mortality.

A healthy diet provides the raw materials that your body needs to produce a baby. It also supplies the building blocks for the extras that go along with pregnancy: increased blood and fluid volume, the placenta, amniotic fluid, and larger breasts, plus the fat stores that the body stashes away for future breastfeeding, says Jennifer Y. Greene, M.D., an obstetrician and gynecologist in private practice in Akron, Ohio.

That means that you need to eat an average of about 300 extra calories a day. The sources of those calories need to be chosen carefully. Pregnant women need extra amounts of just about every nutrient, including vitamin A, thiamin, riboflavin, folate, vitamin B_{12}, calcium, phosphorus, magnesium, and iron, says Yvonne L. Bronner, R.D., Sc.D., spokesperson for the American Dietetic Association and assistant professor of maternal and child health at Johns Hopkins University School of Hygiene and Public Health in Baltimore.

Iron requirements double during pregnancy. The National Academy of Sciences recommends a daily intake of 30 milligrams, beginning in the fourth month of pregnancy. Because it's so hard for a pregnant woman to get all the iron she needs through diet alone, Dr. Bronner recommends a 30-milligram supplement of ferrous iron daily, but be sure to discuss any supplementation with your doctor.

When you're pregnant, your body's need for bone-building calcium also shoots up. You need 1,200 milligrams a day, the amount found in a quart of milk, or even more. One survey showed that women who consumed 1,500 to 2,000 milligrams of calcium daily (the equivalent of five or six glasses of milk) had a lower risk of pregnancy-induced high blood pressure, which can be caused by an imbalance of minerals such as calcium, magnesium, and potassium.

Nutritional Insurance

Here's how to make sure your diet is nutritionally sound.

Go iron-rich. "Pregnancy can create anemia," Dr. Greene says, so it's important not to neglect iron in your diet. But you should learn how to get the most from the iron in foods.

Meats contain a type of iron called heme iron, which is absorbed easily by the body. Look for lean meats such as chicken, turkey, and top round steak (trimmed of visible fat) to boost your iron stores.

The other type of iron, nonheme iron, is found primarily in plant foods and is not as easily absorbed. Generally, you can expect to absorb 23 percent of heme iron but only 2 to 10 percent of nonheme iron.

There is a trick to getting the most iron from nonheme sources: When you eat nonheme foods, eat a food that's high in vitamin C at the same meal—it will increase your iron absorption.

Count on calcium. The National Institutes of Health recommends that pregnant women get 1,200 to 1,500 milligrams per day. Try adding low-fat milk or yogurt or other calcium sources such as canned salmon (with the bones) and collard greens to your menu, says Dr. Bronner.

Eat carefully. If you're a vegetarian, be extra-careful to get enough calories, carbohydrates, and protein. Try eating healthy snacks like yogurt and fruit between meals, says Dr. Bronner. Insufficient calorie intake can cause you to develop anemia or result in development problems that could lead to an abnormally small baby.

Cut back the fat. Prenatal diets should contain some fat, says Dr. Greene, because it's fat that is the basis for the formation of your baby's hormones. But don't go overboard, as too much fat can contribute to excessive weight gain while you're pregnant and make it difficult for you lose weight after you deliver. Fried foods and fast foods are high in fat but contain little nutritional value for you or your baby. Try eating baked or broiled foods instead, says Dr. Greene.

than we used to," says Yvonne L. Bronner, R.D., Sc.D., a spokesperson for the American Dietetic Association and assistant professor of maternal and child health at Johns Hopkins University School of Hygiene and Public Health in Baltimore.

You can't underestimate the importance of a carefully planned pregnancy. Ideally, the physical and mental health of both parents—not just the mother—should be assessed in advance, says Lennox S. Westney, M.D., director of the Division of Obstetrics at Howard University Hospital and professor at Howard University College of Medicine, both in Washington, D.C.

The father has a lot to do with the outcome, says Dr. Westney. Alcohol, drugs, and certain illnesses can affect a man's sperm count, for example, and his state of mind can have a big impact on you and your pregnancy.

For African-American women, getting a head start on a healthy pregnancy is especially important. Our infant mortality rate is still more than double that of White infants, due primarily to conditions that generally can be prevented, such as low birthweight.

Preconception care should begin a minimum of two to three months before conception, Dr. Greene suggests. A year is even better. At your annual or biannual checkup, you can let your doctor know if you're thinking about becoming pregnant. This will give you and your partner plenty of time to undergo genetic screening and counseling for sickle cell disease or other conditions, to cut back on smoking and drinking, to lose weight, and to eat a healthier diet.

Planning goes a long way toward minimizing the risk of low birthweight, infant mortality, and birth defects. For instance, a baby's neural tube, which is the basis for the development of the brain, spinal cord, and associated neural structures, is formed within the first few weeks of pregnancy—long before some women even discover that they're pregnant. If you don't have enough folate, a B vitamin, in your body, your child could be at risk for neural tube defects, which can affect the brain or spinal cord. Folate is found in spinach, broccoli, orange juice, and most beans. Pregnant women need 400 micrograms a day, says Dr. Greene.

Sisters should also try to slide into pregnancy at their ideal weight. "Women more than 20 percent overweight have more problems during pregnancy," Dr. Greene says. Those extra pounds can cause gestational (meaning "during pregnancy") diabetes, toxemia (a condition that causes the buildup of toxic fluid in the womb), and high blood pressure. These conditions lead to difficult deliveries and postpartum weight retention. A woman who begins pregnancy at or near her ideal weight would need to gain anywhere from 25 to 35 pounds during pregnancy, says Dr. Greene.

DOING IT RIGHT

A little troubleshooting can go a long way when it comes to planning and enjoying your pregnancy. These self-help strategies can help ensure that you and your baby come through with flying colors.

Face your fibroids. Lots of Black women live with fibroids and worry that they will interfere with pregnancy. "Not all fibroids are going to cause problems," Dr. Greene says. Some women who have fibroids are able to conceive and successfully undergo childbirth, while others must have them removed and wait a while before conceiving. Ask your doctor about ways to keep fibroids under control before you conceive, he says.

Say good-bye to cigarettes and alcohol. Before and during pregnancy, cigarettes and alcohol can harm you and your fetus. Smoking can increase the risk of stillbirth and infant death. Plus, the babies of smokers tend to be at least a half-pound smaller than those of nonsmokers. And a word to your partner: Smoking while you're trying to conceive can reduce his fertility, says Dr. Greene.

Drinking heavily during pregnancy puts your baby at risk for fetal alcohol syndrome, a pattern of physical and mental defects that may include deformed facial characteristics, growth deficiency, heart defects, and mental retardation. Even though having one drink occasionally may not do any harm, you should stop drinking altogether if you are expecting, says Dr. Greene.

One-a-day is best. Many doctors recommend nutrient-rich prenatal vitamins before and during pregnancy. Ask your doctor about what's best for you and when you should start supplementation, says Dr. Greene.

Avoid stress and racism. It seems that dealing with racism can actually affect you and your baby. Research shows that Black mothers who live in the most segregated cities, for example, have

To reduce the risk of premature labor, miscarriage, or any other prenatal problems, contact your doctor at the first sign of any of the following symptoms, says Jennifer Y. Greene, M.D., an obstetrician and gynecologist in private practice in Akron, Ohio.

- Bleeding
- Fever
- Lack of fetal movement
- Unexpected drop in kick counts
- Blurred vision
- Severe headaches
- Contractions
- Abdominal pain
- Leakage of fluid

the highest infant mortality statistics. And stress in general triggers a host of chemical reactions in your body that can hurt your developing baby.

The best way to overcome these health threats is to build as strong a support network as you possibly can and find ways to stay relaxed and calm.

Physical activity is always a good way to relax. Dr. Greene recommends walking and swimming as well as relaxation techniques such as mild forms of yoga and deep breathing.

Keep that baby moving. As Tula and millions of other women prove each year, you can and should work out. Get into the habit of exercising before you get pregnant, and it will be easier to maintain at least some activity afterward. "Get the go-ahead to exercise from your doctor and ask her to recommend a prenatal exercise program," Dr. Greene says.

Take the right tests. Believe it or not, ultrasound is not the most important test to have during pregnancy, says Dr. Greene. Doctors recommend that you should consider testing for the following conditions.

Sickle cell disease and other blood abnormalities. Sickle cell disease is a genetically transmitted disorder that affects the capacity of hemoglobin in the blood to transport oxygen. This test is given on your first prenatal visit, so it's important to schedule an appointment with your doctor as soon as you find out you're pregnant. If you're aware that either you or your partner has any blood disorders, let your doctor know.

Cervical cancer. Have a Pap smear on your first prenatal visit.

Rh incompatibility. Rh factor is an antigen found on red blood cells. If your blood is Rh negative and your mate's is Rh positive, there's a 70 percent chance that your baby's blood will be Rh positive. If this is the case, you'll need a shot of Rh immune globulin in your 28th week, or last trimester of pregnancy, to prevent your body from creating antibodies that can be transferred to your baby and cause death.

Sexually transmitted diseases (STDs). STDs can cause preterm labor, premature rupture of the membranes, and severe organ involvement of the fetus. The common AIDS/HIV drug azidothymidine (AZT) has been shown to significantly reduce the chance of passing HIV from the mother to the fetus, so early detection is crucial. Tests for STDs should be done on your first prenatal visit and again during the 36th week of pregnancy.

Toxoplasmosis. TORCH titer is the test for toxoplasmosis, which is caused by a parasite that's sometimes transmitted by eating raw or undercooked meat. Cats carry this disease, so tell your doctor if you have one. You should also have tests for measles, chicken pox, rubella, and cytomegalovirus.

Diabetes. You should have a glucose test between the 24th and 28th week to check for diabetes. Since diabetes is often inherited, let your doctor know if there's a history of the condition in your family.

Down syndrome and other genetic problems. Amniocentesis is done to detect possible genetic abnormalities and determine the sex of the fetus, if desired. This test is recommended for women over the age of 35 and is usually given between the 14th and 18th week.

"Risk factors such as cramping, bleeding, leaking of amniotic fluid, and miscarriage are lower after 16 weeks," Dr. Greene says. Until the 20th week, a woman can choose to have an abortion if there is a genetic abnormality. After that, it depends on state laws, she says.

Tend to your teeth. By the second month of pregnancy, prog-

Planning your pregnancy well in advance and following up with regular doctor's visits is the key to successful conception and delivery. Here's the schedule for doctor's visits that's recommended by Jennifer Y. Greene, M.D., an obstetrician and gynecologist in private practice in Akron, Ohio.

- If possible, a year and then six months before conception
- Every month until your 28th week of pregnancy
- Every two weeks after the 28th week
- Every week after the 36th week

esterone levels skyrocket, placing you at risk for gingivitis and eventually tooth and bone loss. Up to 50 percent of expectant mothers have pregnancy gingivitis. Visit your dentist at least every six months, says Dr. Greene.

If you're older, stay in shape. "A number of women are postponing pregnancy until later in life," Dr. Westney says. "The older you get, the more prone you are to risks of high blood pressure and a baby that might be small for its gestational age. The most important thing you can do is to maintain good health before and during pregnancy," he says. Tula serves as a good example.

PREPARING
FOR DELIVERY

By doing your homework, you'll have a better sense of what to expect during pregnancy and delivery and how to plan appropriately. Pick up a copy of *Having Your Baby: A Guide for African-American Women,* by Hilda Hutcherson, M.D., with Margaret Williams.

Get smart. Dr. Greene stresses the benefits of childbirth classes for you and your mate. "They're very beneficial in this day of managed care, with insurance companies seeking shorter maternity stays," she says.

Some women claim that they help and give women a sense of control over the birth, while others say that they're welcome distractions at best. The bottom line is that like most women, you'll be able to deal when the time comes, says Dr. Westney.

Ask your doctor everything. Discuss everything under the sun with your obstetrician. "Explore all of your options," Dr. Greene says. Be sure to talk about various labor scenarios. Specific topics should include whether or not your doctor routinely performs episiotomies, prescribes pain medications, or performs natural childbirth and cesarean births. A doctor who makes decisions about these questions according to the needs of the individual patient should be considered over a doctor who uses the same approach for every patient, says Dr. Greene.

Prepare for pain relief. If you think you might want an epidural (anesthesia to relieve labor pains), ask in advance so that it will be available whenever you need it. "Not all hospitals have 24-hour service," Dr. Greene warns. Hospitals in outlying areas don't always have anesthesiologists on duty overnight.

Don't be disappointed if you find yourself needing an epidural when you had planned to deliver without it. "The main thing is to try to enjoy the birth process," Dr. Greene says. "The epidural is there to help you to relax so that you can enjoy the experience."

Understand cesareans. It's estimated that cesarean section is one of the most frequently performed inpatient operations in the country, according to the Centers for Disease Control and Prevention in Atlanta. The operation can be done with local or general anesthesia. Either way, it typically requires a longer hospital stay and a longer recovery period than a vaginal delivery.

Some women have cesareans because of complications due to abnormal fetal heart rate, abnormal fetal position, failure of the cervix to dilate, or an inability to push the baby out. A few women elect to have cesareans and even schedule them in advance because of preexisting conditions such as severe cardiac disease. Again, discuss the issue of C-sections with your doctor beforehand.

Pick a pediatrician. You'll need one for a checkup when your baby is two weeks old. "Women should make sure they interview someone by the time they're 34 to 35 weeks pregnant," Dr. Greene advises.

Premenstrual Syndrome

ENDING THE MONTHLY MISERY

enrietta Cole has crystal-clear memories of her bouts with premenstrual syndrome. "One of my worst experiences began on a Friday morning a few months ago," she recalls. "I was jolted out of a sound sleep, a full hour before my alarm, by the alternating throbbing and stabbing pains working their way around my pelvis and lower back. At that moment, all I wanted from life was a painkiller, a heating pad, and a cup of tea. I kept wondering how I was ever going to get up from that bed and make it to work."

And this was no average workday. Instead of going to her office, Henrietta had to fly to Toronto to attend a radio announcers' conference. "I had been looking forward to the trip," explains the 36-year-old journalist, "but that morning, I was one evil, tired sister. I just kept thinking how big a pain it would be to have to face the hassles at the Rochester airport and how badly I wanted to pull the covers over my head and stay in bed."

Like millions of other women who experience premenstrual syndrome (PMS), Henrietta spent the rest of that morning dealing with some of the other indignities that her period brought each month. "I stumbled to the bathroom, glanced at myself in the mirror, and discovered that I had broken out like a high school girl. Later, I realized that wearing my fabulous new suit was a lost cause because I had put on at least 5 pounds of PMS bloat. I also could sense the beginnings of a migraine. This PMS attack would go down in history," she says.

Henrietta made it to Toronto, but when she got home, one of the first things she did was to call her doctor and ask what she could do to put an end to her PMS.

DEFINING
THE PROBLEM

Getting a handle on PMS and keeping it from interfering with your life for a few days each month can be tricky. The condition is hard to define, and it can change throughout a woman's life. Most affected women experience only mild PMS, in the form of a random collection of symptoms such as bloating, moodiness, headache, and cramps that range from twinges to stabbing pains. Doctors have catalogued 150 such symptoms, and they affect up to 90 percent of women at some time in their lives.

But severe PMS is a different story. It is a disruptive disease that, thankfully, affects only about 3 to 5 percent of women. Unlike the random and often mild premenstrual symptoms that many women feel, severe PMS shows up like clockwork sometime during the two-week span before a woman's period for at least two out of every three cycles. Then, for the two weeks right after the start of her period, a woman with severe PMS is usually symptom-free.

"Whether a woman endures severe or mild PMS may also have something to do with her culture," says psychologist Nsenga Warfield-Coppock, Ph.D., assistant visiting professor at Catholic University of America in Washington, D.C. It seems that Asian women have the lowest incidence and severity of PMS, while African-American women seem to have very severe cases, she says. Health experts attribute the differences to diet and stress.

"I'm very up-front with my patients. When they have PMS, I know what they're talking about. I have it, too, and our first thought can be that we're going crazy," explains Zerline Chambers-Kersey, M.D., an obstetrician and gynecologist in private practice in Annandale, Virginia. "I tell them to remember that there are still places in the world where women give birth in the fields and get back to working. If you have to lie down once a month, well, be glad you can lie down somewhere. You can handle it," says Dr. Chambers-Kersey.

SORTING OUT
A MYSTERY

Scientists don't agree about the cause of PMS, but it seems to be related to the monthly changes in hormone levels that accompany your menstrual cycle. It's not just the amounts of hormones that determine your state of health, it's their amounts relative to each other.

The female hormones estrogen and progesterone are meant to exist in a delicate balance, and anything that disturbs this balance causes problems. Women in their thirties and forties, who tend to experience more PMS, are also more likely to have been on the Pill or have been pregnant. Both conditions create hormonal changes that may trigger the development of hormonal imbalances.

Progesterone, for example, is thought to have a beneficial effect on mood. It works to regulate blood sugar and brain chemistry, among other functions. So when your progesterone levels start to fall a bit each month while your estrogen increases in preparation for your period, you may become a bundle of raw nerves.

Some health experts think that PMS may be associated with low levels of a brain chemical called serotonin. Serotonin is a neurotransmitter that not only carries messages throughout your nervous system but also influences your mood and regulates your sleep and appetite. Researchers think that low amounts of serotonin may spark mood swings, food cravings, and sleep problems.

And last but certainly not least, that all-purpose health demon—stress—is thought to play a significant role in PMS. The stress connection may also help to explain the rise in PMS after age 30. Women are more likely to have the added responsibilities of marriage, child-rearing, and possibly caring for aging parents during their thirties and forties. Professional obligations, financial responsibilities, and health problems may also add to the pressures of life at this stage. For some reason, the body's responses to stress can bring on an attack of PMS or make the symptoms more severe.

HELPING YOURSELF
TO RELIEF

You may not be able to eliminate PMS from your life altogether, but you can take steps to regain control and minimize your symptoms.

See your doctor. PMS can act like many other health problems, so see your gynecologist and make sure you really have it. Expect her to take a medical history and ask you detailed questions about your symptoms.

Collect the evidence. The only way to be sure your problem is really PMS is to document the timing of your symptoms. Using a calendar or journal, keep a regular written account of your monthly symptoms and their relationship to your periods. Chart both emotional and physical complaints, such as anger, breast tenderness, cravings, and fatigue. This journal will be invaluable for diagnosing your PMS symptoms, because when your doctor asks you how you've been doing, you can give her specific information.

Ask if something's FSHy. If you are in your late thirties or early forties and your PMS seems to be worse than ever, ask for an FSH test. This is a blood test that measures levels of follicle-stimulating hormone (FSH).

During the four to six years before menopause, a period called perimenopause, your body churns out extra FSH because it's trying harder to release an egg, says Dr. Chambers-Kersey. If your doctor tells you that your levels of FSH are high, this is a sign that you're going into menopause. You may want to ask your doctor about hormone replacement therapy to treat the symptoms.

Watch what you eat. "When it comes to PMS, the old saying 'you are what you eat' is true," says Dr. Chambers-Kersey. A diet high in salt, caffeine, and fat is an open invitation to PMS.

Many health experts even think that nutritional deficiencies may cause PMS. The vitamins and minerals riboflavin, vitamin A, calcium, manganese, and magnesium may be key players. Try to eat plenty of complex carbohydrates, such as whole grains, breads, cereals, rice, potatoes, pasta, fruits, and vegetables. Eat protein in moderation, and resist the urge to load up on sweets or drink alcohol, says Dr. Chambers-Kersey.

Get in shape. A half-hour of weight-bearing, aerobic exercise three times a week boosts your psyche through the release of mood-altering chemicals called endorphins, says Dr. Warfield-Coppock. Exercise may also help reduce the severity of cramps and lessen bloating.

Check your treatment options. Research shows that certain new antidepressants—fluoxetine hydrochloride (Prozac), sertraline hydrochloride (Zoloft), and paroxetine hydrochloride (Paxil), to name a few—can be used in low doses to relieve severe PMS symptoms that will not respond to other treatments.

These new medications, known as SSRIs (selective serotonin reuptake inhibitors), have far fewer side effects than older antidepressants. They work by increasing the amount of the mood-regulating hormone serotonin in the brain. Although these medications are useful for alleviating the emotional distress of PMS, they will not eliminate the physical symptoms such as cramping or breast tenderness. Ask your doctor about whether these drugs may be right for you.

Take it easy. Anything that reduces the stress and tension in your life will help with PMS. Prayer, meditation, yoga, and massage are all good bets, says Dr. Warfield-Coppock.

Involve your family. Let your husband and children know that PMS is a real medical condition that can affect your moods and feelings. It's easier for them to be sympathetic and supportive if they know what's going on, says Dr. Warfield-Coppock.

Prostate Problems

MANAGING YOUR RISK

he brothers at the barber shop think Roy White needs to loosen up. After all, they're quick to remind him, he's in prime health, he doesn't have a family history of cancer, and he's only 45.

"Sometimes I feel a little conspicuous myself when I go to the hospital for a free prostate cancer screening," Roy admits. "I'll walk into the waiting room and invariably all the men there will be White and over 60 and looking at me like I'm crazy. But these screenings give me peace of mind. I only have one life, and I want to stick around for a long time. I guess I'd rather have the screening and not need it than need it and regret that I didn't have it," he says.

SILENT
BUT DANGEROUS

The prostate gland is an easy thing to forget. It's an inconspicuous little ball the size of a walnut, hidden away deep in the pelvis where you never see it. But when it decides to act up, it can cause a world of trouble.

The prostate is a male sex organ that produces proteins that liquefy semen and protect sperm from the hostile acidic environments found in the urethra and the vagina.

One of the milder prostate disorders is benign prostatic hyperplasia (BPH), or enlarged prostate, a noncancerous condition that's very common in men over 50. Men with BPH often have a tough time at the urinal because the condition obstructs the urethra, the tube that carries urine from the bladder. The urethra passes through an opening in the prostate gland—kind of like the hole in a doughnut—before it winds its way to the penis. If your prostate is enlarged, it squeezes the urethra, resulting in either a weak stream of urine, difficulty starting the stream, or a strong urge to urinate followed by only a dribble.

These are serious problems, but they pale against a prostate disease that actually takes lives. Of all the parts of a man's body, the prostate is the most likely to develop cancer. And African-American men have the highest rate of prostate cancer in the world. "We get this cancer significantly more often than White men, and we die from it twice as often," says Ronald A. Morton, Jr., M.D., director of laboratories at the Baylor Prostate Center and assistant professor of urology at Baylor College of Medicine in Houston.

While experts don't know why prostate cancer is such a mammoth health threat in our community, poverty probably explains a big part of it because poor people can't afford to buy access to state-of-the-art health care. But that's not the whole story, because affluent African-Americans still have higher rates of prostate cancer than affluent Whites.

"That sort of evidence tells us that African-Americans could have a biological predisposition to the disease," says Dr. Morton. "We don't know for sure, because very few Black men with prostate cancer participate in the research that studies the disease and tests promising treatments." But research at Johns Hopkins University in Baltimore has shown that there is a gene, HPC1, that predisposes men to prostate cancer and may explain the vulnerability of Black men to this disease.

Prostate cancer is more common in men than breast cancer is in women. In 1996, it was estimated that 317,000 American men would be diagnosed with the disease, and another 41,400 would die from it. The cancer appears in older men, develops slowly and doesn't produce symptoms until its later stages.

"Most men will die with prostate cancer, not from it, and never know they have it," says Marc Lowe, M.D., chief of urology at the Group Health Cooperative of Puget Sound (central division) in Seattle.

Just the same, prostate cancer shouldn't be ignored, says Dr. Morton. In other words, many urologists feel that Roy has the right idea: Get tested—regularly. Black men tend to develop the disease at an earlier age than Whites, and by the time they see a doctor, the cancer is more advanced.

"African-American men have a greater chance of having an aggressive form of prostate cancer that grows and spreads very quickly," explains Dr. Morton. That means we can't count on out-living prostate cancer. We need to go after it.

PROTECTING
YOUR PROSTATE

BPH is unavoidable. If you're going to get it, you're going to get it. But when it comes to prostate cancer, you can reduce your risk or catch it early enough to cure it.

Go low-fat. "My personal prevention approach has been dietary," says Dr. Lowe. "It's one of the few things we have control over when it comes to prostate cancer." The American Cancer Society notes that higher intake of animal fat, red meat, and dairy products has been associated with higher risk of prostate cancer. "I eat low-cholesterol foods and foods that are low in saturated fats, and I include soy products in my diet," notes Dr. Lowe.

Try tomatoes. Researchers at Harvard University found that lycopene, a nutrient in tomatoes, may reduce the risk of prostate cancer. Compared to the men who ate the least tomato products, those who ate the most had a 35 percent reduction in their risk of prostate cancer. Tomato sauce appeared to have the greatest effect.

The researchers noted that the African-American men in their study ate tomato products infrequently, which might contribute to the higher rates of prostate cancer that we experience.

Screen it out. African-American heritage and a family history of prostate cancer have both been identified as major risk factors. "If you're an African-American male over age 40, have a routine screening once a year," advises Dr. Morton. To do the exam, the doctor will slip a lubricated, gloved finger into your anus to feel for abnormal tissue in the nearby prostate gland. He will also take a blood sample, which will be tested for prostate-specific antigen (PSA), a blood protein that increases when prostate cancer (or other problems) develops.

"Screening is quick and inexpensive. In fact, it's offered free at many health departments and hospitals, especially during Prostate Cancer Awareness Week each September," says Dr. Morton.

Relax. Prostate cancer may run like wildfire through your family tree, but that doesn't mean that you'll get it. "Sometimes people are so terrified that they will test positive for prostate cancer that they refuse to come in for screening," says Louis J. Bernard, M.D., former director of the Drew-Meharry-Morehouse Consortium Cancer Center in Nashville, Tennessee. "My advice is to relax. No matter what your family history, cancer is never a 100 percent certainty."

Talk about it. "Prostate cancer isn't something Black men normally discuss until somebody down the street gets it," says Dr. Bernard. That's a shame, because the Achilles heel of prostate cancer, like all cancers, is early detection. So if you have a brother, uncle, father, or son over age 40, encourage him to get tested. To locate a support group or get more information, call the National Black Leadership Initiative on Cancer at 1-800-724-1185.

TREATMENT CHOICES FOR BPH

There's nothing you can do on your own to keep your prostate from growing, but here are a few steps you can take to reduce your symptoms.

Clear the pipes. "The most effective treatment for BPH is surgically removing prostate tissue that's blocking urine flow. We essentially enlarge the hole of the doughnut so urine can flow freely," says Dr. Lowe. The procedure has a good success rate (75 to 80 percent) and carries a small risk of impotence (5 to 10 percent of cases) or incontinence (1 percent).

Shrink the prostate. You can also get medication to reduce the enlarged gland or to relax the muscles that control it, says Dr. Lowe. One drug works by blocking an enzyme that converts testosterone into a form that fuels prostate growth. Another relaxes the muscle tissue in the prostate and bladder and makes urination easier.

You should be aware that you must continue to take these drugs for the rest of your life. If you stop taking them, your prostate symptoms will return.

Watch and wait. The third option is doing nothing at all. "If we monitor our patients, about one-third will go on to have worse symptoms, one-third will stay the same, and one-third will improve on their own," says Dr. Lowe.

Call on Mother Nature. Studies in France and Germany have shown that some men get symptom relief with the herbs pygeum and saw palmentto.

Options
for Prostate Cancer

If you have cancer, your doctor will determine whether it's confined to the prostate (the best scenario) or has spread beyond it. At that point, there are several options. Talk these over with your doctor.

Don't act right away. Consider close monitoring but no active treatment. "The risk is that if the disease spreads quickly beyond the prostate, it can kill," says Dr. Lowe. Good candidates for waiting are men whose cancer is at an early stage and older men, usually over age 70. "But each patient should be evaluated individually," Dr. Lowe says.

Consider radiation. People who receive radiation therapy for cancer that has not spread beyond the prostate are just as likely as those who have surgery to remain cancer-free after 10 years, says Dr. Lowe. The best candidates are older men.

Try hormones. Prostate cancer feeds on testosterone. Reducing the hormone doesn't cure the cancer, but it does slow its growth, says Dr. Lowe. This treatment consists of administering testosterone-blocking drugs or removal of the testicles, which produce testosterone. Surgical removal of the testicles may sound radical, but it's common in older prostate cancer patients. (With this treatment, some men notice a decrease in sex drive or occasionally feel warm and flushed but your voice doesn't change and you don't lose your body hair.) Good candidates are men whose cancer has spread beyond the prostate.

Opt for surgery. If the cancer hasn't spread beyond the prostate, it can often be cured by removing the prostate gland and the surrounding tissues, explains Dr. Lowe. This is called radical prostatectomy. The surgery leaves about 50 percent of men impotent and 5 to 25 percent incontinent.

Many men find that prostate surgery leads them to rethink their approach to sexual intimacy. "You don't feel the same sexual tension—the tightness and fullness that builds until you have a climax and you relax. But orgasms happen in your brain anyway, not your body. An orgasm is an orgasm, with or without prostate surgery. Those who adjust the best seem to be men who are open to discussing their sexual relationship with their partners," says Dr. Lowe.

Rape

HEALING THE HURT

laine Moore, 44, has a very clear memory of a traumatic night 26 years ago. "We met at a local community center in Philadelphia. He was an older adult, working at the center. I was naive, 18, and a virgin. I didn't drink or use drugs, and he didn't either. We knew each other for about eight months, and we often went out to hear jazz or get together with friends. I felt perfectly safe. One night we stopped by his house because he said he had to pick something up. Suddenly, he began tearing my clothes off. It was like a nightmare. I was crying and saying no, but he was too strong for me.

"It was painful and I was terrified. I was in a daze for weeks. I didn't understand what had happened, and I didn't know how to talk about it. I told no one. Who could I tell? I didn't think my family or friends would be sympathetic.

"Black people are seldom kind about these things. No one had the right to hurt me like that, but I didn't know that at the time. I was so hurt and ashamed. I was depressed for years," Elaine says with anger darkening her voice. "I tell you, I sure wouldn't handle it that way now."

SEX
WITHOUT CONSENT

A woman is raped every 1.3 minutes in this country. Rape is the act of taking sex by force, and the definition holds whether the person being raped is unconscious, drunk, drugged, mentally incompetent, under 18, or just dressed in a short skirt.

In addition, rape is as much an assault on your health and psychological well-being as it is on your body. It can expose you to AIDS and other sexually transmitted diseases (STDs), unwanted pregnancy, and a lifetime of severe depression and sexual dysfunction.

According to the National Crime Victimization Survey conducted by the U.S. Department of Justice, twice as many Black women are raped as White women. And, unfortunately, tmany still harbor the fears that Elaine had 26 years ago, because rape is seldom reported. Approximately one out of six (16 percent) of rapes are reported, according to the National Women's Survey, funded by the National Institute on Drug Abuse and published in connection with studies conducted by the National Victim Center and the Crime Victims Research and Treatment Center at the Medical University of South Carolina in Charleston.

When it comes to African-American women, the tragedy often doesn't stop with the rape itself. It is extended to a peculiar kind of vilification and anger that the Black community often directs at rape victims, not rapists, says Nelli L. Mitchell, M.D., a psychiatrist in private practice in Rochester, New York. Of reported rapes of Black women, almost four out of five (72.5 percent) are by Black men. Too often, the rapist is a date, a friend, or a relative, yet even though we are more vulnerable to rape, "we are not as compassionate toward rape victims as we should be," observes Dr. Mitchell. "This is why so many rapes go unreported," she says.

Remember how little sympathy Desiree Washington received after she was raped by Mike Tyson? Just as Elaine feared her friends' criticism, Washington was scorned by many women for going to a man's hotel room. "It's like whistling in the graveyard. The women who attacked Washington are trying to say 'I'm not like this person, so what happened to her couldn't happen to me,' " explains Dr. Mitchell.

DEALING
WITH THE RISK

But it can happen to you, warns police officer Cheryl Franks of the Rochester, New York, Police Department Crime Prevention Unit. Anyone can be raped, anywhere and at just about any time. Accepting this fact is an important part of prevention. Women think that if they don't go to a man's place at night, they won't get raped, but that's just one of a million scenarios. Experts agree that rape cannot be completely prevented, but Franks offers these tips to help you minimize your risk.

Respect your own judgment. We are afraid of looking silly if we leave a party or a car just because we feel uncomfortable, but Franks advises that if a situation feels wrong to you, it probably is. Get out as quickly as possible.

Be aware of your surroundings. Even in public places and in broad daylight, pay attention. "Notice who sits near you in a restaurant and who walks behind you on the street," advises Franks. Don't be caught by surprise.

Be wary on first dates. No matter how well your sister or home-girl knows him, a first date is new to you. Consider going on a double date. "Make sure someone knows where you are, who you're with, and when you'll be back. Take money for a cab home and change for the phone," says Franks. A good rule of thumb on dates is: Don't spend time alone with a date in secluded locations. Try to socialize with others in groups or in public places.

Beware of the devil you know. Women have been raped by ex-husbands, doctors, ministers, and fathers. According to the National Women's Survey, 75 percent of rapes are committed by someone the victim knows. Don't assume that you are safe just because you have a relationship with him.

The survey found that 9 percent of victims were raped by their husbands or ex-husbands, 11 percent were assaulted by their fathers or stepfathers, and 10 percent were assaulted by their boyfriends or ex-boyfriends.

Your intimate partner may assault not only you but also your children. "Be careful. In selecting a partner, you're choosing a partner for your children as well," says William Lawson, M.D., Ph.D., professor of psychiatry at Indiana University School of Medicine, chief of psychiatry at the Richard L. Roudebush Veterans Administration Medical Center, both in Indianapolis, and president of the Black Psychiatrists of America.

Don't look like easy prey. Look assertive and unafraid to make a scene if you have to. And don't accept unwanted sexual advances politely, Franks adds. When you say no, say it loud.

Run if you can. It is often too dangerous to fight back, says Franks. Rape is crime of violence, and you are likely to end up being seriously injured or killed in addition to being raped if you attempt to physically challenge the rapist.

RECOVERING
FROM RAPE

If you or someone you know is raped, getting immediate care and support is crucial to living through the experience without long-term physical or emotional problems.

Get to a safe place. Go to the nearest secure building and call the police. Then call your local rape crisis service (you can find the number in the Human Services section in the blue pages of your phone book) or 1-800-656-HOPE, the number for the Rape Abuse and Incest National Network (RAINN) referral service, which will switch you to their nearest participant. "Be aware that the police will probably be direct with you. They may ask, 'What were you doing there at that hour? How were you dressed?' Don't let their candor upset you. You can garner support from trained counselors at a rape crisis center," says Dr. Mitchell.

Call a friend. "But choose her carefully," advises Martha Delain, vice-president of Family Services, a professional confidential counseling service in Rochester, New York. Make sure she is able to support you. "Some friends might get so upset that you may end up comforting them."

Preserve the evidence. "You will want to bathe afterward, but don't. Don't douche, shower, brush your teeth, comb your hair, or clean your hands, face, or clothes. Don't eat or drink anything," says Franks. "Physical evidence that could take your attacker off the street must be preserved," she says.

Get medical help. "You may be injured and not know it," says Dr. Mitchell. A woman who has been raped should go to an emergency room to be cared for. "You may have been exposed to HIV or need morning-after contraception, and the average emergency room is equipped to handle all your needs," says Ruth Louise Hall, Ph.D., assistant professor of psychology at the College of New Jersey in Trenton. The emergency room will also document physical evidence of the rape.

Get psychological help. "Rape is a major cause of post-traumatic stress disorder (PTSD), an anxiety disorder caused by traumatic events," says Dr. Mitchell. To prevent it, you will need immediate counseling and psychological support. A woman with PTSD often has nightmares about the event and may also suffer from depression, anxiety, agitation, and difficulty sleeping. She may have mood swings and cry often. (For more information on PTSD, see page 337.)

"Sufferers tend to relive the event. This can happen through distressing thoughts or playing back the event, either in waking experiences or in dreams," explains Dr. Mitchell. The National Women's Survey found that almost one-third (31 percent) of all rape victims developed PTSD sometime during their lifetimes.

Sometimes a victim can initially handle the emotional trauma, but when she enters a relationship, the flashbacks that cause her to relive the abuse and assault may present problems for her and her partner, says Hall. She adds that a woman needs her partner's support. "Her partner should go into therapy with her if necessary to understand her situation and her needs," Hall says.

Don't accept guilt. If you didn't agree to sex, you were raped. If you were raped, it is important to talk about your feelings of being violated and to seek justice. African-American women often don't report rape because they are humiliated and feel people will judge and blame them. Too often these women have been brainwashed to believe that if they were raped, it was their own fault because they invited it by some seductive action on their part, says Dr. Mitchell.

Get justice. "You should file charges, for yourself and to protect others," says Franks. You must believe in yourself and make the system work for you. Rape crisis services are available to help you through the challenges you face.

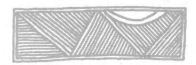

Raynaud's Disease

WARMING UP TO YOUR OPTIONS

ugust in Mobile, Alabama, is sweltering, but at the offices of James Lawrence, M.D., a clinician and assistant professor of pediatric and adult rheumatology at the University of South Alabama College of Medicine in Mobile, the air conditioning is off. Stephanie Johnson, 33, who is wearing a bronze silk cardigan over her matching long-sleeved jumpsuit despite the heat, stretches indulgently.

"I'm so glad that there's no air conditioning in here," she says. "I can't tell you how many movie theaters I've had to leave this summer. They're usually ice cold, and my hands and feet are aching within 5 minutes."

"You don't have to tell me. They ran me out of the supermarket the other day with their arctic-blast air conditioning. And I can't even go near the frozen foods," laughs 27-year-old Hampton Lane.

As they chat, Dr. Lawrence escorts Felicia Oliver, a long, lanky 16-year-old patient and new member of the support group, into the room.

"Remember what I was telling you about dressing for cold weather and air-conditioned areas?" Dr. Lawrence asks the group. "Hats, scarves, and gloves are what you need, I don't care what month it is. And not just any hats, scarves and gloves. Felicia, hold up your hands."

Felicia promptly holds up two hands dwarfed by huge, red, knitted mittens, and everyone bursts out laughing. "That's what I'm talking about!" chuckles the doctor. "I want you to wear ugly gloves. Don't try to be cute, because cute is not warm."

Raynaud's:
The Big Chill

These sisters are not crazy. For them, staying warm, winter and summer, is a priority because they have Raynaud's disease. Even moderate cold causes them excruciating pain and numbness in their hands and feet.

People with Raynaud's experience this reaction because when they feel cold, their blood vessels close too much. So much, in fact, that red blood cells, which carry the oxygen that helps keep our tissues warm and alive, cannot squeeze through. When this happens, the tissues in their hands, feet, and other extremities become starved for blood and oxygen, discolored, ice cold, extremely painful, and difficult to rewarm. "If warmth and circulation aren't restored quickly enough, the tissue actually may die, and ulcers can appear. The worst-case scenario is when people actually lose parts of their fingers and toes," says Dr. Lawrence.

Five to 10 percent of Americans have Raynaud's, and it affects more women than men. No one is sure exactly why, but the female hormone estrogen may have something to do with it. Symptoms usually start between the ages of 20 and 40, but even young teens can develop the disease.

If you are trying to figure out if you have Raynaud's, most medical texts say that a skin color change—from natural to white, then to blue, and finally to red—is the classic symptom. "But these symptoms are common only in textbooks," says Dr. Lawrence. Instead, he suggests that you ask yourself a few questions.

▲ Do your hands (or feet) change color when they become cold, especially when you reach into the freezer or go into a supermarket?
▲ Do your hands and feet hurt?
▲ Does your spouse or friend notice that your hands are always cold?
▲ Have you ever developed an ulcer after exposure to the cold?

If the answers to two or more of these questions is yes, you should see a rheumatologist, a doctor who specializes in disorders that involve inflammation and degeneration of the body's connective tissue.

Raynaud's is a disorder with two names. Both Raynaud's disease and Raynaud's phenomenon refer to the pain, skin changes, and even skin ulcers that cold can trigger. *Raynaud's disease* is the term used to describe these symptoms when they appear with no other signs of a connective tissue disorder. "But Raynaud's phenomenon is the term used when you have Raynaud's and another connective tissue disease such as lupus, an autoimmune disease that is very common in Black women," says Dr. Lawrence. Rheumatoid arthritis also frequently joins forces with Raynaud's phenomenon. Using vibrating tools or instruments can also trigger Raynaud's phenomenon in some people.

To test for either type of Raynaud's, your doctor will look at your nail folds, the fingernail area that is right above the cuticle but under the skin. "I do a nail-fold capillaroscopy, in which I use a microscope lens to look for evidence of a change in the structure of the capillaries," says Dr. Lawrence. A change is associated with the presence of connective tissue diseases.

STAYING SAFE AND WARM

You can't cure Raynaud's, but you can prevent flare-ups if you follow this expert advice.

Go cold turkey. "Smoking is a big, big problem," says Dr. Lawrence. "The carbon monoxide that smokers inhale displaces oxygen in the red blood cells so that the few blood cells that can get through the narrowed arteries of Raynaud's sufferers carry much less oxygen than is needed," he says. This worsens tissue damage. So if you have Raynaud's, do not smoke.

Avoid chill pills. "Diet pills, cold medications with decongestants, and certain migraine medications, especially ones containing caffeine, exacerbate or trigger Raynaud's spasms," says Dr. Lawrence. So you should avoid these medications and caffeinated coffee and cola as well. Birth control pills and hormone replacement therapy may also cause problems for women with Raynaud's.

Take extra care. If you become pregnant and you know that you have a connective tissue disease or think you have Raynaud's, talk to your doctor. Some connective tissue diseases are associated with pregnancy difficulties or an increased risk of miscarriage, says Dr. Lawrence.

Cover up. Carry warm gloves and a warm scarf with you. Learn to always wear a hat, because you lose from 20 to 40 percent of body heat through your head, says Dr. Lawrence. And use potholders or oven mitts when you reach into the freezer or refrigerator.

For unavoidable exposure to the cold, you can try slip-on chemical heat packets, which are available at sporting goods stores. The packets produce heat for up to 8 hours after you activate them by tearing them open or heating them in a microwave. You can buy special mittens that have a pocket for the packet, or you can slip the packet between a mitten and its liner to avoid direct contact with your skin. For your feet, attach the packets to the outside of your socks with the adhesive strip that comes with the packet. Just be sure to avoid direct skin contact with the packets. You can also buy socks, boots, and mittens that are specially designed for skiing and other cold outdoor sports.

TREATING TOUGH CASES

Raynaud's can often be controlled with simple self-help measures, but sometimes you may need special care.

Investigate medications. If you avoid the cold and still experience problems, talk with your doctor about prescription medications such as nifedipine (Procardia), diltiazem (Cardizem), or generic reserpine, which can help control the symptoms but aren't considered a cure. Topical agents such as nitroglycerin ointment (Nitro-Bid) are effective in controlling symptoms in some people.

Go for medical options. If you develop severe ulcers because of Raynaud's, surgery is an option. "An experienced hand surgeon can peel the sympathetic nerve off blood vessels in the palm, and this will markedly decrease the frequency of Raynaud's attacks," says Dr. Lawrence.

Baby yourself. Taking baby aspirin may help some people avoid Raynaud's flare-ups, because aspirin inhibits the function of blood platelets, which help blood clot. If blood clotting is decreased, this may help with conditions where the blood flow is sluggish, says Dr. Lawrence. But talk to your doctor about trying this remedy, because there are some risks associated with decreased clotting ability.

Razor Bumps

A Plan for Smooth Shaving

ust back from the barber's, Ron Monroe surveyed his image in the mirror with disgust and complained to his wife, Lorraine. "That barber didn't cut my beard right. Unless he gets it just right, it looks too sparse, and the gray hairs stick out too much—they're straighter than the others."

Lorraine listened patiently because she knew that although Ron was not a vain person, this beard business was really causing him a lot of heartache and aggravation. Figuring that she had a solution, she suggested that he shave it himself.

"That," he remembers explaining, "is exactly the problem. If I shave it, I get razor bumps.

"A few days later," he continues, "I came home and hurried to the bathroom with a brown paper bag. I told Lorraine that my friend Trent (who has a trim goatee and smooth skin) said that he uses this, and I showed her a can of Magic depilatory shaving powder.

"At first it seemed that Trent had found the answer. But after three weeks of burning, itching, and fighting straggling hairs that had survived all attempts to chemically dissolve them," Ron says, "I gave up and grew my beard back."

For Ron, as for the majority of African-American men, pursuing a close, clean shave was a source of major irritation.

Shear Agony

Dermatologists call this problem pseudofolliculitis barbae (PFB), but ask any brother with a sore, itchy chin, cheeks, and neck and he will tell you that they are plain old razor bumps. Black men in particular are at risk for razor bumps from shaving because the curly texture of African-American hair causes it to grow out of the face and

Unfortunately, razor bumps can be a unisex problem, says Harold Pierce, M.D., a dermatoplastic surgeon at the Pierce Cosmetic Surgery Center in Philadelphia. About one out of five African-American women develops hypertrichosis, or excess growth of facial hair, most notably on their chins. And when women with excess facial hair resort to shaving, pulling, or plucking, they often develop the same unsightly bumps and scarring as men.

About a quarter of African-American women, says Dr. Pierce, face a related condition called post-inflammatory hyperpigmentation. It can result from trauma to the hair follicles caused by leg shaving. Tiny dots—the darkened hair follicles—give the affected skin a peppered appearance. In more extreme cases, the skin has a dry, rough, "nutmeg-grater" texture.

"Shaving and waxing can make matters worse," says Dr. Pierce. "If you still want to remove the hair, depilatories or electrolysis are other options to try." To exfoliate the thickened skin covering the follicles, says Dr. Pierce, your dermatologist may recommend an enzyme cream containing urea (Ureacin).

The solutions to razor bumps are about the same for men and women, says Dr. Pierce, except that women might be more likely to consider trying professional electrolysis, since it works well on small quantities of hair. An electrologist guides a sterile electric needle into the hair follicle and turns on the current, which destroys the hair at the root, but it can take multiple sessions. If you persist with the treatments, the hair will eventually stop growing back. For some people, however, electrolysis itself can cause irritation. It can also be expensive.

One word of caution regarding body hair, for women of all colors. If unusual hair growth suddenly appears on your nipples, chest, arms, or legs, give your gynecologist a call before you call a dermatologist. Sudden changes in body hair in women can signal the presence of an ovarian tumor, since hormone imbalances can encourage such hair growth, says Dr. Pierce.

then curve back on itself, growing into the skin and causing pain, inflammation, and infection.

"Shaving exacerbates the problem by putting a sharp point on a short hair, which then makes it easier for that hair to pierce the skin," says dermatologic surgeon Clarence Wiley, M.D., clinical assistant professor at the University of Kansas School of Medicine and medical director of the Center for Skin Health and Beauty, both in Wichita. "We Black men are at risk because of the actual shape of our hair." Once the hair is inside the skin, the resulting PFB lesions can cause deep scarring as well.

Your Personal Defense Plan

The easiest and best solution for razor bumps has always been to grow a beard, because once the facial hairs grow long enough, they no longer pose a danger to the skin. But a beard is not a panacea. Not everyone likes the look of a beard, and for men in certain professions, growing one is not an option. Here are some other ways to deal with the problem.

Get back to clear skin. Before you try out new approaches to managing your facial hair, consult a dermatologist, who can help soothe and heal your existing razor bumps. Prescription-strength medications containing tretinoin (Retin-A), alpha hydroxy acids (NeoStrata), or cortisone (Hytone) can be very effective, says Dr. Wiley. Tretinoin and alpha hydroxy acids help to discourage new ingrown hairs, infections, and bumps by causing controlled exfoliation (accelerated removal of dead skin cells) of the upper layer of the skin. Cortisone eases the pain and reduces itching, which can help you resist the urge to pick at razor bumps, a practice that Dr. Wiley says can lead to infections and scarring. It's best to get professional help.

Take care of keloids and deep scars. For some men, large scars and dark spots become a serious problem. "I've seen severe keloids that cover a man's entire beard area," says Dr. Wiley. These can be treated with carbon dioxide laser surgery to remove the scar. The surgery is often followed by steroid therapy, which involves injecting cortisone directly into the scar to help flatten it out. A dermatologist may also use steroid patches to help flatten the scars. In some cases, the two methods can be combined.

Try not to shave too close. For most razor bump–prone African-American men, growing a full beard is the only way to protect their skin. You can avoid wearing a beard, however, and steer clear of skin irritations by learning to cut your hair just above the skin but not quite on the skin, says Dr. Wiley. This alternative to shaving will keep the tips of beard hairs just above the surface and prevent them from curling back into your face.

Ask your barber to use clippers to cut your beard no shorter than ¼ to ½ inch, or you can try the same thing yourself at home. When he can't make his weekly barber appointment, Dr. Wiley uses a Wahl brand beard clipper with adjustable settings.

Take another shot at the blade. Some men can find relief from razor bumps by using an electric razor, but others find that this doesn't help. If you've never used an electric shaver before, you may want to give it a try. "It's an option that some men find helpful," says Dr. Wiley.

Try a little magic. Good old Magic shaving powder, as well as similar chemical hair removers or depilatories, work by dissolving the hair with thioglycolate acid–based mixtures that are applied directly to the skin. You then wipe or scrape off the weakened hair, ideally leaving behind nothing but smooth skin. According to Dr. Wiley, however, this isn't always the case. Since depilatories must be used almost daily to be effective in preventing razor bumps, the chemical ingredients can cause irritation. It's great for some guys, such as Trent, but be prepared to give up the goo if you find yourself developing a rash.

Take a shaving break. If even a close-trimmed beard is not in your future, the next best strategy is to ease up on your shaving schedule. Try to shave less frequently and less closely, says Dr. Wiley. For extra care, prepare your beard hair with a good softening agent that contains colloidal oatmeal or oilated oatmeal, like Aveeno Therapeutic Shave Gel. Also, says Dr. Wiley, be sure to shave in only one direction—the direction in which your hair grows. Take a moment to closely observe your face in the mirror and note the growth pattern on your cheeks and beneath your chin, as they may differ.

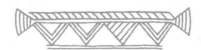

Rheumatoid Arthritis

FENDING OFF SURPRISE ATTACKS

all, willowy, and brown-skinned, with an impressive mane of thick black hair, Elaine Brooks has the type of round, pretty face that makes people think she is several years younger than 34. That's why they are genuinely startled when they see the enlarged and knotted joints that mark her neatly manicured hands. "I often see people trying hard not to stare at my fingers," Elaine says, "but it doesn't really bother me. I try to redirect them a little bit by getting them to look into my eyes."

Elaine's deformed joints are the scars that she carries from an eight-year battle with rheumatoid arthritis (RA). "It started with two sore knee joints that I thought were the result of my spending too much time jogging. I ignored it at first and just cut back on my running schedule. But within two years, I was walking with a cane, and my hands, wrists, and knees were almost constantly swollen and wracked with pain," says Elaine. "It took years of experimenting with different drug therapies and making the rounds to numerous specialists before I found a treatment that sent the disease into remission. I'm pain-free most of the time now, but the damage to my joints is permanent.

"Thanks to a year of physical therapy, I was able to give up the cane," Elaine continues. "To get this far, however, I had to change just about everything about my life: my diet, my exercise routine, my stressful job, even my sleeping patterns—now I get nine hours no matter what. The real test is whether the arthritis will return."

A FULL-BODY ASSAULT

You may think that all arthritis is created equal, but that's not the case. RA differs from osteoarthritis in that it harms a great deal more than your joints. "Rheumatoid arthritis is a disease of the entire body that occurs when the immune system turns against itself," says Margaret A. Fountain,

M.D., an arthritis specialist in private practice and the health editor for a local television station in Baltimore. This type of arthritis affects over two million people, almost three-fourths of whom are women. The rates appear to be similar among Blacks and Whites.

Although osteoarthritis and RA are two completely different diseases, it is possible to have both conditions. The severe damage that RA can cause in the joints can eventually lead to a case of osteoarthritis, the most common type, which results when the joints become inflamed or shift out of place.

"The chief rheumatoid symptom is severe morning stiffness that lasts for hours," says Dr. Fountain. "The stiffness is often followed by inflammation in the small joints of the hands and feet." Other common symptoms include inflammation, heat, redness, pain, and swelling of the joints in a symmetrical pattern (both wrists or both knees at the same time or different times); a low-grade fever; mild anemia (a low red blood cell count); fatigue; and depression.

But the real mystery and misery of RA lie in the fact that it can cause inflammation in almost any internal organ. The heart, lungs, intestinal tract, and blood vessels can all be involved. This inflammation can bring pain, heat, swelling, and redness. Also, the course of this disease is unpredictable. Unlike osteoarthritis, which often progresses gradually over a lifetime, RA can escalate very quickly or suddenly go into remission.

THE IMMUNE ALARM

There are many possible triggers for RA, but doctors suspect that they all begin with the immune system. The trouble starts when your body's disease-fighting mechanism—white blood cells—mistake the tissues of your joints and organs for foreign invaders and attack them, causing painful inflammation and tissue destruction.

RA may also be brought on by a virus or infection that causes your immune system to malfunction and attack your body rather than healing it. "The causes may be many and varied," says Dr. Fountain.

Four times as many women as men develop RA because estrogen, the dominant female hormone, contributes to the frequency and severity of the disease. Doctors are unsure of all of the aspects of the estrogen connection, since RA often goes into complete remission during pregnancy, when estrogen levels are quite high.

Make sure that your doctor understands the full range of your symptoms and other health problems you may have and that he monitors your physical condition for a period of time before deciding if you have RA. "It can take time and patience to diagnose this condition," explains Dr. Fountain.

RHEUM
FOR IMPROVEMENT

You can't prevent RA, but if you have it, you can take steps to keep your symptoms under control. Try these simple self-help tips recommended by leading rheumatologists.

Education is essential. "Every patient's symptoms are different," says Dr. Fountain. "Your doctor should teach you how to understand when your condition is worsening and when you need medical treatment. The severe deformities caused by rheumatoid arthritis, such as the clawlike stiffness of the hands, can possibly be prevented or at least slowed if the patient receives treatment early in the course of the disease."

Proceed with caution. "Be sure to discuss any treatment you are considering with your doctor to make sure you're not doing yourself more harm than good," warns Dr. Fountain. "Arthritis treatment is a big business for charlatans. I've heard of horrible schemes where treatments involved sitting in uranium mines or wearing copper bracelets, which has absolutely no effect on the disease," she says.

Take it easy. Try to stick with moderate levels of activity and choose exercise that doesn't overwork your joints, like moderate walking or water aerobics. "This prevents further damage to your joints and preserves function," advises Dr. Fountain.

Ease into exercise. "If you move your joints when they are hot, swollen, and inflamed, you can do further damage," says Dr. Fountain. Ask your doctor to teach you how to increase your activity level gradually until you can get back to exercising regularly. Working out underwater is an ideal exercise for people with arthritis because the water supports your body and keeps the weight off your joints. So water running or aerobics are good activities to try.

Eat with care. There are no studies proving that food can bring on attacks of RA, but since some people with RA report a connection between food allergies and rheumatoid attacks, you should keep a careful record of how your condition responds to food. "If you begin to suspect that a certain food makes your disease flare up, don't eat it," says Dr. Fountain.

Take alternative action. If you wish to try holistic treatments or acupuncture, be sure to talk things over with your doctor. "I tell my patients that if they take herbs or vitamins, I have no problem with it, as long as it's not in megadoses and as long as they don't discontinue their traditional medications," says Dr. Fountain.

Don't discount drugs. Effective medications for RA include over-the-counter and prescription anti-inflammatory drugs such as ibuprofen (Motrin), analgesics or painkillers like acetaminophen, and prescription steroids like prednisone (Deltasone). Cutting-edge therapy involves the use of chemotherapy drugs such as methotrexate (Folex), penicillamine (Depen), and azathiorine (Imuran). Your doctor should discuss with you which drugs can be effective in your case, says Dr. Fountain.

Sarcoidosis

Getting Your Body Back on Track

ver since Janie Barnes was in kindergarten, she's wanted to be just like her dad, a big-hearted police officer who's widely respected in his Bronx neighborhood for his work with African-American and Latino youth. But she almost didn't get the chance. During her physical for the police academy, a routine chest x-ray revealed swollen lymph nodes.

"I'll tell you, I was stone-cold petrified," admits 27-year-old Janie, waving at a local merchant as she deftly maneuvers her police cruiser through rush-hour traffic. "I had felt perfectly healthy, and when the news came, all I could think of was cancer or something."

It turned out to be sarcoidosis, something considerably less deadly than cancer. Janie's doctors are keeping tabs on her health, but they've given her the green light to do police work. "Working on the police force is my first love," she says, then halts in midsentence and smiles. "Besides my dad, I mean."

Sisters at Risk

Sarcoidosis is a relatively rare disease in which masses of fibrous tissue form spontaneously in the lungs, skin, eyes, heart, or virtually any other organ of the body. The tissue, called granuloma, isn't cancerous. But if it grows unchecked, it can impede or shut down the affected organ, which, depending on the organ involved, can be fatal.

Sarcoidosis is more common among African-Americans, and the death rate is 12 times higher in African-Americans than in Whites in the United States. Among women of both races, death rates are 40 percent higher than among men. "It's not clear whether sarcoidosis actually occurs more in women than in men or if we just detect it more in women because visits to the gynecologist bring women into more frequent contact with the health care system," says Richard F. Gillum, M.D., special assistant for cardiovascular epidemiology at the National Center for Health Statistics in Hyattsville, Maryland.

Besides being more common in African-Americans, sarcoidosis is often more serious. "Blacks have more severe forms of sarcoidosis, and when we die from the illness, we die earlier in life," says Dr. Gillum. Among Whites, the most deaths from sarcoidosis occur between the ages of 80 and 90, but the most deaths among Blacks occur between the ages of 40 and 50. "We're not sure why," he says.

The good news is that only about 5 percent of people with sarcoidosis die from it. In two-thirds of all people with the disease, it disappears on its own with little or no permanent damage. "Lots of sarcoidosis patients feel fine and don't know they have the disease until a chest x-ray comes back abnormal," says O. D. Polk, Jr., M.D., a pulmonary disease specialist and assistant professor of medicine at Howard University College of Medicine in Washington, D.C. "These people—the ones with no symptoms—are often the ones whose illness may resolve spontaneously."

RECOGNIZING THE SIGNS

If symptoms appear at all, what they are depends on which organ is affected. A case of sarcoidosis that is focused in the lungs (the most common target organ), for example, can cause coughing, tiredness, shortness of breath, or mild chest discomfort. With Janie, the disease concentrated on the immune system, which caused enlarged lymph nodes and could have resulted in occasional fevers.

Involvement of the eye typically shows up as blurry vision. And when the disease is concentrated on the skin, there's likely to be bruising. "But 80 to 90 percent of the people who have symptoms come to the doctor's office complaining of tiredness and shortness of breath," says Dr. Polk.

There are lots of unanswered questions surrounding sarcoidosis, including what causes it. Scientists think it begins when an unknown stimulus in susceptible people activates immune system cells called macrophages and lymphocytes. These cells normally scavenge the body for bacteria and other foreign intruders, which they destroy. With sarcoidosis, though, the cells go a bit haywire. They migrate into target organs, where they recruit cells that produce collagen, a tough fibrous protein that's the principal component of tendons. Collagen forms the granulomas, the tissue masses that are characteristic of sarcoidosis.

"Granulomas can range from the size of a quarter to the size of a small fist. You can see how they might interfere with breathing, for example, if they form in the lungs," says Darlene A. Lawrence, M.D., a family physician and associate professor at Georgetown University Medical School and Family Practice Residency Program in Washington, D.C.

SAFEGUARDING
AGAINST SARCOIDOSIS

Sarcoidosis is impossible to prevent—at least deliberately—since we don't understand what causes it. "And treatment of the disease is still evolving," admits Dr. Polk.

Still, there's hope. Sarcoidosis can be treated quite effectively. And remember, many cases clear up nicely even without treatment. Here's what you need to know.

Keep an eye on symptoms. Sarcoidosis is like a forest fire: It's a lot easier to contain in the early stages. "If more than one organ is involved by the time someone sees a doctor, there's a greater chance the disease will worsen," says Dr. Polk. So if you experience unexplained shortness of breath, cough, fever, weight loss, or other puzzling symptoms, don't hesitate to visit your doctor.

Know what to expect. A physician who's familiar with sarcoidosis will give you a thorough physical exam, including a careful check of your skin and lymph nodes. You may receive a chest x-ray, a blood test, and a breathing test. "If someone has worsening symptoms, we take a tissue biopsy of the lymph nodes, lung, skin—whichever organ is involved—to help us reach a diagnosis. Sarcoidosis can mimic diseases like lymphoma or tuberculosis, so an accurate diagnosis is important," says Dr. Polk.

Watch for side effects. If you're diagnosed with sarcoidosis but it's not causing you trouble, your doctor probably won't prescribe medication. But if you are experiencing symptoms, and especially if they're worsening, the standard treatment is steroid therapy.

Steroids reduce the size of granulomas and greatly improve quality of life. "Most patients on steroids can continue to work, and they feel much better. But if you receive steroids, know the potential side effects," says Dr. Polk.

High blood pressure, weight gain, a puffy face, diabetes,

stomach ulcers, susceptibility to infection, and the risk of osteoporosis in postmenopausal women can all be brought on by steroid treatments. "These side effects can be controlled by adjusting the dose," says Dr. Polk.

Get immunized. If you have sarcoidosis that involves your lungs, ask your doctor for an injection of pneumococcal vaccine to prevent pneumonia, says Dr. Polk. And get a flu shot before each flu season, he says. These precautions will help prevent an infection that your impaired lungs might not otherwise be able to fight off.

See your eye doctor every year. Be sure to have an eye examination at least once a year to prevent blindness. Even if granulomas are in another part of your body, they can develop in your eyes and cause damage, says Dr. Polk.

Scalp Problems

DITCHING THE ITCH AND IRRITATION

**I** was checking myself out in the bedroom mirror one day," says Terence Halsey, "and I thought, 'Well, those months of working out and laying off the burgers and fries have really paid off. I look great, if I do say so myself.'

"When my wife, Arlene, came into the room, I asked, 'Well?' and struck a pose in my new black designer jacket. I was angling for a compliment," he says, grinning.

"Terence looked good," Arlene recalls, "but I was distracted by something else about his appearance. I really appreciated the results of Terence's fitness program, but I couldn't help commenting that he looked wonderful, except for all that white dust that I could see on his shoulders."

"When I saw the dandruff on my collar and lapels, I wondered, 'Where did this come from? I've never even noticed it before.'"

"I told him not to worry about it," says Arlene. "A little dandruff shampoo would take care of it. But I did insist that he switch to a lighter-color jacket."

WHAT'S ITCHING YOU

Terence is certainly not the first well-dressed brother (or sister) to find a new look marred by dandruff flakes or a new 'do ruined by an irritated scalp. William Keith, M.D., clinical assistant professor of medicine at Drew Medical School/Martin Luther King, Jr., Hospital and medical director of the Institute for Aesthetic and Cosmetic Dermatology, both in Los Angeles, sees plenty of African-American women and men every day with common scalp problems such as dandruff and scalp irritations from hair dressings and chemical burns from perms and relaxers.

Minor scalp irritation can cause lots of discomfort, but most conditions can be avoided or remedied with a little bit of tender loving care.

Shaking
the Flakes

The scalp problem dermatologists tend to see most often in Black patients is dandruff, or sebhorreic dermatitis, says Greta F. Clarke, M.D., a dermatologist in private practice in Berkeley, California. The reason is simple: Contrary to common belief, it is often an oily scalp, not a dry one, that leads to the itching and flaking we know as dandruff.

Because few of us shampoo on a daily basis (our hair tends to be too fragile and styling too time-consuming), oil accumulates on the scalp and leads to flaking and irritation. There are several things you can do to keep dandruff under control.

Pass on the pomade. Or don't "grease your scalp," as some of us say. "African-Americans tend to have oily scalps, so adding oil to the scalp is unnecessary," says Dr. Keith. If your hair needs moisture, use a conditioner designed for dry hair. For added shine and combability, Keith recommends using a silicone-based shine enhancer, which will also help hold in moisture.

Don't scratch. Scratching may bring temporary relief, but it can lead to inflammation and even broken hairs, says Dr. Keith.

Shampoo at least once a week. "Depending on how they style their hair, many first-time patients come in and tell me that they wait two, three, or even four weeks between shampoos, thinking they're being kind to their hair. In reality, they're being unkind to their scalps," says Dr. Keith.

To thoroughly cleanse your scalp without overdrying your hair, Dr. Keith recommends massaging shampoo into the roots and letting it sit on the scalp for about 5 minutes. Then quickly distribute the lather down the hair shafts and rinse.

Wash with tar. You may need to use a dandruff shampoo if flakes persist. Those that contain tar as the active ingredient, such as Neutrogena Therapeutic T/Gel shampoo, are most gentle, says Dr. Clarke.

Since dandruff shampoos can be drying, Dr. Keith recommends using them only on the scalp and using a milder shampoo on the rest of the hair. After shampooing, use a moisturizing protein conditioner, advises Dr. Clarke. Once the problem is under control, you can taper off the dandruff shampoo, using it only once a month and your regular shampoo at other times.

Go to a pro. If your condition persists after several weeks of home treatment, see a dermatologist, says Dr. Keith. He can prescribe more potent prescription shampoo or a topical steroid treatment.

Cooling
Allergic Reactions

Using chemicals on your hair can cause allergic reactions, especially if you don't test them on a small patch of skin before use. Hair colors and dyes are prime culprits. An allergic reaction may make your scalp itch, become inflamed, or ooze, and your face might swell, says dermatologist Susan C. Taylor, M.D., of Society Hill Dermatology in Philadelphia. The following remedies should help.

Ditch the dye. Hair colors of almost any strength can cause irritation in some people, and black hair dyes may pose a particular problem. If you find that your scalp begins to burn, itch, or flake severely after using dye, stop using that product and consider sticking with your natural color, says Dr. Taylor. If a reaction does occur, wash your hair with baby shampoo several times to remove the excess dye. You can try applying hydrocortisone cream to soothe the skin. For severe reactions, contact your physician.

Get a checkup. Severe scalp irritations can be a sign other health problems. It can also be tough to pinpoint the cause of the problem, so let a dermatologist take a history and help you find the source of the trouble, says Dr. Clarke.

Ask your stylist. Hair stylists are trained to troubleshoot such prickly problems and are skilled and experienced in the proper use of color and other treatments. Yours can recommend an alternative product or service to suit your needs without harming your head. You should also see a professional stylist for big jobs such as coloring or chemical straightening. They're trained to know how to protect your hair and scalp from harsh chemicals, says Dr. Taylor.

Read the fine print. If you must color or otherwise chemically treat your hair at home, follow the package directions on any product you use to the letter. Check new shampoos or conditioners for ingredients that you may be allergic to, such as quaterium 15. Even innocent-sounding plant extracts like jojoba can cause reactions in some people.

Do a patch test. This pretest is a little time-consuming, but it's worth the trouble if it saves you from an irritated scalp. Before trying a product on your hair, follow the manufacturer's instructions and apply the product to a small area of skin in order to see if you're allergic to it. Your stylist should also always do this before providing any new color service, says Dr. Clarke.

Salve your scalp. For itching, try applying a small amount of hydrocortisone cream or ointment directly to the scalp with your fingertips, says Dr. Taylor.

Baby yourself. Switch to a mild shampoo such as baby shampoo until the problem clears up, says Dr. Clarke.

Don't ignore trouble. If you experience dandruff that you can't control, hair loss or breakage, chemical burns that don't heal, bumps of any kind on the scalp, redness, soreness, or other problems, check it out with your dermatologist, says Dr. Taylor.

Sexually Transmitted Diseases

STAYING STD-FREE

rlando Hunt's chart indicated that he was doing well, but a glance at his face told his doctor, Emmet Taylor, M.D., that his patient was in trouble. The moment the tall, well-dressed 32-year-old heard the results of his syphilis test— positive—he collapsed onto the examination table. Then came the clincher: The doctor advised Orlando to tell his wife about the results as soon as possible because she would need treatment as well. Orlando remembers it as one of the worst days of his life.

"'Tell my wife?'" Orlando recalls repeating. "I said, 'She trusted me and now I've got to explain that I cheated on her and that I may have given her this nasty disease? I only stepped out once, but she'll never believe that. She'll never trust me again. She might even leave me!' I was devastated," he says.

As the director of a sexually transmitted disease clinic in the urban area around New Orleans, Dr. Taylor often counsels people who have just discovered that they are infected. He was used to having to weigh his words carefully, but in this case even he was speechless for the moment.

"I wondered how I could prepare this patient for what he would inevitably learn. The truth of the matter was that I had been treating his wife on and off for years. She had probably given syphilis to him," explains Dr. Taylor.

Both Orlando and his wife were eventually cured, but their marriage and their health suffered just the same. "We both paid a high emotional and physical price for infidelity and unprotected sex. And the sad part is, it really wasn't worth it for either of us. It's better to be monogamous, and if you're not, at least use a condom," Orlando says.

You Can't Be Too Careful

AIDS has knocked other sexually transmitted diseases (STDs) out of the media, but each year over one million Americans contract diseases such as chlamydia, gonorrhea, human papillomavirus, genital herpes, and syphilis.

According to government figures, African-Americans have higher rates of most STDs, but most government research is based on information collected from public health clinics, not private doctors' offices. Since a disproportionately high number of Blacks visit those clinics, the study data may be misleading, says Wilbert Jordan, M.D., director of the Oasis Clinic at the King-Drew Medical Center in Los Angeles.

While anyone can contract or transmit an STD, women get gonorrhea and chlamydia at twice the rate men do, and they are also more likely to catch syphilis. The thin mucous membranes of the vagina are more susceptible to the bacteria transmitted during sexual intercourse than the skin of the penis. The semen that often pools in the vagina after intercourse also carries bacteria, so it just makes matters worse for women.

"Bacteria grow very well in the vagina, which puts women at a higher risk for getting STDs than men," explains Nancy Roberson, M.D., clinical associate professor of obstetrics and gynecology at the University of Rochester School of Medicine in New York.

Many people think that they will somehow recognize a person with an STD. Unfortunately, recognizing symptoms of STDs in another person is highly unlikely, since many STDs do not produce symptoms during the early stages of infection. For women, any signs of infection (such as sores) that do show up may be hidden from sight within the vagina. "Many men will not have any symptoms at all," says Dr. Roberson. "And if a man does show signs, it will most likely be in the form of a penile discharge." It's nearly impossible to distinguish a discharge due to infection from that due to sexual arousal if the penis is already erect, she says. Don't try to guess: Use a condom.

Many STDs have also become resistant to treatment. Antibiotic-resistant strains of gonorrhea, for example, were first discovered in East Asia in the 1970s. They were quick to adapt and mutate, and today the drug dosage required to knock out this super gonorrhea is 1,000 times stronger than it was 50 years ago. There are some drug-resistant strains in the Unites States today, but they are still curable with the proper medications. "Soon we may not be able to cure gonorrhea at all," says Dr. Roberson.

Open sores from some STDs also make women and men more susceptible to HIV infection, says Gina Brown, M.D., assistant professor of obstetrics and gynecology at the College of Physicians and Surgeons at Columbia University in New York City. "HIV more easily enters the body through open blisters on the genitals than through healthy mucous membranes," she says.

FIVE COMMON CULPRITS

The good news is that STDs are 100 percent preventable. The first step is to know the enemy.

Chlamydia. Chlamydia is typically silent or symptomless, especially in women. It is one of the most common STDs in America. Chlamydia is easily curable with antibiotics, but since it has few warning signs, it often goes untreated. A woman may not realize she has chlamydia until it turns into pelvic inflammatory disease, an infection of the female sex organs that can cause infertility.

Gonorrhea. Almost 400,000 cases of gonorrhea are reported each year. Often women with this disease have no symptoms at all, but people of either gender who do have symptoms usually experience painful urination and a discharge that begins 2 to 10 days after an infectious sexual encounter. Gonorrhea can be cured, but if left untreated, it can lead to infertility, arthritis, or a rash on the extremities. Gonorrhea can also be passed to a newborn during childbirth, causing a serious eye infection.

Herpes. Before AIDS took over the public's consciousness, and years after syphilis was no longer considered news, herpes was the STD scourge of the late 1970s and early 1980s. Nowadays, no one talks much about herpes, but the disease is still very common. In the United States, 31 million people contract herpes every year—that's one in every six Americans. The herpes simplex type 1 virus usually causes cold sores, but it can also cause genital herpes if it's passed along during oral sex. The herpes simplex type 2 virus is the most common culprit in genital herpes.

Both types of herpes are tricky to spot on your own but easy for a doctor to diagnose. The intensity of symptoms varies from person to person, but generally an outbreak is characterized by the appearance of small, painful lesions (almost like tiny fever blisters) in or on the vagina or penis. Many people also report sharp pains in the hips, thighs, or lower back, or feeling feverish during outbreaks. Many women also find that herpes erupts a few days before their period. Like HPV, the virus can go into long periods of remission.

The virus is most contagious when the lesions are present, but it can also spread during the periods when there are no sores, so someone with herpes should always use a condom, says Dr. Brown. Like syphilis and gonorrhea, herpes can be transmitted from mother to unborn child, causing a very dangerous, possibly fatal infection in the baby. And since herpes is a virus, there is no cure. The pain, duration, and discomfort of the eruptions can be reduced, however, with medication. Getting treatment as early as possible during each outbreak will lessen the severity of sores and shorten their healing time.

Human papillomavirus (HPV). When it comes to dangerous STDs, HPV, also known as genital warts, is one of the most serious (except, of course, for HIV/AIDS). In recent years, doctors have discovered that infection with certain types of HPV often leads to cervical cancer. HPV may appear with or without symptoms. When the warts do develop, they can appear in a woman's vagina, on her cervix, in her anus, or even in her throat if she's been exposed through oral sex. Men who are infected may have warts around the anus, on the penis, or in the throat as well.

Like other viruses, HPV cannot be cured, but it can be successfully treated. Since even a symptomless case of HPV increases a woman's risk of developing cervical cancer, make sure you get regular Pap and pelvic exams if you have the virus.

Syphilis. Affecting about 16,000 Americans per year, syphilis is caused by a spiral-shaped bacterium called a spirochete. It is primarily transmitted through sexual intercourse but can also be acquired through a contaminated blood transfusion or skin-to-skin contact. It is highly curable with antibiotics.

An early sign of syphilis is a painless sore in the genital area. Because the sores are painless, the infection is often missed in its early stages. Later, syphilis may cause extensive skin lesions, heart disease, bone and joint damage, brain damage, blindness, and even death. It can also be transmitted to unborn children. If you have syphilis and are pregnant, it is very important that you be treated before you give birth. That way, your baby will benefit from the treatment as well, says Dr. Brown.

LIVING
WITHOUT STDs

Preventing STDs is simple: Choose abstinence, monogamy, or safe sex.

Get serious. "African-Americans understand that there are risks associated with sexual contact, but many believe it's only a problem if they are promiscuous. Even if you have one partner, you are still at risk," explains Dr. Brown. The bottom line is that both partners must be steadfastly monogamous to ensure protection against STDs.

Forget blind faith. Don't assume that your partner is faithful and uninfected just because he or she says so. Studies suggest that men are less open than women about discussing their sexual histories, and both genders tend to understate the number of their sexual partners.

Dr. Roberson says that a more discriminating attitude toward sexual partners is important. To avoid STDs, make a real effort to know your partners, and know their sexual practices. Spend time together before becoming intimate, get tested before you have sex, and practice rigorous safe sex until you are sure you are seeing only each other, she says.

Use condom sense. If you are sleeping with anyone other than a partner whom you are sure is completely monogamous, insist on using a latex condom. Some people don't know how to use condoms correctly, adds Dr. Brown, but it's easy. It helps if a couple talks openly about it first so they can learn together if necessary, she says.

Make annual visits. Many STDs give no warning signs or symptoms. The only way to be sure you are healthy is to have your doctor conduct the proper tests. If you are sexually active, have a thorough medical exam at least once a year, says Dr. Brown. Visit your physician, gynecologist, or other health care provider.

Self-help is not the answer to dealing with STDs. Reliable medical tests and tried-and-true medical treatments are the only road to recovery. To put it simply, if you have an STD or suspect that you may have been exposed to one, get a checkup, says Dr. Brown. Here's a look at the latest treatments.

Healing genital warts. HPV cannot be cured, but the warts that develop as a result of infection with the virus can be frozen with cryosurgery so that they dry up or dissolve or can be cauterized (burned away) with electricity or a laser. Small warts may be treated topically with a prescription ointment containing podophyllin (Podocon-25). Even after treatment, however, they may recur.

Eliminating gonorrhea and chlamydia. Gonorrhea can be cured with antibiotics, says Dr. Roberson. "Doctors usually treat it with penicillin-type medications or tetracyclines. For drug-resistant strains of gonorrhea, we often prescribe ceftriaxone injections along with a tetracycline-like antibiotic. I often give a second antibiotic at the same time to treat chlamydia because people are so often infected with both diseases at once," says Dr. Roberson.

Beating syphilis. Antibiotics are also the key to curing syphilis. Penicillin is best, says Dr. Roberson. If the disease is left untreated and late-stage complications occur, doctors cannot reverse the damage—such as infertility or neurological disorders—that syphilis can leave behind.

Controlling herpes. The prescription antiviral drug acyclovir (Zovirax) can ease herpes symptoms and greatly reduce the length of the outbreaks. It cannot cure the virus, however, or keep an infected person from spreading the disease.

Many people claim that stress or an overtaxed immune system can cause an eruption, so to help keep herpes at bay, pick a stress-reduction strategy and use it and take good care of your overall health, says Dr. Roberson.

Sickle Cell Disease

LIVING WELL AND THRIVING

eirdre Stone considers herself just another face in the crowd, but you be the judge. The Washington, D.C., native grew up studying tap dancing and ballet, acting in a theater ensemble, and playing jazz piano. Gifted and popular, she was elected president of her junior and senior classes by her college classmates. Today, she's a busy medical student at Meharry Medical College School of Medicine in Nashville, Tennessee, but she still finds time—in between lectures and labs—to do volunteer work at a hospital, something she's done for the past 14 years.

Oh, and by the way, Deirdre has sickle cell disease.

She's a dynamo who mystifies her friends with her high energy and positive outlook on life. "People ask me, 'Aren't you afraid all this activity is going to land you in the hospital?'" says Deirdre, an attractive, brown-skinned woman of 34. "I tell them, 'No, because even people in very good health can end up in the hospital for all kinds of unexpected reasons.' I take sickle cell seriously, but I've tried not to let it get in the way of life."

THE SOURCE OF SICKLE CELL

Deirdre understands the disease that she's lived with all her life, but most of us aren't as well-informed. "Many African-Americans assume that sickle cell disease has already been cured," says Ernest A. Turner, M.D., director of the Comprehensive Sickle Cell Center at Meharry. There is hope on the horizon for a cure, but doctors still have more to learn about the disease.

Sickle cell disease starts with hemoglobin, a substance that enables red blood cells to carry oxygen throughout your body. The hemoglobin forms chains that are made of strings of amino acids, similar

Leon DeLouth is a lot sicker than many people with sickle cell disease. At age 40, he's had hip-replacement surgery, he spends one to two weeks each month in a hospital because of sickle cell crises, and he's gotten so many intravenous medicines that his veins are no longer useable for IVs.

"When I was a child, I was told that I wouldn't live to see age 13," recalls the diminutive artist, who lives in Bakersfield, California. "When I survived my teen years, they told me it'd be a miracle if I lived past the age of 21. Now my doctor says I've lived my life."

And yet Leon says he has no complaints. To the contrary, he says that his life has been pretty good. "My wife and four children have been wonderfully supportive, and I've never had to deal with the really bad problems this disease can bring." Leon recalls a visit to a sickle cell clinic, where he saw people with skin ulcers, bad teeth, and brain damage from the disease. "I realized then that I could be much worse off."

Sickle cell shortened his stature and delayed the appearance of facial hair. He was 30 before he had a mustache. "People look at you and you can see them thinking that you are somehow different. And the fact that my wife, a special education teacher, is the sole breadwinner is hard on my ego. My brothers and I were told as young men that a man supports his family," he explains.

Still, he's making it. Leon's oil paintings—scenes of the Black rural South—are beginning to sell. And he's justifiably proud of his carefully crafted diet, which focuses on such foods as fish, fresh vegetables, and fruit. "I was raised never to use sickle cell disease as an excuse," he says. "I thank God for what I do have."

to a string of beads. When one bead is defective (incidentally, the sickle cell bead is number six), the whole chain of hemoglobin will probably function abnormally. Your body's ability to manufacture hemoglobin is controlled by genes—half from your mother, half from your father. If one gene is normal and the other has a certain glitch in the hemoglobin formula, you have sickle cell trait. People who have only sickle cell trait are usually perfectly healthy because their hemoglobin still functions normally.

If both your mother's and your father's hemoglobin genes are abnormal, however, you end up with sickle cell disease. This double dose of the incorrect hemoglobin formula transforms many red blood cells from flexible disks into brittle, elongated crescents, or sickles, that are too stiff to negotiate the twists and turns of the circulatory system.

A red blood cell can sickle and return to its normal shape many times, but once it does, it develops an inability to properly carry oxygen throughout the bloodstream. In addition, a sickle-shaped blood cell has a shorter life span than a normal cell, so the body of a person with sickle cell disease is unable to make new red blood cells quickly enough to replace the rapidly dying damaged cells. The result is anemia.

What's more, the sickle-shaped blood cells pile up in narrow blood vessels like cars in rush-hour traffic and deprive downstream tissues of vital nutrients. As a result, people with sickle cell disease typically experience crises—periodic episodes of muscle, abdominal, and bone pain, vomiting, blood clots, leg ulcers, and other serious health problems such as kidney disease that can require hospitalization. Children and adolescents with sickle cell disease are also slow to mature physically, and they fatigue easily.

Each person's reaction to sickle cell disease is a little different, however. "While some patients are very ill, most are not, and some have no problems at all," explains Dr. Turner. "It's important not to paint a dismal picture."

Not quite 1 percent of all African-Americans, or approximately 100,000 of us, have sickle cell disease, while another 10 percent or so carry the sickle cell trait.

PREVENTION
THROUGH SCREENING

Sickle cell disease can be prevented, but prevention begins with knowledge. Here's how to protect your family.

Plan your pregnancies wisely. Obstetricians routinely screen mothers-to-be for sickle cell trait. If the mother carries the trait, the

The genetics of sickle cell disease can be a bit baffling. The explanation lies in a rule of nature called genetic dominance. A child's chances of having sickle cell disease are governed by genes that control the production of hemoglobin. If the child's hemoglobin genes are abnormal, meaning that there's a small but important glitch in the hemoglobin formula, she has sickle cell disease. If the hemoglobin genes are normal, the child is healthy.

Any given egg or sperm contains either a normal or abnormal gene for hemoglobin production. If both parents have normal hemoglobin, then naturally the hemoglobin genes—half from the mother, half from the father—that they pass on to the child will be normal.

But if sickle cell disease lies somewhere in the parents' family trees, their eggs and sperm will contain a random assortment of normal and abnormal hemoglobin genes. So a fertilized egg represents one of four possible combinations.

• Two normal genes: The baby will be healthy.

• One normal gene from one parent and one abnormal gene from the other parent: The baby will have sickle cell trait but still be healthy because the gene for normal hemoglobin overpowers the gene for abnormal hemoglobin.

• Two abnormal genes: Because the fertilized egg contains two abnormal genes, the baby will have sickle cell disease. This is why the child of two parents with sickle cell trait has a one-in-four chance of having sickle cell disease. "Keep in mind," says Ernest A. Turner, M.D., director of the Comprehensive Sickle Cell Center at Meharry Medical College in Nashville, Tennessee, "that every pregnancy carries the same one-in-four risk regardless of how many children you have had in the past."

father should be tested, too. "It's not unusual to find fathers who didn't know they had sickle cell trait until the mother gave birth to a child with sickle cell disease," says Gerald M. Woods, M.D., professor of pediatrics at Children's Mercy Hospital in Kansas City, Missouri.

Most states provide family-planning counselors for couples in which both partners carry sickle cell trait. To find these and other sickle cell disease services near you, contact your local health department; the number is listed in your telephone directory.

Make sure your baby is screened. Forty-two states follow National Institutes of Health (NIH) recommendations to screen all infants at birth for sickle cell trait or disease. Check with your obstetrician to make sure your baby is tested.

Talk with your child. For children with sickle cell trait, information becomes more important as they grow to adulthood, since two parents who carry the trait may bear a child with sickle cell disease. Parents need to pass on this information to their kids as they mature. "Otherwise, we will have sexually active young adults walking around with the trait without knowing it," says Dr. Turner.

STAYING HEALTHY

Today, children born with sickle cell disease enjoy better prospects for a normal, happy life than at any other time in history. In 1972, the average life expectancy for people with sickle cell was just 15 to 18 years. Today, it's 42 years for men and 46 years for women. The keys to coping with the challenges of this disease are good medical care and family support.

Use every medical resource. If your baby has sickle cell disease, he or she can receive expert care at one of 10 NIH-funded comprehensive sickle cell disease centers. To find a center near you, contact the National Heart, Lung, and Blood Institute (NHLB) Information Center, P.O. Box 30105, Bethesda, MD 20824-0105. In addition, there are numerous other medical centers that provide comprehensive sickle cell care, including state and public health services. For more information, call your state health department, advises Dr. Turner. Or call the Sickle Cell Disease Association of America at 1-800-421-8453.

Give lots of love. "Without a doubt, family support is crucial to successfully living with this disease. If your child has sickle cell, be with him at the hospital. Most people dislike needles and IVs, especially children, who don't always understand that we are trying to make them well. Tell them, 'Yes, I know this hurts, but we need to do it to help you. We're not punishing you,'" says Dr. Turner.

Deirdre recalls her mother accompanying her on the first day of

Wiping Out Sickle Cell

While a widely available cure for sickle cell disease is yet to be found, a 1996 study of 22 children, ages 3 to 13, with symptomatic sickle cell disease revealed a possible cure, according to the Fred Hutchinson Cancer Research Center in Seattle.

A team of researchers from several leading medical centers discovered that bone marrow transplants were successful in eliminating sickle cell disease from the bodies of 16 of the study participants—a 91 percent success rate. This discovery marks the first time that any procedure has actually stopped the disease.

Unfortunately, however, the bone marrow procedure is not without risks. Two of the 22 study subjects died due to complications from the procedure. "Bone marrow transplantation is one option for a sickle cell disease cure. However, other methods should continue to be investigated and exposed as possible alternatives for cures. Your treatment plan should include gene therapy and the use of pharmaceutical agents that can modify the disease," says Ernest A. Turner, M.D., director of the Comprehensive Sickle Cell Center at Meharry Medical College in Nashville, Tennessee.

school to explain to her teachers that she had sickle cell and would inevitably miss a lot of school. "Once my teachers understood the illness, they let me work ahead of the class so I wouldn't lose ground if I had to be hospitalized," she says.

Relax. "Set reasonable restraints on a child's activities—or your own—but do explore life," advises Dr. Turner. Deirdre couldn't agree more. "My parents raised me like a normal child. Other children whose parents dwelled on the disease grew up being obsessed with it," she says.

Take the initiative. "There are two types of sickle cell patients," says Cage Johnson, M.D., professor of medicine at the University of Southern California in Los Angeles. "Some people are overly dependent on the medical system and expect everything to be done for them. These people suffer, because daily management of sickle cell disease happens at home. Others really take charge of their disease, doing all the right things to manage their health. These people tend to do quite well," he says.

Be your own advocate. What's the worst that can happen when an African-American in the midst of a painful sickle cell crisis goes to a hospital? You guessed it: The hospital staff looks poised to call the vice squad.

"Some Black patients get typecast as drug-seekers because they're Black," says Dr. Johnson. "There's also widespread ignorance about the disease. Not all doctors understand that after years of taking narcotics for pain, sickle cell patients can need high doses for the medicine to be effective. When seeking care, press for what you need," he says.

Ask about hydroxyurea. Research suggests that daily doses of a prescription medication called hydroxyurea (Hydrea) can reduce the frequency of crises and the attendant hospital admissions by 50 percent. "Hydroxyurea doesn't cure the disease, and we don't know about its possible long-term side effects. But it shows great promise for improving the quality of life of patients who have frequent painful sickle cell crises," says Dr. Woods.

Sinus Allergies

BREATHING EASY

fter spending years in the city inhaling traffic fumes and soot, Cynthia Martin thought Tennessee's country air would be a welcome treat. "The country was a wonderful change of pace from the Chicago rat race. I'm a country girl at heart, anyway," says Cynthia. "But a couple of hours after I stepped off the plane, my sinuses started giving me trouble."

The autumn breezes brought the first warning by thickening the already humid air with ragweed pollen. Then she discovered Tennessee's little-known claim to fame: one of the largest collections of hardwood trees in the United States. "I was almost instantly exposed to types of pollen that my poor sinuses had never sniffed before. Within hours, the sinus pain and pressure were unbelievable," she remembers. "By then my asthma had kicked in, so I could barely breathe."

It took a visit to an allergist to make Cynthia's new rural lifestyle livable. Skin tests showed precisely which allergens were making her miserable. Then she worked with her doctor to come up with a plan for minimizing her exposure. "If you don't have allergies, you might think that staying indoors when the pollen count is high and using nasal spray every night is a sacrifice," she says. "But let me tell you: Given the alternative, it's a very small price to pay."

TROUBLE IN THE AIR

"Many people ignore sinus allergies because they're not life-threatening," says Lawrence Prograis, Jr., M.D., deputy director of the Division of Allergy, Immunology, and Transplantation at the National Institute of Allergy and Infectious Diseases in Bethesda, Maryland. "But the fact is that allergies can have a significant impact on your quality of life. Studies show that asthma attacks, like other forms of illness, affect our ability to be productive," he says.

The common symptoms that folks tend to lump under the catch-all term *sinus problems* are actually part of two distinct medical conditions—allergic rhinitis and sinusitis. The first is an allergy triggered by nuisances like pollen, pet dander, feathers, or microscopic insects called mites that live in household dust. The initial sign of trouble is itchy eyes, nose, throat, and sometimes even the roof of the mouth. Then your eyes water, your nose runs, and you sneeze like there's no tomorrow. Your doctor lets you know that you've got allergic rhinitis.

Sometimes allergic rhinitis persists year-round, with symptoms unpredictably varying in severity. At other times it comes and goes with the seasons. Then it's usually called hay fever. In most of the United States, hay fever is a three-season affair. In spring, it's triggered by tree pollen (oak, elm, maple, and so forth). In summer, grass and weed pollen are the culprits, and in fall, weed pollen (especially ragweed) is to blame. If you're under 40 and you or a family member has another allergic condition like asthma or dermatitis, you're at higher risk for developing allergic rhinitis.

Sinusitis, the second well-known sinus demon, is actually an infection of the nasal cavity. Your sinuses are air-filled compartments connected by small canals in which there are tiny hairs called cilia. The cilia sweep the sinuses with cleansing mucus, which then drains to the back of the throat. When the canals are blocked by the inflamed, swollen membranes that accompany a cold, allergic rhinitis, or even a dental infection, the cilia can't do their job. The mucus (plus bacteria or a virus, depending on what's causing the infection) simply has nowhere to drain, and the resulting buildup causes a splitting sinus headache and sometimes a fever. Since the roots of your upper teeth extend very nearly into your sinuses, sinusitis can also cause, and be caused by, tooth pain.

Sinusitis occurs in the course of 1 in every 200 colds. Some people, especially smokers, whose cilia are impaired by the sticky buildup left behind by tar and nicotine, get sinusitis almost every time they get a cold. Pregnant women are at greater risk because the hormones that thicken the mucous membranes of the uterus also thicken mucus in the sinuses.

How can you be sure which type of sinus troubles have a grip

If you happen to be one of the millions of people who are allergic to the venom of bees, wasps, fire ants, or other insects, you should learn to recognize the early warning signs of this potentially fatal allergic reaction and protect yourself. Here's what Lawrence D. Robinson, Jr., M.D., director of allergy and immunology at the King-Drew Medical Center in Los Angeles suggests you do.

Watch your reaction. Most people experience pain and swelling at the location of a bite, but if you start to itch all over, develop hives, feel hot and dizzy, or have trouble breathing, get to a doctor quickly.

See a specialist. If you discover that you are allergic to insect stings, you should consult an allergist to find out how to deal with possibly life-threatening reactions.

on you? "Lots of people say they have a sinus problem without realizing that they have an allergy," says Dr. Prograis. Want one easy way to distinguish allergic rhinitis from sinusitis? Sinus pain and a low-grade fever are clues that you might have sinusitis. Another tip-off is that in sinusitis, the mucus is thick and yellowish or greenish (sometimes indicating an infection), while in simple rhinitis, it's watery and clear.

IDENTIFYING
THE SOURCE

If you think you may have an allergy or sinus infection, here are a few tips on how to recognize it and get it under control from Lawrence D. Robinson, Jr., M.D., director of allergy and immunology at the King-Drew Medical Center in Los Angeles.

Take the skin test. An allergist can track the cause of your sinus allergy—allergic rhinitis—by pricking your forearms with special disposable skin-testing needles, each containing a different allergen. If your skin itches and reddens at the spot where a suspected allergen was placed, you're allergic to it. "It's best to have an allergy test performed by a qualified allergy specialist—a physician who's board-certified in allergy and immunology," says Dr. Robinson.

Know your foe. Your doctor should also be able to tell you if your sinus irritation is an infection—sinusitis—caused by bacteria or a virus. If it's bacterial, the weapon of choice is a prescription antibiotic. But since antibiotics don't work against viruses, you'll have to wait for a viral infection to run its course.

NIPPING THE DRIP

Once you're sure what's causing your sniffles, there are a few steps you can take to reduce the severity of your symptoms and prevent new attacks. Here's what Dr. Robinson advises.

Protect yourself from pollen. If allergy tests show that pollen is your nemesis, tune in to local weather forecasts and stay indoors when the pollen count is extremely high. Limit outdoor activities to 1 to 2 hours and change your clothes as soon as you get indoors and leave them outside your bedroom. If possible, cut back on outings in the morning, when the amount of pollen in the air is likely to be higher than at other times of day.

Nix pet contact. A cat or dog allergy is principally caused by salivary particles that can become airborne and cause your allergic reaction. Pet dander and hair are only secondary factors, so your best bet is to go without contact.

Clean with care. Vacuuming helps, but don't overdo it. "Don't vacuum every footprint; you could stir up so much air that allergies become worse," cautions Dr. Robinson, who recommends a twice-a-week regimen. Special air filters called HEPA devices are the best air cleaners. They're sold as portable units, or you can get a special filter to use with your central air-conditioning or heating unit. Check at a hardware store for both types.

Stock your arsenal. Nonprescription antihistamines containing pseudoephedrine, phenylephrine, or phenylpropanolamine (Benadryl Decongestant, Sudafed Plus) are effective for both preventing and calming episodes of allergic rhinitis. If you're one of the millions of African-Americans who have high blood pressure, however, you should avoid medications with these ingredients and ask your doctor for an alternative, because all of the chemicals listed tend to raise blood pressure.

Try a saltwater solution. When sinuses are irritated, they need to stay hydrated, so try a saline-based nasal spray such as Ocean Spray to moisten nasal secretions and temporarily clear your head.

Drain 'em. You can hasten sinus drainage by using a humidifier or vaporizer to moisturize the air. Or try draping a towel over your head and inhaling the steam from a basin of hot water.

Cool it. Use an over-the-counter medicine such as acetaminophen to reduce any fever.

Say no to chamomile. The pollen-rich flowerheads used to brew chamomile tea can provoke a reaction. Herbalists warn that if you are allergic to ragweed or other members of the daisy or aster family, you should be cautious about drinking the tea.

Skin Cancer

Caring for Healthy Skin

hat Saturday was the first warm day after a bone-chilling New York spring, and Harriet Mays couldn't wait to get to the local pool. So right after lunch, she dashed out into the midday sun with her towel, her goggles, her pool pass—everything but her sunscreen. "I sort of knew better," admits the slender, cocoa-brown athlete and winner of several collegiate swimming awards. "But I said to myself, 'How much damage could an hour or so of sun do?'"

She soon had her answer. That evening Harriet was one hurting sister. Her forehead, nose, cheeks, and lips were swollen into a fiery red testament to the power of the sun's ultraviolet rays. "Not only did I not cover up," she says, "but I spent nearly the whole time in the pool doing the backstroke with my face turned directly toward the sun." It was the first time in her life that Harriet worried about skin cancer, a disease that she knew was pretty rare in African-Americans. "But why tempt fate?" she asks.

Now Harriet keeps a prepacked bag of pool paraphernalia next to her front door, ready and waiting for her next visit to the pool. "Sunscreen?" she asks. "You'd better believe it's packed and ready to go."

Skin Cancer? Us?

Yes, the sun can damage our skin. "Whites get skin cancer more often than we do, but we do get it," says Patricia Treadwell, M.D., associate professor of dermatology and pediatrics at Indiana University School of Medicine in Indianapolis. And when we do, it can be big trouble. "My patients are surprised when I tell them that some skin cancers can kill," says Dr. Treadwell.

UVA and UVB—the letters on your bottle of sunscreen—are actually shorthand for the two types of ultraviolet radiation that can damage skin. Ultraviolet-A (UVA) rays cause long-term damage like premature aging and wrinkling. Ultraviolet-B (UVB) is the stuff that causes sunburn. Both UVA and UVB can cause skin cancer.

Sunscreen ingredients such as benzophenone or oxybenzone filter out some but not all UVA rays. As for blocking UVB, para-aminobenzoic acid (PABA), an ingredient found in many sunscreens, helps keep you protected.

All sunscreens offer some protection against UVB, and many products offer protection against the full range of UVA radiation as well. "Look for a product that promises broad-spectrum protection," advises Rebat M. Halder, M.D., professor and chair of the Department of Dermatology at Howard University College of Medicine in Washington, D.C.

Skin cancer, which is the most common form of cancer in Americans, occurs in three forms.

Squamous cell carcinoma. This is the most prevalent skin cancer among African-Americans. Although it can crop up virtually anywhere, squamous cell carcinoma occurs mainly on skin in areas that get a lot of sun exposure—the face, lips, cheeks, nose, and the rims of the ears. Skin that gets limited amounts of sun, such as that on the hands, chest, abdomen, and lower extremities, can also be affected, especially in areas of preexisting lesions such as scars, chronic leg ulcers (from diabetes, for example), and old thermal burns (from hot liquid spills or fire). Squamous cell carcinoma often starts as a small, wartlike growth and develops into a large ulcerating tumor that can spread to nearby lymph nodes.

Malignant melanoma. This is cancer of the skin's pigment-producing cells, the melanocytes. These cancers are extraordinarily potent. They account for about 5 percent of all skin cancers, but they cause 75 percent of all skin cancer deaths, and they're particularly hard on people with brown skin. "African-Americans get the worst kind of melanomas, a particularly aggressive form of cancer called acral-lentiginous melanoma," says Rebat M. Halder, M.D., professor and chair of the Department of Dermatology at Howard University College of Medicine in Washington, D.C. "And the prognosis is consistently worse for African-Americans than it is for Whites because we often wait so long before we see a doctor," he says.

Malignant melanoma typically starts as a flat, light brown to black molelike blemish about the size of a pencil eraser (¼ inch) and has irregular borders. As it grows, it can develop a variety of colors, such as red, blue, purple, or other shades, and it can bleed or form a scab.

Basal cell carcinoma. This is the most common skin cancer in Whites. It usually shows up on the head or face, often beginning as a bump or scab. This is the cancer that beach-lovers worry about—or should—and it's another reason that Black is beautiful. That's because melanin, the brown pigment that darkens our skin, helps absorb cancer-causing ultraviolet solar radiation, thus preventing penetration into our skin. The darker you are, the more you're protected. "But all the melanin in the world won't guarantee you a zero risk of this cancer," says Dr. Halder.

SCREENING IT OUT

Skin cancer is preventable. Even if you happen to develop it, in the majority of cases it's easy to remedy if you catch it early. "For smaller cancers, we numb the area with local anesthetic, then we remove the diseased tissue either with a scalpel or by freezing it off. For more extensive cancers, we use general anesthesia," explains Dr. Halder. Physicians routinely minimize scarring by using fine sutures. "If we see that a patient is forming a keloid (a harmless overgrowth of scar tissue) as the wound heals, we can inject the tissue with cortisone, which usually stops the keloid from developing and often shrinks it," says Dr. Halder. For advanced disease, the dermatologist follows surgery with radiation or chemotherapy to kill any stray cancer cells.

But here's how to avoid even having to deal with it.

Slather it on. When it comes to preventing skin cancer, sunscreen is your best friend. "Apply it in the morning on all sun-exposed areas of the skin, and reapply it every couple of hours, especially if you

SPF (sun protection factor) is a yardstick for measuring how thoroughly a sunscreen blocks out the sun's rays. SPF is a ratio of how long it takes your skin to burn with and without a sunscreen. So if you're exposed to sunlight that would burn your unprotected skin in a half-hour, a sunscreen with an SPF of 10 will protect you for 5 hours.

SPF 15 products provide adequate protection for most people, according to the Skin Cancer Foundation in New York City. African-Americans with darker skin can sometimes use a sunscreen with an SPF lower than 15, but it isn't recommended, according to Rebat M. Halder, M.D., professor and chair of the Department of Dermatology at Howard University College of Medicine in Washington, D.C. If you want a more precise calculation, here's how to choose an SPF based on your skin tone and the amount of time you'll be in the sun on an average summer day.

Light (tans gradually, usually burns first)		Medium (tans well, burns minimally)		Dark (tans easily, rarely burns)	
Hours in Sun	SPF Needed	Hours in Sun	SPF Needed	Hours in Sun	SPF Needed
1	4	1	4	1	2
1-2	8	1-2	4	1-2	4
3	15	3	8	3	4
4	30	4	15	4	8
5+	30	5+	15	5+	15

sweat or swim. A rating of SPF (sun protection factor) 15 or above is usually enough to prevent skin damage," advises Dr. Treadwell. If you have allergies, try a formula that doesn't include para-aminobenzoic acid (PABA), says Dr. Halder.

Cover up. Pick up a nice hat, a good pair of sunglasses, and a few light summer shirts. "Your best bets are long-sleeved shirts and pants made of light, tightly woven fabric," says Dr. Halder.

Dodge the sun. Avoid working or playing outdoors from 10:00 A.M. to 2:00 P.M., when the sun's rays are strongest, advises Dr. Treadwell.

Start with the kids. Evidence suggests that many carcinoma skin cancers originate in sun damage that occurs during childhood. So shield children from harsh midday sun, and make sure they're covered with protective clothing and sunscreen, says Dr. Halder.

Remember: It's the rays, not the heat. "You can get sunburned on a mountain ski trip, where the thin air can't protect you as much from ultraviolet radiation," says Dr. Treadwell. So use sunscreen whenever you're going to be sun-exposed, even in colder climates, she advises.

Do a once-over. Check your skin twice a year for signs of melanoma by looking for any changes in the size, coloration, or shape of moles, says Dr. Halder. Be sure to examine your palms, the soles of your feet, the webs of your fingers and toes, your gums, the inside lining of your cheeks, and your genital area. If you spot something suspicious, head straight for a dermatologist.

Watch for fake keloids. There's a rare skin cancer that looks a lot like a keloid but is far more dangerous. It's called dermatofibrosarcoma protuberans.

Unlike a keloid, which arises in response to a cut, scrape, or burn, this cancer can appear on nontraumatized areas of the skin. In addition, keloids develop slowly, while the cancer grows quickly. "It may double in size, from the size of a dime to that of a quarter, in three months," says Dr. Halder. See a doctor if what appears to be a keloid is growing very quickly or if the growth is painful or very firm and hard, suggests Dr. Halder.

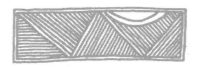

Smoking

Kicking the Butts for Good

When Curtis Johnson was 13, he would sneak off to a country store in his Louisiana hometown to purchase a single cigarette. "They sold them loose, out of a cigar box," recalls Curtis, a handsome management consultant whose café au lait complexion and preference for Creole patois are hallmarks of his South Louisiana roots.

By the time he was in his twenties, Curtis was smoking two packs a day. What had begun as an innocent stab at adult role-playing had become part of his daily routine. "When I shaved each morning, I had a cigarette. When the phone rang, I reached for a cigarette," he recalls. "I was on automatic pilot."

It wasn't dire warnings from the Surgeon General on cigarette packs that convinced him to give it up. It was insistent pleas from his then 10-year-old daughter, Janet. "Jan would mention the dangers of smoking to me and beg me to stop," Curtis remembers. "She was so sincere in her concern."

So one day, he just quit. The first 48 hours were pretty tough, he admits. "I couldn't concentrate on anything for longer than a minute or two, and I couldn't smell a thing." But within a week his sense of smell returned, and eating became a refreshing new experience. "I remember having a bowl of gumbo that had never tasted so good. It was as if I'd grown a whole new set of taste buds," he says.

It's been about 25 years since Curtis last smoked. When he hears smokers talk about how difficult it is to give up cigarettes, he encourages them to keep trying. He's an ex-heavy smoker himself, he tells them. "It feels good to be able to say that," he says.

Where There's Smoke, There's Trouble

Pick a letter of the alphabet, then think of a disease that starts with that letter. The odds are pretty good that smoking either causes it, makes it worse, or delays your recovery from it.

A? Asthma. B? Bronchitis and back problems. C? Cancer of the lungs, mouth, pharynx, larynx, esophagus, pancreas, uterus, cervix, kidney, and bladder. The list goes on and on.

If you want to know why so many of our friends and relatives fall prey to disease and die before their time, you can hardly overstate the role of tobacco. "Smoking is an overwhelming cause of death and disease for African-Americans," says Robert G. Robinson, Dr. P.H., associate director for program development for the Office on Smoking and Health at the Centers for Disease Control and Prevention in Atlanta. "It's the major contributor to heart disease, and it's the one factor that's most preventable. Just don't smoke."

And that's the hitch. Smoking is extremely addictive, both physiologically and psychologically. "There is information out there that says smoking is as addictive or even more addictive than heroin," says Dr. Robinson. "Former addicts have said, 'I have been able to kick a cocaine (or heroin) addiction, but not my addiction to nicotine.'"

Curtis's success at quitting on the first try is very unusual. "People who've never smoked have no idea how difficult it can be to give it up," says Ronnie Hawkins, M.D., a family practitioner in Des Moines, Iowa, and a former smoker. "I still feel cravings after 20 years."

In fact, many African-Americans are at special risk of getting hooked. "Smoking is a social habit rather than a genetic compulsion. In other words, being Black doesn't make you smoke. But it does heighten your risk of exposure to the social stresses that induce people to smoke," explains Gary King, Ph.D., assistant professor and coordinator of the Urban Health Research Program at the University of Connecticut Health Center in Farmington.

Stresses like racism, poverty, and chronic unemployment and underemployment can increase your risk. "It's very stressful to live in a culture that doesn't value us," explains Dr. Robinson. "In focus group interviews, Black smokers tell us, 'I smoke because it's one of the few pleasures in my life. If I had money, I wouldn't smoke.'"

Credit the tobacco industry, too. According to the American Heart Association (AHA), cigarette companies have aimed aggressive promotional campaigns at Black neighborhoods for years. R. J. Reynolds even tried to create a brand (Uptown) for African-Americans, but the effort collapsed when health and consumer groups spoke out in protest, reports the AHA.

Even with all of these inducements to smoke focused on our communities, Black smokers consume fewer cigarettes than White smokers do. But the cigarettes we smoke tend to have more cancer-causing tar and highly addictive nicotine. We also favor menthol brands. This seemingly innocuous additive anesthetizes the lungs, possibly allowing users to draw caustic cigarette smoke deeper into their lungs.

The lungs are the organs that we naturally associate with tobacco damage, but smoking is more than just the primary cause of lung cancer. It also aggravates or causes asthma, chronic bronchitis, emphysema, and pneumonia. And it doesn't stop there.

Tobacco smoke's potent ability to constrict and damage blood vessels contributes to high blood pressure and atherosclerosis, and tobacco's tendency to hasten blood clotting contributes to heart disease, heart attack, and stroke. Smoking causes oral cancers, ulcers, and gastritis (a painful inflammation of the stomach lining). From head to toe, the chemicals in cigarette smoke damage your body in the form of such varied ailments as sinusitis, hernias, and lupus.

Smoking can also harm your baby. Pregnant women who smoke boost their risk of miscarriage and premature delivery as well as increasing the chances that their babies will be born at low birthweights or lose their lives to sudden infant death syndrome.

Finally, secondhand smoke can expose innocent bystanders to some of the same miseries that smokers experience. Rates of lung cancer and coronary heart disease in adults and respiratory disorders and sudden infant death syndrome in children are all higher when people are exposed to secondhand smoke.

Protecting Yourself

Here are a few time-tested methods that will help you keep yourself smoke-free.

Keep saying no. Black teens have smoked less than White teens for the past 20 years, but we need to keep encouraging our kids to do the right thing, says Dr. Robinson.

Become involved. It is crucial to work with friends, family, and community organizations to address tobacco-related issues ranging from smoking around children to cigarette industry advertisements, says Dr. King. "We need to continue to teach children the health consequences of smoking, eliminate cigarettes from vending machines where children have easy access, enforce current regulations that make it illegal to sell to children, resist tobacco industry advertisements and promotions, and work for clean indoor air laws," says Dr. Robinson.

GIVING IT UP FOR GOOD

According to a study from the Louisiana State University Medical Center, among U.S. ethnic/racial groups, African-Americans have the highest prevalence of tobacco smoking, and the quit rate for Black smokers is significantly lower than the quit rate for Whites. Here's how to give tobacco the boot.

Be gentle with yourself. Don't be too hard on yourself if your quitting attempt is short-lived, says Dr. Robinson. "Smokers hardly ever quit on the first attempt. It often takes repeated attempts to quit for good."

Get moving. If you're sedentary, shake a leg, says Dr. Robinson. And if you already exercise, step it up. "Increasing your exercise level helps minimize weight gain and reduce the stress and anxiety that can come with quitting." Plus, it helps produce endorphins, your brain's natural feel-good stimulants. "Once I got the nicotine out of my system, I found that exercise made me feel much better than smoking ever did," says Dr. Hawkins.

Reprogram your automatic pilot. "Identify the things you associate with smoking, then sever the association. Try having your morning coffee without a cigarette or starting your car without automatically pushing in the cigarette lighter," says Dr. Hawkins.

Drink lots of water. "Water helps control your appetite and promotes internal cleansing," Dr. Robinson says.

Patch it up. Nicotine replacement drugs help alleviate the tension, irritability, and other withdrawal symptoms associated with quitting. The nicotine patch (Nicoderm, Nicotrol, Prostep, Habitrol), now available without a prescription, supplies a steady dose of nicotine, but not the other noxious substances in cigarette smoke, through the skin. The patch can be pricey—10 weeks of Nicoderm therapy cost about $250 if you're a heavy smoker—but then, so are cigarettes. "The patch can save you money when you compare what you'd spend on tobacco, and the long-term savings are even greater," says Dr. Hawkins.

Chew on it. Nicotine gum (Nicorette), also available over the counter, works on the same principle as the patch. To reduce withdrawal symptoms, you chew 10 to 15 pieces a day initially, then taper off over three to six months. The cost is about $550 for a 12-week supply.

Bring in reinforcements. "Social support is extremely important," says Dr. Robinson. Tell your family and friends that you're trying to quit and ask for their help. "Bring them into the solution so they don't tease you or smoke around you," he says.

Join a support group. The American Lung Association sponsors Freedom from Smoking clinics through its local affiliates. The eight-session clinics help smokers develop a quitting strategy, use nicotine replacements, control weight, manage stress through relaxation, and prevent relapse. The cost, which is determined by each affiliate, typically ranges from $60 to $100.

Many local chapters of the American Lung Association are working in partnership with African-American churches to provide spiritually based smoking cessation programs. These motivational programs for quitting consist of classes and counseling for smokers that reflect upon scriptural messages and scientific facts about the dangers of smoking. Young people are taught about the ills of smoking and how to counsel others on the health risks of smoking by attending Sunday School programs for children and special youth ministry programs for teens. People who don't smoke also learn how to help and motivate friends and loved ones who are addicted to nicotine.

To get involved in a clinic or to find out about church-based smoking cessation programs in your area, contact your local American Lung Association chapter by calling 1-800-LUNG-USA. Self-help manuals and videos are also available.

Snoring

Putting a Lid on It

"**S**uddenly my head snapped up from the pillow; I jerked awake so fast that a roller fell out of my hair," says Cheryl Allen. "My eyes were open, but I was so disoriented that I saw nothing for a second." She knew that a terrible sound had awakened her, but she wasn't sure what it was.

"A second or so later, I had my answer. Either an ocean liner had sailed into the bedroom or Fred was snoring again," she says, laughing. "There he was on his back, tossing around as if he were being tortured. Even with his mouth open he was attractive, with that pretty chocolate skin and that neatly trimmed beard. Yes, he's cute, I thought, but he's also loud!"

Cheryl knew from experience that it wouldn't help to wake him: He'd only start calling hogs again once he fell asleep. They were going to have to do something about his snoring. "I knew he couldn't help it," she recalls, "but this was getting to be a nightly occurrence, and I needed my rest. All I could think about was the pile of work on my desk at the office. There was no way I could make a dent in it with only 2 hours of sleep. So I scooped up my pillow and a comforter and stomped into the living room. I decided that a few hours of sleep on the sofa was better than nothing."

It's Noisy out There

Fred is not alone. Half of us, Black and White, snore, and a quarter of us do it habitually. When we think of industrial-strength snoring, we tend to picture an overweight, middle-aged man. But women can hold their own, especially if they're overweight. Weight gain, particularly weight gained quickly, makes the tongue propor-

The word *apnea* means "without breath," and that's exactly what happens when you have sleep apnea. People with this condition have brief episodes during which they actually stop breathing. Each time, they partially awaken as the body desperately struggles for air. In some cases, this occurs hundreds of times a night.

Sleep apnea is usually the result of a physically obstructed airway that develops in middle age. While it affects 20 times as many men as women, all women are not immune. "Obese women are definitely at risk," says Andamo Guillaume, M.D., assistant professor of otolaryngology at the King-Drew Medical Center in Los Angeles.

You may suspect that you have sleep apnea if after a night's sleep, you are uncontrollably tired during the day. In most cases, the awakenings during the night are so brief that you probably won't remember them the next morning. If you have sleep apnea, your spouse may notice that your snoring is interrupted by periods of silence that are followed by gasps and snorting, says Dr. Guillame.

If you sleep alone, set a voice-activated tape recorder by your bed and let it run all night. In the morning, listen to the tape to see if there is a pattern of snoring followed by silence and then gasps for breath. This type of snoring makes you a strong candidate for sleep apnea, so see your doctor, recommends Dr. Guillame.

If you have symptoms of sleep apnea, says Dr. Guillaume,

tionately larger in relation to the mouth and throat, and most snoring occurs when there is an obstruction (like the tongue) in those areas.

When it comes to snoring, biology is often destiny: "Larger-than-average tonsils, soft palate, or uvula (that *U*-shaped bit of flesh that hangs down at the back of your throat) can narrow your airway and cause snoring," says Andamo Guillaume, M.D., assistant professor of otolaryngology at the King-Drew Medical Center in Los Angeles.

your doctor may recommend an assessment at a sleep laboratory. You may be asked to stay overnight in the lab, where you'll be observed with videotapes, audiotapes, and a polysomnogram, a record of your sleeping heart rate, respiratory condition, and muscle movements. To make the polysomnogram, technicians will wire your body with electrodes that are hooked up to various monitoring devices.

If the problem is severe, you may need surgery, medications, or other treatments to correct it. But if it's not severe, Dr. Guilluame recommends these tips.

Lose weight. As with regular snoring, weight reduction can work wonders in relieving sleep apnea.

Try a different position. Sleeping on your side can tame sleep apnea by minimizing throat obstruction.

Chill on pills. Avoid taking sedatives, which can cause deeper sleep, more snoring, and more apnea.

Try mechanics. One effective technique is continuous positive airway pressure, or CPAP, in which a jet of air is blown into a face mask that you wear during sleep. The increased pressure inside the mask forces your upper airway to remain open, which reduces or even eliminates snoring, says Dr. Guillaume.

There are other devices that can be prescribed by your doctor to pull the tongue forward and ease snoring and sleep apnea, but many people find that they are uncomfortable to wear.

If you snore, it's because your tongue falls back against your soft palate, which collapses a bit because it loses muscle tone during sleep. When air passes through your throat under pressure, the vibrations create a snoring sound. Snoring can also be caused by a deviated septum, which is a deformity within the nose, or from another obstruction of your airways.

Besides being dangerous to your marriage, snoring can indicate a more serious medical condition such as nasal polyps or sleep apnea, in which a person stops breathing during sleep.

Make peace with your mate and get some rest. Try these simple steps to relieve your nocturnal noisemaking.

Roll over. When you sleep on your back, your tongue falls backward into your throat, partially blocking air flow and causing snoring, says Dr. Guillaume. Sleeping on your side or stomach will usually reduce, if not eliminate, the racket.

Slim down. Although thin people do snore, the problem is more common and usually more severe in people who are overweight, says Dr. Guillaume. Combined with other self-help measures, weight loss is often effective.

Don't drink and doze. "Refrain from alcohol use because it reduces the normal muscle tone inside the throat, which makes airway collapse more likely," says Dr. Guillaume.

Quit the smokes. Smoking irritates membranes in the nose and throat, causing mucus to be secreted. At the same time, it causes tissues inside the nose to swell, which also turns up the snoring volume. So if you haven't already quit, here's yet another reason to kick the habit.

Buy a Band-Aid. They're not exactly adhesive bandages, although they look like them. Special self-adhesive strips made to be worn across the bridge of the nose may help keep airways open. They're called Breathe Right strips, and they are available at pharmacies and sporting goods stores. Dr. Guillame says that they may help some folks find relief.

Go under the knife. If these treatments don't offer relief, another option is surgery to remove some of the tissue that's causing all the noise in the first place. The results are impressive, with about 85 percent of people being cured of snoring and an additional 13 percent showing some improvement, says Dr. Guillaume.

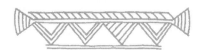

Sprains and Strains

TRAINING TO PREVENT PAIN

arold Jackson, M.D., a California or-
thopedic surgeon and long-distance
runner, was lining up for the start of a
10K race in Oakland when an unusual
sight caught his eye. It was a fellow
runner, a Black man in his seventies
who looked so disheveled he might
have been homeless. "He had long gray hair and a beard, and
he was dressed so unusually," recalls Dr. Jackson. "Dark socks,
beat-up old running shoes, and a racing suit that was probably
20 years old, plus an overcoat." Not exactly a walking Nike ad.

But when the starter's pistol fired, the brother was like a
deer. "Once I saw him run, I realized that he had probably
been doing this his entire life," Dr. Jackson says. "He finished
the race first in his age group, and I'm sure he added that
medal to lots of others he'd won over the years."

Dr. Jackson uses that story to show his patients the
importance of lifelong exercise. "Lots of strains and sprains
happen when people try to work themselves back into shape
too quickly," he says. "If you never get out of shape to begin
with, it's your best protection against injuries like sprains and
strains."

A WHOLE LOT
OF ACHING GOING ON

Strain or sprain, the bottom line is pain. But we're really talking
about two different injuries.

▲ A strain is an overstretched muscle. Muscles have limited pulling
strength, and they can be stretched or torn if worked beyond their
capacity (such as when you dig a garden or go up against a beefy
football lineman).

▲ A sprain is an overstretched ligament, the tough, fibrous band that
holds together neighboring bones. Ligaments are reasonably elastic,

but sudden stress like moving heavy furniture or wiping out on the ski slopes can stretch or snap them or detach one end from the bone.

These injuries can crop up on the job or around the home, but they usually occur at the gym or the track. Doctors treat over 14 million sprains and strains a year in the United States. The most susceptible trouble spots are the shoulders, lower back, knees, and ankles.

"At home or at work, for example, repetitive use of the arms above the head is stressful to the shoulders," says Terry L. Thompson, M.D., assistant professor of orthopedic surgery at Howard University College of Medicine in Washington, D.C. "And most sports, with the exception of soccer, require vigorous use of the arms, which transmit stresses to the shoulders." Any muscle or tendon can be injured if it's too weak to be subjected to a given exercise.

Strains and sprains feel painful and tender, and the injured area may swell as the body sends blood and fluids to the damaged part to help repair it. If you have a hurt muscle that gradually becomes stiff, painful, and tender, often overnight, you're probably dealing with a strain. Strained muscle fibers won't function well until they heal, and they won't function at all if the muscle is torn. Sprained ligaments are often still functional, but if an injury is so severe that ligaments are actually torn, a joint that is sprained may be misshapen as well as swollen and tender.

Making
a Joint Effort

You can help head off sprains and strains by using a healthy pre-exercise routine and proceeding through your workout wisely.

Warm it up. Spend the first 5 minutes of your workout exercising lightly by walking, jogging, or biking, suggests Dr. Thompson. Muscles are cold when you start to exercise, and cold muscles and tendons can snap like pieces of chalk. Warming up accomplishes two things. "It restores good blood flow through the muscles, which helps them function efficiently so you don't have to work as hard," he says. And it makes the muscles flexible so you can gain a full range of motion with less chance of injury.

Stretch it out. After your warmup, spend at least 10 or 15 minutes stretching. "Stretching really decreases ligament injuries," says

Edward A. Rankin, M.D., clinical professor of orthopedic surgery at Howard University Hospital in Washington, D.C. Stretch gradually, without bouncing, and involve all of the major muscle groups, especially the ones you'll be using, he suggests.

"If you've never stretched, ask a coach or personal trainer to show you how, to make sure you're doing it the right way," Dr. Thompson advises.

Fit your equipment. Or more correctly, "make sure your equipment fits you," says Dr. Thompson. Lots of injuries occur because a person borrows someone else's tennis racket that is strung inappropriately for their skill level, or they jog in tennis shoes instead of running shoes, he says.

Go slowly. If you're trying to recapture the fitness of your youth, do it gradually, says Dr. Jackson. "Lots of people make a New Year's resolution to run 4 miles a day," he says. The next thing they know, they're laid up for a week. If you've been out of the exercise flow for a while, do nothing but stretch for the first week or two, he suggests. Then gradually work up to your goals over a period of weeks or months.

Get some variety. Don't immerse yourself in just one exercise, says Dr. Jackson. Cross-training works a variety of muscle groups and makes you less prone to injury. If you swim, ride a bike to exercise your legs, he advises. If you play soccer, use free weights to work your shoulder muscles.

Be contrary. Gym culture is backward, says Dr. Jackson. "Men lift weights, but lots of times they're overweight and they should be doing aerobics, and women do aerobics when they should build up their muscle mass." So live dangerously and try a little role reversal, he suggests. Women who maintain their muscle mass can prevent injuries, especially after menopause, when osteoporosis is common.

DEALING
WITH THE DAMAGE

Okay, so you've overdone it. Here's what you can do to alleviate the pain and help yourself along the road to recovery.

Try RICE. Rest, ice, compression, and elevation are all-purpose remedies for strains and sprains. Rest avoids reinjuring the affected part, ice reduces swelling, compression (with an elastic bandage) minimizes swelling by preventing fluid from rushing to the injury, and elevating the body part above the level of your heart also helps reduce swelling. "Many minor injuries respond to RICE within a day or two," says Dr. Rankin. "If the swelling is persistent, the pain isn't controlled with nonprescription pain relievers, or you can't bear weight on an injured part, that's a sign that you need to see your doctor."

Use whatever works. After RICE, then what? To reduce muscle and joint swelling and pain, Dr. Jackson's patients often use home remedies that range from taking pineapple enzyme supplements (they contain bromelain, which is said to help heal bruises and speed healing) to applying sliced potatoes to their injured joint.

"As long as they are not doing something potentially harmful, I don't discourage people from participating in their treatment in any way that makes sense to them. Even if it's just a placebo effect, you get a benefit without side effects, and that's the ideal combination in medicine," says Dr. Jackson.

Stress

TURNING DOWN THE PRESSURE

herlyn Harris's friends were so impressed with her ambition that they nicknamed her "GC" for Girl Cyclone. But beneath the surface, she was in serious distress. The young paralegal was so overwhelmed with assignments that she had to get two more in-boxes for her already stacked-up desk. And despite all the overtime she put in, the little paycheck she took home was barely enough to feed herself and her two cats. On top of everything else, as the only person of color in her Indianapolis-based law office, Sherlyn felt eyes watching her every move, just waiting for a slip-up.

"I thought that I was handling the pressure just fine until one day when I caught myself feeling more and more frantic and making silly errors," recalls Sherlyn, her tiny dreadlocks catching the afternoon sun. "First I stuffed an important letter to a Milwaukee client into an envelope addressed to a San Diego vendor. Then I placed a high-profile client on hold for a moment and completely forgot about the phone call until breakfast the next morning."

Sherlyn knew that she had to find a way to chill. Now she begins every other workday with step aerobics at the Y, and when the weather is nice, she ditches mass transit for a leisurely stroll home. "Hey, it hasn't made my paycheck any fatter," she jokes. "But it's made a real difference on the inside, where it counts."

ADDRESSING STRESS

Stress may be as universal as traffic jams, pink slips, and lovers' quarrels, but African-Americans still have some pressures that are all their own. In an affluent nation, many of us live with poverty and severe underemployment. And even if we've got a few dollars in the bank, race still matters.

What's Race Got to Do with It?

Every day, whatever their income or social status, Black people face race-related stressors called micro-insults. "I can go into a supermarket dressed in a designer suit, and customers will ask me, 'Do you bag the groceries?'" says William Lawson, M.D., Ph.D., professor of psychiatry at Indiana University School of Medicine, chief of psychiatry at the Richard L. Roudebush Veterans Administration Medical Center, both in Indianapolis, and president of the Black Psychiatrists of America.

At the same time, there's plenty of denial, even from within our own community. "The chances of an African-American heading an American corporation are virtually nil, yet it's common to hear our young adults claim that racism doesn't exist," says Dr. Lawson.

"Many African-Americans find it helpful to remember that they're not responsible for the racism they face," says Terence Killebrew, Ph.D., a clinical psychologist at the Manhattan Vet Center in New York City. "I can work with the most racist boss by reminding myself that I'm not responsible for his ignorance. He has no buttons of mine to push. Only if I'm feeling inadequate can I let him cause me anguish."

If someone you know is struggling with racism-induced stress, let them know that you're there to listen if they feel like talking, says Dr. Lawson. "Racism won't disappear overnight, but that doesn't mean that we can't strengthen our community and ease each other's pain through self-support."

What happens when you combine the everyday stresses of adult life—alarm clocks, difficult bosses, whining children, flat tires, and glaring spouses—with the circumstances that often face African-Americans? Plenty. Stress is defined as any change that you have to adapt to. The more severe the adaptation, the more likely it is that stress will set off mental and even physical reactions: Your breathing quickens, your heart pumps faster, and your stomach churns out more acid.

"If the stresses are frequent or chronic, your body can become hypervigilant (always functioning in overdrive), which is very damaging to the cardiovascular system and organs of your body's gastrointestinal system," says Samuel Gordon, Ph.D., clinical psychologist at the National Rehabilitation Hospital in Washington, D.C.

Stress triggers the release of a powerful hormone known as corticotropin-releasing hormone (CRH) from the brain. In turn, CRH stimulates the release of additional hormones that increase the body's retention of salt and water, thereby raising blood pressure and stressing kidney function. Through this mechanism, prolonged stress could suppress the body's immune system and open the door to some types of infectious diseases or cancers.

So while stress certainly makes us feel lousy emotionally, it can also increase our risk of heart disease, high blood pressure, cancer, and other illnesses.

To make matters worse, even when African-Americans do recognize the dangers of stress, we don't always act to protect ourselves. Black men, for example, are known for keeping their emotions bottled up and responding to overwhelming situations by denying their impact and taking on more stressors, says William Lawson, M.D., Ph.D., professor of psychiatry at the Indiana University School of Medicine, chief of psychiatry at the Richard L. Roudebush Veterans Administration Medical Center, both in Indianapolis, and president of the Black Psychiatrists of America. Psychologists call this behavior John Henryism, named for the legendary Black railroad worker who stoically took on a steam-driven rail machine and then dropped dead of exhaustion.

Other Black men may react to stress by heading in the opposite direction. "They're more likely to opt out of stressful situations because they feel unable to 'be a man' in socially accepted ways, like having a good job or owning a nice home," explains Dr. Lawson.

They may spend what money they have by gambling or buying lottery tickets or abuse alcohol or other drugs to help medicate their pain. "Or they may try to accentuate the one part of their lives they feel they can control—their sexuality—and decide to be a Don Juan," says Dr. Lawson.

Black women handle things a little bit differently. They are more likely to seek support from friends and counselors to help them cope with the pressures of building a career, raising children, or taking care of elderly family members, says Dr. Lawson.

Draining Stress
before It Drains You

You may feel that your life is one big underfinanced, overcaffeinated roller coaster of nerves. But lots of times it's not the stressors that are causing the stress, it's your attitude, says Terence Killebrew, Ph.D., a clinical psychologist at the Manhattan Vet Center in New York City. That means that you can do more about stress than you might think.

Use your support network. It's harder to handle stress alone. When you feel anxiety and tension building up, talk with your partner or close friends and family members and let them know that you need a shoulder to lean on, says Dr. Gordon. Companionship and conversation can be the safety valve that vents the stress before it does real damage.

Find a mentor. "The road to success in business, education, or virtually any other endeavor is paved with the support of mentors—people who have lived through your struggles—who can help you prepare for what lies ahead," says Dr. Lawson. Find a confidante who's older and wiser, he suggests, and ask if it's okay to approach her from time to time for advice or a helping hand.

Walk it off. You don't have to buy an expensive fitness club membership to find stress relief. All it takes is 15 minutes and your own two feet to take a walk at a brisk pace. Research suggests that walking dissipates tension within just a few minutes. The effect is temporary, but it's significant—and it's free.

Work it out. If you can set aside just one half-hour three times a week, you can bring your stress hormones to their knees. "Brisk walking, swimming, and bicycling are great aerobic stress reducers, especially for people who haven't exercised in a while," says Dr. Killebrew. Stretching is also a great stress reliever. As you do it, imagine the tightness and tension leaving your back, neck, chest, and other muscles, he suggests. Before beginning an exercise program, though, be sure to check with your doctor, he says.

Breathe deeply. Feeling stressed and anxious? Here's a simple relaxation technique you can try. Breathe in normally through your nostrils for a count of five, then let the breath out slowly through pursed lips. Try five repetitions, or more if you need to. "Anxiety interferes with thought, so if you can moderate the anxiety, it'll help you think better so you can work your way out of a stressful situation," says Dr. Gordon.

Adopt a pet. If you think having animals around the house is for the birds, maybe you haven't heard about research showing that people with heart problems who own pets live longer. By taking the time to stroke your pet or watch your tropical fish, you can slow down your pace and take a mini-vacation from thinking about stressors in your life, says Dr. Gordon. So if you don't have any pets, think about adopting one.

FOR BROTHERS ONLY

Because Black men react to stress differently than women, here are a few tips especially for the fellas.

Don't be a macho man. The world doesn't need any more John Henrys. You can't be at your best every moment of the day, and you can't be expected to do everything. "Find ways to share your workload," says Dr. Lawson. Delegate what you can in your work at home and on the job so that you can spend more time relaxing.

Ease up on competition. If it rubs you a little raw that your mate gets promoted faster or makes more money than you do, relax. Your partner is there to support you and help you relieve stress, so don't turn her into a source of stress over nothing. "Don't feel threatened by your mate, support her. Your relationship will last and you'll have more fun, too," says Dr. Killebrew.

Let it out. If stress is eating you alive despite these self-help methods, consider professional counseling. In the hands of a supportive and knowledgeable psychotherapist, psychologist, social worker, or other mental health professional, you'd be amazed at the way counseling can work wonders. "When you meet a potential counselor, you should feel that you can establish a comfortable working relationship with him," says Dr. Killebrew.

Stroke

Increasing the Odds in Your Favor

argaree Crosby is a winner and she looks it. At 54, her body is trim and firm, and her caramel-colored skin is smooth and radiant. And she has a lot more going on than good looks.

"I earned my Ph.D. in education from the University of Massachusetts in Boston, and in 1955 I was the first African-American woman to be named a full professor at Clemson University," Margaree says with a proud smile.

But her hard-earned and well-ordered life was thrown into complete disarray on the sunlit morning of July 15, 1995. "I'd been on high blood pressure medication for two years, and I had been told to minimize the stress in my life, but I guess I didn't do that very well," Margaree explains. "That morning, I took a walk outside and returned holding my head. I had a strange feeling, and I went to bed and stayed there all day and night. The next morning I tried to move around, but I couldn't walk without staggering. Finally, I asked my daughter to take me to the hospital.

"By the time we got there, I had lost the strength in my left side. The next day my speech was slurred. I had suffered a stroke. I was really scared," she remembers.

After 2½ weeks in the hospital, Margaree was well enough to begin physical, occupational, and speech therapy. "I cried, but I knew I had to do what needed to be done. I've always been a survivor. I had to do this, too," she says.

She went to therapy as an outpatient. Activities to help her regain motor coordination became part of her everyday life. "I had to walk with a cane. I had to learn to drive again, and I could only say a few simple phrases. But in November, five months after the stroke, my daughter was married, and I walked down the aisle unaided. Now people don't know I've had a stroke unless I tell them," Margaree says.

UNDERSTANDING
STROKE

Stroke, which many doctors call a cerebrovascular accident (CVA) or brain attack, strikes a half-million Americans a year. Of those, nearly one in three dies and others are left seriously impaired. This makes it America's third leading killer and a cause of serious impairment for thousands of people.

How do strokes happen? Your brain needs oxygen to coordinate your mental and physical activities, such as walking, talking, seeing, thinking, speaking, and even swallowing. This steady supply of oxygen comes from your blood, which is carried to your brain by a network of blood vessels. A stroke occurs when these blood vessels rupture or become clogged, cutting off the brain's supply of blood and oxygen. Without fresh oxygen, brain cells start to die quickly. The death of these brain cells causes the loss of muscle control, speech, and other abilities that is so often associated with stroke.

There are two major types of strokes. Ischemic stroke, which accounts for about 80 percent of strokes, results when blood clots block blood flow to an area of the brain. If blood flow is not restored within about 4 minutes, the affected tissue begins to die.

The other major type of stroke, hemorrhagic, occurs when the constant stress of high blood pressure, typically pressure at levels greater than 200/120, weakens and frays small blood vessels until they begin to bleed into the brain, explains Shawna Nesbitt, M.D., assistant professor of internal medicine at the University of Michigan School of Medicine in Ann Arbor. Hemorrhagic strokes appear suddenly and may cause debilitating pain or even death, but they account for only about 20 percent of strokes.

WHO'S
AT RISK?

The prevalence of stroke among African-Americans is not much different than it is among Whites, about 2 percent. African-Americans, however, are almost 88 percent more likely than Whites to die from stroke.

African-Americans are more likely to have high blood pressure, to smoke, and to drink in excess, all of which has a significant effect on stroke risk, says Dr. Nesbitt. The cost of stroke is high in terms of

Stroke's Early-Warning Sign

A TIA, or transient ischemic attack, often called a mini-stroke, mimics what a real stroke would do: It causes weakness; numbness in the face or an arm, hand, or leg; loss of the ability to speak clearly or understand what others are saying; dimness or loss of vision in one eye; and dizziness or loss of balance. But these symptoms rapidly disappear, usually fading in less than 6 hours. If you've had a TIA, your risk of having a stroke is 10 times higher than the risk of someone who hasn't had a TIA, says Shawna Nesbitt, M.D., assistant professor of internal medicine at the University of Michigan School of Medicine at Ann Arbor. The greatest risk of stroke is in the first week following a TIA.

If you think you've had a TIA, see a doctor immediately. With his help, you can probably avert a stroke altogether, says Mark Baganz, M.D., assistant professor of radiology and director of neuroradiology at Howard University Hospital in Washington, D.C. Today, the abnormalities that cause TIAs can often be identified with noninvasive tests such as ultrasound, which uses sound waves to produce pictures of the body, and magnetic resonance imaging (MRI), which allows a doctor to take pictures of your brain. The narrowed blood vessels, usually in the neck, that contribute to TIAs can be surgically reopened, cutting your future stroke risk dramatically.

quality of life, because many do not recover as well or as quickly as Margaree. The good news is that the devastation of stroke can be prevented if we recognize early warning signs and get prompt medical attention.

"We've done a good job of getting the word out that people who think they are having a heart attack must go to the emergency room right away for lifesaving treatment. Now we must get the word out that people need to go to a hospital right away if they are having a stroke," says Mark Baganz, M.D., assistant professor of radiology and director of neuroradiology at Howard University Hospital in Washington, D.C.

Doctors now have drugs that can stop a stroke cold. These clot-busting drugs, as they are called, dissolve the clot that's blocking blood flow to your brain. But the drug must be administered within 4 to 6 hours after the stroke begins. For the vast majority of patients who do not get to the hospital within hours, laments Dr. Baganz, treatments are much less effective.

Is It
a Stroke?

Watch for these warning signs of stroke. If you experience any of these symptoms, particularly if they begin suddenly, don't delay a trip to the emergency room or doctor.

▲ Changes in sensation, including numbness or heaviness, in any area of your body

▲ A headache on one side of your head

▲ Weakness or paralysis that affects one side of your body

▲ Slurred speech

▲ Difficulty walking

▲ Difficulty swallowing

▲ Dizziness or loss of balance

▲ Changes in vision, including blurred, decreased vision on either or both sides

The conditions listed below increase your risk of stroke, so you should talk to your doctor about the best ways to lead a full, healthy life and avoid a stroke.

Getting older. In general, the older you are, the higher your stroke risk becomes. After you turn 55, the risk doubles.

Sickle cell disease. Sickle cell disease can increase your risk of ischemic stroke. In this disease, the red blood cells assume an abnormal sickle shape that interferes with the smooth flow of blood. Sickle cell narrows blood vessels and causes blood clots to form. It is these clots that can lead to stroke.

Lupus. Systemic lupus erythematosus, which affects a disproportionately high number of African-American women, elevates stroke risk because it can cause inflammation of the blood vessels in the brain. The inflammation leads to a narrowing of the blood vessels, which can produce a stroke. People with lupus also have abnormal antibodies in their blood that predispose them to strokes.

Diabetes. People who have diabetes may suffer strokes because the disease may weaken and narrow blood vessels. The high incidence of diabetes among African-Americans doubles their risk of stroke.

POSITIVE CHANGES
FOR PREVENTION

A stroke can happen to anyone. Although there are some risk factors, such as the ones discussed above, that you can't control, there are a lot that you can. Here are some suggestions.

Stop smoking. Cigarette smoking is a big risk factor for stroke, says Dr. Nesbitt. Smoking decreases blood flow and oxygen supply to brain cells, which causes them to die, and the result is stroke.

Nicotine, one of the chemicals found in cigarettes, also has an effect. It's associated with an increase in blood pressure and blood clotting, which also contribute to stroke.

Shed excess pounds. Obesity is a risk factor because it drives up your blood pressure, and more than 40 percent of African-American women are overweight by age 30, says Dr. Nesbitt. It's important to eat right and watch your fat and calorie intake, she says. A daily exercise regimen in which you increase your heart rate for 20 minutes will burn calories and help you shed pounds. Exercise can also help defuse stress, which can reduce your risk of stroke.

Control high blood pressure. Having your blood pressure checked yearly is a good idea, says Dr. Nesbitt. If your blood pressure reading is above 140/90, have your physician recheck it and possibly prescribe medication.

Since lowering your salt intake may help lower your blood pressure, you should avoid high-sodium prepared and canned foods, and don't add table salt to foods that really don't need it, says Dr. Nesbitt. Generally, prepared foods already have a good deal of salt added. Eat fresh or frozen vegetables and add nonsalt seasonings like herbs and spices to give them flavor.

Reduce stress. African-Americans have a different kind of stress. "We are disproportionately represented among the poor, our education levels are often low, which reduces our opportunities, and then we deal with racism," says Dr. Nesbitt. All that stress can send your blood pressure soaring, which can increase your chance of having a stroke. Try meditation, biofeedback, and other relaxing activities such as dancing, reading, walking, or listening to music, suggests Dr. Nesbitt.

Build a better diet. Cutting down on calories to get your weight under control is a great start, but other nutritional factors are important, too. Eat a diet that's low in fat and salt and high in potassium to keep your blood pressure in check, says Dr. Baganz. Indulge in bananas, which are a rich source of potassium and other vitamins and minerals. Also, be sure to get five half-cup servings of fruits and vegetables each day.

Take afternoon tea. Folks who drink black tea seem to have an edge on stroke protection. A study conducted by the National Institute of Public Health and Environmental Protection in the Netherlands suggests that tea drinkers have much lower rates of stroke. Men who drank more than 4.7 cups of tea a day had a 69 percent lower risk of stroke than those who drank less than 2.6 cups a day.

Meditate or pray. Spending quiet time meditating, relaxing, or praying can help ease the effects of stress in your life, says Dr. Baganz.

Cut down on drinking. Let's toast to soft drinks and water. Studies show that alcohol increases the risk of both types of stroke, but especially the more deadly hemorrhagic stroke: The risk is double for light drinkers and triple for heavy imbibers. Alcohol in any form can hike your blood pressure, weaken your heart, thicken your blood, and cause your arteries to go into blood-restricting spasm. If you must drink, do so in moderation, says Dr. Baganz.

THE ROAD BACK

Seven out of 10 people who have a stroke live through it, although the going can be rough. Survivors may be affected in a number of ways, from speech problems to difficulty chewing and swallowing. Of the people who survive a stroke, about two-thirds will need some form of rehabilitation.

Through rehabilitation, the brain can develop new pathways to circumvent damaged connections and switches. As recovery progresses, these still-living cells may take over some of the functions that the dead cells used to perform. They'll need practice.

Doctors and therapists know that, just as Margaree did, you may feel exhausted even thinking about therapy. But the sooner you get into rehab, the better your chances of regaining what you lost. And the more your work at it, the more you'll regain.

Temporomandibular Joint Disorder

SOOTHING A SORE JAW

ost people would never suspect that Pam Greenevale was dealing with a painful health problem—unless they happened to have lunch with her. "Sometimes in the middle of a meal, I just have to stop eating and rest my jaw because of the pain, even though I've started seeing a doctor for treatment," explains the 28-year-old public relations executive.

It took one very embarrassing evening, however, to prompt Pam to get help. "What a night that was," she says, shaking her head at the memory. "I was done, do you hear me—hair fly, dress fabulous, nails perfect—and I was seriously looking forward to having dinner with this guy," she says.

"Well, we met for dinner at one of Baltimore's finest restaurants. The meal was served, and then it happened. I was enjoying myself, making conversation and eating my shrimp, when I got this incredible pain in my jaw. It took about 5 seconds for me to realize that I was unable to open my mouth," says Pam. "You should have seen his face. For some reason he thought I was choking. So he jumped up from his chair, rushed over, and grabbed me from behind, ready to perform the Heimlich maneuver. Thank God, I was able to move my mouth enough to croak out the words, 'Don't! Please stop. I'm all right.'"

"I was so embarrassed that I could barely look him in the eye," she remembers. She managed to get through the meal, but her jaw still hurt, and it made a funny clicking sound. "It was a first date I will never forget. Needless to say, I never heard from that brother again. But I was on the phone to the doctor before 9:00 the next morning. I was determined not to go through anything like that again."

TMD:
A Jaw Breaker

Pam's pain in the jaw was a symptom of what doctors call temporomandibular joint disorder (TMD), a malfunction of the temporomandibular joints, which are two hinges that connect the jawbone to the bones at your temples. If you have TMD, you may get headaches and have unexplained jaw, ear, and facial pain, or you may have difficulty swallowing, says Deborah L. Bernal, M.D., a TMD physical medicine and rehabilitation specialist in private practice in Washington, D.C. You can also experience neck pain, tingling sensations in your tongue, and a clicking or popping noise when you eat, talk, or move your jaw. Like Pam, some people with TMD can barely open their mouths.

TMD can result from a structural abnormality in the joint or teeth. "When you close your mouth, your teeth should fit snugly together. If they don't, your bite won't function properly, and over time, this can set you up for TMD," says Hazel Harper, D.D.S., assistant professor of community dentistry at Howard University College of Dentistry in Washington, D.C., and president-elect of the National Dental Association, an organization of Black dentists.

But most cases of TMD are actually muscular problems resulting from the everyday strain that we place on our jaws. Habits like chewing gum or grinding your teeth put undue stress on the joints and muscles and can lead to TMD, causing persistent soreness in the area in front of your ears and around your temples.

Research shows that anywhere from 40 to 60 percent of the population has some minor TMD symptoms, but only about 5 percent are severe enough to warrant treatment.

Joint Protection

In most cases, TMD can be relieved without medical treatment, so when your jaw starts hurting, try these tips.

Get psychological support. "Often we find that psychological factors like chronic stress, tension, and depression play a role in the disorder. Many people cope with their tension by clenching their teeth, and that act of clenching increases pressure on the cushion in the joint," says Dr. Bernal. Behavioral therapy, using a combination

If you suspect that you have TMD, don't wait: Call your dentist for an appointment and get a thorough examination. Get help and don't wait until the problem is so severe that you get a "lockdown," says Deborah Bernal, M.D., a TMD physical medicine and rehabilitation specialist in private practice in Washington, D.C. "I would suggest that you see a TMD specialist to coordinate your care. Ask your dentist to help you find one. Treating TMD is a pretty complex process." You may need dental work or orthodontic work to correct your tooth alignment, or you may require surgery.

"You can go to the dentist for a bite guard to reduce grinding, if that's the cause of your pain, but that's just the tip of the iceberg," says Dr. Bernal. "Your muscles are still tense, and if you don't modify that behavior, you will still have muscle involvement and still have problems."

In some cases, if the joint is not seriously damaged, chances are good that you can be treated with a variety of conservative therapies. Your doctor can prescribe anti-inflammatory and muscle relaxant medications, physical therapy treatments, and stress-management counseling. In many cases, this treatment may be all you need to relieve your symptoms and protect your jaw from future damage.

In severe cases in which people cannot open their mouths very wide, an acupuncturist can often reduce the facial pain enough to unlock the jaw and allow the healing process to begin, says Dr. Bernal. "Ask your doctor or dentist for recommendations," she says.

You should try all of the conservative treatments before you consider surgery to relieve TMD, says Dr. Bernal. "Some surgeons remove the jaw cushion (the disk that keeps the jaws from grinding together altogether, so there goes your cushioning. Some shave the cartilage to smooth it out, or they shave the bone to clear the space for the joint to move, which can further destabilize the joint. You should exhaust all other measures before considering surgery, because you can't reverse the damage once it's done," she says.

of counseling and relaxation techniques, is often helpful for people with stress-related TMD.

See your dentist. Dental problems, including ill-fitting dentures, can cause TMD problems. "If your teeth don't fit together properly when you close your mouth, you can experience TMD symptoms," says Dr. Bernal. Your dentist can do the dental work or an orthodontist can help you get things back in line with braces.

Fill in the Bs. Nutritional deficiencies, particularly of B-complex vitamins, contribute to the muscle problems that constitute TMD, says Dr. Bernal. Eat more fresh fruits and vegetables as well as beans and brown rice. You could also try adding nutritional yeast, aloe vera juice, or blackstrap molasses to your diet, she suggests.

Juice your joints. If you can't handle chewing hard vegetables or fruit, buy a juicer so that you don't miss out on the basic nutrients that you need. If you have TMD, you also need extra calcium, magnesium, and vitamin D, says Dr. Bernal. Leafy green vegetables are high in these nutrients. Juice up some spinach, celery, and watercress for a high-calcium drink. And spending some time in the sun will stimulate your body to make its own vitamin D, she says.

Heat it up. Applying heat to your sore jaw muscles will help increase blood flow, decrease muscle spasms, and relieve pain. Place two washcloths in warm water, then apply one to each cheek for a few minutes. You could also use hot water bottles (not too hot to the touch) on your cheeks. After you've warmed the area, slowly and gently stretch the joint with a yawn.

Hang up the phone. If you log in more phone time than a popular teenager, you're not going to be able to rest your jaw, so learn to write letters for a while. And when you use the phone, don't hold it between your ear and shoulder, as this position strains the neck and facial joint muscles, says Dr. Bernal.

Testicular Problems
AVOIDING TROUBLE DOWN BELOW

When Kenny Willis played catcher on his high school baseball team, he remembers being summoned to the pitching mound for a little-known but all-important pregame ritual. There, his privacy protected by the umpire, the pitcher, and both coaches, he was told to loosen his belt to show that he was wearing an athletic cup. "That's one thing they never left to our discretion," says Kenny, a husky, genial fellow who looks a little like Joe Frazier. "And I'm glad they didn't."

Kenny, now 42 and the manager of a sporting goods store, remembers a fastball that was deflected off an opponent's bat squarely into his groin. "I tried to act cool about it, but my heart was thumping hard and all I could think of was what would have happened if I hadn't been protected," he says.

Today Kenny makes sure his 10-year-old son, Patrick, a catcher on his Dorchester, Massachusetts, Little League team, never discovers the answer to that question. "I've told him, 'Son, if it weren't for that cup, you might not be here!' Needless to say, Patrick wears his cup to every game."

THE WORST KIND OF PAIN

Sometimes it takes a person of your own gender to appreciate a certain type of pain. Women have childbirth, and men have groin injuries. It can be a tap, a bump, a poke, or a hit from a well-aimed knee; whatever the source, any blow to those two fragile testicles can convince the most macho hulk that there might be something to primal scream therapy after all.

As miserable as it feels, the momentary discomfort of minor testicular trauma doesn't threaten the vitality of these vital organs. Not so with more serious groin injuries. A strong blow to the groin can actually fracture the testicles, or more specifically, the fibrous membrane that holds them together. This is a medical emergency that requires immediate attention. Aside from injury, however, there are several things can go wrong with your testicles.

Torsion. Sometimes a testicle rotates inside the scrotum, twisting the spermatic cord that supplies it with blood. That's called torsion. If the testicle is twisted, the blood supply, and therefore oxygen and nutrients, are cut off. Unless it's untwisted, it will die a slow and painful death within 4 to 6 hours.

Doctors disagree on the causes of torsion. Some say it's due to an anatomic quirk in which the testicle isn't firmly attached to the scrotum. Others blame hyperactive scrotal muscles that twitch when they ought to be chilling out. "The fact that some males experience torsion after orgasm, when the testicles are pulled tightly to the body, lends support for the hyperactive muscle theory," explains Kevin L. Billups, M.D., assistant professor in the Department of Urologic Surgery and director of the National Institute for Men's Health at the University of Minnesota in Minneapolis.

One thing that everybody agrees on is that torsion really hurts. The pain is sudden and severe—a clear message to get to a hospital. Torsion occurs most often in children and teens, but it can also occur in adults. It can happen at any time—after sex, when you're wearing tight-fitting underwear, when your testicles are jostling around during athletics, or even when you're asleep.

Infections. In men under 40 years of age, the most common culprits in testicular infections are bacteria from a sexually transmitted disease (STD) like gonorrhea or chlamydia. The infection can cause inflammation of the testicles, which makes them painful, heavy, and swollen. STDs can also cause epididymitis, a painful inflammation of the epididymis, the spaghetti-like sperm-storage tubes that are coiled up behind each testicle. Men over age 40 may get infections of the bladder or prostate due to enlargement of the prostate, says Dr. Billups. These infections could spread to the testicles.

Celes. This term refers to a noncancerous tumor or a swelling. When a cele occurs in a testicle, it can be uncomfortable. A hematocele, which is a pool of blood, can result from a blow to the testicles,

From ages 17 to 40—the high-risk window for testicular cancer—you should inspect your testicles at least once a month, says W. Bedford Waters, M.D., professor of urology at Loyola University Medical Center in Maywood, Illinois. The exam is quick and easy, and it could save your life.

After a warm bath or shower, when your scrotum is relaxed, take one testicle at a time between your thumb and first three fingers and roll it so that you can feel the entire surface.

A healthy testicle is about the consistency of a peeled hard-boiled egg: smooth and firm but not hard. "Once you've examined yourself a few times, you'll know what a normal testicle feels like," says Kevin L. Billups, M.D., assistant professor in the Department of Urologic Surgery and director of the National Institute for Men's Health at the University of Minnesota in Minneapolis.

If you feel lumps or areas of hardness, notice one testicle is larger than the other, or experience any pain, see your doctor, who may do a number of tests to determine if you actually have cancer. He'll hold a light to the testicle (the light will pass through fluid but not a tumor), and he may do an ultrasound to get a better picture of what's inside. He may also order a blood test to check for various proteins whose levels rise in response to a tumor.

but most celes just develop for no apparent reason.

A spermatocele, a cyst in the epididymis that feels like a round ball resting atop one testicle, is usually not painful. A varicocele is a varicose vein in a spermatic cord, the collection of nerves, arteries, and veins that run to and from the testicle. This condition feels like a bag of worms inside the scrotum and can cause dull pain that disappears when you lie down.

Forty percent of all men with fertility problems have varicoceles. "When we surgically tie off these dilated veins, two-thirds of these men will enjoy higher sperm counts. Varicoceles are the most correctable cause of male infertility," says Dr. Billups. Researchers at the

University of Minnesota are studying altered patterns of testicular blood flow as a cause of sperm cell damage caused by varicoceles.

The majority of celes are hydroceles, which are layers of clear fluid between the scrotum and the testicles that can cause a heavy feeling or a dull ache in the scrotum. "A hydrocele doesn't need treatment unless it is painful or too large," says Dr. Billups.

Testicular cancer. "It's not impossible for African-Americans to develop testicular cancer, but it's rare," says Marc Lowe, M.D., chief of urology at the Group Health Cooperative of Puget Sound (central division) in Seattle. Of the 7,400 new cases of testicular cancer that were diagnosed in 1996, only 80 involved African-Americans. "It's not clear why African-American men are largely spared," says W. Bedford Waters, M.D., professor of urology who specializes in testicular cancer at Loyola University Medical Center in Maywood, Illinois.

Testicular cancer has a cure rate of up to 99 percent if it's detected early enough. The cancer is most prevalent in men ages 17 to 40, says Dr. Waters. It's treated by surgically removing the affected testicles. If a tumor is caught in its earliest stages, surgery may be all that is required. Depending on the type of cancer and how advanced it is, however, your doctor may decide to treat you with a combination of radiation, chemotherapy, or additional surgery to remove diseased lymph nodes.

There is no better way to keep testicular cancer at bay than to examine yourself for signs of its presence at least once a month. The exam takes about 30 seconds.

PROTECTING THE JEWELS

"Whenever you play a contact sport, wear an athletic supporter or similar protector to prevent jostling," says Dr. Billups. Anything that holds your testicles close to your body is better than nothing, he says, so if you don't have a supporter available, briefs are better than boxers. And while a plastic cup may not be comfortable to wear, it provides the most security against contact injury, he says.

If you still manage to injure your private parts, here are some tips to alleviate the agony.

Know the warning signs. Practically any injury to the testicles hurts, at least temporarily. But if you experience pain for more than an hour or notice any swelling, get to a doctor. "These symptoms can be signs of bleeding into the scrotum, or fractured testicle," says Dr. Billups.

Ice it easy. "After a blow to the testicles, an ice compress can help relieve pain and reduce inflammation until you can see a physician," says Dr. Lowe. Place ice in a plastic bag and wrap it in a hand towel to avoid freezing the delicate skin of the scrotum. If ice makes the pain worse, you could have torsion, so seek immediate medical attention.

Give it a lift. Elevate a swollen scrotum by lying down and putting a towel under your testicles. If you have an infection such as epididymitis, this can help ease your pain. "So can sitting in a shallow bath of warm water," says Dr. Waters. But make sure you get medical attention because you'll need antibiotics to clear up the problem.

Thyroid Problems
KEEPING YOUR METABOLISM ON TRACK

 rma Kirby's body was going haywire. The 65-year-old had added 22 pounds to her 140-pound frame in a flash. She was so exhausted that she would sit down to pay her bills and fall asleep. And her strong, gorgeous fingernails were breaking off one by one.

"I had always had beautiful nails, but in a matter of weeks they got as thin as tissue paper," she remembers. Her voice deteriorated to a mere whisper, and her hair was falling out. "My comb would just be full of hair," she says. "At first I just balled it up and threw it away, but then I thought, 'I need to take this to my doctor, because it's just not normal.'"

Erma's doctor thought that her symptoms were being caused by an underactive thyroid gland, and a quick round of blood tests proved his hunch right. The prescription: Medicine to boost Erma's low levels of thyroid hormone. In time, her hair stopped falling out and her nails started to grow again.

After a few months of treatment, she felt well enough to fly from her home in Detroit to Orlando to witness the wedding of her grandniece. "You know, a lot of people complain about their hair falling out, but they never think they could be seriously ill," says Erma, her voice still showing a trace of raspiness. "More than anything, this illness taught me to pay attention to my body," she says, "because when something goes wrong, it has a way of letting you know you need to get help."

YOUR OWN
PERSONAL TRAINER

When megastars like Oprah Winfrey rave about their fitness trainers, don't you wish you had one, too? Think of it: your own personal consultant, who helps you burn just the right number of calories. Well, you can close the Yellow Pages because you've already got one. It's a small gland in your neck.

The thyroid gland is your body's official director of metabolism. From its perch in front of your windpipe, this butterfly-shaped organ makes a hormone called thyroxine. If your body has just the right amount of thyroxine, everything moves along at a nice, smooth pace. But when the thyroid malfunctions and produces too much or too little thyroxine, you've got trouble.

Hyperthyroidism. If the gland is overactive and you have too much thyroxine, you have hyperthyroidism (sometimes due to Graves' disease), which kicks every chemical reaction in your body into over-drive. You feel fidgety, anxious, and unable to relax or sleep, even when you're dead tired. Your heart races so fast that it feels as if it's fluttering in your chest. The smallest exertion leaves you gasping for breath. You lose weight despite eating more. And you perspire a lot.

"People with hyperthyroidism have such rapid metabolisms that you can actually feel the heat emanating from their bodies," says Michael F. Robinson, M.D., an endocrinologist in private practice in Inglewood, California. Other typical symptoms are irritability, diarrhea, weakness, diminished menstrual flow, and occasionally pro-truding eyes. Often people with an overactive thyroid develop a goiter, a visible enlargement of the gland in the neck.

Hypothyroidism. An underactive thyroid, which was Erma's problem, is the result of very low levels of thyroxine. This condition, called hypothyroidism, causes your entire body to slow down so that even simple things like thinking or moving quickly become difficult. You also may become constipated and gain weight despite eating less. "You can run five miles a day and still gain weight if your thyroid isn't working properly," says Darlene A. Lawrence, M.D., a family physician and associate professor at Georgetown University Medical School and Family Practice Residency Program in Washington, D.C.

You may also lose interest in sex, and many women with hypothyroidism find that they develop much heavier periods. Your heart rate can slow from the normal range of 60 to 100 beats per minute to perhaps 50. Other symptoms include dry skin, hair loss, and puffy skin. Puffy tissue can also collect on your vocal cords, causing hoarseness, and in your ears, causing hearing loss.

WHAT ARE
YOUR ODDS?

Males and females do not have an equal risk of developing thyroid problems. For some unknown reason, women with thyroid disorders outnumber men by 5 to 1. About 4 percent of all Americans have thyroid disorders, and African-Americans aren't any more at risk than Whites.

As an African-American, you should clearly convey your thyroid symptoms to your doctor, since some doctors may misinterpret problems like fatigue as just another manifestation of how African-Americans live.

"When a Black woman has chronic low energy, for example, a doctor may overlook an underactive thyroid if he assumes that she's tired because Black women tend to play such central roles in our families and in our communities," says Stephenie Lucas, M.D., an endocrinologist at the Center for Preventive Medicine in Detroit.

Thyroid disorders are also difficult to diagnose for other reasons. For one thing, they tend to creep up on you. "These problems usually don't happen overnight," says Dr. Lucas. "They often occur so slowly—usually over a period of many months—that you may not notice them at first." What's more, the symptoms aren't all that unusual. "What woman hasn't felt cold or had dry skin from time to time?" asks Dr. Lucas.

Although the precise cause of thyroid disorders is unknown, doctors do know that the body's immune system is a major player. In hyperthyroidism, errant immune system cells indirectly overstimulate the thyroid. In hypothyroidism, antibodies—blood cells that normally protect us from infection—mistakenly attack healthy thyroid tissue.

RESETTING YOUR
BODY'S THERMOSTAT

There's not much you can do to prevent thyroid disorders. Genes are the determining factor, not lifestyle. "This isn't one of the 'it's your fault' diseases," says Dr. Lawrence. And there are no effective self-help measures short of seeing a doctor. So let's start there.

Believe in yourself. If you feel you have thyroid symptoms, don't dismiss them, advises Dr. Robinson. Visit your doctor, tell him that you don't feel normal, and ask for a thyroid function test. If your doctor resists, get a second opinion from another physician.

Take those pills. The thyroid function test measures the amount of key thyroid hormones in your blood. If the test suggests that your thyroid is underactive, your doctor will prescribe synthetic thyroid hormone (L-thyroxine) to compensate. Even though some people experience side effects such as nervousness, most people feel normal after a few months on the medication, which must be taken daily for life. Although you will have to buy the medication regularly, it is inexpensive.

Check your options. If the blood screening shows an overactive thyroid, you have three options.

Radioactive iodine. This is one of the most common treatments; it is frequently a single capsule containing radioactive iodine. Once swallowed, the iodine goes directly to the thyroid, where, over a 12-week period, it slows the overactive gland's production of thyroxine. The treatment does not expose the rest of the body to significant radiation, so there's no increased risk of cancer.

The problem with this method is that it's hard to predict the effects of any given dosage; in the majority of people, the radioactive iodine makes the thyroid underactive, so they have to take thyroid hormone each day to get things back to normal.

Medication. Drugs such as methimazole (Tapazole) and propylthiouracil (Propyl-Thyracil) can put the brakes on a galloping thyroid, but they may take 18 months to two years to work optimally. They are effective in bringing about a remission in 50 percent of the people who try them.

Surgery. This infrequently used procedure removes 90 to 95 percent of the thyroid gland and often restores hormone levels to normal for a while. Ultimately, though, people who have surgery for hyperthyroidism become hypothyroid and need to take thyroid hormones.

Surgery always involves some risk. There is a 2 to 9 percent chance of recurring hyperthyroidism even with skilled surgery, and there is a rare possibility of vocal cord paralysis and hypocalcemia (low calcium levels).

Tuberculosis

PUTTING TB IN ITS PLACE

kept going to work even though the cough was absolutely terrible," says Florence Brewster, an accountant in Battle Creek, Michigan. "My whole body just shook every time one rose from my throat. If I had known what I was exposing my co-workers to, I would have stayed home for sure. But I had no idea what was wrong with me. Honestly, I felt 81 more than 31, just about every day of the week.

"When the cough persisted for more than a few weeks, I decided it was time to talk to my doctor," Florence says. "I was sure he would have a prescription or a solution for something as simple as a recurring cough."

Once she heard her doctor's diagnosis, however, Florence was not so sure. "The first time he said 'tuberculosis,' I didn't think I was hearing him right," Florence explains. "Then he said it again, confirming my fears, and explained that the only way for me to get well was to go into the hospital. I was floored. I didn't even know that people got tuberculosis anymore."

After a round of tests to make sure that the original diagnosis was correct, a combination of four medications was prescribed to bring Florence's tuberculosis under control. "I had to take two of the drugs for six months," she says, "but I thank God that I was able to leave the hospital after only two weeks. I'm considered cured now, but I'm still sort of haunted by the fact that, to this day, I have no idea how I developed full-blown tuberculosis."

TB IS BACK

Tuberculosis (TB) has made a dramatic comeback. Older people probably still remember the days when people were shut away in TB sanatoriums until they could be declared cured. Many younger people,

Tuberculosis is a manageable disease if you take the proper steps to prevent it or to treat it if you have been infected. You should be screened annually for TB, for example, if you have come in contact with someone who has it, if you have traveled to or live with someone from a region of the world where TB is widespread, or if you have an illness that compromises your body's ability to fight infection, says Roscoe C. Young, Jr., M.D., a pulmonary health specialist, faculty development fellow at the National Health Service Corps, and professor at Meharry Medical College in Nashville, Tennessee.

If you have symptoms such as unexplained weight loss, night sweats, coughing, loss of appetite, or a low-grade fever, you should see your doctor to be tested. If he suspects that you have TB, he will administer the purified protein derivative (PPD) tuberculin skin test by giving you a small injection on the inside of your arm. If the PPD test is positive, he will order a chest x-ray to see if the bacteria have multiplied and caused tissue damage in your lungs. If the x-ray shows that there has been no lung damage, your doctor will most likely prescribe a drug called isoniazid to help prevent your infection from becoming full-blown TB.

Besides keeping you healthy once you have tested positive for TB, the other main concern is making sure that you don't spread

however, know TB only as the disease of tragic characters in the movies. That's because once doctors discovered the power of antibiotics, more than 40 years ago, TB was thought to be all but banished for good.

Since 1953, there have been effective treatments for TB. With good public health measures and drug treatment, cases were at an all-time low in 1984, says Margaret Kadree, M.D., chief of infectious diseases and director of clinical research at Morehouse School of Medicine in Atlanta.

But in 1985, doctors started seeing a re-emergence of the disease. Funds for TB prevention had decreased, and there was less effective surveillance, says Dr. Kadree. Now a situation exists in which the disease, explains Dr. Young. And since you can only infect others if you have active TB, everything is done to ensure that it remains inactive.

If your symptoms or x-ray indicates that you have an active infection, you will be hospitalized in an isolation room and given drug treatment. The disease is no longer easily cured with the drugs that worked so well 40 years ago, says Dr. Young. Since TB germs have developed resistance to drugs, doctors now prescribe four medications instead of one. You take two of the drugs for 2 months and two for at least 6 months—and sometimes as long as 16 months. You will be allowed to go home after tests show that there are no TB bacteria in your saliva, which means that there is no longer a danger of your passing the disease to someone else.

Once you are sent home, you'll need to continue taking medication to control the TB infection, even if it takes months or years. Once you have TB, it can never be cured by killing off all the organisms in your body, but it can be reduced to an inactive level that is not harmful. It is very important that you finish all of your medications. By doing so, you make yourself less vulnerable to further complications, and there is less chance that a drug-resistant type of TB will develop, says Dr. Young.

the bacteria that cause TB, *Mycobacterium tuberculosis*, have become resistant to the medications that once controlled it. The emergence of diseases such as AIDS, which weaken the immune system and open the door to infection, have also contributed to the increased number of cases.

"TB is spread through the air by such activities as coughing or sneezing," says Dr. Kadree. When someone with an active lung infection coughs, the TB organisms are suspended in the air in tiny droplets of fluid from the person's lungs and mouth. All it takes is one person sneezing and another person inhaling just a few inches or feet away, and the TB is on its way. It doesn't take much to infect you: Just two or three of the microscopic bacteria particles in the air will do it.

How TB
Takes Hold

There are two things that can happen if you are exposed to TB. In the best-case scenario, your immune system is strong enough to fight the growth of the bacteria. Since the seriousness of the disease is determined in part by how much of the bacteria you have in your body, less is best. It is possible to be infected but not have enough of the bacteria to cause damage or spread the disease to others. This is called inactive TB, and the only way you'll know that you are infected is through a simple skin test that shows that the bacteria are present in your body, explains Dr. Kadree.

If your immune system remains strong and the replication of the TB organism is controlled, you can go on for years, or even a lifetime, without knowing that you were infected.

In the worst-case scenario, you are exposed to TB (or you have an inactive case) and your immune system is weakened due to cancer, HIV infection, another illness, or even extreme stress. The TB organisms in your body have a chance to multiply and develop into a full-blown infection. This is what is referred to as active TB, and if it is in your lungs, it can be transmitted to other people when you cough or sneeze.

Active TB of the lungs does its damage by killing off your lung tissue. This damage, which is visible on a chest x-ray, creates symptoms such as coughing, fever, night sweats, and weight loss. The lungs are the organs most commonly affected by TB, says Dr. Kadree, although it can affect other organs, such as the kidneys.

The number of new cases of TB in the past decade has increased 55 percent for Blacks and 25 percent for Whites. Of the 10 to 15 million people infected with TB, only about 10 percent contract active TB. Thirty-four percent of the TB cases in the United States affect African-Americans, although we represent only 12 percent of the population.

TB has always been more prevalent in Blacks because of socioeconomic conditions, not genetic susceptibility, explains Dr. Kadree. We often live in urban centers in crowded conditions with a lack of access to health care. This heightens the likelihood that we will be exposed to TB.

"People from Africa and the Caribbean have a higher risk of becoming infected with TB because the rates of the disease are higher in those areas," says Dr. Kadree.

Children under four years old are especially vulnerable to TB, as are people who live or work in nursing homes, prisons, and any other long-term care facility in which people are housed in close quarters.

KEEPING YOUR
LUNGS TB-FREE

Preventing TB is possible, and so is treating it. If you have TB, of course, you'll need medical attention. But there are steps you can take to keep your immune system strong and avoid contracting the disease altogether. Dr. Kadree offers these suggestions.

Use crowd control. This may sound nearly impossible to people who live in large urban areas, but try to exercise caution during periods when you know that your immune system may be weakened by the flu, exhaustion, or extreme stress.

Eat well. Eat a balanced diet that focuses on five half-cup servings of fruits and vegetables each day.

A balanced diet also limits fat intake to less than 30 percent of total calories and includes 6 to 11 servings of grains or grain products a day. A serving is one slice of bread, half a bagel, or a half-cup of cereal, pasta, or rice. For protein, you may have a 2- to 3-ounce serving of lean meat or another protein food such as tofu, says Dr. Kadree.

Work out. Regular, moderate aerobic exercise, such as walking for 30 minutes three times a week, will help boost your immune system, says Dr. Kadree.

Don't worry, be healthy. If you lead a stressful life, your immune system may not be able to work as hard as it should to keep you healthy, points out Dr. Kadree. Anything that takes the edge off and reduces stress, such as hobbies, meditation, church activities, or even listening to music, can make a difference.

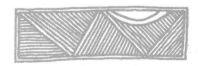

Ulcers

COOLING THE FIRE WITHIN

ne weekend in 1988, Terry Gaskins was snacking on tortilla chips and cola when his stomach started sending him an urgent message: a dull, burning ache that lasted for hours. It wasn't the first time that his stomach had bothered him. "I had felt some vague discomfort before, but it wasn't a big deal," recalls Terry, a strapping young brother with exotic, chiseled features. "This time, though, I had a feeling that something was really wrong."

Terry was right. Like his mother and father before him, he had developed an ulcer. His doctor ordered a prescription antacid, and six weeks later, the ulcer had healed. But the incident helped Terry take stock of the stressors (and stomach-churners) in his life.

For starters, he and his wife had a newborn son, their first child. And his wife had just opened a landscaping business that brought them both a dose of entrepreneurial pride and new-found anxiety. And, as if those changes weren't enough, Terry had earned a serious promotion at the office. Overnight he had gone from being a solitary worker to managing 100 employees.

To manage his stress, Terry ended up going the self-help route. "I bought some stress-management tapes," he says. "They taught me to make sure I was spending some time every week taking care of myself—emotionally, intellectually, spiritually, sexually, and physically. I also learned new ways to relax without making my stomach pain worse. Instead of kicking back with a beer like I used to, for example, I'll go for a long walk."

How's the plan going? Well, it's been nearly a decade since that memorable painful afternoon, and Terry's still ulcer-free.

Equal Opportunity
Pain and Misery

If any sector of the population were likely to be riddled with ulcers (more properly called peptic ulcers), you'd think that it would be African-Americans. But the truth is, ulcers are widespread in the general population: About 10 percent of all Americans develop one at some point in their lifetimes.

The good news is that doctors may have discovered the key to how ulcers develop and why they are so common. "Years ago, we thought we had ulcers figured out. We figured that stress, which psychologists think of as an interruption in the body's internal balance, simply increased the production of stomach acids, which eventually ate away at the lining of the stomach and created an ulcer," says Jules P. Harrell, Ph.D., professor of psychology at Howard University in Washington, D.C. Now we know that there's something else at work.

In many cases, that something may be bacteria—a type called *Helicobacter pylori*, to be exact. While different types of bacteria live throughout the gastrointestinal tract, *H. pylori* is the only organism that flourishes in the harsh environment of the stomach, which is bathed by digestive juices. Some researchers think that the hardy little creatures damage the protective mucous membrane that lines the stomach and duodenum (the tube connecting the stomach and the small intestine), thereby allowing acid and enzymes to attack the stomach lining and cause an ulcer.

H. pylori is found in an estimated 40 to 60 percent of adults, but for reasons that aren't clear, only about 10 percent of people with the bacteria actually develop ulcers. This leads researchers to speculate that ulcers result from a one-two punch. Bacteria set the stage, and then stress and other influences such as smoking and heredity step in and do the rest.

Ulcers can occur in three places: the lower esophagus (esophageal), inside the stomach (gastric), or in the intestine (duodenal). Regardless of location, the symptoms are uncomfortable.

"Most people feel a burning sensation in the stomach, and it's not unusual to feel hungry or to have no appetite at all," says Darlene A. Lawrence, M.D., a family physician and associate professor at Georgetown University Medical School and Family Practice Residency Program in Washington, D.C. People frequently experience belching and coughing, and it's difficult to sleep. The pain is often relieved by antacids or milk, although if you're lactose-intolerant (unable to digest lactose)—as are 75 percent of African-American adults—the milk will probably just make you feel gassy and bloated.

Ulcers tend to run in the family, and people with certain genetic blueprints are more prone to them. They used to be considered a male thing, but women get them slightly more often than men, at least in the under-45 age group. You're more likely to develop an ulcer if you smoke, drink alcohol heavily, or regularly take nonprescription painkillers such as aspirin or ibuprofen.

If left untreated, ulcers can cause bleeding or penetrate the stomach or duodenum and cause potentially fatal peritonitis, an inflammation of the membrane lining the walls of the abdominal and pelvic cavities.

PREVENTION IS THE BEST MEDICINE

The tricky part about ulcers is not diagnosing or treating them, it's avoiding them in the first place. Do your stomach a favor and heed this advice.

Teetotal. Don't drink alcohol, at least not in abundance. Alcohol is an irritant. "It irritates mucous membranes—the kind that line your stomach," says Dr. Lawrence.

Forget the smokes. Tobacco smoke is an irritant, too, reminds Dr. Lawrence. You may wonder how the smoke gets anywhere near the stomach. The back of your throat opens into two passageways, the trachea (breathing tube) and the esophagus (food tube). Inhaled tobacco smoke travels down both, increasing the risk of all three types of ulcers.

Dine before you recline. Give yourself 2 to 4 hours after your evening meal before you go to bed, Dr. Lawrence suggests. It takes that long for the stomach to empty. If you lie down with a full stomach, the mixture of food and acidic stomach juices can splash onto the delicate lining of the esophagus, which is not protected by the same type of mucus as the stomach. That can set the stage for an esophageal ulcer.

Chew well. Digestion starts in your mouth when salivary enzymes start to break down starches. "The more food you can digest in your mouth, the less your stomach has to work and the more quickly food can pass through it," says Dr. Lawrence.

Try yogurt. Make sure the label says that it contains live cultures. That means that it has *Lactobacillus acidophilus*, a form of bacteria that benefits digestive health. "Having more than one type of bacteria in your stomach helps prevent *H. pylori* from taking over," says Dr. Lawrence. She recommends eating at least 2 cups of yogurt a week.

Use care with painkillers. Prescription and over-the-counter painkillers can aggravate or even cause ulcers. These medications reduce naturally occurring antacids that are secreted by cells lining the stomach, possibly allowing acids to start eating through the stomach lining.

"For pain relief, it's a good idea to take small doses of anti-inflammatory drugs that cause the least adverse effects on your stomach. Good choices are a 200-milligram tablet of ibuprofen (Advil, Nuprin) or acetaminophen, two doses of coated aspirin, or low-dose naproxen (Aleve)," says Dr. Lawrence.

Fight stress. The next time you feel stress welling up inside, release it, says Dr. Harrell. Run around the block three times. Go somewhere secluded and yell. Close your eyes and think back to a fun day you had as a child. Take a walk, take a swim, take a drive, take a break, take a nap. Take five. Take control.

BEATING THE PAIN

If you experience ulcer symptoms—gnawing pain or burning in the pit of your stomach, constant hunger, nighttime coughing, or chest pain—see a doctor.

The pharmaceutical arsenal includes antibiotics to eliminate *H. pylori*, antiflatulence medicine to decrease gas, coating medication to help protect the stomach lining, motility medications to speed stomach emptying, prescription antacids to neutralize stomach juices, histamine blockers to reduce stomach acid secretion, and proton pump inhibitors to eliminate acid secretion. Doctors will prescribe one of these medications to start and then move to a combination if necessary, says Dr. Lawrence. If medication doesn't work, surgery can bring relief.

Remember, though, that lots of illnesses cause ulcerlike pain, says gastroenterologist Joanne A. Peebles Wilson, M.D., professor of medicine and associate chief of gastroenterology at Duke University Medical Center in Durham, North Carolina. "Your doctor shouldn't treat you for an ulcer unless the diagnosis has been confirmed with an endoscopy (visual inspection of the esophagus, stomach, and duodenum) or an x-ray of the upper gastrointestinal tract," says Dr. Wilson.

If you are diagnosed with an ulcer, protect yourself by following these ulcer-busting tips.

Eat light and often. Try eating smaller meals more often. Eat four to six meals a day, suggests Dr. Lawrence. "If you reduce the amount of time food stays in your stomach by eating smaller meals, you'll increase the opportunities for the stomach to heal," she says.

Skip the fat. Red meat and fatty foods take longer to digest, and the longer a meal stays in the stomach, the more time acid has to cause problems. So a eating a cheeseburger and fries, for example, is just like asking your ulcer to act up.

Have an after-dinner drink. Try not to drink much during a meal. "Beverages taken with food only dilute mouth juices and stomach acids, which makes digestion more difficult," says Dr. Lawrence. Instead, drink liquids after a meal to help clear food from your lower esophagus, where acid might otherwise wash up to help digest the meal.

Try a new angle. "Place one or two bricks under each post at the head of your bed," says Dr. Lawrence. Sleeping at a an angle helps to prevent stomach acids from touching the lower esophagus. When you lie flat in bed, acids can bathe the esophagus, destroying the lining and setting up the situation for *H. pylori* to attack or a simple ulcer to occur. Just be sure your bed is balanced evenly and sits steady on the bricks, says Dr. Lawrence.

Urinary Tract Infections
Relieving That Burning Feeling

 ucking into the women's room, LaDonna Jones was thinking about the press conference that would begin in just a few minutes to announce the gospel concert series she'd been working on for months. She knew that for the next few weeks, she would be working overtime just about all the time to make sure things went smoothly. But a few moments after she entered the bathroom, she realized that things would be even more stressful than she had expected.

"As I began to go," she recalls, "a familiar pain and burning sensation nearly made me cry. It was the last thing I needed. I had another bladder infection—the fourth one in a year—and I was frustrated. The pain was aggravating enough, but now I would also have to find time to wedge a doctor's visit into my schedule. I knew that I had to do something to get rid of these infections once and for all, so I made a mental note to learn all I could about them."

GETTING TO THE SOURCE

LaDonna's problem, a urinary tract infection (UTI), is experienced by many women of all ages but relatively few men. "Some estimates vary a bit, but by age 40, approximately 35 percent of American women, Black and White, have had at least one UTI," says Evelyn Lewis, M.D., assistant professor of family medicine at the Uniformed Services University of the Health Sciences in Bethesda, Maryland. Although it's not usually a serious medical problem, a UTI can give you some nasty pain and cramping in the lower stomach, burning and pain during urination, and spasms in the bladder and urethra (the tube that carries urine out of the bladder). It can also develop into a dangerous kidney infection if it is not treated quickly and properly.

A UTI begins when certain types of bacteria, including the

Urinary tract infections (UTIs) can occur in men, but they are rare because male anatomy and body chemistry ward them off.

A man's urethra is 8 to 9 inches long; a woman's is 1½ inches. This difference in length means that bacteria have to travel a little farther to cause trouble in men. Also, a man's prostate gland secretions normally discourage bacterial growth. Having an enlarged prostate, however, a condition that is more common in African-American men than in White men, can encourage UTIs by slowing the flow of urine through the urethra. This in turn creates a breeding ground for bacteria and may result in an infection.

In addition to experiencing the same symptoms that affect women, men may have a pus-filled discharge from the tip of the penis and/or an infected prostate (prostatitis), says B. Gerald Hoke, M.D., chief of urology at Harlem Hospital Center and assistant professor of clinical urology at Columbia-Presbyterian Medical Center in New York City.

Here's how to reduce your risks, says Dr. Hoke.

• Cut caffeine, spicy foods, and alcohol out of your diet, as they can irritate the prostate.

• Meet with your doctor to investigate a possible anatomical cause of infection, such as a blocked prostate gland or kidney stones.

• If your doctor prescribes antibiotics to cure your UTI and stave off prostatitis, be sure to take all of the medication, even after you start feeling better.

well-known *Escherichia coli*, find their way into your urethra and then to your bladder or urinary tract. "*E. coli* is by far the most common cause of UTIs," says Dr. Lewis. This type of bacteria is fairly harmless if it stays in your bowel, where it belongs. And, under ideal conditions, the urethra contains protective bacteria called lactobacilli that work to keep *E. coli* and other UTI-causing bugs under control. But once the bad bacteria make the trip to the area around the urethra, the stage is set for an infection. There are also some conditions that increase the risk of getting a UTI.

- Vaginal infections, which can destroy the healthy bacteria that protect the urinary tract.
- Diabetes, which strikes African-American women at a disproportionately high rate.
- Sexual intercourse, which may help push unwanted bacteria into the urethra. Use of a diaphragm and/or spermicides alter normal vaginal pH and decrease the number of protective bacteria.
- And some women, as LaDonna suspected, simply seem to have weak natural defenses against UTIs.

SIGNS AND SYMPTOMS

Recognizing a UTI can be very simple if you listen to your body. The most common symptoms are a burning sensation during and after urination, feeling pressure on your bladder, and bladder spasms. Here are some other clues.

- A frequent and urgent need to urinate that produces only a small amount of urine
- Flulike symptoms, with fatigue and light-headedness
- Strong-smelling urine
- Cloudy or blood-tinged urine
- Painful intercourse

PUTTING OUT THE FIRE

Whether you've had several UTIs or you just want to make sure that you never experience one, Dr. Lewis suggests several steps to protect yourself.

Flush out your system. Drink plenty of fluids, with an emphasis on water, to clean out your urinary tract. Some health experts also suggest that you drink cranberry juice to help reduce your chances of developing an infection. Scientific research has not yet proven the cranberry claim, but a study at Harvard Medical School did show that the acidic juice may help reduce the number of unfriendly bacteria in the bladder.

Take extra care. After using the bathroom, always be sure to wipe from front to back to keep rectal bacteria safely away from your urethra.

Protect yourself before and after sex. Going to the bathroom before and after sex helps to wash out bacteria that may have found its way into the urethra and bladder.

Use soap and water. Cleanse the genital area daily, particularly after sex. Avoid using heavily perfumed soap, as it sometimes causes irritation.

Get plenty of fresh air. Lose your leather pants, nylon panties, Lycra tights, and clothing made of other fabrics that prevent air flow. Switch to 100 percent cotton fabrics or blends that contain cotton.

Reconsider your method of birth control. Spermicides and diaphragms can kill off healthy bacteria, paving the way for a UTI. You also might want to try a new sexual position. The missionary position may cause urethral irritation, which can lead to a bladder infection.

Create a personal prevention plan. If you have a problem with frequent or recurring UTIs, discuss a prevention strategy with your physician. This may include taking an antibiotic before or after sex or taking low doses of an antibiotic daily for 6 to 12 months. Nitrofurantoin (Macrodantin) is an ideal preventive antibiotic because it works specifically in the urinary tract.

Get treatment. Treating a UTI is usually simple. "Your doctor should prescribe a mild antibiotic," says B. Gerald Hoke, M.D., chief of urology at Harlem Hospital Center and assistant professor of clinical urology at Columbia-Presbyterian Medical Center in New York City. "The other thing to remember is that over-the-counter pain relievers don't work well on UTI pain. Instead ask your doctor for a prescription for phenazopyridine hydrochloride (Pyridium), a urinary tract anesthetic that will keep you comfortable until the antibiotics kick in."

Expect to take antibiotics for one to seven days. A three-day regimen works best for curing women with single, uncomplicated UTIs, says Dr. Hoke, but many doctors prescribe a week of treatment, with a follow-up urinalysis to confirm that the infection is gone. Also keep in mind that sulfamethoxazole-trimethoprim (Bactrim), an antibiotic commonly prescribed for UTIs, may cause side effects such as hives in African-Americans.

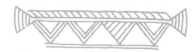

Vaginal Infections

CURING THE ITCH AND BURN

lthough it was 12 years ago, I remember it as if it were yesterday. I had a funny-smelling discharge and an itch that was driving me out of my mind," says 35-year-old Shayna Brown, lowering her voice into a conspiratorial whisper and reaching up to pull her braids away from her face. "After using over-the-counter medicated creams that just didn't work, I finally saw my doctor, who told me that I had trichomoniasis, a sexually transmitted disease. He gave me and my husband pills to take for a week.

"The infection cleared up, but two months later I had it again. My husband had secretly refused to take the pills, and he kept passing the infection back to me. This mess went on for two years! I was really sick of it because I was the one who had to continually go to the doctor. He never developed a single symptom, although he was definitely infected," Shayna says.

UNEQUAL AGGRAVATION

As you can tell from Shayna's experience, women tend to be more susceptible to this type of infection than men, and sexual intercourse increases that risk. Semen, and the bacteria it carries, can pool in the vagina, which is an environment where bacteria can grow well, says Nancy Roberson, M.D., clinical associate professor of obstetrics and gynecology at the University of Rochester School of Medicine in New York.

Men can carry the bacteria that cause vaginal infections without experiencing any symptoms themselves, so they can easily pass them along. This is why it is very important that couples be treated at the same time, regardless of whether or not both partners have symptoms.

"This is an issue we go round and round with," says Dr. Roberson.

Do African-American women get more vaginal infections than White women? Government statistics says yes, but Wilbert Jordan, M.D., director of the Oasis Clinic at the King-Drew Medical Center in Los Angeles, adds that the reporting of sexually transmitted diseases (STDs) and vaginal infection rates is somewhat misleading.

There's no question that we're affected in large numbers by vaginal infections and STDs, but the figures most commonly reported in government statistics come from public health clinics. If Whites notice symptoms of an STD, they're more likely to visit private doctors, who tend not to report such illnesses. Black people are more likely to get treatment at public health clinics, says Dr. Jordan. Since data on our STD rates are reported on much more than the data on Whites, it's possible that it only appears as if we experience higher rates of these illnesses.

THE INFECTION COLLECTION

There are several types of vaginal infections, but three are most common.

Bacterial vaginosis (BV). BV, the most common type, develops when the good bacteria (lactobacilli) in the vagina decrease, allowing infectious bacteria to increase. This imbalance is usually brought about by douching, sexual activity, or other irritants that disturb the ecological balance of the vagina.

Women with BV usually notice a fishy odor, especially after sex, and sometimes develop a white, watery discharge. Fifty percent of women with multiple sexual partners contract BV at some point, but it isn't always spread sexually. A small percentage (2 to 3 percent) of women who develop BV have never had sex.

BV can cause other health woes if left untreated. It can lead to pelvic inflammatory disease (PID), a range of inflammatory disorders within the upper part of the reproductive tract that can cause infertility. Pregnant women with BV have a 40 percent higher risk of premature delivery.

Yeast infections. We often talk about yeast infections and vaginal infections as if they were synonymous, but a yeast infection is a very specific condition. Yeast infections are infamous for the furious itching and cottage-cheese-like discharge that they can bring on. Lots of things can allow yeast to develop, from antibiotic treatment (which wipes out the yeast-fighting bacteria in the digestive tract) to pregnancy, birth control pills, and intercourse. Recurrent yeast infections could be a sign of a more serious problem like an STD or even HIV infection.

Trichomoniasis. This infection, often called trich, is caused by a parasite, *Trichomonas vaginalis*. It is usually characterized by a frothy yellow or greenish discharge that smells foul. Trich is spread by sexual contact and can increase your risk of getting other STDs, including HIV, probably because the infection inflames the vaginal tissues and makes them more susceptible to other infections.

But trichomoniasis is not considered serious because, other than extreme discomfort, there are no long-term consequences if it's left untreated. It won't cause PID or infertility, says Dr. Roberson. This is fortunate, because although it's the least common bacterial infection, half of the women who have trich don't even realize that's what they have. The symptoms are usually mistaken for those of a yeast infection, says Dr. Roberson. Many women simply try to self-medicate with an over-the-counter remedy when they should be seeking proper medical treatment, she says.

STOPPING IT
AT THE SOURCE

Sex with multiple partners leaves you vulnerable to vaginal infections and STDs. For each sexual partner you have, you multiply your risk by the number of their sexual partners. The only real safety measure is abstinence or mutual monogamy, says Dr. Jordan.

Oral-genital contact is equally risky, says Lemuel A. Rogers, M.D., clinical assistant professor of obstetrics and gynecology at the University of Rochester in New York. And a break in the skin of the genital area can make a woman especially vulnerable to any sort of infection, from BV to syphilis and HIV, he says.

Women who have weakened immune systems or chronic diseases are more susceptible to vaginal infections as well. "Someone with AIDS is at higher risk," says Dr. Roberson.

Diabetes also makes a woman more vulnerable to yeast infections, adds Dr. Jordan. The yeast that cause such infections thrive on the sugar-laden vaginal secretions of a woman whose diabetes isn't well-controlled.

Your birth control methods can also affect your risk. A diaphragm may actually lower your risk when used properly, due to the presence of bacteria-killing spermicide, says Dr. Roberson. If the diaphragm is left in place for too long, however, infection can set in. IUDs may cause trouble if the string, which hangs down into the vagina from the uterus, becomes soiled, says Dr. Jordan.

WIPING
THEM OUT

Vaginal infections are fairly easy to prevent and treat. Women's health experts recommend these tips.

Use those condoms. "After abstinence, your next best protection from infection is a condom," says Dr. Roberson. "Picking a brand that's treated with the spermicide nonoxynol-9 also gives you some additional protection from infection-causing bacteria," she says.

Don't douche. Forget all the things you've been told about the vagina being dirty and needing to be cleaned. If you are healthy, your vagina maintains the right chemical balance on its own, says Dr. Roberson.

Make a clean sweep. "After using the bathroom, be sure to wipe from front to back to discourage vaginal infections," says Dr. Roberson. If you introduce fecal bacteria into the vagina, you're asking for trouble, she says,

Scrub up. Before sex, wash your hands and make sure your partner washes his, says Dr. Jordan. BV can stem from poor hygiene, including unwashed hands.

Keep it simple. Natural and gentle preparations are best for cleansing the genital area. Feminine hygiene sprays, perfumed toilet paper, and deodorized sanitary napkins and tampons can all irritate the vaginal area and encourage infection, says Dr. Roberson. Prolonged bubble baths may alter the delicate balance in the vagina and encourage infections as well.

Get regular care. Annual pelvic exams and Pap smears are essential for preventing the consequences of undiagnosed vaginal infections, says Dr. Rogers.

Take all your medication. Vaginal infections are usually treated with antibiotics that act against the specific organism that is causing the problem. Your doctor may prescribe metronidazole (Flagyl, Prostostat) in pill form to cure trichomoniasis and BV.

To be sure that you are truly rid of your infection, take all of your medication, even if your symptoms have disappeared, says Dr. Jordan.

Take care with OTC options. The new over-the-counter products that combat yeast and vaginal itching are not for everyone, says Dr. Jordan. "You must be sure of your diagnosis because OTC treatments for yeast will not work if what you have is actually trichomoniasis," he says. See your gynecologist to be certain that you get the proper treatment.

Enlist his help. As Shayna discovered, it is very important that your partner be treated at the same time you are so that he doesn't continue to carry the infection and reinfect you. "He may say, 'I have no symptoms. I don't think I have anything,' but he still needs to take the medication," says Dr. Roberson.

Varicose Veins

GETTING A LEG UP ON PAIN

iane Pullen remembers a hot, bright Los Angeles afternoon. "My closest sister-friend, Jade Hamlett, and I were dressing for our favorite form of R&R—a long Saturday of Olympic-caliber shopping. When Jade came into my room to see if I was ready to go, she noticed a purplish raised area on my lower thigh.

" 'How on earth did you get that lump?' she asked me. I told her that it wasn't a lump, it was a varicose vein that I was about to hide under a pair of slacks. I was frustrated because I had killed myself making sure I worked out at least four times a week so that I could look good in a pair of shorts," says Diane. "But here it was, the hottest day of the year, and I had to put on pants to go downtown. And besides being ugly, the vein burned sometimes, and it hurt when I got tired. I was only 33 years old and these things were on my legs. I didn't even want to think about what I'd look like at 45."

MORE THAN SKIN DEEP

Diane's varicose veins were passed on to her from her mom (and her grandmom), which is a fairly common circumstance. Treatment helped put an end to her problem, just as it has for millions of other people. But it's hard to feel optimistic when you're looking at those awful, ropy bulges on your legs.

Varicose veins, the swollen, black, blue, and purple veins that are most often found on people's ankles, calves, or thighs, make their way up the legs of one out of every three women and half of the men in the United States. And they don't always stop at the legs. They can also show up near the groin, and darkened veins known as spider veins can appear on the face as well as on the legs.

Unlike varicose veins, spider veins are new blood vessels that form close to the surface of the skin, explains dermatologic surgeon Clarence Wiley, M.D., clinical assistant professor at the University of Kansas School of Medicine and medical director of the Center for Skin Health and Beauty, both in Wichita. Although they are sometimes called broken veins, they are not actually broken. They can be either flat or slightly raised if they are in thick clusters, says Dr. Wiley, and they can be painful.

Women with lighter skin, like Diane, often complain that varicose veins can make their legs look like an old road map. "But in dark-skinned people, spider veins are almost invisible," says Isaac Willis, M.D., professor of dermatology and head of dermatologic research at Morehouse School of Medicine in Atlanta.

African-Americans are not at special risk for varicose veins, but women are two to four times more likely to develop them than men, thanks to the effects of female hormones. Estrogen promotes angiogenesis, or the formation of new blood vessels, and varicose vein development is related to estrogen production, says William Keith, M.D., clinical assistant professor of medicine at Drew Medical School/Martin Luther King, Jr., Hospital and medical director of the Institute for Aesthetic and Cosmetic Dermatology, both in Los Angeles.

For women, varicose veins can begin at puberty and worsen after pregnancy or years of menstrual cycles, since all three events affect the body's hormone balance. Pregnancy also encourages the development of varicose veins because of greater blood volume and the pressure of the extra weight carried by moms-to-be.

Despite their raised appearance, varicose veins don't just suddenly pop up on the surface of the skin. Gravity helps them develop over time. The arteries in your legs carry blood down through your thighs and lower legs, and the veins carry blood back up to your heart. Valves within healthy veins open and close, with great precision, in order to prevent gravity from pulling the blood back downward. But several factors, such as age, hormones, and weight gain, can weaken and stretch the valves so that they can no longer keep the blood from moving backward. As a result, the blood falls back and pools in the veins, painfully stretching the muscular vein walls until they bulge outward. That's when you look down and see a raised vein filled with darkened, stagnant blood peeking out from below your skin's surface.

Even though vein removal is considered cosmetic surgery by some folks, there's absolutely no reason to avoid having it done if you want to, says Isaac Willis, M.D., professor of dermatology and head of dermatologic research at Morehouse School of Medicine in Atlanta. If you have discomfort, burning, or stinging from painful varicose or spider veins, you have good reason to consider surgical removal, he adds.

"Women usually seek treatment in their forties and fifties, but the younger you are, the easier treatment is," says dermatologic surgeon Clarence L. Wiley, M.D., clinical assistant professor at the University of Kansas School of Medicine in Wichita. Visit a dermatologist or vascular surgeon to see if you are a candidate for surgery. Here's a look at your options.

Vein stripping. In this procedure, a surgeon makes an incision and ties off or removes the distended vein. It's moderately painful, requires some recovery time (generally one to two weeks and sometimes up to six weeks, depending on the circumstances), and is usually reserved for severe cases. If the varicose vein is the size of a pencil or greater in diameter, it's considered severe, says Dr. Willis.

Laser treatment. Destroying offending veins in the face with electrosurgery (using a needle to transmit a low-level current that destroys the problem vein) or laser treatment (using an

Varicose veins can pose problems beyond cosmetic concerns. They often burn and hurt, particularly when you are on your feet for long periods or when you lie in bed at night. A varicose vein can also develop phlebitis, a potentially dangerous condition in which a blood clot may block the circulation. Phlebitis can cause extreme tenderness and swelling of the leg, and there is a risk that the clot could break loose and lodge somewhere else, such as in the lungs (a pulmonary embolism).

Since circulation in the area is impaired, the skin overlying the affected vein can develop ulcerations or sores that are slow to heal. It can become a very serious situation, says Dr. Wiley.

ultra-high-intensity light to destroy the vein) is very effective, says Dr. Willis.

"My experience is that the laser works much better when it's used on facial veins," says James Leo Harry, M.D., director of the Owings Mills branch of Vein Clinics of America in Maryland. "There's a different circulatory pattern in the face than in the legs, so you get better results."

Sclerotherapy. The most popular trend in vein treatment today, and the one your doctor will most likely recommend, is sclerotherapy. This simple outpatient procedure involves injecting a sclerosant, or chemical irritant, into the problem vein. "The solution works by harmlessly irritating the inner walls of the veins so that they actually become sticky and collapse in on themselves," says Dr. Harry.

On average, anywhere from four to six treatments may be needed, depending on the person, says Dr. Harry. A few patients may require many more sessions. One word of caution, though: These treatments sometimes cause discoloration. "In brown-skinned people, we can see some darkened pigmentation after sclerotherapy, but it does not occur in everyone and usually fades over time," says Dr. Harry. The darkened pigmentation is not scarring but a normal discoloration caused by the procedure, adds Dr. Wiley.

PUTTING THE SQUEEZE ON VARICOSE VEINS

Varicose veins and spider veins usually run in families: 60 percent of the people who develop them inherit them from one or both of their parents. Even so, you can cut your risk of vein problems.

Don't be a lady. Crossing your legs frequently sets you up for varicose veins that result from habitually blocking the circulation in your legs, says Dr. Willis. Try loosely crossing your ankles instead.

On the Pill? Taking birth control pills or hormone replacement, both of which contain estrogen, can predispose your arteries and veins to inflammation and to spider vein formation, says Dr. Wiley.

Lose weight. Being obese (20 percent over your ideal weight) may also contribute to varicose veins and spider veins.

Move it. The Framingham Heart Study found that women who sit for more than 8 hours a day have a much higher incidence of varicose veins. So stay active if possible.

Slowing Them Down

If you develop varicose or spider veins, there are a few steps you can take to make them less severe.

Garner support. Graduated support hose, custom-fitted for you by your doctor, are expensive, but they may help keep future vein growth to a minimum, Dr. Wiley suggests. Or shop for one of the newer, thinner brands of support hose on the market, such as Park-Davis, suggests Dr. Willis. You can also try wearing support panty hose at night when you go to bed, he suggests. If you find them too warm or confining, try cutting out the crotch to allow air to circulate more freely.

Just walk them away. A 20-minute daily walk eases the pain of varicose veins by strengthening the muscles that support them, explains Dr. Wiley.

Take it easy. Running on hard surfaces can make your veins swell. When you exercise, pick dirt, grass, or soft interior tracks. "High-impact aerobics or any weight-bearing exercise that places great stress on the legs can also potentially increase your chances of getting varicose veins," says James Leo Harry, M.D., director of the Owings Mill branch of the Vein Clinics of America in Maryland.

Keep things moving. Constipation and straining to have bowel movements can put pressure on leg veins. So eat plenty of high-fiber foods such as fresh fruits and vegetables (five or more servings a day) and drink lots of water to keep your system in smooth working order, says Dr. Harry. Nutrition experts recommend that you aim for at least 25 grams of dietary fiber a day.

Take a load off. Putting your feet up eases the pain of swollen veins, so prop your legs on a pillow while relaxing, says Dr. Willis.

Vitiligo

RESTORING THE BALANCE

ackie Monroe looked at her reflection in the bathroom mirror and felt a mixture of anger and sadness. Even though neither emotion was particularly useful in her situation, she felt that she couldn't help herself.

"A few months earlier, I called my mom back home in Louisville and complained that I was getting those little white spots all over my skin, just like my Aunt Audrey," Jackie says. "My mom tried to console me by telling me, 'You're only 26, and you don't look anything like Audrey. Your mind is playing tricks on you.' I wanted to believe her, but soon it became obvious that the widening circles on my face were not a figment of my imagination.

"Some of the spots near my mouth and eyes were as big as a quarter, and they were strikingly white against the rest of my complexion. It frightened me a little, but I also knew it was time to call a doctor and see what I could do," Jackie remembers.

UNDERSTANDING CHANGE

Dealing with this condition, as Jackie would discover, is very difficult for many people.

Are you particularly fond of your pretty brown skin? If so, imagine seeing its color fade away, inch by inch, over a period of months (or years) until it completely disappears. Whether or not you consider your skin your best feature, for most African-Americans skin color is such an intimate part of identity that losing it can be devastating. The rich brown hues of our skin come from melanocytes, which are skin cells. And melanin, the pigment in these cells, gives our skin its color. Vitiligo destroys melanocytes and fades our skin.

People who develop vitiligo see patches of their skin, ranging in size from a half-inch to several inches in diameter, slowly turn milky white. Many people develop a few isolated spots that never spread. But in other people, hundreds of patches eventually cover most of the body, and doctors cannot predict when vitiligo will spread or stay contained in a few isolated spots. Fortunately, most people with vitiligo can be helped, says Harold Pierce, M.D., a dermatoplastic surgeon with the Pierce Cosmetic Surgery Center in Philadelphia.

Vitiligo is no more prevalent in African-Americans than it is in Whites: It affects 1 or 2 out of every 100 people regardless of race, according to the American Academy of Dermatology. "But it is psychologically devastating for dark-skinned people because it results in such a dramatic difference in our appearance," says Julia Boyd, a psychotherapist with the Group Health Cooperative in Seattle and author of *In the Company of My Sisters: Black Women and Self-Esteem*.

Scientists don't yet understand what causes vitiligo, but your doctor can easily diagnose the condition by visual inspection, especially if your skin is dark. If your skin is light, your doctor will use a special ultraviolet light called a Wood's lamp to provide the contrast that helps him make a definitive diagnosis.

MORE THAN SKIN DEEP

Vitiligo has some troublesome running buddies. "Although most patients with vitiligo are otherwise healthy, there are several health conditions that sometimes develop with the disease," says dermatologist Susan C. Taylor, M.D., of Society Hill Dermatology in Philadelphia. Many people with vitiligo also have an overactive or underactive thyroid gland, diabetes, Addison's disease (an insufficient production of hormones in the adrenal gland), or pernicious anemia (a disease characterized by a low red blood cell count).

Last, but certainly not least, is the fact that the loss of pigment brought on by vitiligo also adds up to a loss of protection from the sun and an increased risk of sunburn. So adding a few nice sun hats to your wardrobe and using an effective sunscreen with an SPF (sun protection factor) of at least 15 are health-saving ideas if you have pigment loss.

STRIKING
AN EVEN TONE

"If vitiligo runs in your family, there is nothing you can do to prevent it," says Dr. Pierce. Nearly 36 percent of those who develop it say that another family member has it. Age is also a factor: About half the people who develop vitiligo do so before the age of 20. There is no known prevention and no cure yet, but there are several effective treatment options.

Reach for cover. "Cosmetics may camouflage the white patches," says Dr. Taylor. She suggests that you consider using Dermablend corrective cosmetics (available at department stores, boutiques, skin-care clinics, and some pharmacies), which come in a wide variety of tones and won't wash off in the rain or during exercise.

Color with cortisone. "Topical corticosteroid creams, available only by prescription, can help return color, especially to small areas such as around the eyelids," says Dr. Pierce.

Light it up. A treatment called psoralen and ultraviolet-A (PUVA) light therapy is performed by a dermatologist in her office. "It consists of applying a cream containing the drug methoxsalen (Oxsoralen-Ultra), or taking a pill form of psoralen, then applying ultraviolet light to small, isolated patches of vitiligo. Treatment with PUVA has a 50 to 70 percent chance of returning color in the face, trunk, and upper arms and legs. Hands and feet respond very poorly," says Dr. Pierce.

Try a graft. Dermatologists now use a technique called minigrafting to reverse the effects of vitiligo. "Little punch grafts (top-layer skin grafts obtained with a sharp punch) from pigmented skin, such as those used for hair transplants, are moved to whitened areas," explains Dr. Pierce. "For reasons we don't understand, they stimulate the surrounding cells to produce color within 7 to 10 days. But if a patient tends to develop keloids, we won't try this, because cosmetic surgery may result in additional keloid formation," he adds.

Embrace change. "If the majority of your skin has lost its pigment, bleaching the remaining skin to match it may be your best option," says Dr. Pierce. "We just apply a chemical called monobenzyl ether of hydroquinone on the chest or stomach twice a day, and it takes 12 to 18 months to totally depigment the skin by gradually destroying the remaining melanocytes. We don't have to apply it to the entire body," he says. But when considering this option, remember that it is permanent. "Individuals with dark complexions who are contemplating this form of therapy should have a psychological evaluation preceding therapy because the emotional consequences of depigmentation may be considerable," says Boyd.

Work on inner healing. As Boyd reminds us, not all treatments for vitiligo come from the doctor's office. "Stress-reducing techniques such as biofeedback, breathing exercises, meditation, psychotherapy, and support groups are all good ideas," she says.

"Our society is so bent on how we look that it's very difficult for women (and many men) to cope with a disease like vitiligo," she observes. "And when doctors don't have the answer, we really feel let down. But the answer is to focus on your wellness more than your illness."

Weight Problems

FIGHTING FAT—AND WINNING!

ina Warren is like millions of sisters (and brothers): Her weight goes up and down like a roller coaster at least once a year. "Every woman has an outfit that's her test," says the 28-year-old Washington, D.C., congressional aide. "Since I spend so much time at parties and special events for my job, I have an entire wardrobe of suits and cocktail dresses in different sizes (from single-digit to double). My current summer 'test dress' is a little pale yellow linen sheath. It fit in June, after months of crash dieting, but it was hopelessly tight in August. Now I've moved from the size 8 section of my closet back to the size 12 section," she says.

All Gina wants is a weight-loss program that produces lasting results. "Honestly, I can't afford this four-size wardrobe stuff. I need to get to a healthy, attractive weight and stay there," she says.

FINDING
THE REAL DEAL

Gina's challenge is shared by many. Nearly half of all African-American women and close to one-third of all African-American men are overweight.

The truth hurts: In American culture, overweight is generally associated with being unattractive. But the word from sisters everywhere is that African-Americans see a bigger body as an attractive body. A heftier figure is viewed as a sign of good health and fertility, while thinness is associated with poor health. Lillie R. Williams R.D., Ph.D., chairperson of the Department of Nutritional Sciences at Howard University in Washington, D.C., describes this train of thought as a cultural feast-or-famine mentality: Heavier women could theoretically sustain themselves during famine, while thinner ones would not survive.

Obesity is defined as being more than 20 percent over your desirable weight, whether you're a woman or a man. The measure currently being used to determine appropriate weight for height is called body mass index (BMI). To calculate your BMI, multiply your weight in pounds by 700, divide that number by your height in inches, then divide again by that number. For example, the math for a 120-pound woman who's 5 feet, 4 inches tall would look like this: 120 times 700 equals 84,000. 84,000 divided by 64 equals 1,312.5, divided by 64 again equals 20.5—her BMI. A BMI of between 20 and 22 is considered healthy.

Accurately measuring the health and well-being of our bodies according to measurements like the BMI formula, however, is a little tricky. "Healthy weight is an individual matter. It all depends on whether or not your weight is currently causing health problems or has the potential to cause health problems in the future," says Shiriki Kumanyika, R.D., Ph.D., professor and head of the Department of Human Nutrition and Dietetics at the University of Illinois at Chicago. If you're presently healthy but your BMI is 27 or higher, you may be at greater risk for future health problems than those whose BMI is closer to 22 or less, she says.

Excess weight is linked with health problems such as heart disease, high blood pressure, diabetes, stroke, and even some cancers. No wonder diet centers, weight-loss programs, and other quick-fix gimmicks are just about everywhere you look. Unfortunately, the long-term results are that more than half of the folks who complete weight-loss programs regain what they lost within two years.

This yo-yo syndrome is bad for your health and hard on your wallet. "It's better to maintain a weight than to go up and down. Repeated weight loss and gain can be a strain on your cardiovascular system as well as reducing the elasticity of your skin and setting you up for nutritional problems," says Dr. Williams.

ACHIEVING YOUR PERSONAL BEST

For a perfectly tailored weight-loss plan, see a physician or registered dietitian. In the meantime, these general tips from the experts can get you started on the road to your healthiest weight.

Adjust your view. Focus on healthy eating, not on the bathroom scale. Weigh yourself only once in a while, says Dr. Kumanyika. Don't obsess over results that take time to be noticeable.

Shake it up. Regular, aerobic exercise, whether it's walking, dancing, biking, or another activity you enjoy, is a critical part of weight maintenance. You should exercise for 30 minutes a day at least three times a week, and if you really have a few pounds to lose, it's best to work out four or five days or more, says Victoria Johnson, a fitness trainer in Lake Oswego, Oregon, and star of a collection of hot workout videos bearing her name.

Pump it up. You've probably heard it before, but it's important: Muscle burns more calories than fat, so the more muscle you have, the better. Join a gym, but start slowly. Your local Y will probably have a beginner program to show you how to use weights properly. Or ask a gym staff member to demonstrate the proper technique.

Keep it simple. Work on developing simple, healthy habits such as moderate exercise goals and fat-cutting plans that can realistically become a part of your life. If you push yourself to extremes, you won't be able to comfortably adopt permanent lifestyle changes, says Johnson.

Take a good look. If you're not sure exactly what's wrong with your diet, keep a food diary for a couple of weeks. Jot down your meals and snacks and take a look at your eating habits. You need to know what your personal weaknesses are—like late-night desserts or skipping breakfast—before you can start to make changes for the better, says Lauren Swann, R.D., nutrition consultant and president of Concept Nutrition Counseling in Bensalem, Pennsylvania.

Cut down, not out. When preparing meals, remember that portion control is the key to sensible eating. Buy a scale and start weighing your servings. It's important to eat a variety of foods every day. Even without a scale, you can use these guidelines from the U.S. Department of Agriculture for starters.

▲ Try for three to five half-cup servings of chopped vegetables or fruit; one serving is about the size of your fist.

▲ Eat two to three 3-ounce servings of meat, fish, eggs, or beans; a serving is a piece of meat about the size of a deck of playing cards, one egg, or a half-cup of cooked beans.

▲ Get 6 to 11 servings of grains; a serving is one slice of bread, 1 ounce of dry cereal, or a half-cup of cooked rice or pasta.

▲ Include two to three servings of dairy products; a serving is 1 cup of low-fat milk or yogurt or 1½ ounces of cheese.

The number of servings you need from each food group is based on your activity level and your current weight. If you are trying to trim down, help yourself to the lower number of servings.

Don't forget your favorites. No one can stick to a lifetime eating plan that requires them to give up all the foods they love. Instead, learn to eat smaller portions and try lower-fat versions of the things you can't live without. Have one slice of pizza (minus the extra cheese) instead of two. Or try low-fat ice cream or fat-free frozen yogurt for a change; you can barely tell the difference, says Swann.

Index

Underscored page references indicate boxed text. Prescription drug names are denoted by the symbol Rx.

A

effects on
arthritis, 296
gum disease, 191
high blood pressure, 226
migraines, 305
osteoporosis, 14, 191, 275, 296, 320–21
pregnancy, 275, <u>344–45</u>
temporomandibular joint disorder, 437
food sources of, 191, 275, <u>344–45</u>
hormone replacement therapy and, 296
iron and, 14
postmenopausal women and, 296
supplements, 321
Calcium channel blockers, 227
Calluses, 173
Cancer. *See also* Breast cancer
alcohol and, 7
cervical, 74–78, 349
colorectal, 90–94, <u>92</u>, 215
esophageal, 203
hepatocellular carcinoma, 219
lymphoma, 287–90
ovarian, 324–27
prostate, 358–61
skin, 403–9, <u>406</u>, <u>408</u>
basal cell carcinoma, 407
dermatofibrosarcoma protuberans, 409
malignant melanoma, 406–7, 409
squamous cell carcinoma, 406
testicular, 441
Carbohydrates, 91, 142, 311
Cardiovascular conditions, 207. *See also* Heart disease
Cardizem (Rx), 370
Carpal tunnel syndrome (CTS), 69–73
Carrots, ovarian cancer and, 327
CDC. *See* Centers for Disease Control and Prevention
Ceftriaxone (Rx), 392
Celes, testicular, 439–40
Center for Counseling and Health Resources, 135

Centers for Disease Control and Prevention (CDC), 165, 167, 219, 283, 351
Cereals, in Food Guide Pyramid, 311
Cerebrovascular accident (CVA), 428–33, <u>430</u>
Certified professional ergonomic evaluator (CPEE), 71
Certified professional ergonomist (CPE), 71
Cervical cancer, 74–78, 349
Cervical cap, <u>45</u>
Cervical problems, 245
Cesarean delivery, 351
Cetaphil soap, 23
CFS. *See* Chronic fatigue syndrome
Chamomile, sinus allergies and, 404
Cheese, cavities and, 191
Chemical irritation, of eyes, <u>146</u>
Chemotherapy, 287, 289–90, 361, 378
Childbirth classes, 350
Chlamydia
effects on
fertility, 244, 246
testicular problems, 439
menstrual spotting and, 299
the Pill and, 335
treating, 392
Cholesterol. *See also* Fat, dietary
Accutane (Rx) and, 4
atherosclerosis and, 35
bile and, 182
diabetes and, 209
exercise and, 210
gallstones and, 183
high-density lipoproteins, 210–11, 296
lipid analysis and, 296
low-density lipoproteins, 210–12, 296
Chronic anxiety, 16
Chronic bronchitis, 67
Chronic fatigue syndrome (CFS), 79–82, 93, 150
Chronic pain, 83–85
Cigarettes. *See* Smoking
Cimetidine, 183, 204

Hallux valgus, 173
Hammertoes, 173
Harvard Nurses' Health Study, 62
HDL, 210–11, 296
Headaches, 196–200, <u>199</u>. *See also*
    Migraines
Hearing problems, 127–31, <u>128–29</u>
Heart attack, 202, 207, 209, 212
Heartburn, 201–5
Heart disease, 206–12
    atherosclerosis, 33–36, 207, 223
    Black women and, <u>208–9</u>
    factors affecting
        Accutane (Rx), 4
        alcohol, 7
        diabetes, 209
        diet, 210–11
        exercise, 210–11
        genetics, 207
        high blood pressure, 206,
          208
        overweight, 210, 216
        smoking, 211
    left ventricular hypertrophy (LVH),
        206–7
    preventing, 210–12
    stroke and, 241, 428–33, <u>430</u>
    types of, 207
    women and, 207–10, <u>208–9</u>
Heat treatments
    for osteoarthritis, 317
    for sprains and strains, 437
Heel spurs, 172
Helicobacter pylori bacteria, ulcers and,
    453, 455–56
Heme iron, 12, <u>13</u>, <u>345</u>
Hemoglobin, 10–14, 349, 392–93, <u>396</u>
Hemorrhagic stroke, 429
Hemorrhoids, 213–16
HEPA filter, 31, 403
Hepatitis, 217–21
Hepatocellular carcinoma, 219
Herbs, to treat
    lupus, 282
    menopause symptoms, 296
    menstrual irregularities, 301

    motion sickness, 308
    prostate problems, 360
    sinus problems, 404
Heredity. *See* Genetics
Hernia, hiatal, 202–3, 205
Herpes, 389–90, 392
Hexadrol (Rx), 29
High blood pressure, 222–27
    atherosclerosis and, 34
    diagnosing, <u>24</u>
    effects on
        headaches, 198
        heart disease, 206, 208
        kidney ailments, 269
        stroke, 432
    factors affecting
        alcohol, 7
        caffeine, 226
        calcium, 226
        diet, 223, 225–26
        dietary fiber, 225
        exercise, 225
        genetics, 223
        smoking, 226
        stress, 222–23
    managing, 224–27
    medications for, 226–27
    racism and, 223
High-density lipoproteins (HDL),
    210–11, 296
High-efficiency particulate (HEPA)
    filter, 31, 403
HIV, 228–34
    blood test for, 232
    cervical cancer and, 76
    coping with, 232–33
    immune system and, 229
    pregnancy and, 233, 349
    preventing, 43, 230–32, <u>231</u>
    sex and, 230–31
    support for, 234
Hodgkins' disease, 287–88
Home Access test, for HIV/AIDS, 232
Home remedies, for stomachache, cau-
    tion with, 21
Hormonal drugs, 143. *See also specific types*

National Cancer Institute (NCI), 59, 62, 76, 311
National Council on Alcoholism and Drug Dependence, 9
National Crime Victimization Survey, 363
National Heart, Lung, and Blood Institute (NHLB), 397
National Institute on Drug Abuse, 363
National Institutes of Health (NIH), 59–60, 120, 134, 296, 327, <u>345</u>, 397
National Kidney Foundation, 271
National Medical Association, 55, 65
National Resource Center on Domestic Violence, 118
National Victim Center, 363
National Women's Survey, 363–64, 366
NCI. *See* National Cancer Institute
Nebulizer, for asthma, 29
Nedocromil (Rx), 29
Neostrata (Rx), 3, 373
Nephrons, 268
Neutrogena products, 2, 23–24, 138, 384
NHLB, 397
Nickel allergies, 108, 266
Nicoderm, 414
Nicorette, 414
Nicotine. *See* Smoking
Nicotine gum, 211, 414
Nicotine patch, 211, 414
Nicotrol, 414
Nifedipine (Rx), 370
Night owl insomnia, 259
NIH. *See* National Institutes of Health
Nitro-Bid, 370
Nitrofurantoin (Rx), 460
Nitroglycerin ointment, 370
Nonheme iron, 12
Non-Hodgkins' lymphoma, 288–89
Nonsteroidal anti–inflammatory drugs (NSAIDs). *See also specific types*
kidney ailments and, 271

to treat
back pain, 40
carpal tunnel syndrome, 73
endometriosis, 143
headaches, <u>199</u>
menstrual cramps, 301
Norplant, 41–42, <u>50</u>
Nortriptyline (Rx), 161
Norvir (Rx), 232
Norwalk Agent, food poisoning and, 167
Novopranol (Rx), <u>199</u>
NSAIDs. *See* Nonsteroidal anti–inflammatory drugs
"Numbing," post-traumatic stress disorder and, 341
Nuprin. *See* Ibuprofen
Nutrition, 310–14, 356

O

Oatmeal baths, for itching, 109, 139
Obesity. *See also* Overweight
atherosclerosis and, 34–35
body mass index and, 476
eating disorders and, 133
heart disease and, 210
ovulation disorders and, 244
stroke and, 432
Obsessive-compulsive disorder, 16
Occupational Safety and Health Administration (OSHA), 130
Ocean Spray nasal spray, 404
Odors
migraines and, 304–5
motion sickness and, 308
Oil, moisturizing, 23
Oil of Olay soap, 23
Oligomenorrhea, 300
Omeprazole (Rx), 204
Oral contraceptives, 43, <u>44</u>. *See also* Pill, the
Orasone (Rx), 29
OSHA, 130
Osteoarthritis, 315–18, 376

Premarin (Rx), 297
Premenstrual syndrome (PMS), 352–56, 354
Prilosec (Rx), 204
Primatene products, 27
Procainamide (Rx), 279
Procardia (Rx), 370
Progesterone (Rx), 354
Progestin (Rx), 143
Promethazine (Rx), 309
Pronestyl (Rx), 279
Propranolol (Rx), 199
Propylthiouracil (Rx), 446
Propyl-Thyracil (Rx), 446
Prostaglandins, 300
Prostate problems, 357–61
Prostatectomy, radical, 361
Prostate-specific antigen (PSA), 359
Prostep, 414
Protease inhibitors (Rx), 232
Protein, 116, 311, 356
Proton pump inhibitors, 204
Protostat (Rx), 465
Proventil (Rx), 29
Prozac (Rx), 82, 161, 257, 356
PSA, 359
Pseudoephedrine, 89, 137, 403
Pseudofolliculitis barbae (PFB), 371–74, 372
Psoralen and ultraviolet-A (PUVA) therapy, for vitiligo, 473
Psychophysiologic insomnia, 259
Psychotherapy, to treat
    anxiety disorders, 17, 18
    depression, 105–6
    eating disorders, 135
    impotence, 238
    inhibited sexual desire, 256
    painful intercourse, 330–32
    panic attacks, 18
    spouse abuse, 120–21
    temporomandibular joint disorder, 435, 437
    vitiligo, 474
Psyllium, 215–16, 263
PTSD. *See* Post-traumatic stress disorder

Pulmonary embolism, 468
Purified protein derivative (PPD) test, for tuberculosis, 448
Purpose soap, 2
Pustules, 2
PUVA therapy, for vitiligo, 473
Pygeum, 360
Pyridium (Rx), 460

R

RA. *See* Rheumatoid arthritis
Racism
    anxiety disorders and, 15
    high blood pressure and, 223
    pregnancy and, 347–48
    stress and, 424
Radioactive iodine treatment, for hyperthyroidism, 446
Ragweed allergies, 404
RAINN, 365
Ranitidine, 183, 204
Rape, 362–66
Rape Abuse and Incest National Network (RAINN), 365
Rash, butterfly-shaped, with lupus, 279
Raynaud's disease, 278, 367–70
Raynaud's phenomenon, 368–69
Razor bumps, 266, 371–74, 372
Red blood cells, 11
Referred pain, 128
Reflex sympathetic dystrophy (RSD), 83–84
Reglan (Rx), 264
Rehabilitation programs, for alcoholics, 9
Rehydration solutions, oral, 168
Relaxation, to manage
    breast surgery recovery, 57
    high blood pressure, 226
    insomnia, 260
    irritable bowel syndrome, 263
    premenstrual syndrome, 356
    tinnitus, 129
    vitiligo, 474

Tums, 204
Tylenol with Codeine No. 3 (Rx), _199_
Type I (insulin-dependent) diabetes,
    111, _112–13_
Type II (non-insulin-dependent)
    diabetes, 111–15, _114_
Tyramines, headaches and, 200

U

Ulcerative colitis, 91, 249–52
Ulcers, 370, 452–56
Ultrasound, 142, _424_
Ultraviolet-A (UVA) radiation, _406_
Ultraviolet-B (UVB) radiation, _406_
Undecylenic acid, 180
U.S. Agency for Health Care Policy and
    Research, 38
U.S. Center for Substance Abuse Treat-
    ment, 125
U.S. Department of Agriculture
    (USDA), 311
U.S. Department of Health and Human
    Services, 123
U.S. Department of Justice, 118, 363
Urea, _372_
Ureacin (Rx), _372_
Urge incontinence, 240, 242
Urinalysis, for kidney disease, 271
Urinary tract infections (UTIs), 457–60,
    _458_
Ursodoxycholic acid, 183
USDA, 311
Uterine problems, 330
UTIs, 457–60, _458_
UVA radiation, _406_
UVB radiation, _406_

V

Vaccinations, 221, 382. _See also_
    Immunotherapy
Vaccines for Children Program, 221

Vacuum devices, for impotence, 238
Vaginal dryness, 329, 331
Vaginal infections, 461–65
Vaginismus, 330, 332
Valproic acid, _199_
Varicoceles, 440–41
Varicose veins, 466–70, _468–69_
Vascular headaches, 197–98, 302–6
Vegetables. _See also specific types_
    in Food Guide Pyramid, 312–14
Vegetarianism, 12
Veins
    hemorrhoidal, 213–14
    varicose, 466–70, _468–69_
Vein-stripping procedure, _468_
Violence
    domestic, 7, 117–21
    prevention programs for, 340
    rape, 362–66
Visine, 187
Vision problems
    diabetic retinopathy, _114_
    glaucoma, 184–87
Visualization, for breast cancer recovery,
    _57_
Vitamins. _See specific types_
Vitamin C
    effects on
        cervical cancer, 78
        colds, 88
        gum disease, 191
        lupus, 282
    iron absorption and, 14, 152
    sources of, 312
    supplements, 14
Vitamin D, 305, 321–22,
    437
Vitamin E, 78, 212, 282
Vitiligo, 471–74
Vitron C, 14
Vocal cord paralysis, with thyroid
    surgery, 446

W

X

Y

Z